FRANCE
ON THE
BRINK

Also by Jonathan Fenby

Will China Dominate the 21st Century?

The Battle of Tsingtao

Tiger Head, Snake Tails: China Today

The General: Charles de Gaulle and the France He Saved

The Penguin History of Modern China

Alliance

The Sinking of the Lancastria

China's Journey

The Dragon Throne; China's Imperial Dynasties

The Seventy Wonders of China

Generalissimo: Chiang Kai-shek and the China He Lost

Dealing with the Dragon

Comment peut-on être français?

Piracy and the Public

The International News Services

The Fall of the House of Beaverbrook

FRANCE
ON THE
BRINK
SECOND EDITION

A GREAT CIVILIZATION
IN THE NEW CENTURY

Jonathan Fenby

Arcade Publishing • New York

Second Edition

Material from chapter 12, 'A French Life,' first appeared in different form in the *Guardian* 'Weekend' magazine in 1995.

Map by Neil Hyslop

Arcade Publishing books may be purchased in bulk at special discounts for sales promotion, corporate gifts, fund-raising, or educational purposes. Special editions can also be created to specifications. For details, contact the Special Sales Department, Arcade Publishing, 307 West 36th Street, 11th Floor, New York, NY 10018 or arcade@skyhorsepublishing.com.

Arcade Publishing® is a registered trademark of Skyhorse Publishing, Inc.®, a Delaware corporation.

Visit our website at www.arcadepub.com.

10 9 8 7 6 5 4 3 2 1

Library of Congress Cataloging-in-Publication Data is available on file.

Cover design by Brian Peterson
Cover photo © by Thinkstock

ISBN: 978-1-62872-317-5
Ebook ISBN: 978-1-62872-406-6

Printed in the United States of America

To the memory of
Alter and Fanny

CONTENTS

PREFACE

The first time I went to France, I didn't like it much. My godmother had invited me to join her on holiday in Brittany in the late 1950s to look after her children. I have two memories of the trip: daringly calling out, '*Ah, les flics!*' at the police on the seafront and trying to learn to sail on a boat with a grizzled Frenchman who kept yelling about '*le foc*'—the mizzen sail, not a Breton approximation of a four-letter swear word.

Forty years later, I was sitting in my office by the harbour in Hong Kong, having edited the *South China Morning Post* through the territory's return to China. It had been a breathless summer, with no time to think of anything except work. One Wednesday in August, I was seized by a single thought. My wife was in France, taking the waters at an obscure spa in the wilds of the Cévennes. In three days' time, she and three of our closest friends would drive to a favourite restaurant and hotel in a medieval village by the Aveyron River. My diary was embarrassingly empty. So I booked a ticket for that night, flew to Paris, changed airports and boarded a little plane to the town of Rodez. Once there I hired a car, drove twenty miles, and was sitting in the garden by the river when they drove over the humpbacked bridge on Saturday afternoon.

France gets you that way. Its lure is the reason for this book. I had wanted to write an account of the state of France for some time; what got me started was the virulence and scale of the protests that were set off by President Chirac's decision to resume nuclear testing in the summer of 1995. Why, I wondered, did France arouse such strong emotions? What is it that is so unusual about this nation and its people? And then, looking at the morosity which spread across the country from the mid-1980s, how does one reconcile the superior sheen which France displays to the world with the realities of double-digit unemployment, rising to 3.3 million in defiance of presidential pledges to bring it down, a rampant extremist party of the far right and a people who reject the elite that has ruled them for decades?

Without a healthy France, there is no Europe. That is why the state of the land between the Atlantic and the Rhine, the Mediterranean and the Channel matters so much, and why, for all the pleasures and stimulation it offers, France needs to get a grip on itself.

For a foreigner to try to grapple with such matters may seem arrogant. But I hope that three decades spent either living in France or watching it closely from abroad have enabled me to take the pulse of the nation, though I know that many friends living in Paris, the Berry or the Auvergne would disagree with my concerns about their country. My starting point is certainly not that of a Francophobe; rather more that of a lover who entertains some fundamental worries about the object of his affection.

The first edition of this book was published in 1998. France was in a quite confident mood as the last century ended. When a French version appeared, I was taken to task especially by reviewers in right-wing newspapers for my criticisms of the country. A leading commentator in *Le Figaro* noted that I claimed to be a friend of France and concluded with the cliché that 'with friends like M. Fenby, France does not need enemies.' I can only note that the same newspaper has taken to levelling the same kind of criticisms at the way the country is run as I laid out at the time. I would claim that the weaknesses and strengths, which I identified first time round, remain—and, indeed, have in some cases been magnified on the debit side. However, while still on the brink, France has not toppled over. How it has managed this is one of the themes of this new edition.

So much has happened in the last fifteen years that this is really a new book, but I hope it has the advantage of putting the current state of the country in a longer historical context stretching back to

Charles de Gaulle and the founding of the Fifth Republic in 1958, with particular focus on the period since François Mitterrand became the first President of the Fifth Republic to be elected on a left-wing platform. Those three decades form a continuum which both explains the brink along which France is walking and how its politicians, of right and left, have repeatedly chosen short-term fixes or indulged in evasion of harsh realities to perpetuate that state of affairs, leading to the current uncertainties lapping round the presidency of François Hollande. The book seeks, therefore, both to present a portrait of France today and a longer-range account of the evolution of the country, from the centres of power in Paris to the provinces, from the economy to gastronomy, from the immigrant issue to the fading of old icons with the backdrop of the history that has formed the nation.

It is based on half a century of experience, encounters and observation both personal and drawn from my work as a journalist in France for *Reuters*, the *Economist*, the *Times*, the *Guardian*, the *Independent*, the *Observer* and other publications in Britain and the United States. I could never have undertaken this book, let alone finished it, without the help of my wife, who has given me roots-by-marriage in France and whose assistance has been as invaluable as it has been rigorous. Hundreds of people have contributed to my knowledge of France and given me material for this book. I owe a special debt to my colleagues in the French press and broadcasting; in particular to *L'Express*, *Le Monde*, *Libération*, *Le Figaro*, *Le Nouvel Observateur*, *Le Point* and RTL. I have indicated their specific contributions at various points in the text, but, beyond that, they have given me a far broader insight into France over the years as friends and colleagues.

Louis and Lya Wartski and their children have been an invaluable well on which to draw since the mid-1960s. Roger Galéron was a particularly moving witness of one day in 1942. The late André Passeron was my first and best guide to French politics, while Louis Marcerou opened windows on to France that I could never have found elsewhere. Paul Webster was an essential companion at historic moments in the 1990s as well as unearthing valuable material on the saga of François Mitterrand, which he generously made available before his untimely death. As well as conversations with people across the country, I have benefitted more recently from the timely observations of André Villeneuve, from the analysis of John Peet and from continuing exchanges with a range of academic observers of France, opinion pollsters and journalists for the French publications cited above.

I owe a special debt to the inhabitants of Mourjou and Calvinet in the Cantal, and in particular to our generous and ever-dependable host in the chestnut country, Peter Graham. Among the Anglo-New Zealand tribe to be found in those parts, Keith Walker, Brian Oatley and Peter and Win Campbell have provided information and food for thought over the years in the Place de Église. Ginette Vincendeau has been both a valuable source of material and a stimulating verbal sparring partner. Bernard Edinger has always been there when facts needed to be checked or leads followed up, while Simon Caulkin, Jack Altman and David Lawday have been friendly sources of ideas through more years than any of us would like to acknowledge. Jenny and Peter Thomas in the Gard and Lisa and André Villeneuve in Italy provided most welcome hospitality while I was working on the new edition of this book; André has been a source of constant ideas about France wherever we are.

I would also like to thank the following for their often unwitting contribution over the years: Jacques Attali; Raymond Barre; Jean-Philippe Beja; Pierre Bérégovoy; Luc and Annie Besnier; Jean-Louis Bianco; the Baron Bonnefous; Denis and Genevieve Brulet; Claude Cheysson; Jacques Chirac; Mary Dejevsky; Roland Dumas; Albert Duroy; the Estienne family and others who stayed on in the village of Saint-André-de-Rosans; Nicole and Michèle Fagegaltier, and their father; Philippe and Claire Ferras; Anne Freyer; Marie-France Garaud; Valéry Giscard d'Estaing; Jacques and Annie Hudes; Denis Jeambar; Serge July; Pascal Lamy; Jean-Marie Le Pen; Jean-Yves and Michèle Libeskind; John Litchfield; Gerald Long; Serge Marti; Dominique Moïsi; Christine Ockrent; Micheline Oerlemans; André Poitevin; Louis-Bernard Puech; Martine Schultz; Dominique Strauss-Kahn; Margie Sudre; the Vincendeau family and John Vinocur.

The chapter on the National Front draws, in part, on Alexander Fenby's thesis on the party, and Sara Fenby kept me up to date on the latest relevant French writings while I was on the other side of the world. In Hong Kong, Winnie Tarn, Joseph Leung and other colleagues helped in producing the original manuscript, for which deep thanks to them.

Though our paths diverged, Faith Evans set the ball rolling, and Gillon Aitken gave valuable advice. Paul Theroux suggested a vital connection. Christopher Sinclair-Stevenson's enthusiasm made all the difference both times round. I am grateful to Philippa Harrison for having decided to publish the first edition book and to Richard Seaver for the first US edition, to Andrew Gordon for his expert editing and backing first time round and to Cal Barksdale for his attentive and supportive work on this version, along with his colleagues at Skyhorse.

But, in the end, it all comes down to Renée, without whom none of this would have been possible and who has, once again, provided the most expert and devoted first reading anybody could ask for, putting me right on points of detail and, more important, providing stimulating big picture thoughts and the insights only a native of the Hexagon can truly possess. If this book is dedicated to her parents, it exists because of her.

April 2014

Note

Since this is a book in English, the Anglophone version of place names have been used where they exist, i.e. Lyons, Marseilles, Brittany, Burgundy.

Because of movements in the currency markets, euros and French francs have not been converted. At the time of writing, the euro stood at 1.36 to the US dollar.

FRANCE
ON THE
BRINK

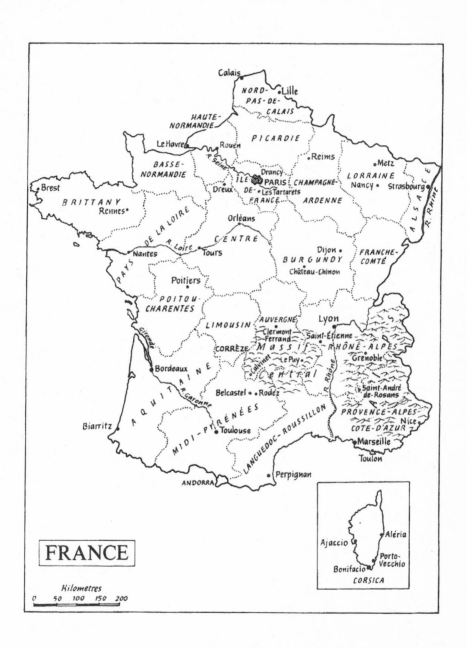

Calais

NORD-
PAS-DE-
CALAIS

Lille

HAUTE-
NORMANDIE

PICARDIE

Le Havre

Rouen

R. Seine

Reims

Metz

BASSE-
NORMANDIE

Drancy

PARIS

LORRAINE

Brest

Dreux

ILE
DE-
FRANCE

Les Tartarets

CHAMPAGNE-

Nancy

Strasbourg

ALSACE

R. RHINE

BRITTANY

Rennes

ARDENNE

PAYS   DE   LA   LOIRE

Orléans

CENTRE

Nantes

R. Loire

Tours

Dijon

BURGUNDY

FRANCHE-
COMTÉ

Poitiers

Château-Chinon

POITOU-
CHARENTES

LIMOUSIN

AUVERGNE

Lyon

Clermont-
Ferrand

Saint-Étienne

RHÔNE-ALPES

CORRÈZE

Massif

Grenoble

Bordeaux

Cavines

Le Puy

Central

R. Rhône

Saint-André
de-Rosans

GIRONDE

Belcastel

Rodez

AQUITAINE

R. Garonne

PROVENCE-ALPES

Nice

Biarritz

MIDI-PYRÉNÉES

Toulouse

LANGUEDOC-ROUSSILLON

CÔTE-D'AZUR

Marseille

Toulon

ANDORRA

Perpignan

FRANCE

Kilometres
0   50   100   150   200

Aléria

Ajaccio

Porto-
Vecchio

Bonifacio

CORSICA

1

A SPECIAL PLACE

Nations and their peoples often go through mood swings spurred by victories or defeats, good times or bad, booms and slumps. But none displays such a disjunction as France between its people's view of their country's role in history and their feelings about contemporary life. On the one hand, they are convinced that the home of Joan of Arc and Louis XIV, Napoleon and Charles de Gaulle, Balzac, Victor Hugo and the Impressionists, the Eiffel Tower and the Arc de Triomphe occupies a special place in the world, a land that stands apart from others on account of its history and its character.

Its model of a strong state, social protection for its citizens and the mantra of 'liberty, equality, fraternity' from the Revolution of 1789 makes France unique, 'a beacon for the human race,' according to Jacques Chirac, its president from 1995 to 2007; he concluded the first volume of his memoirs by dedicating his electoral victory to the 'patriots . . . who have made France a tolerant, fraternal, inventive and masterful nation.' His successor but one, François Hollande, is equally clear. 'France's destiny is to be a global nation,' he declared on one occasion. 'Europe needs a strong France,' he said on another, 'and the world needs an influential France.' In 2013, an official committee advised the government that 'as soon as France touches something, she makes it more intelligent, more unexpected, sharper, more productive. France always puts the breath of inspiration into what she undertakes.'

Once, the hexagonal land that looks both to the rest of Europe and to the wider world was known simply as the 'Great Country.' 'Live like God in France,' was how the Germans put it. But, as the twenty-first century progresses, the nation has sunk into what its people describe as '*morosité*.' They are deeply worried about the state of the economy, the integrity and ability of politicians, immigration and society. Beyond that lies the deeper and even more troubling matter of national identity as successive administrations have failed to revive the country's confidence. Opinion surveys report a widespread desire for a strong leader to restore the national direction, but the failure of mainstream political parties to provide reassurance leads many to vote for extremist parties. Those gripped by exasperation fall back as their preferred form of expression on the French habit of angry demonstrations, sometimes spilling over into violence. 'Behind the generalised protest movement lies a deep doubt about the continuation of the French model,' remarks the head of a polling service.

The fallout is everywhere and is gaining in scope and speed. The people turn quickly against those they chose to rule them; within a year of Hollande's election in 2012, his popularity rating had slumped to 30 per cent and then went on dropping. Sharp reverses at municipal elections in March 2014 forced him to change prime minister and reshuffle the government. The French consume more tranquilisers and antidepressants than other West Europeans. A study by the consultants Deloitte in late 2013 reported that a quarter of young graduates thought their futures lay abroad, double the number eighteen months earlier. Concern about law and order—*insécurité*—is a constant theme; 70 per cent of those questioned in a survey in 2013 said they thought the justice system worked badly. Such concerns are not new.

'There is too much violence in our country, too much insecurity—in schools, on public transport, in the streets,' President Chirac said in 1998. 'Every day new limits are broken beyond which our society will disintegrate.' More and more people have admitted to sympathy with racism. Nicolas Sarkozy, who won the presidency in 2007, based his political career largely on presenting himself as a tough enforcer of law and order during his spells as Interior Minister in charge of the police. The new prime minister of 2014, Manuel Valls, had become the most popular member of the previous government in the same post with a similarly tough line.

A nation which has always prided itself on its internationalism and its links with the world has been turning in on itself, fearful of what lies beyond its borders be it cheap goods from China, immigration from new member states of the European Union in central and eastern Europe or 'Anglo-Saxon finance' (meaning Wall Street and London). Opinion surveys show low support for the capitalist system and for globalization. In the 2012 presidential election one-third of the vote went to candidates hostile to the European market economy, and Sarkozy undertook to press the EU Commission in Brussels to adopt protectionist measures if re-elected. The following year, polls found that support for the European Union in France had dropped below 50 per cent. Only a fifth of those questioned said they viewed European economic integration in a positive light, while 72 per cent wanted restrictions on access to welfare for migrants from other EU states.

Still, there are plenty of reasons for that pride even if, as we will see, quite a few of them contain worms in the bud. Though its sixty-five million people rank only twenty-first in the population league, France is home to the world's fifth-biggest economy at $2.7 trillion dollars. Its companies stand fourth in *Fortune* magazine's global rankings. It possesses nuclear weapons and a permanent seat on the United Nations Security Council. It has the most important bilateral defence agreement in Europe—with Britain—and President Sarkozy announced his country's return to NATO's integrated military structure in 2009, four decades after General de Gaulle quit it in search of national independence.

Frenchmen led the creation of the European Union, with de Gaulle, making sure that Paris assumed the political leadership of the community. Jacques Delors—one of two presidents of the EU Commission from France—piloted the development of the single market embracing twenty-eight countries. A Frenchman was the commission's Secretary-General for thirty years. Four of the last six managing directors of the International Monetary Fund (IMF) have been French. Jean-Claude Trichet was the first head of the European Central Bank from 2003 to 2011. Pascal Lamy served as Director-General of the World Trade Organization from 2005 to 2013.

France has one of Europe's most extensive and least crowded road networks, and as big a railway system as Britain and Italy put together. The state Post Office set up the world's first online data network for households, and the government took the lead in developing both the supersonic airliner and the high-speed train. The health service has long been a subject of national pride and joy, and a subject of international envy for its standards of care. The French eat high levels of butter and eggs while maintaining a low rate of heart disease and an obesity level one-fifth of that of Americans. A Europe-wide investigation reported that their children were the healthiest on the continent.

The Hexagon occupies a unique geographical position. On its west is the Atlantic Ocean reaching across to the Americas. To the south lie the Mediterranean, the Pyrennean frontier with Spain and the border with Italy. Up on the east side, it has Switzerland, Germany and Belgium as neighbours. To the north, across the narrow Channel, is the nation which has so often been France's prime rival and sometime ally, 'perfidious Albion.' Bounded by water, mountains and flatlands, France is neither a land power, like Germany, nor a maritime one, as Britain used to be. Away from Europe, traces of its empire, second only to that of Britain and covering 4.8 million square miles at its apogee in the 1920s and 1930s, persist from former colonies in Africa and Asia to territories stretching from the North Atlantic to the South Seas which Paris insists remain as much part of the republic as the Auvergne.

The royal courts of the Bourbon monarchs were among the outstanding centres of power up to the eighteenth century. France then gave the world the template of the modern revolution, which brought together the ideals of liberty, equality and fraternity, and promulgated the sacred nature of the rights of man. Though the Revolution of 1789 led to totalitarian terror and the autocratic rule of Napoleon Bonaparte followed by the restoration of the monarchy, the republican ideal had been established at a time when kings and emperors ruled the rest of Europe. This ideal was briefly reborn in the revolution of 1848 only to be crushed by the Second Empire of Napoleon III. But then the Third Republic, born in the ashes of military defeat at the hands of Prussian-led Germany in 1870, established a durable form of non-monarchical, non-Napoleonic rule, lasting until the second defeat by Germany in 1940. After the interregnum of the Vichy collaborationist regime, a Fourth Republic came into being, but, brought low by instability in its legislative-dominated political system, economic woes and the poisonous war to hold on to Algeria, gave way to the presidential regime established by Charles de Gaulle in 1958, which endures to this day.

Through this long story of regime changes stretching over two and a quarter centuries, France has given the world the metric system, Braille, pasteurization, tinned sardines and liposuction. Baron Pierre de Coubertin was the father of the modern Olympics. The Tour de France cycle race is watched each year by more on-the-spot spectators than any other annual sporting event on Earth and is televised in more than 160 countries. This is the land of *les Misérables*, Edith Piaf and Brigitte Bardot, claret, the camembert and the cancan. The 'French lover' stands for sexual sophistication, and *l'amour* has a special potency, whatever the performance realities.

The French built the Statue of Liberty and the Suez Canal. They invented the vegetable mixer, denim and champagne, not to mention disposable razors, the pressure cooker, the sewing machine and the non-stick frying pan, which gave Ronald Reagan his Teflon nickname. The Perrier spring is synonymous with sparkling water round the globe. Nicéphore Niépce pioneered photography in the early nineteenth century. The Lumière brothers made the first moving picture in 1895. The Club Méditerranée set the model for informal, all-inclusive holiday resorts, and it was a Parisian who commercialized the bikini swimsuit, employing a nude dancer to show it off after the regular models refused to do so.

French cultural history is unmatched, dating back to a 32,000-year-old cave painting. Which other nation can boast writers such as Rabelais, Molière, Corneille, Racine, Stendhal, Flaubert, Balzac, Hugo, Zola, Baudelaire, Proust, Camus and Dumas *père et fils*? The Ancien Régime produced the greatest court diarist in Saint-Simon. Voltaire dreamed up Candide and Panglosse, and Beaumarchais provided Mozart with Figaro. The whole planet knows *The Hunchback of Notre Dame*, 'Bluebeard,' *Around the World in Eighty Days* and *The Three Musketeers*. France counts more Nobel Prizes for literature than any other country. Philosophy stretches back over a thousand years to Abélard, followed by Montaigne, Pascal, Descartes, Diderot, Comte,

Bergson, and the Existentialists, Structuralists and Post-Structuralists of modern times.

In art, the list is equally impressive—from Poussin and De la Tour through Corot and Cézanne to Manet, Monet and Renoir, Matisse and Braque, not to mention the sculptor Rodin or the caricaturist Daumier. The list of great composers goes from Lully and Rameau to Debussy, Ravel, Berlioz, Fauré, Bizet, Satie and Poulenc. Claude François, a French singer who subsequently electrocuted himself in his bath, was responsible for the music of 'My Way,' while another, Sacha Distel, co-wrote that alternative anthem, 'The Good Life.' The French language includes subtleties that escape Anglophones—and six hundred synonyms each for the penis and vagina listed by linguistic expert Pierre Guiraud.

The first parachute descent took place two centuries ago from a balloon above the Parc Monceau in Paris. A seventeenth-century prelate, Pierre de Fermat, set out the theorem which took three centuries to prove. Albert Binet invented the intelligence test. Michel Lotito of Grenoble, *Monsieur Mangetout* (Mr. Eat Everything), distinguished himself by consuming nine tons of metal, including a light aircraft. Other Frenchmen set new standards for the speed eating of snails—275 in fifteen minutes—and shucking oysters—2,064 an hour.

As the world's favourite international holiday destination, the Hexagon attracted eighty-three million visitors in 2012—ten million more than at the turn of the century. According to the historian Emmanuel Le Roy-Ladurie, 'France is, first of all, a woman. A beautiful woman.' It is a land hymned in Charles Trenet's lyrical song, 'Douce France' (Sweet France), to be loved in its people's hearts whether in joy or pain.

No nation of comparable size, and few that are much bigger, can equal its variety of landscape and life. Where else provides rivals to the châteaux of the Loire; the walled city of Carcassonne; the majestic papal palace of Avignon; the jewel church of Vézelay and the Romanesque beauties along the pilgrim trail towards Compostela; the hilltop fortresses of the doomed Cathar heretics in the Pyrenees; the cathedrals of Chartres, Reims or Albi; the central square of Nancy or the Dominican church and hidden medieval townhouses of Toulouse; the Spanish-accented charm and Fauvist colours of the anchovy port of Collioure on the Mediterranean; and the nineteenth-century elegance of Biarritz on the Atlantic and

Deauville on the Channel, not to mention the celebrated esplanades of Nice and Cannes?

The list goes on and on—the great gorges not just of the Tarn but also the equally spectacular ravines of the Ardèche, the Verdon and the Hérault, the rough beauty of the Cévennes and the Auvergne and the bucolic pastures of Normandy and the Limousin, from the towering peaks of the Alps to the lavender fields of the Drôme and the softness of Anjou, from the wild horses of the mountain plateaux of the Spanish border and the pink flamingos of the Camargue to the storks nesting on the rooftops of Alsace and the seagulls wheeling over the vast D-Day invasion beaches of Normandy.

Paris provides a unique range of architecture, history and personal memory—Roman relics of the Arènes de Lutèce, Renaissance mansions of the Marais around the Place des Vosges through Baron Haussmann's construction of a city centre under Napoleon III and on to the legacy of steel, glass and concrete bequeathed to the capital by François Mitterrand in the 1980s and 1990s. The Centre Georges Pompidou in the Beaubourg district has lured five times as many visitors as originally planned and had to close for two years to repair the resulting wear and tear. France's capital has some of the most famous monuments and open spaces in the world—the Eiffel Tower, the Louvre and Arc de Triomphe, the Place de la Concorde, the quays of the Seine, Notre Dame Cathedral, the Tuileries gardens and the Bois de Boulogne— but also a wealth of smaller jewels, quiet cobbled court-yards, exquisite houses large and small, street markets, glass-roofed nineteenth-century shopping galleries, churches and squares. Paris is sometimes dismissed these days as having fallen behind such throbbing temples of twenty-first-century urban life as London, New York, Berlin or Barcelona. But, if that is the case, it still remains unique in its own special way and one would be a fool not to acknowledge as much.

Despite all the tales of outrageously priced cups of coffee on the Champs-Élysées, Paris is not among the most expensive world cities to visit. Its famously abrupt inhabitants are as likely to be in a hurry as rude—and will be as short with their fellow citizens as with visitors. From China to Argentina, cities in search of glamour call themselves the 'Paris of the East' or the 'Paris of the Americas,' and they are not wrong given the city's international renown to so many different kinds of people.

For more than a century, the City of Light was the magnet for exiles ranging from White Russians and Jews to Communists and the Duke and Duchess of Windsor in their memento-filled villa in the Bois de Boulogne. Karl Marx burnished his theories during a stay in the capital. Ho Chi Minh and Pol Pot studied Marxism and Leninism in France's capital. Deng Xiaoping joined the Chinese Communist Party there while in France as a teenager and retained a taste for croissants all his life. The Ayatollah Khomeini spent the last spell of his exile in a Paris suburb. Today, some of the best-known foreigners in the city are international soccer players, including the incomparable Swedish striker Zlatan Ibrahimovic, bought for huge sums by what may be the richest club in the world, Paris Saint-Germain, which has been transformed under Qatari ownership.

One of the troop of foreign writers and artists who came to live there, Walter Benjamin, called Paris the capital of the nineteenth century; a bit later, another resident foreigner, Gertrude Stein, dubbed it 'the place where the twentieth century was.' Henry James and Edith Wharton were denizens of France. Charles Lindbergh became a world hero as a conqueror of distance when he landed at Le Bourget airfield in 1927. In his film *Midnight in Paris*, Woody Allen paid an ultimate homage to the French capital's role in the American literary imagination.

The city was home to Picasso and Modigliani, and a last refuge for Oscar Wilde and Marlene Dietrich. Ernest Hemingway and Scott Fitzgerald sized up their penises in a Left Bank café lavatory. Paris and France adopted Josephine Baker and Sidney Bechet. Fats Waller got a chance to play the 'God box' in the organ loft of Notre Dame, and jazz musicians fleeing American racism found a home away from home in the Hotel Louisiane above the Rue de Buci street market on the Left Bank. Richard Wright and James Baldwin, among other African American writers and artists, found refuge in Paris, too. In a different musical mode, Jim Morrison's grave is still a pilgrimage spot for Doors fans on the northern slopes of the city.

A Paris publisher was the first to print Joyce and Nabokov. George Gershwin sailed home in 1928 with a collection of Paris taxi horns to use in *An American in Paris*. Eugene Ionesco and Samuel Beckett wrote in the language of their adopted country. Asked why he lived in Paris, the Irishman replied, 'Well, you know, if I was in Dublin I would just be sitting around in a pub.' Cole Porter made April the city's month. Gene Kelly and Fred Astaire gave it the sheen of musical romance for cinema audiences around the globe. Humphrey Bogart comforted Ingrid Bergman in Casablanca by assuring her, 'We'll always have Paris.' Even Hitler had to admit that, while levelling London or Moscow would not have disturbed his peace of mind, he would have been greatly pained to have had to destroy the capital of France— when he finally gave the order to do so in 1944, it was not executed.

Not to be outdone, other French cities, towns and regions have attracted their stars, too. The still two-eared Van Gogh drew his inspiration from Provence. Salvador Dali proclaimed Perpignan station to be the centre of the universe. Medieval popes took up residence in Avignon. Chopin made beautiful music with George Sand in the dank flatlands of the centre. Robert Louis Stevenson trekked through the Cévennes on a donkey. Madonna named her daughter after the pilgrimage shrine of Lourdes, and Yul Brynner's ashes were laid to rest in a monastery in the Loire Valley. As for the Côte d'Azur, Scott Fitzgerald's 'pleasant shore of the Riviera' became such a mecca for the smart set of the 1920s that they could believe they had invented it. Later, Somerset Maugham held lugubrious court in his villa at Cap Ferrat, and Graham Greene denounced the local political mafia as he saw out his last years in one of the less fashionable towns of the coastline.

France's gastronomic leadership has come under severe challenge from global rivals, but reports of its demise are premature. One problem is the number of top chefs from the Hexagon who work abroad. Inventiveness has taken the place of old stereotyped menus in the twenty-first century; molecular cooking can be found at a top restaurant in the little-visited Corbières region of the south as well as in smart establishments in the capital. But, for all the excellence of cooks in countries which used not to count a single Michelin three-star restaurant, the underlying traditions of France's regional gastronomy provide a foundation few other nations can rival. A French name is still prized by exponents of culinary excellence. So New York has Le Cirque; Los Angeles, Ma Maison; London, Le Gavroche and Tante Claire; and both Stockholm and Hanoi L'Opéra. In California, the celebrated chef Alice Waters called her restaurant Chez Panisse, while Napa Valley gastronomes flock to the

French Laundry and diners at steakhouses in Santa Monica cut their meat with knives from the small town of Laguiole in the Aveyron department more than five thousand miles away.

Laying claim to a Hexagonal heritage, brasseries and bistros flourish round the world. Tokyo's Ginza shopping avenue is swamped with French outlets, and Japanese gourmets can spend a fortune eating the potato purée of three-star chef Joël Robuchon in a full-scale replica of a Loire Valley château constructed with stone imported from France. Across the sea from Japan, North Korea marked the elevation of the Great Leader Kim Jong-il by ordering 66,000 bottles of French wine. Shanghai has a Café de la Seine on the riverfront and a brasserie called Chamselisee. (Say it fast with a local accent and all becomes clear.)

As in gastronomy, France is no longer the unchallenged leader of world fashion, and its top couture houses employ British, Italian and Russian designers to give them a contemporary edge. But these designers still want to work in what, for the global imagination and marketing, remains the city that epitomizes high style. Boutiques from Oslo to Osaka call themselves by French names. Rag-trade workshops around the globe stitch in 'Arc de Triomphe' or 'Tour Eiffel' labels. Paris still means fashion, even if the frocks are financed and dreamed up by people who can't speak to the limo driver on the way home. It was, after all, Christian Dior who invented international haute couture, and his successor, Yves Saint-Laurent, who carried on the tradition—even if, as his lover and manager once said, he was born with a nervous breakdown.

France's rays reach round the globe in other ways, too. Archaeologists reckon that the greatest symbol of Britain's prehistoric past, the stone circle at Stonehenge, was probably the work of invaders from Brittany. The remains of a tenth-century monastery transposed from Saint-Michel-de-Cuxa in the Pyrénées-Orientales department stand above the Hudson River in New York, while the televisual *Friends* have a poster of a park in northern Paris on their wall. Frederick the Great named his palace in Potsdam Sanssouci, and his successors called their supreme military medal Pour le mérite. The French architect Joseph Ramée was the progenitor of the American campus plan with the Union College of Schenectady. Louisiana is home to half a million Cajuns descended from French settlers who were ethnically cleansed from their Acadia in Nova Scotia by the British and who keep their language alive on the bayous 250 years later. In the 1990s, Hollywood got into the habit of gobbling up French films for trans-Atlantic versions; 'Another week, another Hollywood remake of a French movie,' as *The New Yorker* remarked.

Japan has its version of the Eiffel Tower, and a reproduction of the Alsatian town of Colmar is being built above the tropical forests of Malaysia. The Tianducheng development in China's Zhejiang Province has been built with Parisian boulevards and a full-scale replica of Monsieur Eiffel's edifice. The most expensive hotel suite in Korea is modelled after the Palace of Versailles. An Indochinese sect counts Louis Pasteur and Victor Hugo among its saints, and Cambodians smoke cigarettes named after the actor Alain Delon. Pupils at schools on the resort island of Phuket in Thailand learn to play pétanque.

Bitter opposition to France's nuclear tests in 1995 did not cause the Australian Prime Minister to abandon his hobby of collecting French clocks or stop a Japanese firm from tripling its orders of Beaujolais nouveau. In the 1960s, an aged African dictator tried to get his country turned into a department of France, while the leaders of the Indian Ocean island of Mayotte announced that they wanted to become part of France 'like the department of Lozère.' Duke Ellington defined himself as a drinker of Beaujolais; James Dean found solace in Saint-Exupéry's *The Little Prince*; and Ella Fitzgerald was once spotted reading a book by Jean-Paul Sartre in her dressing room, though what she made of it is not recorded.

Linguistic backwoodsmen have long fought against the spread of English, but have met with little success—in 2013, the state railway system started to offer English language lessons on its service from Rheims to Paris. The use of English can, indeed, reach ridiculous lengths, or depths, as when newspapers write of planes having *crashé* instead of using the perfectly good French word *écrasé* or inventing neologisms that do not exist in English. But, if anybody bothered to calculate whether more words of French origin are used in English than vice-versa, French would come off much better than its fearful defenders might think.

Chic, after all, is smarter than smart. *Faute de mieux*, invitations in London or Hong Kong come marked RSVP or Pour Mémoire.

Generals have aides de camp, media organizations call their foreign offices bureaux and America's greatest artistic gift to the world probably takes its name from the use of the chattering verb *jaser* by Creole speakers in New Orleans. Hotel concierges and waiters the world over address women as 'madame.' In filmdom, even producers like to be called auteurs. Gourmets eat in restaurants; tourists buy souvenirs; bourgeois folk gather at the table for dinner or rendezvous at a café. Negligees and culottes may no longer be in style, but women still wear brassieres (except in France where they don the *soutien-gorge*). Comedians thrive on double entendres. Dead-end streets are known as cul-de-sacs—though the French prefer *impasse*, *cul* being a somewhat rude term.

Louis Pasteur, Joseph Guillotin and the Marquis de Sade bestowed their names on posterity. The .caped cloaks of the Limousin region of France provided the synonym for motorcars with hoods. Extreme patriots and opponents of women's rights take their label from an enthusiastic Napoleonic veteran, Nicolas Chauvin. Gymnasts somersault more easily thanks to the garment invented by the trapeze artist, Jules Leotard. Disciplinarians should flick their whips towards Colonel Martinet for the strict order he imposed on Louis XIV's infantry. Napoleon's name was used by the US Secret Service as its code name for Frank Sinatra. The extremely grand Vicomte de Turenne, on the other hand, might be less than charmed to know that, outside the history class, his name is perpetuated by his habit of using his helmet as a soup bowl.

The French have a term for their special nature—*l'exception française*. They have been accustomed to seeing themselves as standing apart from their neighbours, superior to the shopkeepers across the Channel, the laborious, plodding Germans or the mercurial Italians. The supreme monarch, Louis XIV, was not all-victorious, but no European doubted that his Sun King court at Versailles was the centre of the universe—and just imagine the outcome if his successors hadn't made a hash of the Anglo-French wars in the mid-eighteenth century and had become dominant in North America.

The most famous Corsican may have ended up in poisoned exile on an island in the Atlantic, but Bonaparte still seemed to the philosopher Hegel to be master of the world and inspired Beethoven to write the *Eroica* Symphony. A century and a half later, Charles de Gaulle could be, as the American diplomat Charles Bohlen told Franklin Roosevelt, 'one of the biggest sons-of-bitches that ever straddled a pot'; yet, like Napoleon, his style of government provided a new adjective for the vocabulary of power. Wherever they go, the French take their country with them—from restaurants in Indochina to their unrivalled network of lycée schools around the world, which ensures that French children follow the central curriculum from Bonn to Beijing. Wherever they go, one government minister declared, the French carry Europe 'on the soles of their shoes.'

The urge to be exceptional is, in the words of the commentator Dominique Moisi, a fundamental part of national existence. As the novelist Julian Barnes puts it, the French embody 'otherness.' They are conceited rather than vain, the British politician Roy Jenkins judged. Their national vision of history is unabashedly Franco-centric, co-opting foreign rulers since Charlemagne and, as far as possible, glossing over uncomfortable episodes such as the collaboration with the occupying Nazis or the nature of colonialism in Indochina and Algeria. The Republic, which President Hollande described in 2013 as 'our most precious possession,' founded on 'virtue, honesty and honour,' is hallowed by the political left and right alike. Immigrants are expected to conform to the rules of the Republic even if that means Muslim women being prosecuted for wearing the *niqab* head covering and their children learning, until recently, about 'our ancestors the Gauls.'

In keeping with its vision of exceptionalism, France ended the twentieth century in a optimistic mood, led by the neo-Gaullist Jacques Chirac, its confidence boosted by victory for its virtuoso soccer team in the 1998 World Cup. Under a tight money policy dictated by the Bank of France, the franc rivalled the German mark in strength. Strong exports and limited imports had boosted trade performance since 1992. The budget deficit was forecast to fall to 2.5 per cent of gross domestic product by 1999—just over half its level in the mid-1990s. Such was the international confidence in the economy that, at one point, France was able to pay lower interest than reunited Germany on its bonds. The annualized inflation rate fell to 0.3 per cent. A hybrid administration made up of a centre-right president and a Socialist government undertook a major programme of privatization of state assets.

The value of the Paris Bourse soared, with the trading volume rising by 39 per cent in 1998 alone. Foreign investors accounted for half the turnover. France became the fourth-biggest recipient of global investment as companies such as IBM, Motorola and FedEx developed their operations in the Hexagon, and Toyota decided to build a four-billion-franc plant in Valenciennes in the north of the country rather than in Britain.

French companies were world leaders in tires, cosmetics and yoghurts. Air France was the fourth-biggest international carrier. The state was a major force in the European Airbus consortium, whose development was steered by a Frenchman. A hundred space rockets had been launched from the base in French Guyana. Électricité de France was Europe's biggest energy exporter. A French firm built the world's largest flight kitchen at Hong Kong's new airport; another installed almost half the new telephone lines in China. The AXA-UAP group counted as a major global asset manager, and the Société Générale bank snapped up one of London's last independent investment houses, Hambros. The luxury goods firm LVMH established itself as a top world player. The French state even found itself owning MGM in Hollywood and the Executive Life insurance group in the United States as part of headlong expansion by the publicly owned Crédit Lyonnais, which made it Europe's biggest bank for a while.

In international politics, independence was a constant theme. The tone was set in 1940, when Lieutenant-General de Gaulle insisted on his Free French command in London being the only Allied European force not to be integrated under the British and used recurrent rows with his host and with the hostile FDR to stress his autonomy, even if he depended on the Allies winning the war to enable him to return home. After returning to power in 1958, the General presumed to act as a bridge between East and West and denounced the division of Europe, if only because it had been enshrined at the Yalta summit of 1945, to which he had not been invited. France insisted on freedom to target friend and foe alike with its nuclear force. A little later, its President left the French chair at Common Market meetings empty for months when he didn't like the way the embryonic community was going. But there was also solidarity at major crisis points during the Cold War.

Under presidents of right and left, the Gaullist heritage has been an enduring element in France's relations with the rest of the world. French leaders take a global view as if they had an automatic right to pronounce on the affairs of others. Policy paths that might seem contradictory are justified by French logic or interests. The first President of the left caused concern in Washington by taking Communists into his government, but then gave determined backing to American missile policy in Europe. His successor from the right cancelled summit meetings with some of France's closest partners for alleged lack of solidarity with Paris, but then announced a major reorganization of the armed forces which affected its allies without prior consultation. The French can be 'masters of splendid ambiguity,' as Britain's former Foreign Secretary, Douglas Hurd, noted. Margaret Thatcher wrote—in evident exasperation—of President Mitterrand 'speaking in paragraphs of perfectly crafted prose which seemed to brook no interruption.' Secretary of State Madeleine Albright recalled the inscrutable comment of a French diplomat about a proposal affecting various European organizations: 'It will work in practice, yes. But will it work in theory?'

'The French are by nature inclined to bully the weak and to fear the strong. Although they are boastful and vainglorious, as soon as an enterprise becomes difficult they abandon it; they are better at start-ing things than following them through.' That was the judgement of Marquis Tseng, the Chinese minister in Europe, who negotiated with the French over Vietnam in 1881. Echoing the familiar description of the French cavalry as being magnificent when it advances but ragged in retreat, this is a verdict which many, including some friends of France, would regard as an apposite piece of Oriental wisdom. But when I put the notion to a French professor, she gave me a Gallic response from a 1930s film: 'The locomotive of your ignorance runs on the rails of my indifference.' *Et schlack*—so there!

So what was there to worry about? This was clearly a more than unusual nation with a great deal to be proud of. But lift the cur-tain, look behind the mirror, and the reasons for disquiet become all too evident. '*Tout va très bien, Madame la Marquise*,' as the butler told his employer over the telephone in a famous French comedy song of the 1930s. The château and the stables are burning down, your favourite mare is dead, your husband has killed himself, but, apart from that, everything's all right, ma'am: *Tout va très bien, tout . . . va . . . très . . . bien.*

The song has been highly apposite because this has been high-anxiety time in the Hexagon. Just consider the contrasts between all those reasons for pride and early-twenty-first-century reality, between the glossy image and what people actually see when they glance into the national mirror, which is rendered particularly sensitive because of the sharp rejection of external criticism by a people who seem even more self-protective than most others.

The high note on which France ended the twentieth century turned out to be a passing illusion. The recovery from the economic mistakes made by the first Socialist administration of the Fifth Republic under François Mitterrand was long and painful, leaving persistently high unemployment and a large state deficit, while French competitiveness declined, especially vis-à-vis its increasingly powerful neighbour, Germany.

A gauge of public opinion showed that people regarded eleven of the years between 1980 and 1995 as having been 'bad times.' Going further back, surveys between 1973 and 1990 found that only 12–13 per cent of the French said they were 'very satisfied' with their lives, compared with more than 30 per cent in Britain, Denmark, Belgium, Ireland, Luxembourg and the Netherlands. Polls in the mid-1990s showed a steady 55 per cent expressing pessimism about the future. The suicide rate increased to one of the highest in developed nations.

So the good times around 2000 were probably always destined to be a blip, occurring at a time when President Chirac had been obliged to appoint the Socialist Lionel Jospin as Prime Minister after his supporters lost legislative elections in 1997. The first round of the presidential contest of 2002 produced a seismic outcome when divisions on the left and a poor Socialist campaign pushed Jospin into third place in the first round of voting behind Jean-Marie Le Pen, leader of the far right National Front.

This handed Chirac an overwhelming win in the second round run-off, but, for many, it was a vote against Le Pen, not for the incumbent. There was renewed national self-esteem when the dashing Foreign Minister Dominique de Villepin led opposition to the invasion of Iraq in 2003, earning his country the sobriquet 'cheese-eating surrender monkeys' (courtesy of *The Simpsons*) from across the Atlantic and getting French fries renamed Freedom fries in Washington. But the new administration produced little in new policies or reform as tension between the need for modernization and the power of vested interests blocked movement.

The electoral cycle should have swung back to the Socialists in 2007 when Chirac's twelve years as head of state ended (the term had been cut from seven to five years in 2002). But the party of the left suffered from serious internal dissention. Its candidate, Ségolène Royal, the first woman to run for the presidency as the standard bearer for a major political movement, sometimes seemed to be running against those who should have been backing her. Though her partner and father of their four children, François Hollande, was the party's manager, some prominent Socialists hardly hid their reservations about her headstrong campaign, which appealed mainly to old left values rather than crafting a new doctrine of social democracy. In a crucial television debate, she floundered and Nicolas Sarkozy romped home promising modernizing reforms, especially in the economy, and a tough clampdown on crime and disorder.

Sarkozy, a man known for his extreme energy and short attention span, failed to follow through and reverted to more conservative policies as France was buffeted by the financial and economic crisis which broke in 2007 and then gathered pace and engulfed the euro common currency zone. While Sarkozy performed well on the international stage, Germany's growing authority made it all too apparent that the balance of power in Europe had shifted decisively against France, while the President became associated with flashy 'bling' tastes and rich friends. He embarked on his presidency suffering from extreme personal pressure as his marriage fell apart and led to divorce; then he told the world that he found love with a new wife, the Italian star model and singer Carla Bruni. However much the President deplored it, their frequent appearance in gossip magazines took him even further away than before from the gravitas the French still expected from their president. As we will see in chapter 14, just about everything that could have gone wrong for him did, and he seemed incapable of rebalancing the boat he had built for himself with his relentless pursuit of power.

By the time he faced re-election in 2012, Sarkozy's unpopularity was such that he was doomed to defeat, even if his strongest challenger, Dominique Strauss-Kahn, had to withdraw from the contest after his imbroglio with a maid in a Manhattan hotel. Propelled to the front rank after making his career as a backroom manager of the Socialist Party, François Hollande duly won the presidency, but his score was not the triumph that might have been given the outgoing head of state's low rating in public esteem. At the first round of voting, in which ten candidates ran, he took 28.6 per cent of the vote, compared with 27.2 for Sarkozy The second round, in which only the two front-runners compete, was won by 51.6 to 48.4 per cent, with 25 per cent registered electors abstaining or casting spoiled ballot papers.

Still, the left triumphed at subsequent legislative elections and controlled most of France's regions, departments and cities. The new leader promised to be a 'normal' president and to unite the country around a programme that would spare France the austerity being imposed on indebted nations of southern Europe and the United Kingdom. Well-meaning, didactic in the manner of a friendly teacher, François Hollande was man with whom one would have liked to spend an evening talking about France, but the country needed something more than normalcy and earnest assurances that things would get better in due course.

He showed resolution in foreign affairs by sending troops to turn back Islamic fundamentalists in Mali and then to try to restore order in another former colony, the Central African Republic. He was among government leaders who boycotted the Sochi Winter Olympics of 2014 to protest Russia's human rights record. His expressed readiness to participate in an attack on Syria after the Assad regime used poison gas against rebels and civilians earned France the accolade of 'our oldest ally' from Secretary of State John Kerry. But this had low popular backing and the subsequent agreement between the United States and Russia's Foreign Minister, Sergei Lavrov, to opt for diplomatic pressure left him isolated—a cartoon on the French Huffington Post showed Hollande eavesdropping outside a door marked 'Kerry-Lavrov—Do not disturb.' It was captioned

'The Butler.' France then temporarily blocked an agreement with Iran over its nuclear programme, which Kerry had helped to craft, on the grounds that it was not sufficiently firm. That earned a tweet from Senator John McCain of 'Vive la France,' and the French President was greeted as a hero in Israel.

In February 2014, Hollande paid a state visit to the United States, during which the atmosphere seemed to bear out Kerry's accolade. The French leader's description of himself as a social democrat a month earlier was seen in Washington as a sign of moderation, but, above all, he was welcomed as somebody who was ready to have his country undertake its share of international military operations—who was freer of the parliamentary control that shackled Britain's government and more ready to step up to the plate than Berlin. Indeed, before their black-tie dinner at the White House and their visit to Thomas Jefferson's Virginia home, Hollande and Obama explicitly called, in a joint newspaper article, for their allies to participate more in burden sharing. French commentators saw a stronger bond than under Sarkozy, but there were limits—the Frenchman was not invited to address Congress as his predecessor had been.

Despite this strong performance abroad, when it came to domestic affairs, the impression in Hollande's first eighteen months in power was one of lack of resolve and of an administration reacting to the latest shift in opinion, giving way in the face of demonstrations and failing to arouse more than a minimum degree of public trust in its policies while the President's private life became a matter of very public attention. Its decision to impose tax increases to reduce the state deficit caused rising discontent—Hollande and Pierre Moscovici, his first Finance Minister, both acknowledged the problem, and some National Front candidates in local elections in 2014 switched their main rhetoric from immigration and crime to high taxes. But Hollande's expressions of understanding did not assuage people who saw their standard of living declining and their payments to the state increasing. Unemployment rose to a record 3.3 million by the end of 2013, and very few people saw the prospect of a significant recovery with the state's debt having ballooned from 20 to 90 per cent of Gross Domestic Product (GDP) since the mid-1970s (the television station France2 worked out that if all government liabilities were added up and expressed in terms of hundred-euro notes, the pile would be one storey higher than the 164-foot Arc de Triomphe).

In his televised address to the nation for the 2014 New Year, Hollande declared himself to be a social democrat, a suspect breed to many in his Socialist Party. He announced a more business-friendly policy direction, with a cut in the payroll tax on companies by 30 billion euros to reduce their average wage bill by 5 per cent in return for what was called 'a responsibility pact' under which firms would hire more workers. There would also be less regulation. But a corporate tax break introduced in 2013 was to be eliminated, meaning that the overall saving for employers would be half the headline figure he cited. He also acknowledged that the tax level was too high, said the state had become 'too heavy, too slow, too costly' and pledged cuts of 50 billion euros in spending—though this had already been implicit in his promise to get the budget deficit down to the European Union's target level of 3 per cent. Business leaders welcomed his announcements, and there was support from West Germany, too. But trade unions were unpersuaded, demanding guarantees of job creation from companies—'The President has held his hand out to business, and business has eaten his arm off,' a leader of the Force Ouvrière labour federation commented. The left wing of the Socialist Party was also hostile, while the head of the employers' federation commented that 'there is no sign of improvement.'

After losing one hundred fifty towns and cities in municipal elections three months later, Hollande dropped his first Prime Minister, Jean-Marc Ayrault, and replaced him with the popular Manuel Valls, who had spoken disparagingly in the past of old-style Socialism and criticised the thirty-five-hour work week. But Hollande still felt the need to balance factions in the Socialist Party, where he had spent all his adult life; he was more a prisoner of his party than any previous president had been. So he appointed two senior left-wingers to balance Valls and insisted that he still wanted growth, not austerity. As the economic data continued to decline, Paris asked the EU for more time to put its financial affairs in order, but the Commission in Brussels took a tough line and a leaked German paper said that Europe's most powerful nation thought France had not earned more flexibility.

The President's affair with an actress—revealed at the start of 2014—and his subsequent breakup with the official First Lady, Valérie Trierweiler, his partner for seven years, threatened to overshadow his declarations, at the same time, of the change in economic policy. He refused to comment and the French media were generally respectful of his privacy, but when he visited Britain in early 2014, he could not avoid questioning, to which he replied with a curt refusal to comment.

As ministers squabbled in public, France's second Socialist President became a target for mockery from right and left alike. A photograph of him visiting a school showed him grinning gormlessly; the French news agency and Thomson Reuters killed the shot but not before it had been posted on Wikipedia and had featured on a Saturday night prime-time television entertainment programme as backdrop to a satirical song about 'Monsieur Normal.'

In a phrase that also caught on, Jean-Luc Mélenchon, the hard left leader, described Hollande as the captain of a *pedalo* (pedal boat) caught in a storm. From the vociferous right, activists from the movement against same-sex marriage whistled at him at the Armistice Day commemorations on November 11, 2013. By the end of that year, his approval rating was down to one-fifth of those questioned. The left-wing newspaper *Libération* ran a simple but trenchant front page headline: 'A question of authority,' while an opinion survey reported that 86 per cent of those questioned said that 'authority' was the word that went least well with the head of state. His hope was that Valls would save the day, but the way in which he had been forced to make the change of prime minister hardly spoke of presidential clout and he still felt the need to balance Socialist factions by naming two leading left-wingers to counter the new premier from the right of the party.

A majority of voters had hoped that Sarkozy would bring strong leadership, but he was undone by his own inconsistencies and his failure to confront the forces defending the status quo. Then they thought that Hollande would bring growth and a more inclusive style of ruling to square the many circles surrounding the nation. But, as he admitted at the end of 2013, he had underestimated the depth of the economic crisis facing France and soon appeared to be caught in the different pressures on him, transfixed by his desire to maintain support from the left that opposed structural reform. In the sixteen years since I pointed to the problems with France in the first edition of this book, it is extraordinary how little changed and how the fault lines have deepened under governments of right and left alike. *Plus ça change, plus c'est la même chose* as the saying goes. France sticks to its ways inherited from centuries past and seeks to live by its own values however the world outside evolves.

Year by year, surveys show the French are deeply worried about their present well-being and their future, the economy, law and order and immigration and disappointed in the institutions that form the core of the hallowed state while growing more mistrustful of one another. A World Health Organization (WHO) report in 2011 found that they were more likely to suffer from a 'major depressive episode' than eighteen other countries surveyed. This was followed two years later by a Gallup poll which reported that the French were among the most pessimistic people on earth. Another survey published the same year hammered home the message—70 per cent of those questioned thought their country was in the grip of a 'collective depression.'

In the spring of 2013, *Le Monde* reported that three-quarters of respondents thought their country's democracy was not working well, and 62 per cent saw politicians as corrupt. More than 70 per cent wanted a 'true chief,' a strong leader to pull the nation together, among them plenty of voters for the Socialists. There was talk of the need for a Sixth Republic, with less top-down authority and greater bottom-up democracy, but it was not clear how this would improve matters. The malaise was of a different order and was unlikely to be fixed by constitutional tinkering. By the spring of 2013, some news magazine covers were speculating as to whether the country was on the brink of another 1789, with discontent so widespread that the regime would crumble.

In this context, many see protectionism as an answer to global economic challenges, supported by the far left and right and, in essence, by some in the mainstream. Disenchantment focuses easily on immigrants. A survey conducted for *Le Monde* in early 2013 found that 62 per cent of respondents said they no longer felt at home in their own country as they used to. Three-quarters considered Islam incompatible with French society. Concern about immigration coalesces with worries about public and personal security, urban 'no-go zones' and crime waves in cities such as Marseilles. French Jews feel a rising wave of anti-Semitism, leading some to emigrate to Israel, as historian Georges Bensoussan reported immigrant school pupils clapping when their teacher mentioned Nazi extermination camps. A comedian parades his 'anti-Zionism' and wishes that gas chambers still existed to deal with a Jewish critic. Of course it is all a joke and Jews have no sense of humour, his fans say, but it is not, and they do.

Fear ramped up following a rampage in the southwest in 2012 by a French-Algerian terrorist and petty criminal, Mohammed Merah, who shot dead three Muslim soldiers and four Jews, three of them children, before being killed by police after a thirty-hour siege. Violent riots recur in outer city housing estates inhabited mainly by immigrants where youth unemployment can reach 50 per cent and relations with the police are tense. After one outburst in 2009, the Commissioner for Diversity and Equality warned that 'we are creating a social civil war in this country. I believe we are digging a ditch that leads straight into apartheid.'

At New Year, hundreds of cars are regularly torched in big cities. In July 2013 rioting ripped through the town of Trappes outside Paris after police asked a Muslim woman to remove her face-covering veil as required by legislation outlawing visible religious symbols in public places. Her husband, a convert to Islam, was arrested after fighting with police—after which the violence erupted.

An increasing number of people are cast out of society. The numbers living in cardboard boxes on the sidewalks of Paris and other big cities grows steadily. The national statistics office talks of a 50 per cent increase in homelessness between 2001 and 2012 and puts the total number of people living rough at 141,500. Charities say many more people are in danger of losing their homes or living on the edge—a poll in 2009 reported that 56 per cent of the French feared they could be homeless one day.

Books and magazine cover stories on national decline augment the gloom. The economist Claudia Senik reckons that the French are, on average, 20 per cent less likely than other Europeans to regard themselves as happy. She traces this not to objective factors but to 'values, beliefs and their perception of reality.' Central to that is the contrast between the nation's view of itself and the harsher conditions that crowd in from all sides and raise fundamental questions about the ability of the country to live up to the national identity it has forged for itself.

Great city though it remains, Paris lost its status as the global cultural centre some time ago. The much-vaunted education system produces a turbocharged elite but leaves many others by the wayside. No French university figured among the world's top twenty in global rankings in 2013. At school, pupils hesitate to ask questions for fear of showing ignorance and making mistakes, according to surveys by the Organization for Economic Co-operation and Development (OECD). Rote learning is the norm in a system designed to pick out winners that has little time for the rest. In the international ranking for 2012, France stood twenty-first out of sixty-five countries for reading and twenty-second for mathematics.

The motorway network may be among the best in Europe, but twice as many people die on the roads each year in France as in Britain with much the same population. The impressive high-speed train system helped to plunge the state SNCF railway service into major losses; in 2013, a third of lines were running at a loss and passenger numbers declined because of high ticket costs and competition from cheap airlines.

Bureaucracy stifles enterprise; the French labour code runs to anywhere from 955 to 3,200 pages according to which version you consult. Government is particularly complex, from the central government in Paris through regional and provincial administrations to local authorities in communes and cantons, with an overlapping array of ministers, prefects, civil servants, mayors and councils which is calculated to contain a *mega-millefeuille* of 37,000 different bodies. In the southern metropolitan area of Marseilles and Aix-en-Provence, there are six separate layers of administration and ten different authorities for public transport. When the EU Commission in Brussels set out to reduce red tape, Paris demurred, invoking consumer, worker and environmental protection. A joke at the time of the revelations about US electronic snooping in 2013 had it that, while the Americans could track everything that was being said in France, the complications of the way government works is such that they could not understand what it meant.

Some 400,000 directives reach down, from stipulating how far mail boxes can stick out from walls to a limit of half a boiled egg to be served to infants at kindergarten lunches. The cost to local authorities has been put at 1.9bn ($2.5bn) over a period of four years while business regulations are reckoned to impose an annual burden of 7.5bn ($10bn). 'The country is in danger of paralysis,' Alain Lambert, head of the French government's Consultative Commission on Evaluation of Norms warned, while the Prime Minister acknowledged in 2013 that the tax system had become 'too complex, almost illegible.'

As for half the population, France lay forty-fifth on the World Economic Forum's gender equality ranking in 2013 (Germany was fourteenth, the United Kingdom eighteenth and the United States twenty-third). Women are, on average, paid around 30 per cent less than their male counterparts. There are two women among the seventy-three historic figures honoured in the Panthéon mausoleum to the nation's great figures, the scientists Marie Curie and Sophie Berthelot, who are commemorated with their husbands. The 2014 contest for the mayor's office in Paris, the most important local government post in the country, was between two women, and female politicians have held senior posts in government since the 1970s; but, according to the International Parliamentary Union, the professed home of equality lay thirty-eighth among world nations in 2013 in the proportion of national legislators who were women, below Germany, Italy, Switzerland and Belgium, though ahead of both Britain and the United States. When it comes to the wider spectrum of legislators, senior officials and managers, the female-male ratio is 0.63.

The only woman to have been prime minister, Edith Cresson, has called French politics a 'closed men's club.' Elisabeth Guigou, a former European Minister who later became Minister of Justice, complained of the 'below-the-waist jokes' directed at her in parliament; she once stared down a macho male minister when he suggested that she could increase her popularity by wearing crimson lingerie. A former Environment Minister faced demonstrators waving placards reading: 'Dominique, get back to your housework and leave us alone.' Political parties are required by law to impose male-female parity in their candidates for election, but they generally prefer to ignore the stipulation and pay whatever fines are levied.

Several incidents in 2013 showed how deep-rooted sexism can be. A female minister from the Green Party was accused by the centre-right of 'lacking respect' when she turned up to a Cabinet meeting in jeans and was then wolf-whistled in parliament when she appeared in a flowered dress. In October of that year, a right-wing

legislator returned to the Chamber of Deputies from what was
described as a 'well-oiled' dinner and sat on the red velvet benches
making clucking sounds at a female deputy who was speaking. Male
colleagues egged him on. The Speaker eventually ordered him to
stop; he subsequently apologized and was fined a quarter of his
monthly salary.

For all its woes, it is important not to forget that France remains
fundamentally a rich country with the traditional strengths laid out
at the start of this chapter. In terms of global reach, it remains
a considerable actor. Politically, for all its fumbling at home, the
Hollande administration was ready to get involved militarily abroad
in a way that Britain, Germany and the United States shrank from. It
has major international pulpits and leadership of major global bodies,
notably the IMF. Its defence agreement with the UK is the strongest
within Western Europe. Despite policy differences between Paris and
Berlin, the half-century-old Franco-German friendship treaty under-
pins a vital relationship in a continent that saw three wars between
the two nations in seventy-five years.

The record numbers of visitors drawn to the Hexagon show the
strength of its attractions. Its overseas departments and territories,
which successive administrations insist are an integral part of France
and which elect representatives to the legislature in Paris, span the
globe from the islands of St. Pierre et Miquelon off the coast of
Canada to Réunion in the Indian Ocean and to Tahiti and French
Polynesia in the South Pacific, a colonial hangover to be sure, but
still a footprint across the world. The economy has become less
competitive internationally, but still contains major global enterprises
and a residual strength as an agricultural supplier. France is the
fifth-largest destination for global foreign direct investment. There
is even finally an attempt now to fuel up a high-tech sector with a
million-square-feet hub in Paris.

There are those who reject criticism. From the Finance Ministry,
Pierre Moscovici calls for an end to 'French bashing.' The *New York
Times* columnist Roger Cohen argues that the French are living off
their malaise much as the British live off their royal family. 'It's a
marketing ploy with its degree of affectation; an object of fascination

to foreigners rather than a worrying condition,' he goes on, attributing to the French 'a fierce form of realism . . . a bitter wisdom . . . a bracing frankness.'

But there is no disputing the rot which has set in since the early 1980s. The popular disenchantment built up over the last three decades puts the functioning of the republican state at risk. At the municipal elections of 2014, the abstention rate hit a record 38 per cent. France has demonstrated a large capacity for survival, but the stakes grow ever higher in a more complex world where the achievements of the past count for less and less, and heritage assets bring diminishing rewards. It is a time of high anxiety in the Hexagon. Year by year, the survival act becomes more difficult to pull off and the outside world grows ever more challenging, with the increasingly alarming danger of drifting away from the strong economies of northern Europe and joining the struggling nations of the south.

The roots of the concern are not new, but time has been no healer. Politicians have been unable to come up with answers and are increasingly seen as incompetent and out-of-touch. Scandals have engulfed prominent figures since the 1980s. Most recently, those guilty have included the Budget Minister, who had been meant to oversee more rigorous control of government finances, but was found to have had a secret bank account in Switzerland. In 2013, extreme right-wing candidates eliminated mainstream Socialists in the first round of voting in a series of legislative by-elections. Meanwhile, the centre-right opposition plunged into fratricidal infighting as speculation rose about a comeback bid by Nicolas Sarkozy less than two years after the electorate had rejected his presidential re-election bid. A minister was quoted by the news magazine *L'Express* as saying at the end of 2013 that the 'climate is almost one of insurrection.' As well as the widespread anti-tax protests which united labour militants, shopkeepers and small business bosses, the old conservative-Catholic right-wing was rejuvenated by the massive rallies against same-sex marriage that were notable for the number of young demonstrators. (The government's majority in the Chamber of Deputies ensured that the measure passed into law.)

The National Front leader, Marine Le Pen, daughter of the movement's founder, epitomized this outbreak of what the French call *ras-le-bol* (had enough). She took almost 18 per cent in the first round of the 2012 presidential election as she led her movement out of the obscurantist ghetto, fostered by her reactionary Catholic father, nostalgia for the Vichy collaborationist regime and for French Algeria, crude anti-Arab racism laced with anti-Semitism and a general in-your-face bully boy approach to politics. Highly intelligent, alert, media-savvy and far more open on social issues than the traditional hard right, she made the most of her freedom to speak her mind, denouncing the mainstream politicians of left and right, preaching nationalism and attacking the European system.

One poll a year after Hollande's election showed that he would finish behind Marine Le Pen in a new vote with 19 per cent support, compared with 23 per cent for her and Sarkozy taking 34 per cent. Meanwhile, old-style leftists, including the once-powerful Communist Party, formed a Left Party whose candidate, Jean-Luc Mélenchon, won 11 per cent in the first round in 2012, denounced the administration as having sold out on Socialist principles and propounded nostrums for national recovery that often sounded similar to those of the far right in their nationalism and anti-Europeanism. Le Pen and Mélenchon were sworn enemies who thrived off of one another. In 2012, the demagogic left-winger fought a parliamentary election against her in a depressed area of northern France which she had been cultivating. He got only half as many votes as Le Pen in a constituency whose economic condition should have made it a happy hunting ground for him; she was blocked at the run-off by an anti-Front coalition, but the orthodox Socialist scraped home with 50.1 per cent of the vote.

If the appeal of parties of the hard right and left bodes ill for mainstream politicians, it is hardly a surprise, given the way that governments have repeatedly failed their voters in the past three decades. Though he cut an unimpressive figure, François Hollande could not be saddled with the blame for the state of the nation, as his administration foundered only a year after his election to the Élysée. France's problems stretch back to the 1980s as president after president fell short of his undertakings to an extent even a cynical electorate found hard to stomach. The country retains considerable strengths that could enable it to live up to the role it likes to see for itself, and, in the process, make it a much happier place. But a failure of leadership has led to it teetering along the brink of even greater troubles as it looks desperately for a way out of the trap into which it has cast itself.

2

BEHIND THE MASK

Diminishing faith in leaders is a general phenomenon in the West, as is widespread impatience with the political class, which is seen as a self-perpetuating elite, be it inside the Washington's Beltway or at Westminster, let alone Italy, where a man like Silvio Berlusconi was able to cling on to power for so long. In France, these two sources of discontent have a particular impact because of the nature of the political class and the assumptions built into the core of the system created by Charles de Gaulle in the late 1950s.

Whatever their failures, French politicians enjoy great longevity. Governments come and go, but the same figures, most of them male, remain centre stage. Even when a new cast steps up, there are long-serving old stagers among them. This tendency has been buttressed by the practice of 'cohabitation,' under which, when the opposition party wins a legislative election, the President accepts that it forms a government (until he can unseat it). However much they may differ in rhetoric, politicians are ready to get on together in the pursuit of power when necessary.

Some rising stars fall by the wayside, of course, like the one-time Socialist heavyweight Dominique Strauss-Kahn, brought down by his encounter with a hotel maid in Manhattan in 2011 and subsequent allegations of long-running sexual misconduct. Others seem fated to remain on the edge, such as Ségolène Royal, who ran unsuccessfully for the Socialists in the 2007 presidential contest and who, despite her fiercely loyal following, has never been fully accepted by her party's establishment. Leading centrists, such as the eminently sensible François Bayrou from the Pyrenees, are eternal outsiders, who hold ministerial office from time to time but then are caught in the eternal civil war between left and right, in which they are expendable once they have served a temporary purpose.

The tradition of long political lives dates back more than two centuries to two great survivors from the era of the French Revolution. The former bishop Charles Maurice de Talleyrand-Périgord exercised his diplomatic skills and ability to amass cash under Napoleon's Empire and the restored Bourbon monarchy alike, while Joseph Fouché transformed himself from a relentless advocate of terror under Maximilien Robespierre's Committee of Public Safety into Napoleon's police chief and then a key figure in the restoration of Louis XVIII in 1814–15. Seeing the two men together, the writer François-René de Chateaubriand dubbed them 'vice leaning on the arm of crime.' But political longevity really came into its own during the Third Republic, which stretched from the defeat of Napoleon III's force by the Prussians in 1870 to the invasion by Nazi Germany seven decades later.

France's longest-lasting regime was run by moderate men of the political centre who believed in consensus and cutting deals, except when it came to their opposition to the power of the Catholic Church. The Radical Party, whose moderate actions belied its name, dominated the political scene along with groups glorying in names such as the Opportunistic Republicans. The legislature ruled supreme, especially the lower house of parliament, the National Assembly in the Palais Bourbon by the Seine, though the Senate in the stately Palais du Luxembourg provided a plush home for elder statesmen. There was constant horse trading between its most prominent members for ministerial posts with the ultimate aim of reaching the prime minister's office in the eighteenth-century Hôtel Matignon in the rue de Varenne on the left bank of the Seine. In the forty-three years between the creation of the Third Republic and the outbreak of World War One, France had forty-eight prime ministers.

The bosses of big cities, with their large electorates, were major power brokers, but so were the representatives of the farmers of what was still predominantly an agricultural nation, with deputies playing their role in protecting the fruits of the land—for instance, those from the mass production wine-growing country of the southwest ensured that French soldiers were kept well lubricated. The system of accommodation and lifetime political careers reached down through departments and provincial cities to villages, where elected mayors held office for decades as if owning a franchise of the local store.

The way things worked meant that the late-nineteenth-century politician Charles de Freycinet, a reliable servant of the Republic who is little remembered today, could serve for four terms as Prime Minister, while the totally forgotten Armand Dufaure occupied the position five times. Before, during and after World War One, the expansive Aristide Briand headed eleven governments and was a minister in twelve others, spending ten years in all at the Foreign Ministry on the Quai d'Orsay. His great rival, the stiff, spear-bearded conservative Raymond Poincaré, was at Matignon three times as well as serving as President of the Republic from 1913 to 1920. Edouard Herriot, Léon Blum and Edouard Daladier each also served three terms as Prime Minister. In the twenty-one years between the two great wars, France had thirty-three premiers before defeat in 1940 ushered in the collaborationist regime based in the spa town of Vichy under Marshal Philipe Pétain.

After the Liberation of 1944, Charles de Gaulle became the first Prime Minister of the new Fourth Republic. When he strode out of office rather than accept the logjam of party combinations, figures from the pre-war epoch re-emerged along with younger men in the parliamentary ranks of the legislature in the Palais Bourbon by the Seine. Politics resumed its familiar pattern, though, with a powerful Communist Party playing the role of an outsider while governments were constituted of Socialists, Christian Democrats and surviving Radicals.

As prime minister and sage of the left, Léon Blum kept alive the ghost of the left-wing Popular Front he had headed in the mid-1930s. Other fixtures included Robert Schuman, an Alsatian bachelor with a numbingly sedative speaking style who became a pioneer of European integration; Paul Ramadier, the sharp Socialist leader; Vincent Auriol, his party colleague with a cherubic expression and well-honed political skills; the exceedingly clever centrist Edgard Faure; and Antoine Pinay, a conservative economist who had voted to grant power to Pétain in 1940.

There were rare exceptions to those who played the game, notably the intransigent Pierre Mendès France, a brooding figure advocating a more austere and moral form of politics, who became Prime Minister for eight months as the only man who could implement France's retreat from its colonies in Indochina; once he had achieved that, the politicking of his colleagues and enemies soon got rid of him. The Communist boss Maurice Thorez, who had spent the war in Moscow, was another outsider, but still, he commanded electoral battalions of industrial workers.

The frequent swapping of top government posts between a small circle of politicians persisted as France got through twenty Prime Ministers in the eleven years of the Fourth Republic. Characteristic of the way politics operated was the Radical Party's Henri Queuille, an unassuming—and anything but radical—doctor from the deeply rural Corrèze department in central France. He held no fewer than nineteen ministerial posts between 1924 and 1954, including three spells as Premier. The watchword of the 'good doctor Queuille' was simple—'[P]olitics,' he said, 'is not the art of settling problems but of shutting up the people who pose them'—not by force but by persuasion and inducements of all kinds.

From time to time, outsiders posed a passing threat. In the 1930s, 'green shirt' rural fascists caused temporary alarm while right-wing nationalist leagues staged large and violent riots outside the Palais Bourbon. Under the postwar Fourth Republic, a movement of small shopkeepers and artisans from the provinces, led by an accomplished agitator, Pierre Poujade, had a significant electoral impact for a few years. Though they played the parliamentary game and participated in several governments immediately after the Liberation of 1944, the Communists spent most of the Fourth Republic positioned on the margins, under orders from Moscow and able to wield the blunt weapon of strikes through their control of the country's biggest trade union federation.

In the United States, Richard Nixon is the only postwar president to have won the White House after having run unsuccessfully as his party's candidate in a previous election. In contrast, the occupants of the Élysée between 1981 and 2007 were men who had failed in their earlier attempts to achieve the supreme prize, but who did not let defeat deter them. François Mitterrand, the first leader of the Fifth Republic elected on a left-wing platform in 1981, was an ultimate survivor who had entered parliament in 1946 and became a minister for the first time the following year. He held a string of government posts under the Fourth Republic before running unsuccessfully for the presidency against de Gaulle in 1965 and against Valéry Giscard d'Estaing in 1974. Jacques Chirac, Mitterrand's successor, became a minister for the first time in 1967, Prime Minister in 1974 and Mayor of Paris in 1977 before finally entering the Élysée in 1995; his long pursuit of the top prize and the number of official posts he held earned him the soubriquet from a former editor of *Le Monde* of the 'Resident of the Republic.'

With a ministerial career that began only in the 1990s, Nicolas Sarkozy set himself out as a new broom when he became President in 2007. His backstory was, however, suitably lengthy. Elected Mayor of the prosperous Paris suburb of Neuilly in 1983, he became a National Assembly deputy in 1988. After being named Budget Minister in 1993, he deserted his original patron, Chirac, to side with Edouard Balladur, the rival candidate for the Gaullist presidential nomination in 1995. But after Chirac had beaten off Balladur and won the Élysée Sarkozy returned to his first mentor's camp and made his mark with tough law-and-order rhetoric as Interior Minister in charge of the police and fighting crime, though some of his outbursts, such as the need to 'Hoover up' (or vacuum up) delinquents in immigrant housing projects earned him an unsavoury reputation.

His successor, François Hollande, was more of a newcomer, at least as far as government was concerned, having never held national office before he became President. But he had been First Secretary of the Socialist Party for eleven years and a classic backroom operator whose career as an adviser dated back to the early Mitterrand era of the 1980s. And, as Hollande stumbled to record low opinion poll ratings, the talk was of a comeback by his predecessor, a man nobody thought was ready to count himself out despite the rejection of 2012.

The new Socialist administration of 2012 was, inevitably, filled with fresh faces, since the party had been out of government for more than a decade and had not held the presidency since 1995. Few people had heard of the Prime Minister, Jean-Marc Ayrault. Most ministers were newcomers to power on a national level. But one member of the government kept alive the old tradition of longevity and an ability to bounce back from reverses that would have been terminal in many other countries.

The debonnaire Laurent Fabius first held ministerial office (for the budget) under Mitterrand in 1981, thirty-two years before he became the second-ranking member of the Ayrault government as Foreign Minister. In 1985, Mitterrand had appointed him as Prime Minister at the age of thirty-seven. He was replaced when economic problems, notably high unemployment, led the Socialists to defeat in legislative elections the following year. His spell at the Matignon was dogged by two major scandals. One involved French agents sinking the *Rainbow Warrior*, a ship crewed by protestors against French nuclear tests in the Pacific; the government admitted responsibility and the Defense Minister resigned. The other was over allegations that the government had allowed doctors to give haemophiliacs transfusions of HIV-infected blood; a judicial inquiry acquitted the former Prime Minister of personal responsibility.

Becoming First Secretary of the Socialist Party, Fabius led it to a big defeat in parliamentary elections in 1993, but came back to government as Economics Minister for two years in the Socialist government at the turn of the century. Along the way, he spent two spells as Speaker of the National Assembly before going on to head the successful campaign against a new European Union constitution in a referendum in 2005. That got him dismissed from the Executive Committee of the Socialist Party, which had campaigned for a 'yes' vote. In the primary vote for the left-wing candidate to oppose Nicolas Sarkozy in 2007, he finished third, but bided his time and gained his reward in 2012. Though loyal to the new head of state, Fabius marked his status as an elder statesman by referring to Hollande by his name rather than as *Monsieur le Président*, as was usual among ministers.

On the other side of the spectrum stands an equally urbane figure, Alain Juppé, long-time Chirac lieutenant who was appointed as Prime Minister in 1995. By coincidence, both men showed a receding hairline from early on in their political careers. Known as 'the computer,' who lacked human feeling as he set out to impose drastic reforms to boost the market and cut state spending, he aroused such unpopularity that the right crashed to defeat in 1997, ushering in the cohabitationist Socialist government of Lionel Jospin, a one-time Trotskyite whose own record in senior positions reached back to having become First Secretary of the Socialist Party in 1981.

Juppé hit a roadblock in 2004 when he was handed a fourteen-month suspended jail sentence and barred from holding political office for a year after being convicted of abuse of public funds as Chirac's principal aide at the Paris City Hall. Undeterred, he bounced back in 2006 to win election as Mayor of Bordeaux, a long-time Gaullist fiefdom, and entered the Sarkozy administration, first as a Minister of State and then as Minister of Defense and subsequently Foreign Minister. After the left's victory of 2012, he was spoken of as a possible leader of the centre-right if another figure who had tasted defeat—Nicolas Sarkozy—did not try to stage a widely expected comeback.

Nothing keeps politicians like Fabius and Juppé down, and they bring with them bags of experience. But, exemplars of upper-drawer survival as they are, they hardly stand as signs of the regeneration French politics needs as voters look for new directions away from the self-confirming political class of successive republics.

The permanence of the ruling caste in France is bolstered by the education system, which is designed to produce an elite ruling class for the republic. Those on top ensure that this is perpetuated, without much apparent concern for those who may be unable to keep up with the high-pressure learning involved. Discussion of change swiftly runs into opposition from teachers' unions, who are wedded to the approach honed over more than a century. 'The result is inevitably conservative,' educational expert François Dubet has observed, 'since each element in the system fears losing its position if the system is changed.'

The link between the education system and the depressed state of the employment market is evident, as Hollande acknowledged when presenting his televised message to the nation for 2014. 'A key focus is the need to ensure that the country's education system and professional training infrastructure provide people with the right skills to succeed in a globalised economy,' the Organization for Economic Co-operation and Development (OECD) wrote in a report in 2013. One prominent French information technology entrepreneur, Xavier

Niel, has taken matters into his own hands by setting up a college in northern Paris where students work on computer programmes with little or no supervision, following their own paths to innovation.

But the educational establishment has shown every sign of rebuffing reform that would make it more flexible and adapt it to the changing world. Teachers can be sure of consideration from Socialist governments since they constitute one of the party's big electoral battalions, and their powerful unions, which are adept at appealing to republican values to block change, intimidate administrations of the centre-right. Access to universities is free, so students do not have to incur the kind of debts common in the United States and Britain, but the drop-out rate is higher, and the OECD judges the French educational system as one of the most unequal among developed nations because of the gap between the performance of good and weak students. It has also found that the impact of the socio-economic background of students on their performance is one of the highest among rich countries. As a former minister has reflected, 'We make fine speeches about equality of opportunity, but France is the European country where the selection of elites is the fiercest, and the division between good and bad pupils perpetuates the cleavage between social classes.'

Only one President of the Fifth Republic, Georges Pompidou, came from a really modest social background in the village of Montboudif in the Auvergne, though he went on to a leading lycée in Paris and then achieved worldly success as a banker at Rothschilds and a patron of the Parisian cultural scene. Traditional national pride in the education offered by the Republic is, thus, sadly undermined by the realities of what it offers the mass of students, especially those most in need of the state's help.

This is evident at the top of the educational tree in the super-colleges, known as the *Grandes Écoles*, which produce the men and women who run the nation. At any one time they have around 65,000 students. Only 5 per cent of students finishing high school get into the preparatory classes for admission to them; most are youth from the middle and upper classes who have time to devote themselves to study and whose social and cultural environment melds with what the examiners require. The irony is that the selection process which is meant to serve republican values ends up favouring the children of the existing elite, who apply the same thought processes when they come to administer France.

The apex of the system is to be found at the École Nationale d'Administration, known by its initials as ENA. Only one hundred students graduate each year from ENA, a high-octane elite that includes Presidents Chirac, Giscard d'Estaing and Hollande, who met his long-term partner, Ségolène Royal, when they were in the same class at the college. The roster of Prime Ministers runs through Michel Rocard, Edouard Balladur, Alain Juppé, Laurent Fabius, Lionel Jospin and Dominique de Villepin. Other Énarques become senior civil servants, including the powerful prefects who administer France's departments or top executives of companies ranging from oil groups and automobile makers to aerospace, steel and chemicals, defence, transport and banks. Some head international organizations such as the European Central Bank or the International Monetary Fund.

Set up after the Liberation by de Gaulle's fervent follower, Michel Debré, ENA aims to produce an irreproachable mandarin sect whose only duty is to serve the nation above and beyond partisan politics or personal advancement. As the General told the students of 1959, 'You are called by your vocation to exercise the most important and most noble function which exists in the temporal sphere—I mean, the service of the state.' A report drawn up for another elite college, the École Normale Supérieure, took a less lofty view: 'ENA creates a self-reproducing caste which has completely conquered the key political positions and confiscated the apparatus of the state, making politics very technical with the same approach by left and right,' it declared.

'The big failing of top civil servants is their superiority complex towards ministers,' a former minister observed. 'Their class, made up of technocrats and technicians of governments and administration, only really respects the President of the Republic.' They are the experts—so why search any further, why prize practical experience over abstract reasoning at the highest level? 'When one looks for people who can understand industry, public finance or the reform of the social security system,' noted a former chief of staff at the Prime Minister's office, 'one quickly turns to the pool which provides the administration—forever.' When the Prime Minister of a neigh-bouring country expressed concern about the zigzags of Chirac's

European policy, a French elder statesman reassured him that, whatever the politicians might say in public, the officials had laid down the unalterable tracks for the future behind the scenes—and so it proved.

As an unelected elite, the Énarques personify the importance of central planning in France. Under the Fourth Republic, Jean Monnet, the 'Father of Europe,' headed a government agency that laid the foundations for the modernization of French infrastructure, which was put into effect under de Gaulle and his successors. The motorway, the telecommunications network, the nuclear energy industry and the high-speed train were among the results, along with less successful outcomes such as the soulless suburban projects that are home to much of France's social tensions. But the basic criticism is that the elite knows how to work out logical solutions that seem good on the computer screen or on printouts, but which do not connect with the real world and everyday demands of a population that has its own ideas about where it wants to go and increasingly distrusts the governing class.

'The idea is that brightest kids in the class can go on to run the country, but it doesn't work,' says Peter Gumbel, a Paris-based British author who has made a study of the French education system and who lectures at the Sciences Po, a college in Paris. 'Those in this elite come from much the same upper middle-class backgrounds and they are not running the country well. They may be smart and swots and get grammar and maths but they don't have experience, or necessarily ability.' The Énarques, as one jibe goes, are like super-intelligent aliens who have landed in a strange planet, France. A joke runs like this:

A young man stops his car in the countryside. He goes over to a farmer in a field with his dog and a flock of sheep.

'If I can tell you how many sheep you have here without counting them, will you give me one?' he asks.

'Okay,' says the farmer.

'Eighty-one,' says the smart young man.

'That's amazing. How did you know?' asks the farmer.

The young man does not reply. Instead, he picks up an animal and walks back to his car.

'Now, let me try something,' says the farmer. 'If I can tell you where you were educated, will you give me my animal back?'

'Of course,' says the young man disdainfully.
'You're from the ENA,' says the farmer.
'How did you know?'
'Because that's my dog you have under your arm.'

The diminishing faith in politicians and the elite around them is especially resonant in France because of the nature of the Fifth Republic instituted in 1958. Even more so than the US President, France's supreme leader is expected to personify the nation and its global influence. He is meant to bring the country together above party politics. That aspiration has never reflected reality, not even on the part of the founder of the regime. Germans and their leaders are ready to seek compromise, not the French.

To agree with one's opponents is generally seen as a sign of weakness in a country where, as we will see in a later chapter, divisions are endemic and consensus-minded figures do not get far. This is the legacy of wars of religion, conflicts of royalists and revolutionaries, church versus state, left and right, and the tension between the view French have of themselves as progressives and the deep strength of conservatism. Within each of these broad groups there are multiple subdivisions, for instance warring factions of royalists and revolutionaries were as alienated from one another as they were from their ideological opponents. Some dedicated Catholics rejected the Revolution and refused to celebrate Bastille Day or sing the national anthem while others preached the need for social reform and acceptance of 1789.

However outmoded the cause, however great the rejection by the electorate, politicians cherish the abiding belief that they were right and the voters wrong. So redemption must lie somewhere down the road if only one perseveres. No need to re-examine one's credo; all one needs to do is to persevere.

Take as a prize example the founder of the National Front, Jean-Marie Le Pen. He soldiered on as the leader of the extreme right through recurrent electoral failures from the 1950s until he handed the National Front baton to his daughter, Marine, half a century later. At times, the bluff, blustering former paratrooper could muster only a few per cent of the vote. He was repeatedly written off but always bounced back and finally got his recompense by forcing the Socialist candidate out of the presidential election of 2002 to earn a place in the run-off against Chirac. Inevitably, he went down in a huge defeat, but he had been vindicated, and, ten years later, Marine posed the biggest electoral threat the mainstream had faced under the Fifth Republic.

The very system under which French politics has been conducted for more than half a century combines a fundamental dichotomy. The Fifth Republic is both quasi-monarchical and extremely democratic. It harks back to the Napoleonic dictatorship in offering strong executive leadership, but also produces frequent elections at national and local level, each one confirming or denying the legitimacy of those in power.

The President of the Fifth Republic has a greater range of authority than any other Western leader, but popular sentiment has proved volatile in allowing him to exercise that power effectively. Five years after sweeping to the presidency and winning a legislative majority as well in 1981, the Socialists were defeated by the centre-right and Mitterrand had to take Chirac as Prime Minister. A couple of years after Chirac won the Élysée in 1995, the rout of his supporters by the left at a parliamentary election forced a second period of cohabitation, this time with a president from the centre-right and a Cabinet from the centre-left. Subsequently, both Sarkozy and Hollande managed to win big legislative victories to go with their presidential triumphs, but that did not stop a swift decline in popularity and internal dissention.

Taking office in conditions of near civil war in 1958 after a long period of legislative supremacy and political instability, de Gaulle was intent on establishing the powerful executive he had always thought necessary for France to live up to the high ideals he had for it. In place of the squabbling politicians of the Fourth Republic, the French needed a single strong leader—in the first instance, himself. Instead of a network of political parties, none of which could obtain a majority to rule and so were consigned to endless maneuvers and self-preserving deals, the country of which the General had 'a certain idea' required, he believed, a political movement devoted to its chief who would carry out clear policies.

The result was a pyramid of power topped by the head of state, initially appointed by an electoral college, but, since 1965, chosen by the electorate at large and the legitimacy conferred by universal suffrage. Until 2002, the President served for a regal seven years, with François Mitterrand spending fourteen years in the Élysée between 1981 and 1995. Since 2002, the term had been cut to five years, but his successor, Jacques Chirac, still racked up a dozen years in the palace. Compare that to the eight-year term limit across the Atlantic, or even the ten years maximum stay at the top in China.

The President is commander-in-chief with the power to send troops into operations without consulting the legislature beforehand. He (it always has been a man) runs foreign policy as well as intervening in any domain that interests him; one former minister told me that he was blessed because the head of state of the time had no interest whatsoever in his field of responsibility. If a member of the government cuts an individual swathe, as Dominique de Villepin did as Foreign Minister in opposition to the invasion of Iraq, he acts as the President's point man.

The occupant of the Élysée is not only head of state and head of the executive branch of the administration (and co-prince of the tiny tax haven of Andorra in the Pyrenees). He also appoints the Prime Minister to lead the government and approves the list of ministers, which is announced from the steps of the presidential palace, not from the Premier's office at the Matignon. When ministers fall out, it is the president who is called on to decide between them; thus, when the Interior Minister squabbled with Socialist colleagues about immigration and prison policies in 2013, everybody watched for the signal from the Élysée with the Prime minister reduced to the status of a bystander— in the end, François Hollande, as so often, chose to compromise, seeking to exercise sweet reason but ending up by satisfying nobody.

On top of his other powers, the head of state can use the Bonapartist device of a referendum on issues affecting the constitution, appealing to the people of France over the heads of their elected representatives in parliament. De Gaulle set the pattern of using such votes to rally national support for himself as he warned that it was 'me or chaos.' He gained massive backing for ending the war in Algeria and for the new constitution, each of which built up the stature of *le grand Charles*.

Other referendums have been less successful, with one on the strengthening of the European Union in 2005 bringing defeat for a proposal put forward by China and backed by the main political parties. De Gaulle gave the process an inner logic by pledging that he would resign if he lost such a national vote—and did just that after his proposals for political reform were rejected by the electorate in 1969. Chirac felt no such need to leave when the European vote went against him, and subsequent rulers have been careful in their use of the plebiscite, since it can easily bring together different opposition forces in a single vote. Still this blunt weapon remains at their disposal.

While he is meant to represent the nation as a whole as a supreme guide, the President also heads a powerful political movement, and his actions have inevitable sectarian consequences. De Gaulle may have despised the political combinations of the Fourth Republic and cast an anathema on their chiefs, but his followers set up a powerful party to back him. Mitterrand, one of those Fourth Republic survivors for whom the General had no time, made sure he enjoyed the solid support of the Socialists during his long tenure and, in keeping with his nickname of 'the Florentine,' played consummate destructive politics with the Communists in his first years as President. Chirac built up a neo-Gaullist movement whose only real coherence lay in supporting him. His successor, Sarkozy, re-jigged the Chirac machine in his own version of centre-right Union pour la Majorité présidentielle (Union for the Presidential Majority), or UMP party. Then Hollande was elected in 2012 as leader of the Socialist machine he had managed for more than a decade.

When the departure of presidents removes the glue of power, their parties often splinter. This happened after the death in office in 1974 of de Gaulle's successor, Georges Pompidou. In the ensuing election, Jacques Chirac, whom Pompidou had described as his 'bulldozer,' led a breakaway Gaullist faction that opposed the party's official candidate, Jacques Chaban-Delmas, and sided with the centrist Valéry Giscard d'Estaing, enabling him to win the crown. Chirac then showed an aversion to his former ally at the next presidential contest that contributed to his defeat by Mitterrand and opened the door to a protracted war between the two men plus the former Prime Minister Raymond Barre, which greatly helped Mitterrand to win re-election and which will be described in more detail later in this book.

When the 'Florentine' finally stepped down in 1995 at the end of his fourteen-year term in the Élysée, strife broke out in the Socialist ranks, contributing to the disastrous presidential poll of 2002 when the Prime Minister, Lionel Jospin, was eliminated in the first round ballot by Le Pen. In 2007, the electoral cycle should have turned to the left after Chirac's dozen years, but internal bickering in the Socialist Party and the choice of a polarizing candidate in Ségolène Royal facilitated Sarkozy's victory. Five years on, Sarkozy's defeat in 2012 and his (perhaps temporary) retreat from politics led to bitter conflict between his former Prime Minister, François Fillon, and the UMP party leader Jean-François Copé, with other figures lurking in the background, including the unsinkable Alain Juppé.

The head of state sits atop vast acres of patronage through the pervasive, powerful state apparatus. If he chooses to do so, he speaks ex cathedra on any subject under the sun; talking of one of his grand cultural projects in Paris, Mitterrand declared, 'I choose, I decide, I build.' When he cast a quizzical look at the colour of the desks in the offices of the new opera house at the Bastille in Paris, they were replaced. In what may not be an apocryphal story, another President was told on a trip abroad that his country no longer had a leading world novelist. 'When I get home, I'll call a ministerial meeting to deal with the matter,' he replied.

It is not surprising that, in the half-century after de Gaulle established the Fifth Republic, commentators came to speak of 'our president-monarchs' and noted how many of the trappings of power that surrounded the kings of Versailles were echoed in more modern form at the Élysée, even down to Mitterrand's mistress and their child, maintained at the state's expense. But these trappings need to be exploited carefully. Giscard contributed to his own defeat by accepting diamonds from an African dictator. Mitterrand's indulgence towards cronies plunged his last years into a morass of scandal as we will see. Chirac was dogged with gossip about his country château and his private life, as well as court cases after he left office arising from the financing of his political party from the coffers of the Mayor's office of Paris, for which Juppé received his suspended prison sentence.

Rejection of Sarkozy was fuelled by his taste for 'bling' and the public view of him as a headstrong, narcissistic character who did not have the gravitas appropriate to the position he held. All in all, the power invested in the presidency and the expectations of how that power should be deployed may be all too much for a single human being. This is not surprising since the job was a highly personal creation, reflecting the multifaceted character of a unique figure who, more than any other, marked the France of the last hundred years.

Born into a royalist, reactionary family in 1890, Charles André Joseph Marie de Gaulle was brought up in a staunchly conservative milieu which left him with a deep belief in traditional values. At the same time, however, he was a ceaseless innovator, including his championing of tank warfare when a military instructor in the 1930s. He was, in the words of the writer and passionate Gaullist André Malraux, a man from the day before yesterday and the day after tomorrow.

He believed in discipline but flew to London to proclaim resistance against the legitimate regime in France in 1940 and headed the Free French for four years until the Liberation of France in 1944. Fourteen years later, he staged his second great rebellion against the country's established legal authority to bring about the end of the Fourth Republic in 1958. He was aloof in public and believed that leaders should not have friends—'I respect only those who stand up to me, but I find such people intolerable,' he once said. But he was deeply human in private, devoted to his homely wife, known to the French as 'Aunt' Yvonne, and to his second daughter, Anne, who had Down's syndrome. He drew strength from her suffering. As he led his tank division into battle against the Germans in 1940, he told the unit's chaplain, 'She is my joy; she has helped me to rise above all setbacks and all honours, and always to aim higher.' After she died in 1948 at the age of twenty, he told his doctor that 'without Anne, I should perhaps not have done what I have done. She gave me so much heart and spirit.'

Despite his rock-like hauteur, the General exhibited more than his fair share of contradictions. Though convinced of the need for top-down authority, he was a real democrat, having observed that dictators usually come to a bad end. So he resigned after losing the referendum vote in 1969; indeed, it is arguable that the vote was a political suicide note by a man who knew it was time to go. A champion of the French Empire, he agreed to the independence of Algeria. A man brought up on the right, he presided over a big expansion of the state and social welfare policies, both after the Liberation of 1944 and under the Fifth Republic, and said that the 'power of money' was the greatest threat to France.

While he spared no expense in glorifying his nation, this product of French Social Catholicism was personally frugal and took little advantage of the perks of office—even paying the electricity bills for his quarters at the Élysée. No economist, he imposed a tough programme to stabilise the economy in 1958. A sharp critic of party manoeuvres, he was an adept and ruthless player of the game when it suited him. A fierce opponent of US 'hegemony,' he took France out of the unified military structure of the NATO alliance and treasured national sovereignty in its most basic form; but he proved a staunch supporter of Washington in the Cuban missile crisis and over Berlin.

Like his country, de Gaulle believed he had a unique role to play and a destiny to pursue through his unusually long life. He fought in the trenches of the First World War, was wounded three times and was given up for dead at the epic Battle of Verdun before being held for two years as a German prisoner of war. He raised the standard of resistance in the Second World War, saved the nation from impending civil war in 1958 and founded the political system that endures to this day. 'When de Gaulle the man looks at de Gaulle the historic figure, he understands that the historic de Gaulle has to act as is expected of him,' he wrote in terms that few other leaders would permit themselves. The nation was the bedrock on which everything rested, though he lamented that his fellow citizens were not worthy of their fatherland—he sometimes referred to them as *veaux*—literally calves but best translated as sheep.

Had the General not run for re-election in the first popular ballot for the presidency in 1965, he would have gone down with his reputation as high as he would have wished, the leader of the Free French who had saved his country's honour and the founder of a new republic. He always attracted criticism, sometimes visceral as from the extreme proponents of holding on to Algeria who tried repeatedly to assassinate him, as well as diehard political opponents such as Mitterrand and Mendès France. But, he had established an executive-led government after nearly ninety years of legislative supremacy, presided over the strengthening of the economy and won huge majorities at crucial referendum votes. He had engineered the Franco-German friendship treaty, the key European act of the postwar era, and excluded Britain from the European project to ensure that it was conducted on lines chosen by France. He had stood up to the United States and encouraged André Malraux, whom he appointed as Culture Minister, to launch an ambitious programme to glorify the arts and clean up historic buildings. Not all he did was welcome to other nations, notably the US and UK, but it was what France wanted and what he saw as the right, almost sacred, course for his country.

However, when the seventy-five-year-old President stood in the 1965 election, he looked old and out of touch and, for once, performed poorly on television. His main opponents, the younger, sharp-featured Mitterrand and the reassuring pro-European centrist Jean Lecanuet, seemed to represent the future. Mitterrand's alliance with the Communists gave his left-wing platform the support of serious numbers. The result was that the General polled 44.6 per cent at the first round. This was well ahead of Mitterrand's 31.7 per cent and Lecanuet's 15.5 but humiliatingly short of the overall majority which the General felt was his right. He hesitated about whether to withdraw in the face of such a slight but, inevitably, plunged into the second round campaign more effectively than before and was rewarded with a 55 per cent majority over his opponent.

Yet the shine had gone off the General's rule. He was now a mere mortal, and an old one at that, increasingly out of touch with his time as shown by his fumbling, uncomprehending reaction to the student riots and general strike of 1968. That summer, the Gaullists rallied for a last hurrah under their historic leader, but, victory achieved, the General promptly sacked the man who had run the government for him, Georges Pompidou. Like an old king, he banished the dauphin who was gaining too much authority in order to buttress his own. He also personally affronted his former Premier by failing to intervene to stop rumours spread by his opponents alleging that his wife had been involved in orgies organized by Yugoslav gangsters. This only created an even more dangerous situation for the President, since the affable, able, chain-smoking Pompidou emerged as an alternative to the giant who had been brought down to earth. The choice was no longer between de Gaulle and chaos but between a seventy-eight-year-old icon and a viable successor.

Foreign policy became more erratic, with the General's cry of '*Vive le Québec Libre*' in Montreal and his description of Jews as 'an elite people, sure of themselves and domineering.' He attacked the United States on any occasion that presented itself but got nowhere with his efforts to forge a Franco-Soviet relationship. Pompidou described him privately as 'an old, disenchanted man.'

The end came, with pathetic inevitability, when de Gaulle lost his last referendum vote at the beginning of 1969. It was on a marginal subject of regional government and reform of the upper house of parliament, the Senate, which was proving obstructive—a far cry from the great issues of the past, the new constitution and independence for Algeria. A week before the vote, de Gaulle knew that he was going to lose. His former Finance Minister, Giscard d'Estaing, who represented the modern technocratic strain in France's governing class and who had deplored the General's 'solitary exercise of power,' led centrist voters into abstention or opposition. Aides at Pompidou's headquarters in Paris worked on plans for a new government and opened discreet consultations with Giscard and other centrists.

As always, de Gaulle had pledged to resign if he suffered defeat and, on this relatively trivial issue, he kept his word. Before the French voted, his belongings had been packed into removal vans to be taken to his country home at Colombey-les-Deux-Églises in the flatlands of eastern France if the vote was lost.

The referendum proposals were rejected by 52.4 per cent of voters. Speaking on the telephone located in a cubbyhole under the stairs at Colombey, the man who had saved France twice instructed that his resignation statement should be issued immediately. Later, he described the whole episode as absurd.

Pompidou was elected as President of the Republic with 58 per cent of the second round vote. De Gaulle and his wife stayed in virtual seclusion at Colombey, where he worked on his memoirs, took long walks in the woods and received a few visitors. He made trips to Spain and Ireland, the second timed to coincide with the election in France so that he would not be present to see his one-time dauphin installed in the Élysée. He made no public comment on current affairs, though in private letters he wrote of the 'crisis of mediocrity' in the country and deplored the way his successor invoked his name. He died of a sudden heart attack on November 9, 1970, while playing solitaire as he waited for the evening television news. 'General de Gaulle is dead,' Pompidou said in an address to the nation. 'France is a widow.'

Though it is now more than four decades since the General died, his shadow hangs over France today, not only in the republic he bequeathed but in the way he encapsulated so much of his nation as none of his successors has managed to do. While competent, cultured and highly intelligent, Pompidou, who died in 1974 of complications from cancer, lacked the aura the French like to detect in their rulers; when he attended an evening reception for the British Queen, his dinner jacket was ill-fitting. His squinting look and the cigarette dangling from the corner of his mouth denoted a fixer rather than a leader.

Under his presidency, the Gaullist tent was extended to take in centrists who had backed Lecanuet in 1965. Britain was allowed into the Common Market. The industrial modernization conducted under de Gaulle was pushed ahead. The Prime Minister, the Gaullist Resistance hero Jacques Chaban-Delmas, who was handsome and popular but suffered from an unfortunately metallic voice, promoted a 'New Society' to make the country a fairer place. That led the President to sack him for veering too far to the left. The General's mix of policies from all sides of the spectrum was ditched in favour of business-friendly policies. The power of money, which the General had so detested, was heightened. The state and big business worked together to rule the roost.

This was particularly evident in the capital, which was in serious need of modernization. That meant some old monuments had to go. The sprawling open-air wholesale food markets at Les Halles were torn down and replaced with shopping malls and clothes stores, many quite tawdry as the area became a haven for drug dealing. There were contributions to the city's allure, notably with the great modernistic art museum the Centre Beaubourg, which was re-named for the President after his death. But the ugly Montparnasse Tower loomed over the Left Bank, and the banks of the Seine were turned into multi-lane highways. Real estate boomed and fortunes were made as in the great modernization of Paris conducted by Baron Haussmann under Napoleon III a century earlier.

After the five years of Pompidolien pragmatic conservatism, France turned away from Gaullism in 1974 to elect the brilliant, conceited and ultimately fragile Valéry Giscard d'Estaing. The left had revived, with Mitterrand heading a unified ticket backed by the Communists. The Gaullists were split, with Pompidou's protégé, Chirac, leading his pro-Giscard splinter group while Chaban-Delmas got just 15 per cent of the vote in the first round of presidential voting. In the second round, after televised debates in which the former Finance Minister came over as the more competent operator, the centre-right unified behind him and he emerged the narrow winner. Seven years later, dragged down by the country's economic troubles after the oil shock of the 1970s and by allegations about a gift of diamonds from Jean-Bedel Bokassa, the loathesome dictator of the Central African Republic, Giscard was defeated by the perennial pretender Mitterrand, who became the first President of the Fifth Republic elected on a left-wing platform. Those events, and the saga that ensued, are the subject of later chapters in this book.

To incarnate France and its greatness is an impossible task to perform in an age in which the nation does not enjoy the stature the General imagined. It calls for discrimination in the exercise of power, which can hardly be expected of politicians who have spent their lives fighting their way up the ladder of power. It has been prey to the debilitating effect of recurrent scandals involving politicians on all sides and, at times, lapping round the man in the Élysée.

François Hollande thought the way out of this trap was to be a 'normal' president when he came to office in 2012. He would shed the trappings of grandeur. He would cease to be the head of one party pitted against the rest. Unlike his predecessor, Sarkozy, he would not be a self-willed individualist walled off by aides who sought to keep even the Prime Minister from tête-à-tête contact with their master. Instead he would be a reasonable ruler listening to all sides, considering the options and acting in the general national interest to achieve a synthesis that would represent the general will. In fact if not in name, his would be a new, Sixth Republic.

But such humility sat uneasily with the nature of the office. When Hollande spoke in everyday terms of having a 'tool kit' to deal with the country's economic woes, he struck a false note that did not go down well with a population expecting leadership from the top rather than sweet reason. He was soon hosting policy meetings at the palace for Socialists only, chairing negotiations with trade unions which he should have left to ministers and getting involved in disputes between ministers over minor issues that should not have required presidential attention. His synthesis did not work well in a nation where conviction in politics is a matter of faith as it were.

His manner, that of a neighbour or somebody with whom one might have a reasonable conversation over a glass of wine or two, did not marry comfortably with the presidential function. The French are generally uncensorious about the personal lives of their rulers, including the revelation that Mitterrand's wife had had a live-in lover who went out in the morning to fetch croissants for the three of them. But Monsieur Normal provoked snickers when his partner, a journalist with the magazine *Paris Match*, seemed to call the shots in their ménage and strayed into politics by coming out in support of an opponent of her predecessor, Ségolène Royal. Pictures of the two women at Socialist events were grist to press photographers. Then the alleged affair with actress Julie Gayet, eighteen years his junior, came to light at the beginning of 2014, with a report in the *Closer* celebrity gossip magazine of the President being driven on a motor scooter by a bodyguard for his nights in a flat with her, the bodyguard bringing croissants in the morning. In a 2012 campaign video she had praised him for 'the force of his oratory.' Hollande's insistence that his private life was his own affair did not stand up for long. His twice-divorced former partner, with whom he had been living outside marriage since 2004 was hospitalized for shock at the public disclosure; she said it was like being hit by a high-speed train or falling from a skyscraper. Continuing her job as a journalist at *Paris-Match* magazine and undertaking a high-profile charity trip to India, she said did rule out writing a book on her time with the President.

After hesitating for several weeks, Hollande announced in an eighteen-word statement that she was no longer France's First Lady. It was all too mundane, too 'normal' in the worst kind of way for the office Hollande held and, far from enhancing his standing as a ladies' man in a country where male chauvinism is still rife, added to his reputation for dithering deviousness, for lacking the necessary presidential style and, like his predecessor, for having allowed his private life to distract him from matters of state. A poll published by *Closer* reported that two-thirds of those questioned did not think he struck 'the right tone' in ditching Ms Trierweiler.

The *Economist* had some fun imagining a reversal of Franco-American presidential behaviour roles in which Barak Obama had an affair with Hillary Clinton followed by Katie Couric, who was installed in the White House as First Girlfriend only to be thrown over for Jennifer Aniston. Looking back, it wondered at the reaction if George W. Bush had divorced Laura and wed the singer Beyoncé (just as Sarkozy had divorced his wife before marrying the supermodel Carla Bruni) or if Bill Clinton had been driven to the houses of mistresses by official cars for assignations which the driver subsequently termed 'three minutes, shower included' (as Chirac's chauffeur alleged about that President's behaviour).

The clear system of government and political allegiances envisaged by de Gaulle has broken down over the decades since his death. That has vitiated the advantages which France still possesses but which are not being made the most of as the country sinks into a morosity that produces the negative poll figures scattered through this book.

Periods of cohabitation between left and right, in 1986–8, 1993–5 and 1997–2002, might have produced a degree of unity and mutual understanding. Instead, they underlined the way in which everything is subordinated to the pursuit of electoral victory: in each case, the Prime Minister's main concern was to become President at the end of his term at the Matignon.

De Gaulle had sought to tear France from the rut into which it had sunk as the Fourth Republic proved unable to deal with the problems facing the nation in its economy, its politics and its colonial war across the Mediterranean. His prime aim was to restore French greatness and reinforce its national identity. The strengths to which he wanted to appeal are still present, but, half a century on from the early years of the Fifth Republic, the rut is there again as the system that governs France has become inward-looking, a means of self-preservation for politicians and the rest of the ruling class, with little prospect of a second rescue effort.

3

ECONOMIC MATTERS

Nowhere is the lack of new horizons more evident than in the economy. Again, it may seem at first glance that France has little to worry about. It recorded a gross domestic product of $2.6 trillion in 2012, placing it below the United States, China, Japan and Germany and just ahead of the United Kingdom. Its economy is the second-biggest in the European Union. The Crédit Suisse bank ranked the Hexagon as the fourth-wealthiest nation in 2010 in aggregate household wealth.

But such numbers cover a multitude of problems caused by a combination of domestic weaknesses and the changing challenges of the global economy. GDP growth since 1978, when it reached a high point of 1.6 per cent, has averaged just 0.5 per cent. Among the thirty-four OECD countries, only Italy and Japan have recorded lower per capita growth over the last quarter of a century. While holding fifth GDP position globally, France drops to nineteenth place among developed industrial nations when measured in purchasing power parity, which takes into account the cost of living.

The French model has made the Hexagon a global symbol of the big state, which provides around a quarter of all jobs. Public spending has been up to fifteen points above the average for OECD countries since 1980. The level of expenditure means high taxation, which has reached 46 per cent of GDP and was further increased under Hollande to try to reduce the budget deficit. Still the state's debt amounts to $2.1 trillion, and interest payments on that are the biggest item in government expenditure. No wonder that the ratings agencies, Standard & Poor's, Moody's and Fitch, all downgraded France as the level of debt continued to increase while the other seventeen eurozone countries cut back on their exposure. At the end of 2013, Standard & Poor's delivered a second blow by reducing the rating from AA+ to AA, putting France on a par with Belgium in its index of creditworthiness.

The agency said the Hollande administration's use of tax increases to cut the budget deficit had run out of steam while its limited reforms would not substantially raise medium-term growth prospects and continuing high unemployment weakened support for further significant fiscal and structural changes. The government insisted that its measures would reap longer-term benefits. Critics were 'underesti-mating France's ability to reform, to pull itself up,' Finance Minister Pierre Moscovici argued as the numbers showed a slight improve-ment in the summer of 2013. But, by the third quarter, quarterly growth contracted once again to end flat for the year.

At the end of the last century, the proportion of national product devoted to public spending was roughly equal in France and Germany; today it is ten points higher in the first country than in the second. Overall public debt increased from 68 per cent of GDP in 2008 to 89 per cent when Hollande took office in 2012. The state deficit has regularly burst through the 3 per cent limit set by the European Union; in mid-2013, the EU Commission in Brussels had to give France an additional two years on the original deadline set to bring its public deficit back under the ceiling by 2015.

The country's share of world output has fallen steadily from 4.4 per cent in 1990 and 3.6 per cent at the start of the twenty-first century to a forecast of 2.5 per cent in 2015. With membership of the eurozone precluding the devaluations used by previous administra-tions to boost price competitiveness, France's share of world exports has dropped steadily. The trade deficit is equivalent to 2 per cent of GDP. French firms are handicapped by having to pay the highest level of payroll tax in the world—43 per cent compared with 11 per cent in Britain and 5 per cent in the United States. Social security contributions by employers amount to nearly 30 per cent of total labour costs compared with 17 per cent in Germany and 10 per cent in the UK. Though somewhat modified, the thirty-five-hour working week introduced by the Socialist government of Lionel Jospin remains a drag on output and saddles companies with overtime payments.

Manufacturing has steadily contracted, accounting for 18.5 per cent of activity compared with 80 per cent for services. The index of manufacturing activities fell sharply in 2011 and remained below Germany, Britain and Italy through 2013. The World Economic Forum's Competitiveness Index puts France in twenty-first place (with Germany sixth and Britain eighth), and the World Bank's 'Doing Business' rankings accord it thirty-eighth position. The International Institute for Management Development in Switzerland places it twenty-eighth out of the sixty most competitive global economies.

The reasons are not hard to find. A report by the OECD singled out French 'economic regulation, product regulation, impositions by local policies, state control of the details of business operations and barriers to entrepreneurship.' The IMF says the Hexagon has begun to lose competitive ground to Spain and Italy as they cut wages and costs after the euro crisis; wages in Spain and France rose to an equal point between 2007 and 2011, but those in Spain have subsequently dropped by seven points while those in France have risen by three points, putting the Hexagon five points ahead of Germany and sixteen points ahead of Britain. While recognizing the country's enduring strengths, the OECD warned that excessive regulation and high levels of taxation are gradually eroding the economy's ability to compete and said that improvement was 'essential to boost the economic growth needed to create jobs and allow citizens and businesses to develop their full potential.'

The head of the employers' federation reckoned in 2013 that French firms paid fifty billion euros more annually than their German counterparts did in taxes and social charges. The IMF urged an over-haul of the labour market and a focus on 'quality fiscal adjustment in order to strengthen incentives to work and invest.' A report com-missioned by the Hollande administration on the economy in 2012 concluded that France faced 'a crisis of confidence' and laboured under 'a cult of regulation'; it called for a major reduction in pay-roll taxes and what the author, businessman Louis Gallois, called 'a competitiveness shock.'

The President took little immediate notice of it. Instead, he commissioned ministers to draw up ideas as to where the country could be in ten years' time—as if they had that much time. The France of tomorrow, they said, 'would be a safer place where justice was quicker and cheaper and where today's stressful experience of finding affordable housing would be transformed into "a pleasant moment in one's life."' The apparatus of the state would be made 'stronger and quicker.' Less cheerily, the Finance Minister warned that France would drop to eighth or ninth place in world economic rankings by the middle of the next decade.

The crystal ball gazing contained no answer to the central puzzle— how to reflate the economy and restore national morale while pushing through spending cuts required to reduce the budget deficit and to put state finances on a sounder basis. The administration tried to convince the public that the tax rises were only the first step in the process of restoring public finances and that cuts to public expenditure would replace them as the main weapon in the future; but that did not assuage a population which was loathe to see a reduction in the benefits it draws from state spending.

Morosity became the national watchword among the French, based on a combination of economic troubles, social change and a fear of the changing world around them and of what the future may hold; a survey by the Pew Institute in 2013 found that only 9 per cent of the French thought that their children would live better than they did (compared with 33 per cent of Americans, 28 per cent of Germans and 17 per cent of the British). All of this comes together to generate something close to a national identity crisis, spurred by factors ranging from the closure of shops and changing eating patterns to immigration and the balance of power in Europe. 'The natives have not budged, but everything has changed around them,' the philosopher Alain Finkielkraut wrote in his 2013 book entitled *L'identité malheureuse* (*The Unhappy Identity*). 'Are they afraid of the Stranger? Do they close themselves off from the Other? No, they feel they are becoming foreigners on their own soil.' Finkielkraut's volume shot straight to the top of the bestseller list.

A persistent trade deficit meant that, in 2012, the French market share of global exports was one-third of the 1993 level and less than half that of Germany. When the European common currency was launched at the start of the new millennium, France's labour costs were below those of its neighbour; now they are higher. Industrial output bumps along at the same level as two decades ago. Profit margins are far below those in Germany and lag 25 per cent behind the EU average. Company closures are more frequent than on the other side of the Rhine.

Though the hourly productivity of French workers is good, the goods they produce are less and less competitive because of their short working week. The news magazine *Le Point* calculated in 2013 that they put in an average of 1,679 hours a year, compared with 1,904 in Germany; time worked annually per inhabitant in France was 11 per cent lower than across the Rhine, 22 per cent less than in Scandinavia, and almost 40 per cent below South Korea. French employees take an average of seven more vacation days a year than the Germans.

The pension system is far too expensive, costing 14 per cent of GDP. The French stop work early—the average age for stopping work is 60.3 years in France, compared with 62.6 in Germany, 64.1 in the UK, and 65 in the US, rising to 67 for those born after 1959. A long-term crisis is taking shape as people born in the baby boom generation reach pensionable age; the ratio of those of working age to those aged over sixty is set to shrink from 2.6 to 1.5 in the coming twenty years. Still, Hollande cut the retirement age back to sixty after Sarkozy had raised it to sixty-two. As a result, the deficit of the pensions system is set to increase from fifteen billion euros in 2013 to twenty-one billion at the end of the decade. On top of this are the shortfalls for the systems of family allowance and unemployment pay, totalling 7.4 billion euros, respectively. With the highest birth rate in the EU except for Ireland—an average of two children for every adult woman—state help for families now amounts to 4 per cent of GDP, nearly double the level across the range of developed countries. The Hollande administration says it will cut back on this kind of spending, but nobody knows quite how that is to be achieved without the kind of cuts which a Socialist government would find it impossible to implement, even if it really wanted to do so.

Companies are subject to large welfare contributions for their staff. The labour market is inflexible. Though membership is low by European standards, at 1.7 million, or 7 per cent of the labour force, trade unions continue to wield considerable power in key parts of the state sector, such as the railways. Governments generally prefer to compromise with them rather than risk the kind of conflicts that brought down Alain Juppé as Prime Minister in 2007.

These kinds of costs and constraints have had their political effects, both in the unhappiness at home and loss of status abroad. Despite his tardy recognition of reality at the start of 2014 with promises of a change in economic policy, Hollande rejects austerity of the kind implemented in Britain to reduce the budget gap, but the effect of low growth and increased taxes means that people have less disposable cash and suffer from stagnant or falling standards of living. In Europe, the Gaullist equation of Paris keeping its grip on the political leadership tiller while Germany remains content to concentrate on its economy no longer functions as, however reluctantly, Berlin has become the continental leader. Though still valuing the relationship across the Rhine, Chancellor Angela Merkel did not cast a kindly eye on Hollande's efforts to tax and spend his way out of the economic downturn, and his calls for a European 'economic government,' which would encourage other countries to draw closer to the French model. Across the globe, states know who to look to first—when China wanted to turn back punitive European Union duties on its solar panel exports in 2013, it enlisted Merkel's aid to good effect; though backed by France, the EU Commission in Brussels had to retreat.

France does not relish playing second fiddle, and the implications for its national psyche are profound, reflected in sometimes scratchy relations between Paris and Berlin and the rise of French parties which want to unpick the European project and follow the path of national sovereignty. Support for the European Union fell to 40 per cent in a Pew poll in mid-2013—this in a country which has always seen itself as central to the construction of the continent.

The malaise has been greatly sharpened by continuing high unemployment, which a Pew Institute poll in 2013 reported was the major concern of 80 per cent of French respondents. The jobless rate has dropped below 8 per cent in only one year during the last two decades, and neared 11 per cent as Hollande went into the second year of his presidency—the highest level since 1998 and double the rate in Germany. It was forecast to stay above 10 per cent at least until 2015. In all, 750,000 industrial jobs have been lost in a decade. The number of people out of work for more than three years stood at 500,000, compared with

300,000 three years earlier. A quarter of those aged under twenty-five were on the dole, compared with 16 per cent for developed nations as a whole, Germany's 5 per cent and 7–8 per cent in the US and UK.

The French model has helped to compound the effect of slow or negative growth on job creation. Regulations designed to defend workers have acted as deterrents to employment, since firms cannot easily cut the workforce if business turns sour. Generous unemployment benefits of between 57 and 75 per cent of earnings make the need to find work less urgent than it might otherwise be, and insufficient training opportunities for the jobless handicap those who do seek employment. The universal application of the minimum wage means that unqualified young people are crowded out of jobs—employers naturally prefer older people with some training or experience; but proposals to set a lower rate for those without qualifications have run into stiff opposition from the Socialists who make up President Hollande's majority. Eighty per cent of the jobs created in 2012 were on short-term contracts. Alternatively, companies move jobs to cheaper labour markets in Eastern Europe and far-away developing nations while shutting down operations at home as margins tighten. Between 2007 and 2010, big French firms cut their workforce in France by 4 per cent while increasing their workers abroad by 5 per cent, leading the pugnacious Industry Minister, Arnaud Montebourg, the National Front and an assortment of politicians on the left to denounce globalization as the cause of high joblessness.

Some of the country's most celebrated companies have shown the strain. The big car manufacturer PSA Peugeot Citröen, which makes 60 per cent of French cars, became emblematic of the woes of French industry as it slipped to ninth rank among global auto companies, producing three million light vehicles in 2013, compared with nine to ten million each for Toyota, Volkswagen and General Motors—and seven million for the healthier Renault, which benefits from its international alliances. After its use of its French plants fell from 80 per cent in 2011 to 64 per cent two years later, PSA announced plans to shed 10 per cent of its hundred-thousand-strong workforce. It shut down a big factory outside Paris. Its outgoing Chief Executive renounced his twenty-one-million euro pension package, which had been criticized by the government for clashing with the cuts and closure. The Peugeot family, which had controlled the firm for a century, was even ready to loosen its grip on ownership with an agreement for both the government and a Chinese car maker to take stakes in return for much needed capital.

Meanwhile, Air France said it would cut its workforce by 8,000, and the bankruptcy of a big road haulage firm threatened to throw 2,000 staff out of work. Companies unveiling closures and staff reductions ranged from the Michelin tire maker to the Alcatel-Lucent telecommunications equipment firm, from retail groups to media outfits. The major defence contractor EADS announced that 1,700 posts were to go in France as part of a Europe-wide contraction.

A steel mill at Florange in the Lorraine region of eastern France became a potent symbol of the challenges the Socialist administration faced in seeking to stem the tide of joblessness. A plan by the owner, ArcelorMittal, to close the furnaces was a central issue in the 2012 presidential battle. Hollande visited the site, climbing on top of a trade union truck to pledge to defend the steel industry. But at the end of the year, the owner, which had said it would maintain employment when it bought the site in 2006, announced that it was shutting down part of the operation, causing six hundred redundancies. Industry Minister Montebourg advocated nationalization and declared that the Indian Mittal family was not wanted in France. That sparked a violent argument with the Prime Minister, who opposed a return of state ownership. Montebourg thought of resigning but pulled back. Jean-Marc Ayrault then negotiated a plan to mothball the furnaces until a plan for low-carbon steel making backed by the European Union came into effect in 2016.

The President pledged to visit the plant every year to check that investment was going into it—on a trip in 2013, he insisted that 'steel in Lorraine has a future' and announced the creation of a government-funded research centre. But he was met with a marble tombstone engraved with the word 'BETRAYAL' when he visited Lorraine earlier in the year. Legislation known as the 'Florange law' was introduced to require companies to prove they have exhausted all options for selling a plant to a new operator before closing it. In the case of Florange, there was no buyer. The furnaces were closed; by the end of 2013 all but 40 of the 629 workers there had taken early retirement or gone to work at other company sites. A cartoon in *Le Monde* showed the President standing on a truck with a bullhorn and telling a desolate landscape of rusting steelworks with not a worker in sight, 'My friends, I've returned!'

Consumer confidence has crashed. Savings rates are high as people fear worse times. Investment by non-financial companies dropped each quarter between the start of 2012 and the fall of 2013, and a survey showed that firms intended to continue to hold back. 'We need as little uncertainty as possible, but instead there is more and more,' the chief executive of the big construction materials company Saint-Gobain told a conference in the summer of 2013. That brought a dismissive response from Finance Minister Pierre Moscovici that he was being 'inelegant and facile.' Who could be surprised that Saint-Gobain was committing itself to invest in the United States and China? France has been a laggard in robotization; the Hollande administration promised to boost the sector, but the investment remained quite limited and one leading manufacturer seeking funds to expand agreed to be taken over by Softbank of Japan in the absence of domestic support.

Though George W. Bush was mocked when he was reported to have remarked that the trouble with France was that it did not have a word for entrepreneur, there is a resonance to the charge; French innovators score well in international rankings, but the system does not encourage them. Bureaucracy holds them back. The tax system penalizes them if they succeed. In 2010, Crédit Suisse ranked France as the European country with most wealthy people. Yet, with some notable exceptions and a thriving IT community in the old rag trade district of the Sentier in Paris, they tend not to have made their fortunes from cutting-edge industries, but from safer and older pursuits or from inheritance.

To be sure, France houses big companies, many of them long-established global players. It also has a very large number of very small firms. Ninety per cent of all enterprises have ten or fewer employees, and the average workforce is only fourteen. Firms tend to halt their expansion when they reach forty-nine employees because an array of thirty-four laws and regulations kick in for them if they go to fifty or more. What is largely missing are the medium-sized firms which form the core of Germany's success. An estimate cited by the *Economist* in a survey of France in 2012 put the number of medium-sized enterprises at just over four thousand, half the number across the Rhine or in Britain.

As a generalization, it is fair to say that the French are not very keen on business. Only 15 per cent of them questioned in an international poll in 2010 thought that capitalism was a system which worked well—compared with 45 per cent in Britain and 55 per cent in the United States. Hollande himself confided in a television discussion before becoming President that he disliked rich people and, during his campaign, identified finance as the main enemy of the nation. Arnaud Montebourg has branded bankers as 'parasites.' A businesswoman was quoted by the *Economist* in 2012 as saying that the rich were stigmatized in the same way as the Jews seventy years earlier. Bonuses and generous pension packages for company chieftains have come under even stiffer criticism than elsewhere. Bankers are widely seen as profiteers, though a survey by the European Banking showed that the number receiving bonus payments above one million francs in 2012 was just 177, compared with 2,714 in the United Kingdom.

There is nothing new in this; de Gaulle inveighed against the 'forces of money,' and Mitterrand denounced its power even as he hobnobbed with financial predators. The financial crisis that began in 2007–8 amplified such sentiments. Bashing the wealthy is a popular pursuit for politicians in difficulties. So it was not surprising that, though he extended some fiscal relief to companies and scrapped an increase in capital gains levies on small firms, Hollande embarked on a round of tax increases presented as a means to make those with plenty of money pay their proper contribution to aid the nation's strained finances. The most headline-grabbing move was to levy a marginal rate of 75 per cent on salaries above a million euros, with a similar payment required from the rich self-employed.

After the Constitutional Court ruled against the measure, it was modified to make payment due from the companies doling out the big pay rather than on individuals. Still, Jean-Paul Agon, chief of the world's biggest beauty products firm, L'Oréal, told the *Financial Times* that it would become 'almost impossible' for France to attract leading business talent, while one of Hollande's advisers was reported to have said the measure would turn France into 'Cuba without the sunshine.' Soccer clubs staged a strike against the blow at their ability to employ highly paid stars in the extremely competitive European soccer market. David Cameron, the British Prime Minister, said his country would 'roll out the red carpet' for French business people wanting to cross the Channel. The actor Gérard Depardieu registered as a Russian citizen in 2013 to escape French taxes. France's richest man, the luxury goods tycoon Bernard Arnault, said he was going to move to Belgium but then decided not to do so.

The amount the tax brought to the treasury was minimal in relation to the size of the state debt; but the political symbolism and the anti-rich sentiment in his own party meant it was politically impossible for Hollande to abandon his campaign pledge on the matter even if he had wished to do so, which seemed unlikely. Indeed, he declared, 'We will still ask more of those who have the most.' Opinion polls reported 60 per cent support for the move. In the French model, the state and its needs come before individuals, particularly if they are wealthy.

However, the reliance on taxation soon turned out to have rather less popular implications. Increases in levies hit ordinary people, notably through the VAT sales tax, which brings in 185 billion of the total of 432 billion raised annually. The Prime Minister had given the country to understand that tax rises would hit only a tenth of the population, but everybody seemed to be hit, leaving many feeling deceived as well as poorer. Anti-tax demonstrations swelled. As a columnist in Le Monde put it, using the English phrase employed under Margaret Thatcher about Britain's contribution to the European Union, the national mood was one of 'I want my money back.' The populist tribune Jean-Luc Mélenchon trumpeted that France was 'in 1788,' with the revolution just round the corner. The proportion of those who said they felt they were middle class fell from 65 per cent in 2010 to 59 per cent three years later, when 40 per cent classed themselves as economically 'modest' or 'badly off.' Average wealth per inhabitant in Germany was 13 per cent above that in France. This was the logical outcome of a process which had been going on for more than three decades and has to be placed in a historical context—a fact that shows how difficult it will be to achieve a significant recovery.

The root of this disconnect between the French and the way the global economy has evolved can be traced back to the fourteen-year presidency of François Mitterrand, who is not going to emerge from this book as the sage ruler above the throng that has become the fashionable depiction of him. He was a supreme narcissist, with few if any principles, who was described by one of his Prime Ministers, the serious social democrat Michel Rocard, as being 'allergic to economic and financial arguments.' As his initial dreamlike project of pumping up growth crashed in the early 1980s, unemployment and inflation soared and the franc was devalued. But the idea of the state which could provide a comfort cocoon for the people of the Hexagon was not abandoned. When that nice idea proved impossible to deliver, the result was widespread alienation and cynicism, which were augmented by a series of scandals that swirled around prominent members of the court at the Élysée (as will be laid out in a later chapter) and also affected some of the country's leading companies.

At the end of the twentieth century, close to fifty chairmen and chief executives of big firms had been fined, gone to prison or were under investigation for illegal behaviour of one kind or another. Executives at the SNCF state railway system, which hugely inflated revenue forecasts on a major new high-speed line, handed out construction contracts without public tendering and with costs inflated by up to 75 per cent for favoured firms. Quizzed about some unusual items in his accounts, one of the contractors said he had given SNCF executives Porsche, Ferrari and Mercedes cars, jewels worth a million francs, and up to twice as much in cash. Thirty of the country's major public works firms were eventually fined a total of 388 million francs in the affair, but this was only half of what the news magazine *L'Express* estimated the corruption had cost the railway network, which, as it happened, racked up the second-biggest loss of any company in the world in 1996.

The Crédit Lyonnais bank, then still in state ownership, got involved in a series of dodgy deals, including its foray into Hollywood in association with a shady Italian financier. Its breakneck international expansion, which made it Europe's biggest bank for a time, eventually required a rescue package that would end up costing the taxpayers fifteen billion euros. Another major French enterprise, the Elf oil company, ran into even deeper trouble in an enormous corruption scandal with political overtones.

Elf at the time was the only French firm to figure in *Fortune* magazine's ranking of the top forty companies in the world; its core operating area was in Francophone Africa, from where it drew 60 per cent of its oil. It was especially close to the long-time dictator of energy-rich Gabon, Omar Bongo, who had been picked as his country's ruler in 1967 by the French *éminence grise* for Africa, Jacques Foccart. French political parties, led by the Gaullists, found Gabon a handy source of illicit funding, with Elf providing a useful conduit.

The firm bought a fine white country house outside Paris from one of President Mitterrand's golfing partners and invested in luxurious real estate for its executives to use around the world. There was a report that, during these transactions, one hundred million francs had somehow got lost in the process in offshore accounts in the Channel Islands, the Isle of Man and the Caribbean. The Elf boss, Loïc Le Floch-Pringent, a Socialist former civil servant with a neat beard and a taste for high living, made liberal use of his company credit card, once allegedly charging it with 68,000 francs' worth of compact discs in a single day. Looking after business friends, he got his company to help a textile magnate who was in legal trouble and was subsequently jailed for having taken out a backdated insurance policy on a factory which had burnt down.

After police and a tough examining magistrate delved into the oil firm, ten executives were hauled in—a couple of others skipped the country or refused to come across the border from Switzerland to be interrogated. Le Floch, who had lost his job at Elf when the Socialists were defeated in legislative elections but was then put in charge of the SNCF for what turned out to be a short tenure, was detained and locked up in a special cell in the Santé prison in Paris. He was accused of having abused his position as chairman and chief executive to seek 'enrichment of himself, his family and friends' through Elf's Swiss and African subsidiaries. Allowed to retain his own clothes, he was forbidden scarves, ties, belts, paper handkerchiefs or a bath towel larger than 1.2 metres square.

A stream of politico-financial revelations followed, including secret bank accounts, alleged payments to the Christian Democratic Party in Germany and a murky affair involving bribes paid to secure a contract to sell French frigates to Taiwan. In a series of trials between 2003 and 2010, Le Floch was sentenced to four separate prison terms. Subsequently freed, he was then arrested and held for a year in Togo after a complaint by one of his former associates.

Then there was the case of the hard-charging businessman Bernard Tapie, appointed Minister for Urban Affairs by Mitterrand in 1992. At the time, he was seen by at least some Socialists as a breath of fresh air, a man who knew the real world and who could go head-to-head with that other bruiser, Jean-Marie Le Pen. But his ministerial career was brief and, in 1997, he was sent to prison for a year for a corruption affair concerning the Olympique de Marseilles soccer club, which he had owned.

The swaggering Tapie was no stranger to trouble and never gave up on a fight. The most protracted of these stemmed from Crédit Lyonnais' purchase of the troubled Adidas sports goods firm from him in 1992, The bank then sold it on for a great deal more. Alleging sharp practice, Tapie launched a legal action which dragged on into the new century.

Beside such colourful cases, disclosure of the secret Swiss bank account of Jérôme Cahuzac, Hollande's first Budget Minister, or revelations that the Socialist Presidential Campaign Treasurer of 2012 operated companies in tax havens seemed quite mundane. A long-running affair involving allegations of illicit funding for Sarkozy by France's richest person, Liliane Bettencourt, heiress of the L'Oréal empire, rumbled on until a judge decided in 2013 that there was no case against the former President. Dominique de Villepin, Prime Minister from 2005 to 2007, was said to have been complicit in fake records of illicit financing through a Luxembourg bank for a list of prominent French politicians. Though the list turned out to be a false, the question remained of why it had been conjured up and for what ends. Then the leader of the UMP party was alleged to have indulged in a dodgy agreement with a company that arranged political rallies and publicity; a close associate of Sarkozy was revealed to have secretly taped confidential meetings with him; and police admitted having tapped Sarkozy's telephone as they investigated allegations that his 2007 presidential campaign had received funding from Libya.

Stock market scandals erupted involving rogue traders, notably the case in 2008 of Société Générale's Jérôme Kerviel, who was convicted of involvement in losses for the bank of 4.9 billion euros in hidden trades—he was released from the fine in 2014. An echo of the past came when, nearing his seventieth birthday, the still combative Tapie popped up to continue his fight with the Crédit Lyonnais and got an adjudication awarding him more than expected. This gave rise to allegations that the decision was political payback for him switching support from the left to Sarkozy. Christine Lagarde, the Finance Minister at the time who had gone on to head the International Monetary Fund, was dragged in. Tapie went on television to deny such charges, but police put under investigation Stéphane Richard, the CEO of France's telecommunications company Orange, who had been Lagarde's chief of staff at the time of the adjudication. The overall effect of the repeated *affaires*, as the French call them, was to diminish the reputation of the political class at a time when citizens had plenty of other reasons for their low opinion of the men and women who ruled them.

That made politicians unwilling to bring in the kind of reforms introduced in Germany at the beginning of the new century by the Social Democratic Chancellor Gerhard Schröder. When Sarkozy was elected in 2007, commentators saw his victory as a sign that the electorate was at last ready to embrace a change in the economic and social system as had been promised during the campaign. But, as we will see, President Sarkozy failed to live up to the rhetoric of Candidate Sarkozy. He did make some changes in the pensions system, but held back from deeper measures and reacted to the global economic crisis with traditional spending medicine. One of his advisers, Alain Minc, has admitted that the President was simply afraid to confront the unions and the social uproar that real reforms would arouse. François Hollande claimed to have a 'tool kit' he would deploy to revive the economy and unveiled a grand plan to invigorate thirty-four industrial sectors, ranging from biotech medicines to renewable energy, and to create 450,000 jobs. But its effects were to take ten years and, in the more immediate term, every step forward by the new administration brought one backwards or turned out to contain less substance than was required or be plainly counterproductive.

Thus, in the summer of 2013, an increase in pension contributions was announced to try to reduce the spiralling deficit. But there was no move to increase the retirement age as recommended by the European Commission. To do that would have risked igniting demonstrations and anger in the Socialist-supporting public sector; a survey showed that only 44 per cent of respondents favoured such a step. As a result, companies found themselves saddled with even more social costs, and contributors had to pay more, too, reducing the disposable incomes they could spend on the consumption needed for the expansion Hollande promised.

When the PSA car company reached an agreement with its workers in the fall of 2013 to work longer hours and accept pay restrictions in return for a halt to the plant closure programme, commentators hailed it as a sign of a new reasonableness as preached by the Socialists in the Élysée. But the following night, the television news led with reports of violence in Brittany by local farmers and fishermen angry at an increase in the tax on the transport of their produce, and poultry processing workers threatened with the closure of their plant. The protests escalated with routine smashing of the sensors set up on main roads to monitor heavy trucks. In line with other policy retreats, the government suspended the tax which had set off the Breton protests. This gave the demonstrators cause for celebration but did not dispel their underlying disenchantment with the administration, while it annoyed environmentalists who had pushed the measure and added to the impression of weakness on the part of the administration when it faced a challenge from the grassroots.

Coming on top of extensive legislation protecting workers whatever the economic environment, the recurrent strikes and demonstrations for which France has become a by-word hardly encourage foreign companies to set up in France and prompt French firms to look overseas. Between 1999 and 2011, inward investment of 279 billion amounted to just one-third of the sum France invested abroad in the same period. Foreign investment dropped by 77 per cent in value in 2013, the biggest fall of any major economy. An American businessman, Maurice Taylor Jr., head of the Titan International tire company, summed it up in early 2013 in a letter to the Industry Minister explaining why he was turning down an offer to take over two factories in northern France about to be shut down with the loss of 1,173 jobs.

'Do you think we're stupid?' Taylor wrote. 'I've visited this factory several times. The French workers are paid high wages but only work three hours. They have one hour for their lunch, they talk for three hours and they work for three hours. I said this directly to

their union leaders; they replied that's the way it is in France . . .
Titan has money and the knowhow to produce tires. What does
the crazy union have? It has the French government. The French
farmer wants cheap tires. He doesn't care if those tires come from
China or India or if those tires are subsidized. Titan is going to buy
Chinese or Indian tires, pay less than €1 an hour to workers and
export all the tires that France needs. In five years, Michelin won't
be producing tires in France. You can keep your so-called workers.
Titan is not interested in the factory in North Amiens,' concluded
Taylor, nicknamed 'The Grizz' and described as 'rough-hewn' by
Forbes magazine.

It is easy, therefore, to see France as being on an inexorable
downward spiral caused by national habits and expectations as well
as by the laws of economics. Yet the picture needs to be nuanced
beyond a straight tale of doom and gloom to understand the context that explains why the country has been able to teeter on the
brink for so long without crashing down. To start with the state,
while it is undoubtedly too big and too expensive, the heritage of
central planning launched under the Fourth Republic has produced
excellent infrastructure. The coordinated system of development, with
private enterprises working within a government framework, has, for
instance, done wonders in the national motorway network that other
advanced economies can only envy.

While the high birth rate comes with a cost on family assistance
programmes, it has given France a young population in an ageing
continent and, looking further afield, contrasts with the much lower
rate in the expanding economies of East Asia. France remains the
fifth-largest recipient of foreign direct investment in the world and,
though its high-tech entrepreneurs have largely deserted the Hexagon
in recent decades for Silicon Valley, London or other more friendly
destinations, there are now moves to foster innovations at home, with
a 120-million-euro project to open a 1.1 million square feet incubator
hub in Paris and a pledge of 215 million euros from the government
to take stake in start-ups. Tech companies based in France attracted
405 million euros in venture capital finance in the first half of 2013,
a 13 per cent increase on the same period of the previous year.

On the labour front, for all the noise they make, French trade unions are really quite weak overall. Their strength is concentrated in a few public sector areas such as the railways. The rate of penetration of the workforce is low by European standards. Membership as a proportion of the total labour force is below that in Britain, Germany and the United States. 'The problem in our country is not that we have too powerful unions, but that they are too fragmented and too small,' said Sarkozy when he was Interior Minister. They claim repeated victories over government by staging big street demonstrations and are helped by the way in which those democratically elected administrations prefer to buckle in the face of their pugnacity and allow themselves to be blindsided by appeals to 'republican values' and the revolutionary tradition of liberty, equality, fraternity—however fragile it may have become in practice. But at least some union leaders are starting to acknowledge that labour problems in France should be put in the wider European and global context, and that a common approach with employers is needed to improve competitivity in place of the traditional confrontations.

On the wider economic scale, France retains significant strengths. Though its share of world agri-food trade has dropped since the 1980s, it still ranks among the three major exporters of home-grown farm products alongside the much larger land areas of the United States and Brazil. It is the world's top tourist destination. French companies are prominent across the world, scoring strongly in high-end goods and services, notably fashion and luxury products, pharmaceuticals, armaments and food and wine in most of their forms.

Total, the country's largest enterprise by revenue, is the eighth-biggest global oil and gas undertaking. AXA, second in France, is a big player in global insurance. After some hiccups following the onset of the crisis in the eurozone due to their exposure to troubled economies, French banks regained their health; BNP Paribas, ranking third among companies at home, was the fourth-largest bank on earth measured by assets in 2013. Carrefour, fourth among domestic firms, is the world's second-biggest retailer. Accor ranks fifth among global hotel groups, and Jean-Claude Decaux is the largest outdoor advertising company on earth.

L'Oréal leads the world in cosmetic and beauty products groups. Air France, merged with KLM of the Netherlands in 2004, was for a time the biggest airline in terms of total operating revenues and international passenger-kilometres. Danone taught the Chinese to love yoghurts and other milk products. Luxury goods from LVMH, Christian Dior, Hermès and their peers are sported by fashionable folk from Sao Paulo to Shanghai. Thales and Dassault Aviation are major global players in aerospace and defence, while vehicle makers Renault and PSA Peugeot-Citröen and Michelin tires have wide international reach. Alstom is an engineering and transporting giant, Vinci and Bouygues are strong in building and infrastructure, Saint-Gobain in construction materials, Pernod Ricard in beverages plus an array of computer companies and international publishers.

Quite a few have serious problems, such as PSA and Air France. Areva has run into difficulties with its nuclear power plant programme overseas and faces opposition from the left-Green coalition at home. Alstom suffers from a decline in big public sector infrastructure projects round the world and at home along with stiff competition from General Electric and Siemens and has run into headwinds given fallen demand for the thermal power plants which it builds—plus it has a mountain of debt that led it to announce a package of job cuts. Yet this is not a nation that has lost its underlying economic clout; Veolia, GDF Suez and Areva are big in utilities across the globe, while EDF is a major energy supplier across the Channel and is building Britain's first nuclear power station in two decades (with a dose of funding from China). The big French banks outperformed the European banking stocks index, with shares rising 33 per cent in 2013 and strengthened balance sheets. Privatization, which began in 1986 under François Mitterrand's presidency when Jacques Chirac was Prime Minister, presents an interesting case study of the tensions between economic development and the state as it loosened its grip on industry and finance.

First to go was Saint-Gobain (set up by Jean-Baptiste Colbert in 1665). Then came the TF1 television channel, the Paribas bank, which was merged with BNP, followed by the Société Générale. The Suez group was taken to market and merged with the state-owned gas company. The giant Compagnie Générale d'Élecricité became Alcatel. Renault, Total and Arcelor followed. The process continued in banking, aerospace and utilities under governments of left and right, with the Socialist Lionel Jospin showing himself as keen a privatizer as anybody. In all, the state sold off thirty-five companies plus nine highway operating firms.

When the process began, opinion polls reported wide support, but there were drawbacks. The job cuts which often followed were, naturally, unpopular; a banker involved in privatization discussions at the end of the twentieth century recalls how the politicians spent more time worrying about the reaction of the public sector unions than they did about the best offer price for the market. There was controversy about how large a stake the state should retain, since privatization did not mean that it lost interest in the national champions it seeks to promote.

Allowing foreign investors to buy into what had been public assets was not a popular notion for the French, particularly when less comfortable working practices might be imported from abroad. But by 2013, non-French investors held 46 per cent of the shares of the forty biggest companies quoted on the Paris Stock Exchange. As domestic shareholders became net sellers, foreigners bought fourteen billion euros worth of stock in 2012. There was discomfort at the realization that what had once been the treasure of the state was up for grabs and that fund managers in New York, London and Asia could determine the course of major companies, but the trend appeared inexorable.

In European terms, France may fall short of German standards of success and rectitude, but it has still fared significantly better than southern European members of the common currency zone. Despite its large state debts and Sarkozy's refusal to embrace austerity, France did not become a target for the bond vigilantes in the crisis that enveloped the eurozone from 2009. Nor did the election of a Socialist President who had pledged to increase taxes on the rich and seek growth through yet more public spending lead investors to demand sharply higher interest rates on French government securities. Indeed, the stock market rose and investors turned to French bonds as they fled Italy and Spain. The danger was, in the words of the American analyst John Maudlin, that the country would become 'dependent upon the kindness of strangers' who could prove fickle if they decided that Hollande's policies could lead to the country to follow the southern European trail. But that possibility remained only latent through 2013 as French bonds remained strong, and even

Mr. Grizz changed his tune. Six months after the incendiary letter from the American, Arnaud Montebourg announced that he had received an offer from Titan to buy one of the two tire plants on offer, saving 333 jobs, and to invest 'tens of millions' of euros in it. The saga became more cloudy, however, as workers took action and negotiations appeared to run into the sand. However, recognizing the widespread view of France as an unattractive place in which to invest and the danger to the two million jobs provided by foreign companies, Hollande held a meeting of their executives in February 2014 to reassure them that they would be well treated—some were enthused; others preferred to wait and see.

So, behind the image of a state-dominated land living on past glories lies a nation that still enjoys considerable strengths, if only it could make more of them. The problem is that the country and, above all, its leaders, seem to prefer to maintain a status quo which offers less and less for the majority of the population and augments the national feeling of unhappiness. Given the array of comfort blankets on offer, it is easier not to take the risk of shaking up the system and to sink into a spiral of decline, cushioned by the belief in the nation's exceptional nature.

In its annual report on France in 2013, the OECD, which happens to be based in Paris, came up with a list of recommendations that makes eminent sense and could be achieved by a serious administration intent on reversing that spiral. Research and innovation should be reinforced, particularly among small- and medium-sized companies; public sector efficiency should be improved with fewer regulations; taxation should be cut and labour market reformed while measures should be undertaken to control real estate prices, whose high level attracts capital away from more productive sectors. That shopping list lays out what France should have done over past decades, and policy-makers know it. So why has little been achieved?

The fundamental problem, as with other areas of today's France examined in this book, is political. Since Giscard d'Estaing lost the presidency in 1981, after he and his Prime Minister, Raymond Barre, implemented necessary tough measures in response to the oil shock of the late 1970s, leaders of both left and right have fought shy of policies which would involve pain for the population. As a result, there has not been a balanced budget since their time. As the banker Michel Pébereau remarked in an official report in 2005, the reaction of successive administrations in the past thirty-five years to economic and social problems has been to spend more money. When things are bad, extra expenditure is seen as the way to revive the economy; when the situation improves, spending has to be maintained, or even increased, to ward off the possibility of a downturn. In this vicious circle, the French find it hard to live without high public spending, but they pay for the benefits in the shape of a highly taxed economy in which structural reform is rendered more and more difficult by entrenched interest groups, by the expectation that the state will always bail them out and by the lack of political will to do otherwise.

So far, the narcotic has proved irresistible, and a spell of cold turkey would mean political disaster, as Sarkozy soon concluded. The result is that the French economy diverges from the twenty-first-century global norm, remaining rooted in a nostalgia for the *Trente Glorieuses* (Glorious Thirty Years) that began in the 1950s when inflation and devaluation cushioned the country from harsher realities. Many French would hold up that divergence as a sign of national identity, indeed of pride. They do not want to be like the 'Anglo-Saxons,' by which they mean the 'Anglo-Americans.' The snag is that they live in a globalized world in which retreating into a cocoon has made no sense since the failure of the Mitterrand experiment in the early 1980s.

François Hollande summons up all the earnestness at his command to talk of a future in which his country will enjoy full employment and a new industrial revolution with social justice and good housing for all. How this is to be achieved is left unexplained. It would certainly mean some short-, and not so short-, term pain in search of long-term gain. It would mean accepting policies which the President, and voters, rejected in the 2012 election. Though parallels have been drawn with the initial Mitterrand economic experiment in 1981, the comparison is not very apt but has worrying aspects. Hollande's programme has been nothing like as audacious as that of his Socialist predecessor, but the real differences lies in the state of France's economy in 1981 and now—then the national debt was 22 per cent of GDP, the budget deficit was small, there was growth and

France had a currency of its own which it could devalue; today, the situation on the first three counts is much worse, and competitive national currency games are ruled out—indeed, the strength of the euro puts French exporters at a disadvantage when they can afford it least.

So long as Berlin calls the shots, the eurozone crisis is not going to be solved on Hollande's terms by boosting public spending. Any real resolution of the crisis by the creation of a fiscal authority over the zone's member states would mean a surrender of the national sovereignty the French prize so highly—and increased German dominance.

These are not simply economic issues. They involve fundamental political and social questions—and France's entrenched view of itself. Coming to grips with the need for change and adapting to a world in which the driving forces are beyond the control of the Énarques in Paris constitute a challenge many people in the Hexagon would prefer to avoid. Calls for reform resounded through 2013. The French central bank advocated a 'profound change in public policy,' and drew attention to the 'particularly generous' benefits to the unemployed. The OECD warned of 'significant downside risks' if action was delayed. The President of the European Commission, Manuel Barosso, said the two years breathing space granted to France to get its deficit in order must be used for structural change. Olli Rehn, the Commissioner for Economic and Monetary affairs, added that 'tax increases have reached a fateful point,' while former German Chancellor Gerhard Schröder wrote that reforms such as those he introduced in Germany were necessary in France 'because of excessive debt as well as demographic developments and international competition.'

The snag is that Schröder's policies brought electoral defeat. The first rule for politicians in France, as elsewhere, is to get elected or re-elected, and the examples of Giscard d'Estaing in 1981 and Alain Juppé in 1997 demonstrate the penalty of imposing unpopular measures, however necessary. So they shrink from imposing medicine which may repel voters—it took a de Gaulle to implement the tough economic moves that set the Fifth Republic on its feet in the late 1950s. Rather, the reaction of voters to growing challenges over the past three decades has been to seek solace in a new administration rather than facing uncomfortable realities—from Mitterrand's dream of 1981 to Hollande's promise of growth in 2012.

Comfortable as that may in the short term, the longer-run impact has been debilitating, like a patient putting off having the necessary operation. The Pew survey of international attitudes in May 2013 showed the impact. Far from generating confidence, the lack of reform left only 9 per cent of French respondents saying they thought conditions in their country were currently good, compared with 75 per cent in Germany. As for the future, just 20 per cent said they were satisfied with the way the country was going. Only one-third approved of the government elected only a year earlier. A vast majority wanted a change of policy but had little idea what it might consist of. Something different was simply bound to be better—a confession of failure from a country that could not see a coherent way forward.

There were many other factors at work, as we will see, but the economy lay at the root of the national unhappiness as Hollande retreated in the face of popular revolts, and his search for a reasonable consensus doomed him to be seen as irresolute or evasive as he avoided confrontations and issued assurances that everything would come all right in the end. As he proved sadly mistaken in his pledge to reduce unemployment in 2013 and changed tack to say he merely meant that the rate of increase would be reduced, he appeared to be downright dissembling, expecting the French to join him in a make-believe world that could only cut away at his credibility. 'His pledge of new economic policies at the start of 2014 remains to be translated into effective action. 'When it comes to taking decisions, Mr. Hollande is a study in ambiguity, a leader who seems strangely averse to the idea of leading,' wrote the *Financial Times*. He was overshadowed by Chancellor Angela Merkel, whose supremacy contrasted so sharply with his weakness and who had the great advantage of presiding over a flourishing nation.

Had France's economy been stronger or had there been at least a clear strategy, the outlook might have been brighter. But such solace was not on offer, as the best data showed only tiny improvements and high unemployment had become endemic. The changing nature of French society, and the unhappiness it causes, plays into the hands of politicians ready to exploit morosity by offering a vision of a return to the past in which the troubles of the early twenty-first century would be swept aside and France would miraculously regain its true essence.

Again and again, since Giscard paid the price for recognizing the need for austerity in the face of the oil shock of the late 1970s, French leaders have preferred to put short-term political advantage ahead of policies which might incur popular displeasure. Mitterrand, Chirac and then Sarkozy all followed this path to varying degrees. They have gambled on achieving growth through consumption fuelled by state spending rather than seeking stronger industrial growth through production. In the process, manufacturing and exports have contracted and the state's cash injection has not boosted the happiness of citizens, while wealth inequality of households grew more than in the United States and the UK between 2007 and 2011.

With occasional and partial exceptions, the political elite has let France down by its short-sightedness, personal ambition and lack of resolution—and by its abiding belief that the people of the Hexagon will always prefer the easy way out. Given the nature of the available leaders and the increasingly unappealing reality confronting them, it may not be surprising that the French have been tempted by yet more dreams over the past three decades. But this could bring no remedy to the discomforts of the late twentieth and early twenty-first centuries in cities and the countryside, in the changing nature of society and in the loss of traditional anchors. So let us now move away from the world of the economy, the Élysée, Matignon, government and the Énarques to consider the condition of the symbols that have defined France for so long and whose fate plays so powerfully into the current condition and mood of the nation.

4

VANISHING MADELEINES

Modernists and technocrats may scream, but a set of images defines France—the beret and the café, dark pungent cigarettes, the baguette breadstick and red wine, the accordion, garlic and the Seine. The front of a book on the French by the noted British academic Theodore Zeldin features a beret along with a baguette, a striped jersey and a packet of Gitanes. The cover of a survey I wrote for the *Economist* on France had a man carrying a baguette and another with a beret leaning on a bar bearing glasses of red wine. A compact disc compilation of French songs by a British record firm is subtitled 'The garlic and Gauloises world of French accordionists and singers.' At the reconstruction of the citadel at Verdun, where hundreds of thousands of French soldiers perished repulsing the German advance in 1916, the table is laden with baguettes and bottles of red wine. No film set in Paris would be complete without a scene in a café—and every documentary about the capital has to have a long, lingering shot of the Seine and its bridges.

So how are these particular symbols faring? Naturally, they have been affected by modernization, just as the Wild West is not what it was and British gentlemen have given up wearing bowler hats. High-rise blocks and multi-lane highways cover the banks of the rivers outside Paris where the Impressionists painted some of their most beautiful scenes and Henri Cartier-Bresson captured a working-class quartet having a picnic on the grass above fishing boats in one of his most iconic photographs. Under Pompidou, the right bank of the Seine was turned into a multi-lane speedway.

That is part of the cost of material progress and comes with significant compensations; today's inhabitants of Nogent-sur-Seine enjoy a lifestyle that the painters and picnickers could not have imagined and, when there are no logjams, it is much quicker to get from the Alma to the Hôtel de Ville than it once was. But, though every country has its icons from the past which have come under growing assault from the present, the shifting sands of contemporary life have a particular impact in France because of the way in which they affect the symbols that have framed so much of the image of the nation both for foreigners but also, crucially, for the people of the Hexagon themselves.

In the 1930s, the prominent commentator Georges Duhamel wrote in defence of a country 'whose soul, inhabitants and products are diverse, motley, changing and ingenious. From milk, this simple and elementary food, we Frenchmen know how to make more than one hundred kinds of cheese. All are good, healthy, strong, substantial and amusing. All have their history, character and role. In this feature alone, I recognise the genius of my country, in it I understand that she has produced so many great men in all professions . . . I belong to a peasant people which has cultivated lovingly for centuries fifty different plums, and which finds in each one a deliciously incomparable taste.' He followed this with a grave warning that, unless traditions, values and identities were defended, American-style modernity would overwhelm the Hexagon.

What is one to make, then, of the proliferation of fast food led by McDonald's 1,300 outlets, the decline of the café and the traditional bakery, or the adoption of rap and hip-hop in place of the melodies of Charles Trenet and Georges Brassens or the heartfelt chants of Edith Piaf? How is one to judge the evaporation of brown tobacco smoke that once hung around the essential image of France, or evaluate the loss of unchallenged leadership of the culinary world which could be taken for granted for so long? For English-speaking expatriates in the Hemingway-Fitzgerald tradition, how is one to interpret the transformation in 2013 of the Paris-published *Herald*

Tribune, which first appeared in 1887, into the international edition of its owner, the *New York Times*?

Start with the arts and intellectual tradition of which France is so proud, with Sarkozy declaring in 2007 that, like the United States, 'we think our ideas are destined to illuminate the world.' France insists on *'l'exception culturelle'* to justify tariff barriers to protect itself from foreign competition. As the American writer Donald Morrison put it in his 2008 book, *Que reste-t-il de la culture française?* (English title, *The Death of French Culture*), 'Nobody takes culture more seriously than the French. They subsidize it generously; they cosset it with quotas and tax breaks. French media give it vast amounts of airtime and column inches. Every French town of any size has its annual opera or theatre festival, its Maison de la Culture and, in its churches, weekend organ and chamber-music recitals.' But, as Morrison added, 'There is one problem. All of these mighty oaks being felled in France's cultural forest make barely a sound in the wider world.'

Much of the French cultural establishment, naturally, lined up to criticize the author when he first made his case in a cover article in *Time* magazine. Yet it is difficult to gainsay his overall conclusion. France still has a vibrant cultural scene, but it is very hexagonal and cannot claim the supremacy it once did. As Antoine Compagnon, who wrote an essay to accompany Morrison in his book, put it, 'We have long thought ourselves the best, but France these days is an average cultural power, a good average cultural power.'

While disputing Morrison's views, Olivier Poivre d'Arvor, head of the government's programme to spread his country's culture globally, responded to the article by writing that the French should be reminded that 'nothing can be taken for granted, that it is necessary to fight, including at home, to reaffirm the importance of this culture.' The philosopher Jean Baudrillard summed up a growing sense of insularity when he told an interviewer in 2005, 'We accept only what we invented.'

This is an overstatement, but not in a way that favours France. Foreign books figure prominently in the bestseller lists; America films attract big audiences; French popular music groups absorb rap, hip-hop and reggae. However, there is little traffic the other way—even Hollywood has cut down on its adaptations of French films. As for

Sarkozy's claim, one might ask crudely, 'Which ideas did you have in mind?'

France's global impact as a home of new thoughts has seriously diminished. The days of Personalism, Existentialism, Structuralism, Post-Structuralism, Deconstructionism and all the other -isms that sprang from Saint-Germain-des-Prés, the Sorbonne and other intellectual hot houses have gone—some would welcome this given the way in which some French thinkers tended to pursue their reasoning to the point of absurdity or rendered them simply incomprehensible to mere mortals.

There is no doubting the lowering of France's global intellectual clout. A survey of 20,000 readers conducted by the magazines *Foreign Policy* in the US and *Prospect* in Britain ranked just two Frenchmen, Baudrillard and Alain Finkielkraut, among leading global public intellectuals (the US had thirty-one and the UK, twelve). Appearing on television talk shows or giving long, and often quite vapid, interviews accompanied by a striking photographic portrait seems to be the main aim of today's thinkers. 'There are no more French intellectuals,' Baudrillard said in the 2005 interview. 'What you call intellectuals have been destroyed by the media. They talk on television, they talk to the press and they are no longer talking among themselves.'

Despite its stout defence of its literary tradition, the country ranks only twelfth in the world publication stakes as recorded by the United Nations, with 42,000 titles in 2011, compared with 328,000 in the United States and 150,000 in Britain. Very few French novels get translated. The largely forgotten poet and essayist Sully Prudhomme was the first winner of the Nobel Prize for Literature in 1901, followed by the Provençal versifier Frédéric Mistral in 1904 and then seven other laureates before Jean-Paul Sartre turned down the award in 1964. Since then, there have been only two French laureates—novelists Claude Simon in 1985 and Jean Marie Le Clézio in 2008.

French cinema remains strong, buoyed by generous government subsidies and the protection of *l'exception culturelle* against competition from abroad, especially Hollywood-though foreign films topped the box office receipts for more than half of 2012 and six of the top ten biggest-grossing films of all time in France have been American. Paris has more cinemas per inhabitants than any other world city. With over 200 million tickets sold each year, France is the third-biggest film market in the world after the United States and Japan. That reflects a high degree of self-sufficiency, with films recovering up to 90 per cent of their costs domestically, a source of strength and an encouragement to the country that invented the motion picture; but it has the effect of lessening the impact of French cinema globally.

Other icons are undergoing less salutary changes. France's 100,000 restaurants increasingly use cheap ingredients from industrial suppliers to balance the rising price of fresh raw materials and, in particular, increased wages which have spiked up by 40 per cent since 2000 and make up almost half of the running costs of most establishments. Sales to French restaurants by the ready-made unit of the giant Nestlé group have jumped from 40 to 60 per cent this century. In 2013, a grouping of owners of hotels and eating places said that one-third of all establishments in the country served up meals made entirely or partly outside. This may well be an underestimate; one leader of a movement to encourage fresh food reckons that the true figure is 70 per cent when ingredients like frozen fish are included. Star chef Alain Ducasse says most of the country's restaurants do 'only industrial cooking.'

Legislation was introduced in 2014 requiring restaurants to designate fresh dishes made on the premises as *fait maison* (homemade), the point being that fare without such a label would be presumed to have been bought in from an industrial supplier. Daniel Fasquelle, a National Assembly deputy who was among those behind the law, said it was a matter of preserving 'our heritage.' Ducasse and fellow kitchen star Joël Robuchon have begun to offer quality seals for establishments that meet high standards for their cuisine; Ducasse estimates that only one-tenth of France's restaurants would qualify.

Now take the staff of life, bread from France's *boulangeries* and their prize exhibit, the elongated baguette loaf with its pointed ends, crunchy surface, soft doughy interior and inimitable aroma; the author of a book entitled *Vive la Baguette* says it should sound like a drum if you tap its surface and that it ought to 'flatter the palate with its slightly-caramelised hazelnut flavour.' The baguette stick has its cousins: the fatter, torpedo-shaped *bâtard*; the smaller *flûte*, *bâton* and *ficelle*; and the more distant relations of the circular *boule* and the large *miche* loaf. Alongside the white flour of the baguette are the darker *pain de campagne* and various organic breads and bran and multigrain loaves, with combinations of wheat and rye, kernels and nuts (an old country speciality that goes particularly well with cheese). Bakers have experimented with bread infused with any number of herbs and spices and even asparagus. Then come croissants for breakfast and brioche to start the day or go, toasted, with foie gras—not to mention *pain au chocolat* and *aux raisins*, Proust's memory-evoking madeleines and all the pastries on offer on the *boulangerie* counter for mid-afternoon and any other sweet-toothed time—*éclairs*, *babas au rum*, fruit tarts, *beignets* and the wonderfully named *pets de nonne* (nun's farts).

But it is still the baguette and its relations which are meant to rule the baker's roost. The place of bread in national life was consecrated by a competition involving a hundred bakers each year for the Grand Prix de la Baguette and the honour of supplying the President of the Republic. Jacques Chirac, who ate one and a half baguettes a day, told the National Bakers' Federation that their product was 'one of the great charms of our civilization.' As part of the overseas aid effort, an expert from eastern France was sent to teach bakers in developing countries. Historians identify the price of bread after a series of bad harvests as a contributor to the French Revolution, and the fall of the Bourbon monarchy and Marie-Antoinette will forever be associated, even if erroneously, with her saying that, if the people did not have bread, 'let them eat cake'—*brioche* was the word attributed to her, though there is no record of her having uttered it. The theft of a loaf of bread by Jean Valjean set off the saga of *Les Misérables*. For most French people, it was difficult to start a meal without a chunk of baguette by the plate. Bread plays the same role as rice for Asians; it is more than a simple means of calming the pangs of hunger or mopping up sauce.

Sandwich shops around the world sell their food in baguettes (even if they are run by American, British or Asian entrepreneurs). The sourdough loaves of the Parisian baker Lionel Poilâne are on sale thousands of miles from his headquarters on the Left Bank in Paris. A second-generation baker who was apprenticed to the trade at age fourteen and built up a collection of 1,500 books on bread, he proclaimed that it 'is at the heart of French food' and 'the key to social peace and stability for every French government.' His *miches* stay fresh for a week; 'I make bread the way it was made in the fifteenth century,' he said—in wood-fired ovens in the cellar of his bakery.

However, there was an awkward reality lurking in the background. Three-quarters of the bread produced in France in the 1990s came from outlets that called themselves bakers. But a lot of what the French ate was made from frozen dough or originated in mass production plants elsewhere though sold as if it had been manufactured early that morning on the premises. The expansion of supermarkets meant that more and more people bought loaves made in such plants.

Chirac might have stigmatized industrial bread as 'not even a Christian food,' but how many young people wanted to take up a trade that required them to rise in the middle of the night to make the dough, divide it by hand into sticks and then monitor the baking in the oven. Much quicker, easier and more economical to use frozen dough containing two or three times the normal dose of yeast to increase the end volume by up to 30 per cent. Mechanical shaping of the sticks toughens the inside of the baguette, while modern hot-air ovens do not give a thick crunchy crust. But how can the extra labour and care required by the traditional methods compete with industrial production and supermarket margins when most consumers did not seem to care too much, some even being content to buy pre-packed, pre-sliced loaves to toast?

Traditional bread makers remain in the country and upmarket urban enterprises. On the southern slopes of the Massif Central, an Auvergnat bakes his bread once a week in the oven in his farmhouse and drops the big round loaves off to grateful friends in big flour bags. But, in general, as people grow richer and more citified, they eat less bread. A century ago, the average French person consumed 219 kilograms a year. By 1967, that was down to eighty-two kilos. Around 2000, it fell below sixty kilos. By the second decade of the last century, the average French person ate only half a baguette a day compared with almost a whole one in 1970, and more than three in 1900. Women consume a third less bread than men do. Parisians average only thirty-six kilos a year; the national record for bread eating is in the poor, deeply rural southwestern department of Gers. Not surprisingly, the number of small bakers has nearly halved from 54,000 in 1960 to some 35,000. 'Eating habits are changing,' Bernard Valluis of the bakers' lobby group explained in 2013. 'People are too busy or work too late to go to the bakery. Teenagers are skipping breakfast.'

Bakers took to the streets periodically to demand protection from supermarket competition, calling on the government to identify the baguette as an element in France's civilization. Seeing a national treasure in danger, legislation has been introduced to restrict the name *boulangerie* to establishments that bake their bread on the premises. The decline in the number of bakeries slowed. A government decree laid down the permitted ingredients for baguettes—wheat flour, water, salt plus yeast or a raising agent. Bread served to children with school meals was improved to catch them young. An apocalyptic television commercial thundered, 'If you don't eat bread anymore, one day there won't be any!' A European Union report in 2010 found less industrial bread production in France than in Germany, Britain and the Netherlands. The bakers launched a fresh campaign in 2013 to trumpet the contribution of bread to good health, conversation and French civilization under the slogan '*Coucou, tu as pris le pain?*' ('Hi there, have you picked up the bread?'). In 2014, 187 Paris bakers entered a twenty-year-old competition to find the best baker in the capital; 50 loaves were immediately rejected for not being the right size (55–65 cms long) or weight (250–300 grams). The winner. Anthony Teixeira, whose father took the prize sixteen years earlier, starts work at three a.m. and makes 1,500 baguettes a day at his bakery in the 14th arrondissement. As part of his prize, he will be entitled to deliver forty baguettes to the Élysée Palace each morning for a year. Bread was an icon under threat from the evolution of modern life, to be sure, but it was still able to fight back against the homogenized, flaccid product of factories and fast dough.

More problematic is the fate of the greatest French social landmark of all, the café. For Balzac, it was 'the parliament of the people.' A century later, the novelist Nathalie Sarraute sat writing at the same table every morning for forty years. The poet Léon-Paul Fargue hailed the café as the soundest of French institutions: no revolution, he wrote, had been able to rock its foundations. That was in 1946. Seven years later, Robert Doisneau took one of the great photographs of everyday French life at the Bouillon Tiquetonne café in the Paris market district of Les Halles. A man in a thick jacket and cap stands in front; an accordionist is on the right by the wall-sized mirror; a stout gesticulating woman fills the middle ground; empty glasses and wine bottles sit on every table. The reality of today is a long way from Fargue's postwar world. Surveys report that half the French hardly ever set foot in a café.

In 1910, France had 510,000 cafés and bars; by 1960 the total was down to 200,000, and it has dropped to a fifth of that today. Between 1960 and 1995, the ratio of cafés to people fell by a factor of five. In villages, there is not enough custom. In big cities, people patronize other places to drink and eat. Knocking back a quick calvados on the way to work or propping up the zinc bar while downing a pastis or three on the way home is no longer in fashion. Clients wanting wine are more likely to go to specialized establishments where there is a wider and better choice.

Sandwich shops and fast food outlets have edged out the classic basic fare on offer at cafés. Starbucks made its first appearance in France on the Avenue de l'Opéra in Paris in 2004; by 2013 it had thirty-eight outlets in the capital, ten more in the surrounding region and three in Lyons. Legislation against smoking and drunk driving has had its effect. Waiting on customers is not an attractive profession for the young. Online access to the horse racing betting system has replaced the need to go to the *café-tabac* to place a wager.

Bernard Quartier, president of the National Federation of Cafés, Brasseries and Discothèques, says café owners were 'in synch' with society in the 1960s but then got out of touch with customer requirements. Television keeps people at home in the evening. The exodus from the land has deprived thousands of country cafés of customers. A fast food outlet is estimated to cut the trade in nearby cafés by up to 35 per cent. Even the tax system was tilted against cafés; the food they serve is subject to value added tax at the maximum rate of 20.6 per cent, whereas take-aways were hit for only 5.5 per cent. Owners and managers marched in protest in Paris and got satisfaction when the Sarkozy administration lowered their tax rate, but then the government under Hollande put it up at the end of 2013.

McDonald's provides a good example of a malaise that stretches to encompass mass culture in general and resonates with geo-political apprehensions. When the first Golden Arches went up in Strasbourg in 1979, Big Macs and fries became the focus of worries that the French way of life was under threat. That fused with a longstanding strand of disdain for things American, which has always sat oddly with the way the French have often taken up trends from across the Atlantic. The acute commentator Marie-France Toinet pointed out that 'the fascination for and rejection of Americanism' felt by her fellow citizens was 'not so much a debate about the United States as about themselves, about their society, their goals and their methods. It is, so to speak, a Franco-French debate, where arguments about America—often half-baked—are just an excuse or a pretence. The French hold up the United States as a mirror to look, in fact, at themselves.'

At the time of the Strasbourg opening, it was *de rigueur* to sneer at *'le Big'* as immortalized by John Travolta in *Pulp Fiction*. The location of the first outlet, in a city on the edge of France with a European vocation, may not have been a coincidence. But then there were controversies about the chain opening up in historic sites, including the Louvre. The Paris authorities stopped the golden arches being erected on a building where Picasso and Matisse once bought their paints. The southern city of Uzès, which has been busy building itself up as a place that reflects old French ways given a modern gloss, banished its McDo to the fringes of the urban area. In August 1999, a self-appointed scourge of fast food called José Bové became a national figure, and a hero to many, when he broke up the site of a new McDonald's restaurant in his hometown of Millau in the southwest.

His action was mainly to protest at the slapping of high US tariffs on the Roquefort cheese made in the area as part of a trans-Atlantic trade war; commentators agreed that Washington was using bully boy techniques in the sacred area of food. *Le Monde* depicted an America 'whose commercial hegemony menaces agriculture and whose cultural hegemony insidiously ruins culinary customs, the sacred gleams of French identity.' Bové warned ominously that 'the Americans could cancel your business at the push of a computer button.'

Despite all this, McDonald's had nearly eight hundred outlets in France by the turn of the century. The number expanded at the rate of almost 80 per cent a year between 1995 and 1999 when the company announced that Europe was its most successful region globally and that France was one of the leading countries within the continent.

Its success has been, in large part, because of savvy marketing that takes French tastes and feelings into account as well as providing facilities many national competitors lacked. In 2002, an 'advertorial' placed on behalf of the company in the magazine *Femme Actuelle* warned against obesity in children. 'There is no reason to eat excessive amounts of junk food, nor go more than once a week to McDonald's,' it said. (The company in the United States said it disagreed with the advertisement.)

'It has been tough for us to become integrated in the French market,' said Eric Gravier, the chain's Vice-President of Corporate Affairs in France. 'We were attacked because we had this image of globalisation.' The counter-punch was to downplay the flashy red and yellow branding and the bright lights to try to create the image of what Gravier characterizes as 'a cosy place with nice, warm colours with free wireless, where you might like to stay for an hour.'

The chain gave out nutritional information to help clients balance their meals. It opened Ronald McDonald Houses for what was described as a relaxing coffee break at Nantes in southern Brittany and Limoges in Central France. It also stepped up its environmental programme by cutting carbon gas emissions. To cater for French taste, a new product was introduced, complementing the beef patties and toasted bun with Emmental cheese, Batavia lettuce, tomato and mustard sauce. 'Enough to delight the most delicate palates,' the company declared. It then added a new desert—Crunchy Pineapple— free with each Happy Meal, plus organic yoghurt and apples, all designed to increase infant consumption of fruit, it explained. In 2011, it set up a model farm in the Pas-de-Calais where it grew its own potatoes. Above all, at a time of persistently high unemployment, nobody except the most gastronomically chauvinistic economist or politician could gainsay the 25,000 jobs McDonald's created.

There were still plenty of critics and food purists ready to make retching noises at the very mention of *un Big*. A Socialist deputy, Thomas Thévenoud, accused the firm in 2012 of failing to abide by an agreement that, in return for having their sales tax cut under Sarkozy's VAT changes, restaurants and cafés would reduce prices and take on more staff. As a result, he charged, McDonald's added 190 million euros to its profits but invested only 136 million of this sum in higher pay and improved conditions. The firm riposted in a full-page newspaper advertisement that it had respected the tax pact, and insisted that Thévenoud's figures did not add up. The argument descended into number juggling, but it was clear that the food chain was being singled out. Most restaurants had got away with not reflecting the tax cut in their prices; nationalist, populist politics made it simpler to point the finger at the American giant rather than corner bistrots or gastronomic temples.

McDonald's is far from alone in the fast food stakes. In 2013, 54 per cent of restaurant turnover went to fast food outlets and sandwich shops as workers had less time to eat in the middle of the day and eschewed heavy fare which French-owned chains proliferate—Quick hamburgers, originally Belgian but now controlled by an investment from the government in Paris; Flunch, with two hundred outlets; the three-hundred-plus Paul bakery shops and Speed Rabbit Pizzas—to name but four. Lower down the food chain, greasy spoon burger joints proliferate in areas such the Halles district of Paris or round the railway stations of major cities.

In some places, however, cafés still prosper; walk down the Cours Mirabeau in Aix-en-Provence or the grands boulevards in Paris and there are crowded terraces. But too many smaller establishments in country towns have become dominated by the television set blaring from one corner. The microwaved food they serve lacks any local connection. In villages they exist only on the back of subsidies from the local authorities. 'We often say that cafés are a part of France's national heritage—from a social, cultural and even architectural perspective,' says Christine Pujol, the head of an industry group that represents cafés and restaurants. 'It's very saddening to think that these places could disappear and that they will stop playing the social role they have been playing for so long.'

The pungent smoke of another cliché has wafted through national life for most of this century. Tobacco entered the French consciousness after the ambassador to Portugal treated his injured cook with a patch made from a herb imported from the New World in 1559. News of its therapeutic qualities got back to France, and the ambassador was soon supplying the court with tobacco grains. The Queen used them against headaches, and such was their popularity that Louis

XIV restricted worshippers at mass to only one sniff of the stuff from the spiritual staff. By the beginning of the eighteenth century, there were 1,200 snuff and tobacco establishments in Paris; the smartest still exists in the Place du Palais Royal. In 1818 the special property of tobacco was given a name, inspired by the original ambassador to Portugal, Jean Nicot. Three centuries after his discovery, the manufacture of cigarettes began after French soldiers came across them while fighting in Spain. The very word comes from the French for a 'small cigar.'

Along with the cigarettes themselves, the outlets where they are sold are a feature of the urban landscape with their red *tabac* signs outside. There are 27,000 such establishments in the country at the last count, and the people who run them are intent on keeping the monopoly for themselves in the old tradition of monopolistic trades. They won a lawsuit in 2013 to prevent a company selling electronic cigarettes from its own shops; anything that bears the name of cigarette has to go through a *tabac*.

Tobacco causes 73,000 deaths a year, according to Health Minister Marisol Touraine in 2013. Among men, lung cancer is the leading cause of early mortality, well ahead of alcoholism. It is a particular killer among the working class, but a killer which has long been close to the Finance Ministry's heart. Tobacco taxes came in under Cardinal de Richelieu in the seventeenth century, and a state monopoly followed. As well as the tax takings, the state cigarette company, Seita, provided large revenues to the public purse in three decades of nationalization; today, privatized Seita ranks as one of the country's dozen biggest agro-food businesses. In a country which looks after its agriculture, tobacco is an important crop and is given appropriate government protection.

It was not until recently that French politicians had any reservations about being photographed dragging on a cigarette in a way that would have been unacceptable in, say, the United States. President Pompidou frequently had one dangling from the corner of his lips. Chirac was snapped with one sticking out from the middle of his mouth while deep in conversation with a young Nicolas Sarkozy. A classic photograph of the Tour de France from the 1960s shows a cyclist giving a teammate a light from his stub as they freewheel at the head of the pack. At a time when the rest of the developed world was cutting down, the number of cigarettes smoked in France rose from 85.7 billion to 97.1 billion during the 1980s. Twenty per cent of men smoked more than fifteen a day. Then, in 1991, the government got tough.

There had always been isolated pockets of anti-tobaccoism. If a client at the restaurant run by the godfather of modern cuisine, Fernand Point, was seen lighting up during a meal in the 1950s, coffee and the bill were immediately brought to the table, even if the crayfish or poularde en vessie had not yet been served. Some anti-smoking measures were introduced in public buildings in the mid-1970s. When these were extended to provide for no-smoking areas in restaurants and cafés, they were much honoured in the breach. One café in the Paris suburbs put up a notice proclaiming that its owner would rather go to prison than infringe his customers' right to smoke; another designated a single table in the middle of the premises as the no-smoking area. When my wife asked for the tobacco-free zone in a Left Bank restaurant, she was told simply, 'Outside.' (The owner insisted that the odour of perfume was far more detrimental to the enjoyment of food than tobacco fumes.)

A serious-minded Socialist Health Minister, Claude Évin, introduced legislation in 1991 to ban smoking in canteens, public areas in hotels, lifts and offices containing more than two people. Offending individuals or employers were threatened with fines or imprisonment—the state railway was found guilty of failing to put up big enough anti-smoking posters at a station in Lyon. Cigarette advertising was outlawed. A stamp showing André Malraux was doctored to airbrush out the cigarette between his lips.

The consumption of cigarettes fell steadily through the 1990s, and the Jospin government at the turn of the century announced plans to increase taxes on cigarettes and tobacco—not, of course, to raise revenue, but as a way of discouraging young people from smoking. In 2008, smoking was banned in public spaces, offices, schools, government buildings, railway and bus stations, museums and restaurants, with a 500 euro fine for transgressors.

People came to respect the rules over time even if it meant smokers huddling together in isolated clumps outside offices, hotels, restaurants, shops and museums like heretics ejected from the mainstream of French life. Their fortitude and refusal to give up their habit meant that the decline bottomed out in this century, though a sharp price rise in 2013 appeared to dissuade the money-conscious smokers. Some fourteen million people smoke in France today, and consumption by young people increased between 2008 and 2011 to reach nearly 33 per cent of male and 30 per cent of female seventeen-year-olds. A medical study in 2012 put the cost to health service of nicotine-induced sickness at eighteen billion euros and a total cost of double that if one includes smokers kept from work, forest fires started by discarded cigarettes and so on. That far outweighs the eleven billion brought in by tobacco taxes.

What has changed is the kind of cigarettes people puff. For decades, there was something exotic about French brands; even their names were peculiarly resonant. When cigarettes swept the nation as the nineteenth century turned into the twentieth, smokers could choose from 242 different products. There was a name for everybody to identify with—Odalisques and Jockeys, Boyards and Havanaises. The Hongrois brand changed its name to Gauloises in 1910 and became the market leader ten years later. Gitanes-Vizier put a woman on its packet in 1927, the year it dropped the Turkish second half of its name. The Belle Epoque brand, *elegantes de luxe*, turned butch after the First World War by altering its name to Amazones. For chauvinists there were Celtiques, Royale and, most simply, Les Franchises; those with more distant horizons could buy packs of Congo, Maryland or Égyptiennes.

Despite the range of choice, French cigarettes were epitomized for decades by Gitanes and Gauloises, in conventional white paper cylinders or more exotic maize paper. Gitanes had a characteristic flat box that opened like a drawer; Gauloises were tapped out of a soft packet with a card-shuffling motion. In the last century, smoking Gauloises was linked to the image of World War One infantrymen, the *poilus*, Resistance fighters, Picasso, Sartre, Camus and, during his time down and out in Paris, the British writer George Orwell.

No French film was complete without a cloud of smoke round Jean Gabin or Jean-Paul Belmondo; no existentialist nightclub or corner café was authentic without the tobacco haze; no Paris taxi ride was real without a throat-twitching, stomach-churning stink wafting back from the driver. *Les brunes*, as these pungent smokes were known, accounted for 86 per cent of sales. The songwriter Serge Gainsbourg, who lived in a perpetual cloud of smoke, appeared quite content when Catherine Deneuve told him in a duet that, while God puffed Havanas, 'you are only a smoker of Gitanes.'

It was Gauloises that led the charge towards change in 1984 when it introduced a light, American-type tobacco with a filter, known as Gauloises Blondes. Gitanes followed suit and its light brand sold as many as its brunes. When Marlboro went on sale in France in 1924, it was as a niche product aimed at women, complete with a red tip to go with their lipstick. Seven decades later, the brand took 17 per cent of the market, with Chirac among its users. Foreign brands accounted for almost half total sales; filter tips had come to rule. Perhaps that is why French films seem to show less smoking these days. Gérard Depardieu drawing on a Stuyvesant wouldn't be quite the same as the gangs of the great films noirs plotting their heists in a pall of smoke you can smell off the screen. And even the packet for Gitanes Blondes took on a new look from the other side of the globe. Its flip top box showing a little yellow figure dancing against the traditional black gypsy silhouette on a stonewashed jean background was the work of a Japanese designer.

If brown tobacco and cafés are essential elements in the traditional image of France, another is red wine, which became a national habit as rail transport enabled the mass production of the southwest to be taken to urban centres, and the supply of *pinard* rotgut to soldiers in the trenches of World War One introduced the drink to troops from parts of the country like Brittany, Normandy and the north where it had not been commonly consumed before. Cafés and bars made wine readily available everywhere, with the high point in consumption reached in the 1950s and 1960s.

Decline was slow to set in. Three decades ago, more than half of French adults still consumed wine on a near daily basis. Today only 17 per cent do so, and the proportion who says they never touch the stuff has risen to 38 per cent. Over a longer time frame, the decline is consistent—in 1965, the French drank 160 litres a year per adult head of population; by 2010 that had plummeted to 57 litres, and there were forecasts that it would fall further to 30 litres. In 2014, China overtook France as the nation that consumes most red wine. The drop in the number of people taking wine as a regular part of their meals was accompanied by a sharp jump in those replacing it with mineral water, up from 24 to 43 per cent between 1980 and 2010, and a tripling of soft drinks and fruit juices to 15 per cent. For all his attempts to personify French values, Jacques Chirac made no secret of his preference for beer (although, after being elected, he at least had the patriotic decency to switch from his preferred Mexican brew to Kronenbourg). Sarkozy is a teetotaller.

For older people, wine at table is part of the national way of life. For the middle-aged it is a pleasure; they tend to drink less but spend more on better-quality bottles. For the young, drinking wine is less and less frequent and faces growing competition from other liquids, alcoholic or not. Binge drinking involves spirits not wine. 'What has happened is a progressive erosion of wine's identity, and of its sacred and imaginary representations,' say the authors of a 2013 report for the International Journal of Entrepreneurship. In a health-conscious age, a report in 2009 that alcohol was responsible for 49,000 deaths a year hardly helped sales—though other medical experts said moderate consumption was good for you—while campaigners lobby for a tax on wine as a dangerous product.

Though some French restaurants still label the foreign section of their lists as '*vins d'ailleurs*,' the industry has faced growing international competition not just from traditional Europeans rivals in Italy and Spain but, above all, from the New World, primarily from Australia and the United States to begin with, and then from Chile and Argentina, followed by South Africa and New Zealand. As long ago as 1998, the wine critic of the *New York Times* declared the best reds of California and Oregon to be worthy rivals of the great Burgundies. Lower down the quality ladder, Australian wines outsell French products in Britain where purchases of French growths have fallen by 38 per cent in volume and 13 per cent in value. Top-end buyers, increasingly from Asia, kept the luxury wine market afloat, but, when it came to the everyday consumers, the French system of labelling wine by producers and regions, from top Bordeaux châteaux and tiny Burgundy properties to ordinary varieties from the southwest, put off consumers who simply wanted a reliable brand name or a generic mention of shiraz, merlot or cabernet sauvignon.

In 2011, export of wines and spirits earned France more than ten billion euros in a year for the first time, constituting the biggest source of income from abroad except for aerospace. Champagne is the leading alcoholic export by value, followed by cognac brandy with claret from Bordeaux in third slot.

Overall sales were up by 3 per cent to 4.1 billion euros to Europe, by 29 per cent to 2.5 billion to Asia and by 9 per cent to the Americas. Income rose by 10.5 per cent, according to the Federation of Wine and Spirits Exporters. But the increase was due mainly to higher prices, as rich buyers and speculators, especially in East Asia, piled in to top-quality wines as a new asset class. Sales volume increased by only 2.4 per cent and is 12 per cent down on the beginning of this century. Vineyards cover one-third of the land they occupied before they were devastated by the phylloxera disease in the mid-nineteenth century. The number of people employed in making wine has more than halved since 1970 to 30,000.

Some sociologically minded food writers worry that the trend among the middle-aged to drink less but to move upmarket will make consumption an elitist pursuit, removing the traditional link between the French and the product of their grapes. This is part of a broader shift away from traditional meals at which the family and friends gathered convivially around the table towards individualized eating, snacks and fast food. 'The traditional family meal is withering away,' food writer Perico Legasse told the BBC in 2013. 'Instead we have a purely technical form of nourishment, whose aim is to make sure we fuel up as effectively and as quickly as possible.'

There are other significant factors at work. The proportion of French people consuming alcohol on a daily basis dropped from 15 to 11 per cent between 2005 and 2013. The wine industry has been buffeted by recurrent scandals mainly involving the use of strong wines from elsewhere to fortify choice growths in thin years. The pursuit of higher yields, sometimes by late watering, which makes grapes swell, jeopardized quality in some areas. So did the addition of sugar to the fermenting grape juice to increase the alcohol level. Questions were raised about pesticides getting into wine. When the consumer magazine *Que Choisir* detailed some of these failings, it aroused a storm of protest—not from drinkers but from the wine industry which tried to get the article withdrawn. Faced with the pesticide revelations, the growers' association said it was best to treat this as a private matter since the public might not understand the complexities involved.

Muslim immigration has brought France a lot of abstainers. The closure of village cafés and bars reduced the haven for companionable consumption. Drugs provided competition among the young. Long business lunches have been cut short. Upwardly mobile executives and their bosses are likely to prefer mineral water to wine in order to keep a clear head; a deal is more likely to be sealed these days in a conference call than over a well-lubricated lunch at a three-star restaurant ending with a celebratory vintage cognac. Computer keyboards require accuracy not inebriation. The ebbing of tough manual labour and hard work in the field has brought the end of the traditional litre of rough red to fortify efforts. The shockingly high figures for drunk driving accidents, responsible for 40 per cent of deaths on the roads, led to government crackdowns. People seek solace in anti-depressants and tranquilizers rather than from draining *un ballon de rouge*.

The industry is stepping up its game in reaction. The largest wine-producing region in the southwest makes excellent wines as well as its usual multitude of *vins de table*. The French believe that their wines as a rule are the best in the world, and they are right. Foreigners, especially from Asia, pay tribute by buying up fine vineyards when they can, and a French company has taken the message to the other side of the world by planting three thousand hectares of quality grapes in China to nurture the nascent wine industry there.

All right, so things are changing, but one fact about the French is surely unshakable—they stink of garlic. Indeed, they may be so imbued with it that they don't notice its aroma: a gourmand academic from London, Keith Walker, once ate a whole chicken stuffed with forty cloves and rode the train back to Paris from Orléans without anybody wrinkling their noses. The truth is, however, that France does not even rank in the world's top half-dozen producers or consumers of the vegetable. Yes, there is an association devoted to its folklore and promotion in the middle of France, whose members parade at jolly ceremonies wearing hats shaped like the clove. But the leading

academic expert on garlic is in the United States, and the South
Koreans use far more of it than the French. The self-proclaimed
garlic capital of the world is Gilroy, California. The International
Garlic Information Centre is to be found in East Sussex. New York
has a Garlic Seed Foundation. At an 'officially regulated tasting' of a
dozen varieties held there back in the autumn of 1995, there was a
French entry, but Spain took the prize.

One by one, the landmarks crumble, change, or are not quite
what they seem to be. The franc has given way to the euro. The
post office, which formed an integral part of national life with its
yellow vans and 90,000 delivery staff trekking out to the most isolated homesteads, is contracting fast as email means that the number
of units it handles is forecast to fall from eighteen million as recently
as 2007 to ten million in 2018.

France may still be the centre of the iconic game of pétanque,
with *boulodromes* in village squares, but the world championship was
won in 1997 by Tunisia. An immigrant from North Africa, Ridha
Khadher, won the national bread competition in 2013. The madeleine on display at the house in the country town of Illiers-Combray
which has been turned into a museum to the memory of Marcel
Proust's most famous novel is made of plastic. Foie gras is imported
from Central Europe. Snails come from as far away as Taiwan. A
sommelier from Japan carried off the top prize at a Bordeaux wine
fair. That essential element in traditional French hygiene, the bidet,
is now installed in fewer than 10 per cent of new bathrooms. The
famously rotund Michelin Man, Bibendum, was slimmed down for
his centenary in 1998.

When it comes to headgear, France now has only one firm
still making the berets of the Basque region, long another familiar
national icon. With sales of 160,000 in 2013, it has to contend
against cheaper competition from China, India and the Czech Republic. As for another icon in the Doisneau café photograph, you have
to go a long way to hear an accordionist in the flesh these days, and
he is likely to come from Eastern Europe. Despite the invention of
'rock-musette' combining accordions with heavy bass-lines and a few
retro-restaurants complete with strolling players, France's principal
accordion factory, in François Hollande's provincial fiefdom of Tulle,
produces fewer than a thousand instruments a year, compared with

six thousand before the Second World War. A French soccer star with the Arsenal club in London, Laurent Koscielny, joined a group who put up 600,000 euros in 2014 to save the century-old Maugein factory from closure as it faced cost competition from instruments made in Eastern Europe and China and its labour force dwindled down to 20 from 300 in 1939. One of the last heroes of 'the piano of the poor,' Jo Privat, ended his days as a born-again star in Japan after work dried up in France.

Meanwhile, churches cut services, and France now counts more psychiatrists than priests. The French clochard tramp immortalized by the actor Michel Simon in the anarchic 1932 film *Boudu sauvé des eaux* is quite likely to be a homeless immigrant. At the Élysée Palace, Sarkozy stopped serving that most fundamental dish, cheese, while an American runs the *Michelin* gastronomic guide.

In the south, Marseilles is no longer famed for its colourful old port, with terrace restaurants serving pungent bouillabaisse fish stew, pastis and rosé wine, or for the iconic characters immortalized in the films of Marcel Pagnol, but instead is known as the scene of racial tension, political in-fighting, crime and drug trafficking. It was proclaimed Europe's capital of culture in 2013 and the authorities undertook a big renovation programme centred on the old docks; but 20 per cent of the city's inhabitants live below the poverty line, and there were fifteen gang killings in the first nine months of 2013. In the worst hit districts, up to half the young people are out of work. The city had four police chiefs in two years. The mayor of the worst crime-afflicted area called unavailingly for the army to be sent in to restore order in 2013.

That prime symbol of France, the franc, dating back to the revolution in its decimal form, gave way to the euro common currency in 2002, and supervisions of monetary policy moved to the European Central Bank in Frankfurt. The system of featuring departmental numbers on vehicle plates has gone so they can no longer be used to teach children that fifteen denotes the Cantal and eighty-three the Var or enable motorists to dismiss bad drivers as coming from unruly or backward parts of the country. Adoption of English terms continues apace, sometimes with the use of words in ways that would puzzle people from across the Channel—as when television viewers are said to *scotché* in front of their sets or a beauty treatment is described as a *relookage*. Social media has brought neologisms to horrify linguistic purists—*followé*, C for *c'est* and a ministerial tweet that *nous live-twitterons*, though literary critic Bernard Pivot, whose tricky spelling tests attract 25,000 contestants, published a book of tweets that respect classic French—and a poll showed that, while 62 per cent of those questioned found French complicated, 64 per cent did not want its rules simplified.

Even the sacrosanct ban on Sunday trading has come under attack from retailers which want their customers to be able to buy their goods all week. Exceptions to the law have produced a patchwork of regulation. In September 2013, fourteen department stores selling home improvement products in the Paris suburbs decided that they had had enough and ignored the law to open their doors on Sunday, their staff wearing T-shirts proclaiming, in yet another Anglicism, '*Yes weekend*.' Trade unions protested that staff were being forced to put in more work, even though they seemed quite happy to earn the extra cash. The legal tangle thickened when competitors took action to make the shops close. The outcome remained messy, but another feature of French tradition appeared to have succumbed to the rhythm of modern life.

Modern society and fear of AIDS have undermined the image of the headstrong French lover—in an opinion poll at the turn of the century, men expressed their preference for a partner who would bring a condom in case he forgot his rather than for an impromptu unprotected coupling. As for the prostitutes with gold-plated hearts and a repertoire of repartee who have been part of the popular imagination, from Manon Lescaut through Toulouse-Lautrec's easy ladies to Irma la Douce, they are being banished to the outer reaches of cities or replaced by students who advertise their attractions electronically or by sex workers shipped in from Eastern Europe and Brazilian transvestites in the Bois de Boulogne where they work in vans and tents among the trees. Official figures put the number of prostitutes in France at 20,000, 80 to 90 per cent of them from Africa, Asia and Eastern Europe, but the Union of Sex Workers believes there are far more. Fifty-two pimping rings were broken up by police in 2012, two-thirds of them run by foreigners. In 2013, controversial legislation was passed to fine their clients with the minister involved saying she wanted to 'abolish' prostitution. But critics, including sixty celebrities who signed a petition against the law, warned that this might drive the women further into the shadows.

Though the beginning and end of August is still a time for huge traffic jams, the month-long summer vacation that month is becoming less sacrosanct, with people ready to go away for shorter periods. The new boss of the Club Méditerranée has added one-day breaks in France to the organization's traditional offering of long stretches in exotic places. Executives can get twitchy sitting on a beach when their companies may be heading for restructuring. In any case, smart phones and Wi-Fi mean they never really get away. In 2013, François Hollande took only one week's summer vacation and limited his ministers to two—to be spent in the Hexagon. His partner, Valérie Trierwieler, said he spent most of the time catching up on answering letters; it was not all hardship, however, since the President spent his break in a former royal hunting lodge at Versailles equipped with a tennis court and swimming pool.

Money-conscious holidaymakers have been avoiding the Riviera and frequenting cheaper areas of the country. Those who still go south rent simple *gîtes* away from the coast. The mood swung against the conspicuous consumption of the Côte d'Azur in favour of the more bracing and less polluted west coast, from the gilded palaces, suntans and overpriced lounging chairs on the beaches at Nice and Cannes to woolly jumpers, sailing and family walks through the windswept Celtic heather.

The change of scene is not just a matter of the amount of cash spent—Brittany can be as expensive as the Mediterranean—but more a matter of mood. 'I see in this fashion the generation of those in their forties who have done it all,' says the publisher of magazines for the smart set of the south and the west coasts. 'They want a return to the family, which is even more sacred to them because they are often starting out for the second time after a divorce. They remember the quiet family holidays in Brittany during the 1950s. For years, they made fun of them, but now they realise they weren't so bad after all.'

There has even been an offensive from across the northern border on one worldwide French icon, claiming that French fries are actually a Belgian invention. The home team, however, appears to have a good defence on this score, pointing out that Thomas Jefferson spoke of 'Potatoes, Fried in the French Manner' thirty years before Belgium even came into existence as a country.

In a final cliché challenge, the river along whose banks lovers traditionally stroll on the screen, in romantic imagination and in real life, may even be misnamed. The Seine rises in Burgundy, hundreds of kilometres from the capital. On its way to Paris, it joins another Burgundian river, the Yonne, at the town of Montereau. Their waters are, from then on, known as the Seine. But the custom is that when two rivers meet, the one which has the largest volume of water gives its name to the combined flow. And the flow rate of the Yonne at the junction is 105 cubic metres per second while that of the Seine is only 75 cubic metres. The Mayor of Montereau has no doubts: 'The rivers are of different colours. It is easy to see that the Yonne beats the Seine.'

In this moving set of stereotypes, however, one thing seems certain: the name of France's best-known river will not be altered. We will not stroll along the Quais de l'Yonne. But plenty else is changing in the countryside where the Yonne, the Seine and all France's other great rivers flow, for the most basic of all madeleines is undergoing a metamorphosis which is more crucial to the nation than all the Virginia cigarettes, euro banknotes or McDonald's in the world.

5

Country Living

If there is one thing which the French have long held particularly dear, it is the rural land that covers some 90 per cent of the surface of their country. Flying high over France on a cloudless day one is struck by the extent of the uninhabited spaces, the fields and forests and empty land dotted with occasional villages. This is not the great space of the American West, the Russian steppes, Amazonia or the jungles of Africa, let alone the deserts of Asia. But, for crowded Europe, it is quite impressive and has shaped the nature of the country.

Famous regions live on the foundations of a rich history—Burgundy, the Bordelais and Brittany, the Loire Valley and Normandy, not to mention the great swathe of the Midi across the south from the Alps to the Pyrenees where the people speak with a distinctive accent and Paris was, for centuries, far away. Then there is an abundance of lesser-known *terroirs* with their own identities. Consider the Béarn on the mountain frontier with Spain, home of the Fourth Musketeer, d'Artagnan, of little-known but excellent wines and the ever-hopeful centrist politician François Bayrou; the Massif Central, with its dozens of upland and valley communities and the Gévaudan, where a monstrous wild beast was once said to roam; the 370-square-mile marshland of the Marais Poitevin in the west of France, where the easiest means of transport is by flat boats on canals covered with duckweed, and eels abound; or the *pays de cocagne* around the old city of Albi, where the countryside is rich and seductive and the great medieval fortress cathedral depicts in an enormous mural painting the horrors that sinners face at the Last Judgment.

In the nineteenth century, writers living in Paris recorded their journeys to such strange and primitive places like Brittany, the centre of France or the wild Languedoc with amazement bordering often on fear. This was like a foreign country to them. Balzac had a journalist in his 1844 novel, *Les Paysans*, reflect that 'you don't have to go to America to see savages.' Stendhal and Victor Hugo recorded their astonishment at the solitude and backwardness they encountered when they travelled far from Paris, the former writing of 'that fatal triangle which stretches between Bordeaux, Bayonne and Valence. There they believe in witches, cannot read and do not speak French.' Edmond Michelet, the leading historian of the day, regarded Brittany as 'a country quite different from ours . . . scarcely French.' For him, the Vendée in the west of the country, which had risen up against the Revolution and suffered the equivalent of ethnic cleansing as a result, was the home of 'strange people,' and the Midi in the south 'a country of ruins' marked by murderous violence.

Centralization, modernization, the railways and the postal system changed all this, followed by the telephone. Then came motorways, high-speed trains, air travel, the pioneering Minitel online system and the Internet. The French *paysan*—translated as peasant but denoting attachment to the rural locality, the *pays*—has been deserting agriculture ever since the growth of big urban centres and manufacturing in the nineteenth century. From 1860 to 1960, dropped by a third. Most recently, the share of GDP represented by agro-food in France has fallen from 7 per cent in 1980 to 3.5 per cent today, at sixty-seven billion euros. The number of people employed in farming has dropped steadily. In the 1980s nearly five people worked for each one hundred hectares; today the number is around three.

Despite the decline in their relative contribution to the economy, farmers remain a politically powerful group as shown by the difficulty governments of left and right had over the decades in agreeing to the needed reductions in the European Union agricultural subsidies; though cut from earlier levels, they will still account for 38 per cent of the community's budget for 2014–2020, running at some fifty billion euros a year and with France taking 20 per cent. The ability of French farmers to mount demonstration is unmatched, be it with cortèges of slow-moving tractors snarling up traffic or protestors dumping manure outside town halls. When the Hollande administration buckled in the face of protests from farmers in Brittany in 2013, the main newspaper in the hard-pressed industrial region of the Nord was moved to wonder why unemployed workers there did not benefit from similar favours from Paris. The reason was simple; politicians reckon that agriculture and its travails pluck at national heartstrings in a way that the closure of rustbelt factories does not.

The Agriculture Ministry is a highly sensitive government post. When Mitterrand appointed a woman, Edith Cresson, to the job, she was greeted with sexist derision by male farmers. Chirac made his name as the relentless promoter of France's interests when he held the position from 1972 to 1974; so much so that his German counterpart, Josef Ertl, told him during one heated negotiation that he was mad and should see a psychiatrist. For Chirac, agriculture was central to France's well-being and to the very essence of the nation. In his memoirs, the former President waxes lyrical about 'the view of well-kept land, of a fine animal in a farmyard, the fruit of the most perfect symbiosis between nature and man.' Forty years after his time as Agriculture Minister, he was mobbed by a crowd at the annual farm show in Paris where, though visibly in poor health, he admired prize steers, sampled vegetable juices and embraced exhibitors.

His successor had a more testing time on his visit to the show in 2008, which provided one of his occasional outbursts of bad temper in public. When Sarkozy reached out to shake a farmer's hand, the man drew back and said, 'Oh no, don't touch me, you'll dirty me.' To which the President snapped back, 'Get lost then, you bloody idiot, just get lost!' He spent only two hours in the cavernous exhibition hall on the outskirts of Paris. In contrast, five years later François Hollande extended his visit to ten hours, saying that he could have stayed for a week if he had not had other things to do.

Though he announced measures to help small farmers and stock breeders, Hollande's Socialist administration was not popular among those working on the land who generally trend to the right. He was booed in October 2013 when he visited a farm show in the Auvergne, where small-scale upland agriculture provides a precarious livelihood, though he responded with a Chiracian statement—'The difficulties of your work are more and more burdensome, costs are higher, markets are more volatile; this must stop because, when husbandry falls back, the whole sector collapses.' Still, the Agriculture Ministry budget was cut by 7 per cent for 2014 and European Union subsidies, though considerable at sixty-three billion euros for France in the 2014–20 period, are on the decline too. Modern reality is catching up with the old countryside.

Rural depopulation has a long history. The appeal of urban jobs, a falling birth-rate and the huge loss of life from country communes in the First World War reduced the population of some country regions significantly from early in twentieth century, and the outflow has speeded up. The quintessentially rural Creuse department, for instance, has lost half its population since 1901. Forty per cent of those have gone in the last fifty years, and the number of residents is still falling year by year. It is now the least populated department in the country. In 1929, France had almost four million farms; by the 1950s, that number had halved, and the total has now dropped below three-quarters of a million. More than a million agricultural jobs have vanished since 1970.

World Bank figures show the number of people living in the French countryside declining from almost 15 million at the start of this century to 10.45 million in 2008 to 9.02 million in 2012. Farmers and farm workers make up less than 7 per cent of the active population, only one-third of the level of the early 1970s. Over the same period, more than 50,000 country shops and small rural businesses shut down. The French have a word for the emptying of the countryside, la désert-ification—not that the wide-open spaces of the middle of the country bear any resemblance to the Sahara. The official definition of this is a population level of thirty people or fewer per square kilometre. That makes half the land area of France into a green desert.

Itinerant farm labourers who were a feature of life at harvest time have become rarer. So have the bands of rural artisans who developed particular skills and roamed the country offering their services— masons from the Limousin, tree cutters from the Forez region around Roanne, chimney sweeps from Savoy, wet nurses from Burgundy. Despite buoyant prices in some northern areas, the average price of agricultural land in France has fallen continually since 1980.

If the depopulation appears to have bottomed out, this is not because more people are working on the land. Rather, people have been moving to the countryside to take advantage of grants offered by rural towns to foster small-scale manufacturing or to benefit from cheaper housing costs when improved transport enabled them to commute to an urban job. Some villages report an increase in the number of single mothers on welfare who have left cities where they cannot afford to live. Low-cost airlines from abroad have brought tourists to previously isolated areas where some buy cheap properties.

Still, rural residents are older—a quarter are over sixty compared with 21 per cent nationally. In the Auvergne, nearly half the farmers are over fifty-five, and in the Indre department of central France the number of people over sixty-five is double the national average. Those who live in the countryside have a slightly higher poverty level than urban dwellers have. A study for the European Commission in 2008 found that one farm in five either lost money or earned less than the minimum wage. Fertility is lower in the countryside than in towns. Fewer women are in work in rural areas than in urban centres.

But farming, forests and country land still cover twenty-eight million of France's fifty-five million hectares of land. (Thirty-seven per cent of this is cultivated, 34 per cent is forest, 19 per cent grassland and the rest marshes and scrub.) In contrast, inhabited areas represent only 9 per cent of the national territory. Fields, forests and uncultivated regions, including rugged highlands and mountain ranges, stretch as far as the eye can see, interspersed with rivers, villages, the occasional town and the even more occasional city. There are still extensive areas where hardly anybody lives and where you can walk all day without seeing another human being, not only in the great sparsely populated 'desert' of the middle of France and the Massif Central, but also not so far from cities, such as the region behind the Mediterranean coast round Montpellier where the scrub-covered rocky defiles stretch to the horizon as buzzards swoop and wild pigs come out at dusk.

Two-thirds of farms are still run by a single family, and the image of the individual farmers cultivating his small holding or tending a flock of sheep remains a potent one. Yet the nature of agriculture has altered. On a national scale, agriculture has become highly mechanized as big units dominate. The bulk of subsidies from the

European Union go to large farm businesses. In 2010, 174 agricultural companies got grants of more than a million euros each, for a total of one billion of the common currency; most were big groups and some of the biggest recipients were sugar and banana producers in France's overseas territories, far from the poor upland farmers often depicted as the reason why taxpayers across the continent have to pay for French agriculture through their taxes.

But even industrialized agriculture felt the strain on global competition in the new century. The intensive factory farms for poultry and pigs, which had become a major element in the agricultural economy of Brittany alongside the traditional crops of cauliflowers, onions and artichokes, encountered heavy pressure from a strong euro-currency, cheaper exports from competing producers, particularly Brazil, and the removal or reduction of some EU subsidies in 2013. Intensive factory farms and slaughterhouses closed, as did a big plant processing smoked salmon for its Norwegian owner. Protests by workers escalated into violence with attacks on official buildings and highways and clashes with police, facing the Hollande administration with yet another challenge. Meanwhile, chicken breeders in southern France who let their birds live freely in fields and live much longer before being killed reported rising revenues at higher prices as customers went for quality rather than buying simply on price.

The pull of the rural world goes much deeper than mere economics. It is a pole around which national sentiment has revolved. But now it, too, is changing more than the French would wish to admit. Ninety per cent of rural households do not contain anybody working in agriculture. Farms are being deserted, villages are emptying. Pig factories flourish while the streams are empty of crayfish. Foie gras is as likely to originate from Eastern Europe as from a farm in the Périgord—though bands of Romanians and Bulgarians are accused of raiding the French countryside for wild mushrooms which they take to sell in Spain. The seeds for Dijon mustard come from Canada. Traditional evenings around the village fountain exist only in books and on the screen. The French may cherish the idea of the rural bourg with its weekly market and its links with the surrounding countryside, but small-scale rural commerce is being killed off by supermarkets and hypermarkets down the road. All of which is so disorienting because what is vanishing has been crucial to the nation's idea of its own basic character.

Country life has deep roots in the French imagination. The tale of a harassed town dweller escaping to peace and contentment in a rural idyll is a constant theme of popular books and films. France has a set of diverse and thriving regional cultures. Many of its greatest writers have drawn on their direct link with a country region—Balzac with the Loire Valley, Flaubert with Normandy, Mauriac with the Bordelais, Mistral, Giono and Pagnol with Provence. As Jacques Chirac has pointed out, the regional appeal in fiction lies in 'the rediscovery of a source of popular memory which the French are afraid of losing forever.' Upmarket pop singers record hymns to their native corner of the land, and regional cultural centres keep traditions alive, if sometimes rather artificially. A remarkable encyclo-paedist, Marcel Lachiver, has collected 45,000 rural terms in a book running to 1,816 pages. In the heart of France, the annual literary fair of Corrèze draws 100,000 people to the departmental capital of Brive la Gaillarde.

For some who have risen to the summit of power and glory, the link with the countryside is a political necessity and a source of repose or memories. Charles de Gaulle retreated to the agricultural Haute-Marne in eastern France after resigning the premiership in 1946, spending a dozen years amid the forests and bleak countryside awaiting the occasion to return to power. Georges Pompidou, though more at home in Parisian intellectual salons, made much of his origins deep in the Auvergne as did his successor, Giscard d'Estaing, who, after he left the Élysée, became that same region's patron in the capital, lobbying for a spectacular highway through its mountains and for a park to celebrate its extinct volcanos. Through his long political career in Paris, François Mitterrand never shook off the sentimental attachment to his native region of the Charente, which his fellow southwesterner François Mauriac described as 'an unchanging landscape where I can still believe I am an adolescent.'

Both Jacques Chirac and François Hollande, who originate, respectively, from Paris and Normandy, made the quintessentially rural department of the Corrèze their adopted homes. The former bought a château there and was to be seen patting the rumps of cows at farm shows (his wife was elected as a local councillor), while the latter got news of his presidential victory in 2012 in the provincial capital of Tulle and celebrated briefly there before hopping on the plane to Paris. Among Fifth Republic Presidents, only Nicolas Sarkozy showed scant interest in the countryside and preferred the smart life in the capital, something that came to be held against him—and not simply by the stroppy farmer in the Paris exhibition hall in 2008.

French townspeople have more country homes than any other Europeans. A million and a half people count themselves as hunters; they often go shooting in packs drawn up around the killing ground. Accidents are not uncommon, and it is best to give them a wide berth. Scratch an urban French man or woman of the older generations and they will speak nostalgically of the village or small town where they grew up or where their parents hailed from. Until austerity began to bite, their taxes paid for services hard to find in similar regions of many other advanced economies—for the electricity network which took no account of distance or inaccessibility, airports that handled a hundred or so travellers a day, the country train network with its neat little stations and the highly efficient postal system which supported rural offices with tiny turnovers. In person or through television, many more join the great annual celebration of the countryside that is the Tour de France, as riders sweep across the plains, climb the mountains, swoop down on the coasts and rocket through a hundred villages in *la Grande Boucle* which brings the nation together.

In a nation which has always appreciated feminine virtues of an old-fashioned kind, the land was long depicted as female, as in historian Emmanuel Le Roy Ladurie's description of his country first and foremost as a beautiful woman. This is '*la douce France*' immortalized in Charles Trenet's songs. Today's writers shrink from genderized descriptions, but Balzac had no inhibitions about describing his native Touraine as 'a woman going to meet her lover,' or nature as resembling 'a woman rising from her bed,' and the Loire estuary as an older woman 'swollen with all the disappointments and tribulations of life.'

Though more modern stereotypes have now imposed themselves, the traditional national imagination is peopled with stock characters who popped out from the hedgerows or came hobbling up the lane: the ruby-cheeked priest preaching to a tiny congregation of old women and the earnest left-wing teacher trying to instil republican values in a class of bored children; the dried-up widow in black peering at passers-by from behind her curtains and the amply-breasted, loosely dressed village flirt who leads the farm boys off into the long grass; banquets without end on market days and the old-fashioned farmer eating his soup as his wife stands humbly behind him; the poacher lying in the bushes watching for rabbits on the edge of the local hunting estate and the gamekeeper who waits until the owner has driven back to town before inviting his friends around for a feast behind the château. It was not all a matter of imagination. In one village we visited regularly, an old woman sat for many years watching the passers-by from behind her curtains, and the priest drank cheap wine from tumblers as his housekeeper served his meagre supper.

Bernadette Chirac recalls that, when her husband began campaigning in the Corrèze in the 1960s, local dignitaries held dinners at which their wives remained standing behind them after serving the dishes. Then, in her role as a local councillor in the department, she soldiered through the eight-hour annual festivities of the local firemen. Some years ago, I spent a long Sunday at an open-air banquet in the grounds of a hunting estate amid the forests and lakes of the Sologne region, where the increasingly drunk gamekeeper denounced his absent employers, opened their finest wines and terrines of foie gras—and ended the day by lurching off into the woods with his wife.

France was long a patchwork of local pays; as François de la Rochefoucauld put it in the seventeenth century, 'The accent of the country where one is born remains in the spirit and the heart as it does in the language.' The untranslatable expression 'la France profonde' refers not just to areas like the great central region stretching from the Limousin through the volcanic peaks of the Massif Central to the Cévennes, for it is not just a matter of geography. Rural France has been a state of mind. Towns were held to breed politics and division; farmers got on with life in a down-to-earth manner, and stood together in adversity. 'With bare arms and pure hands, we will go to clean up Paris,' proclaimed a pre-war quasi-Fascist rural movement, the Green Shirts. Sixty years later, the President of the Republic spoke feelingly of 'a land peopled by humble, brave, honest and hard-working folk.' Though the Ile-de-France region around Paris was, as its name suggests, the kernel of the nation from the

Middle Ages, there is a lingering and unshakable feeling that the real France lies in the countryside, not in the capital.

Farmers, proclaimed Jacques Chirac, 'are the gardeners of our country and the guardians of our memory.' Provincial, rural knowledge is a natural gift as opposed to an acquired skill—folklore rather than culture, a natural wisdom absorbed from the ebb and flow of the seasons instead of being learned from books. The country was a place where people had proper old French names rather than being called after American film stars, where the tombs in a graveyard by the Aveyron River deep in the Rouergue region commemorate Albertine and Armand, Baptiste and Blaise, Calixte and Célestin, Firmin, Germaine and Marise, and where the living old folk get a twice-yearly free banquet of soup, asparagus quiche, stuffed veal, duck, cheese, dessert and cakes at the Michelin-rosetted restaurant opposite the church. Like Bouvard and Pécuchet, Gustave Flaubert's classic couple of city-dwellers who think they have found paradise in a crumbling farmhouse in Normandy where the vegetables wither, the cabbage is inedible and the neighbours mocking, the French stood ready to be swamped by a rural idyll.

Much of this was always rubbish; 'the land is tough,' as a local landowner remarked to Bouvard and Pécuchet while their haystacks burned down. The hold of the rural world has on the national mind is diminishing. The exodus to the cities means that, while their parents or grandparents may have a misty-eyed memory of the rural idyll, the younger generation feels little connection with the fields. Villages are attractive as sites of second homes, not as places in which to stay in the family abode. The immigrant communities have no reason to be sentimental about the pays of France. Holidays are increasingly spent abroad. The incomers to villages are as likely to be British, Belgian, Dutch or German as French seeking rural repose—in the Aveyron department, which is linked to the UK by a budget airline, 17 per cent of residences are second homes; local people celebrate that they can sell off tumble-down houses and old barns to the foreigners for renovation.

Add in other disruptive elements—many more people die on country roads than on motorways; villages are usually dead after nightfall, with the old cafés and the communal evenings they fostered a matter of memory. Getting in the harvest is no longer the social occasion it once was. Farmers are notoriously aggressive demonstrators. There has never been any shortage of village money-grubbers. Rural folk today are as likely as anybody to name their children after pop stars and film idols. The highest rates of suicide are in largely agricultural areas of the northwest. The countryside's good sense often equates to reactionary conservatism.

However, the countryside still counts in the area where it really matters—the stomach. Food in France is linked to the land in a way that is not the case in many other nations. This, after all, is a country where an academic writes a 152-page treatise on one sort of Auvergne cheese and where, for many years, food pirates found it worth their while to buy cheap brown lentils from the Cantal department, die them green and pass them off as the prized pulses from the neighbouring Haute-Loire. Paris has excellent chefs, but it is the regions, the pays, which make French cuisine what it is. A 440-page compendium of national menus by the Maîtres Cuisiniers de France contains only half as many pages on the Ile-de-France region around the capital as on Brittany, Guyenne or Languedoc.

Pollution may have driven the famous sandre fish from the Loire River, and the boeuf bourguignon served up for dinner may have been produced on an industrial estate, but food remains rooted in the countryside, and most of the top restaurants are still located in the provinces. Each product has its specific local link. The best butter comes from the meadows of the Charente, the sweetest melon from Cavaillon in the south, and your favourite wines from any one of a hundred individual vineyards, each with its own taste. Those green lentils from Le Puy have an Appellation d'Origine Contrôlée to honour and protect their excellence, as do poultry from the wetlands of the Bresse east of Lyon, nuts from Grenoble, potatoes from the Ile de Ré in the Atlantic, and the olive oil from Les Baux-de-Provence and from Nyons in the foothills of the Alps. These are national treasures, as much a part of France's glory as Notre Dame or the nuclear strike force. The AOC accolade has even been extended to a foodstuff not consumed by humans, the 100,000 tonnes of hay harvested each year on the plain of Crau at the mouth of the Rhone, which is exported as far away as Hong Kong for the delectation of thoroughbred racehorses.

To illustrate how the countryside and village life imbue French gastronomy with its real strength, let us take a short tour around some of France's deeply rural areas. Start at the village of Saint-Bonnet-le-Froid, a lost place in the Haute-Loire department known mainly for its annual mushroom fair before it became the home of a great cook. Son of the local café owner, Regis Marcon wanted to be an artist but turned to the kitchen instead. After travelling to London and learning his trade under the Roux brothers there, he returned to his native village and transformed the family café into a restaurant and simple hotel—at the same time running the village petrol pump. He used the extraordinary natural local ingredients, and made a few mistakes along the way—his cèpe mushrooms in vinegar were inedible back in 1986. But by the mid-1990s, Marcon was a deserved gastronomic star. His food remained rooted in the countryside around him. He constructed an annexe to his hotel in the glitzy style French chefs seem to enjoy, but his menu built on local fungus was a marvel worthy of its three rosettes in the Michelin guide.

Head southwest across the rugged heights of the Massif Central across the Auvergne to Laguiole in the wild Aubrac region, a trim town famed for its knives and its cattle. When I first visited it in the 1980s with my wife and two children, a café-restaurant on the high street offered exceptional fare from a local man, Michel Bras, who had been taught to cook by his mother. We ate in the large back room, drank wine recommended by Madame Bras, and slept in two huge beds in a cavernous room under the eaves. Bras moved to a proper restaurant in the town and then built a space-age establishment on the hill above, with bedrooms opening out directly onto the Aubrac plateau with views reaching forever. He has three Michelin rosettes and was named seventh-best eating place in the world by *Restaurant* magazine in 2008.

An intense marathon competitor (he finished 5,000th out of 40,000 in one New York event) with a somewhat scholarly mien, he runs regularly across the plateau, with its woods and lakes, collecting rare herbs from the pastureland as the changing seasons give the area very different characteristics; bitterly cold and snowy in winter, balmy in summer, but always with the forces of nature present in the wide-open countryside. Though sophisticated and precise with a mastery of complex taste combinations, his cooking has roots deep in his *terroir*, notably the *gargouillou* dish which combines up to three dozen vegetables and herbs. His enthusiasm for such dishes is irresistible—'he who loses himself in his passions loses less than he who loses his passions,' he wrote in the front of a book of his recipes for my wife and myself.

To the south, in the rocky terrain and vineyards behind the Mediterranean coasts of the Aude department, the hamlet of Fontjoncouse is just another tiny place abandoned by time and the rural depopulation. It has no café, no shops, and just 130 inhabitants. The streets are deserted except for an occasional dog. Houses are boarded up and sport '*A vendre*' sale boards. The only tourist attraction is a path leading up to an old church on a ridge with good views over the rugged countryside and the Corbières wine country.

No reason for the traveller to stop, it seems, while driving between the region's celebrated mediaeval abbeys or on the way to the coast between Narbonne and the Spanish border. Except that Fontjoncouse does possess one highly unusual attribute: a restaurant whose chef has, like Marcon and Bras, won his third Michelin star. It took the convivial, bearded Gilles Goujon eighteen years to reach such heights. Bitten early on by a love of cooking, he saw photographs of the pope of modern French gastronomy, Paul Bocuse, wearing medals he had won for his work and thought, 'I want to do that!' So he worked his way up the restaurant chain at celebrated establishments before taking over the Auberge du Vieux Puits in Fontjoncouse after three of its previous owners had gone bust trying to operate in such a backwater.

In the early years, there were sometimes only two or three customers a day, or none at all. A breakthrough came when a television producer ate at the restaurant and returned to make a programme about it. Business picked up. In the space of ten years, Goujon accumulated his three rosettes from the red gastronomic guide. Like all these restaurants deep in the countryside, the menu draws heavily on local produce—fish from the Mediterranean forty kilometres away, mushrooms, meat from nearby butchers and the characteristic goat and sheep cheese of the Roussillon region.

Goujon speaks enthusiastically of the quality of raw materials on offer at the markets, some grown by exiles from northern Europe who have settled in the area in search of sun and cheap house prices and turned to small-scale bio-agriculture. Razor clams are set in a pungent garlic sauce accompanied by *petit gris* snails, almonds and a frothy, garlicky *bouillon*; the pork and lamb are accompanied by a plethora of small vegetables and little pastry concoctions, each with its own distinct taste and, in the case of the pork, a ball of andouille tripe. Other influences also intrude. The pigeon comes with dates and pastilla, and a signature starter consists of an egg white with the yolk replaced by a pungent mushroom purée sitting on truffles, with the yolk turned into a sabayon sauce that is poured over the dish. The wines draw on the best of the rapidly improving growths of the area. Corbières used to be cheap plonk sold in litre bottles with tear-off caps. Now it lives up to the potential of soil and a climate naturally suited to vines.

As will be clear by now, France has a habit of throwing up great restaurants in out-of-the-way places run by chefs who know how to make the most of their neighbourhoods, be it in a distant part of the rural world or in the drab railway junction town of Roanne where the great Troisgros clan of cooks has held sway since the 1930s. For another rural experience head to Belcastel, named by the tourist board as one of France's most beautiful villages, where the Fagegaltier sisters have transformed the simple café in the deeply rural department of the Aveyron once run by their rock-like father, who was born on the plateau overlooking the valley of the river which gives the department its name.

He started out building roads and other public works and rose to become a foreman. 'I had a place in life,' he remembers. 'I could have gone away. But then I met my wife by chance. We were mature—I was thirty, she was twenty-eight. We decided to stay here.' They ran the café by the old bridge across the Aveyron, specializing in frying the little fish plucked fresh from the river outside. One day, a retired miner came to stay and began fishing in the river. Before long, he returned and fished some more. Eventually, he became a fixture, spending the last fifteen years of his life in the village, where he was remembered years later as 'the king of whitebait.' One day, father Fagegaltier recalled, a party of a dozen people turned up unexpectedly—'and within fifteen minutes, we'd caught enough fish to feed them all.'

Like him, his daughters could have moved on—they have dipped a toe in the celebrity chef circuit with an expedition to Tokyo, where the jet lag was a problem. But the excellence of the dishes served up by Nicole Fagegaltier, the sister who does the cooking, would be unthinkable away from their roots. The food is so good that one guide named them the best-value restaurant in the whole country. Nobody who has eaten there would argue, and Nicole received a supreme local accolade when she won a cookery competition and was rewarded with her weight in prunes.

Again, it is the rural-based dishes which make their mark—cèpe mushroom tart, salt cod, veal and lamb with variations of herbs and berries in the sauce, stuffed cabbage, cream of bacon to accompany the sweetbreads, all washed down by Marcillac wine from over the hills with their deep red soil. For the big menu, you need a solid appetite—on one occasion, this might mean artichokes and asparagus with truffles and powdered ham, red mullet with sweet onions flavoured with anchovies, duck liver with young turnips and a sauce made from a local liqueur, sweetbreads, local cheeses and four desserts; on another, crispy potato cake with shrimps and cèpe mushrooms, sea bass and leeks with cèpe oil, grilled duck's liver with green beans and a sauce using a Marcillac liqueur, pigeon breast in breadcrumbs with garlic and rosemary oil, local cheeses and four desserts. At one recent Sunday lunch, every table except ours was taken by local family parties, and several of them were eating the big menu.

In times of trouble, the country is a source of valuable supplies: one of the staple Second World War tales is of food being smuggled into Paris, preferably involving a squealing pig which has to be kept quiet while the police patrol passes by. At such moments in history, the contrast between town and city becomes all the sharper. While food was hard to come by in the occupied capital, a marriage banquet in an isolated village in the centre of the country consisted of a macédoine of vegetables, ham and butter, homemade foie gras, rolls of ham with cream, guinea fowl in sauce, chicken with truffles, vegetables, turkey with watercress, cheese platter, apple pie, almond cakes and fruit, with red and white wine, champagne and liqueurs.

For some, at moments of great danger, the countryside provides an even more important succour as a haven to escape into the vastness that is rural France. The isolated town of Le Chambon-sur-Lignon, with its reserved Protestant inhabitants, won fame for sheltering thousands of Jews from 1940 onwards. When the German army swept by on its regular patrols, the refugees were hidden in the rough countryside of the windswept plateau that surrounds the town. After the war, Chambon was offered a Garden of Thanksgiving in Israel but, in its modest manner, refused the honour.

Two hundred kilometres to the east, it was the snow on the foothills of the Alps that dazzled a five-year-old Jewish girl who didn't know what she was escaping from. 'We arrived in the village in wintertime,' she recalled half a century later. 'Snow covered the countryside. I was five and tired from the long journey. My father carried me on his shoulders up the path that led to our new home, the farm of the Vieux Colombier which we had rented in the Free Zone to escape from the persecution in Paris. Years later, the family would repeat my first words when we got there: "Oh, look at the white snow, it's like pre-war snow." I had heard everybody saying, when they saw anything good, that it was like before the war—so I guess I thought that was the best thing I could say about the snow.'

Her father had been taken prisoner by the Germans in 1940, and had escaped from his camp. His wife and two children avoided deportation from Paris to Auschwitz by a mixture of hiding and good luck; some of their relations died there. In 1942, they decided to flee the city. The little girl was entrusted to her nine-year-old brother.

The two children were taken to a group of passeurs, people living by the demarcation line between the occupied zone of France and the Vichy-run 'Free Zone' where the Germans had not yet arrived. Some passeurs took Jewish children to safety in the south; others sold them to the Nazis. This brother and sister were lucky. Their mother travelled separately to join them in the Free Zone, hiding in a crate of coal on a goods train from Paris. Before it left the capital, police with dogs searched the train for people like her fleeing death, but they did not find her. When she emerged from the crate and met relatives in Grenoble, they could not help remarking on her face.

Despite her attempts to scrub it off, the dust from the coal remained. At such a tragic time, they asked, how did Fanny have the vanity to put on mascara?

In the Alps, life was different. The father came from rural stock in Poland: he told rousing stories about repelling bandits and riding through the family forests with a rifle in his hand. In Saint-André-de-Rosans, the war was far away. 'Our farm was one kilometre from the village,' the daughter recalls.

'We lived in the back of the building. A family from Marseille and then a group of resistance fighters were in front. We had a garden and a courtyard where the poultry ran. One evening my brother and I gave the chickens the wine left over in the glasses from supper. They tottered about, completely pissed. On one side of the building was a mysterious room; later I was told it was occupied by a member of the collaborationist militia.

'My brother, five years older than me, went to the village school and learned to talk the local patois with his mates. Once, I remember, the whole village was gripped by fear: word spread that a German was marching across the square. But it was only a teenager who thought it was a good joke to dress up in a Wehrmacht uniform—where he got it from we never knew.'

The family pretended to be Turks and called themselves Vartil rather than Wartski. Not that the demons stalking France at the time would have been fazed by a name. Appearance counted for more, and there they were fortunate in their father.

'One day, the schoolteacher came up to our farm. He'd slung a satchel over his shoulder so that it would look as though he was out hunting or picking berries. "They're here," he warned. My mother, my brother and I ran up the hill to hide in another farm. My father stayed behind, working in the garden. The Germans, who were retreating from Italy, stopped and said they had been told that Jews were being sheltered in the area. At a time like that, all they could think of was rounding up some more of us. With his green eyes and blonde hair, my father looked like a Kirk Douglas Jew. He shook his head and said no, he didn't know of any Jews in the area. So they drove on, and nobody in the village betrayed us.'

But even far away in the countryside danger remained ever present. The Wartski-Vartil parents kept an empty tube of toothpaste in their barn with rolled-up banknotes tucked inside. They told their young son, 'If anything happens to us, take the money and look after your sister—and God help you.' Northeast of Saint-André, an anonymous tip-off in March 1944 led the Germans to a farmhouse near the mountain village of La Martellière, in which eighteen Jews were staying with a resistance group led by a rabbi. All were sent to a transit camp on their way to their deaths. One escaped. The others were deported to Auschwitz, where all but one died. Fifty-three years later, a plaque with the names of the dead was unveiled in the village—and still nobody knew who had tipped off the Germans.

In the 1950s, the girl who had sheltered in Saint-André went back to live in her wartime haven six hundred metres up in the southern foothills of the Alps for a year to fight off tuberculosis.

'In the summers then, Saint-André-de-Rosans was always busy,' she recalls. 'The women gathered around the fountain to gossip and exchange secrets as they did their laundry in the public wash house. Farmhands sipped pastis while they waited their turn to play pétanque in front of the three cafés round the main square. On summer evenings, the young people danced to the music on the portable gramophone—*le pickup*—set up outside Madame Roland's café down the main street; the priest warned us we were courting damnation. In the winter, after supper, we wandered from house to house, chatting and listening to the old folk recounting their memories in the local Provençal dialect. Our favourite stopping-off point was the post office, where Madame Estienne had a wireless for us to listen to the hit shows from Paris. The schoolteacher taught all his pupils in a single class. Those who graduated to secondary school moved to the town down on the plain to study.

'At weekends, we sometimes went to visit relations in nearby villages for lunches that stretched on till the evening. Each commune and village had its own fête, held in August when the harvest was in. The day labourers who moved around from village to village would join in before going on to their next place of work. We danced late into the night under lanterns in the trees. The music was by little country bands in which the accordion player was always the star.

'Once a month, the travelling cinema came by. A white sheet was hung on the wall of the mayor's office and the whole village trouped in, everybody bringing their own chair. The sound and picture sometimes got out of sync. The noise of the projector drowned out the actors' voices. There were gaps while the projectionist changed the reels. None of that mattered. It was always an evening to remember.

'The food sprang from the earth, and I can still taste the flavours to this day. The salad of big shallots with walnut oil from Leon Jean's farm. The gratin of wild herbs which Granny Augustine collected on the slopes above the village in the skirt of her apron held out in front of her as far as her arms could reach. The thrushes and rabbits which the Estienne boys brought back from their poaching expeditions.'

Now fast-forward to the 1970s. Like the rest of France, Saint-André has been modernized. The houses have running water. The jolly Madame Estienne is delighted that she no longer has to press the nuts and olives from her garden: she can buy her oil ready-made in a plastic bottle. Washing machines have destroyed the convivial gossiping round the communal wash house, while easing the lives of the women of the village. There is only one café in the square now: it serves meals for tourists as well as pastis for the locals. Most of the elderly people have died or moved to old folks' homes. Madame Roland is as alert as ever in her café. Every year, she goes on a package tour for pensioners, once all the way to Ibiza.

The young people have left to work in the town on the plain or farther afield. Several are in Marseille; others in Lyon or Paris. Some come back in the summer with their families to spend their holidays with their parents. The village fête is still held in August. One year, we meet two of the Estienne sons there. At night, one of them leads half a dozen of us out on the ridge beyond the farthest-flung farm, from where there is a superb view of the Milky Way. The other son is the life and soul of the party, organizing beds for visitors and roasting a whole lamb on a spit in the garden of a mill he is rebuilding nearby. Following in the footsteps of his father, Venance, he has become a postman. Venance delivered the letters on foot across the hillside, winter and summer in snow and sunshine. The son drives the mail in a van in the Paris suburbs.

In the early 1980s, the ruin of a chapel opposite Madame Roland's café was declared a historic monument and added to the official route of the Romanesque churches of southern France. By then, the village had so few inhabitants that many of the fields were left untended.

But the remaining villagers nurtured the dream that the tourists visiting the ruins might stay, seduced by the beauty of the place. They could walk in the fields, climb the neighbouring rocky outcrop of Mont Risou and write postcards to their friends in Paris congratulating themselves on having found an undiscovered corner of paradise. A potential new source of revenue seemed to be there for the taking: Madame Roland installed showers in the rooms below her café. But tourists these days want swimming pools and tennis courts, good food and service—not stuffy rooms in the basement of a village café run by an eighty-year-old.

So the visitors stopped, looked and drove on. Before they left, some wandered through the narrow, winding streets between the crumbling stone houses with their collapsed beams and heaps of fallen masonry on the floor. We were told that we could have a fine old ruin if we simply paid the legal fees. But there was nobody around to rebuild the houses, install bathrooms and kitchens and make sure the walls weren't going to fall in. And who wants to live in a place where the only distraction is a village fête once a year and where the remaining inhabitants are dying all around you?

'It's so sad,' lamented the woman who had first gone to Saint-André as a little girl in the war and took me back there after we married. 'Saint-André is one of the most beautiful villages on Earth. When we were feeling energetic, we used to climb Mont Risou and light bonfires on the top for the festival of St John. You could see the glow from far away.'

On the paths around the village, the scent of lavender still hung heavy in the air—ancient, straight-backed Melanie gathered it to sell to the perfume makers of Grasse down south. Up the hill, in the farm to which my wife and her mother and brother had fled when the Germans came through, Monsieur Richard dispenses his homemade pastis and advises against a third glass—can it be the long-banned absinthe that drove Verlaine crazy? On the slopes below, the goats munched the wild herbs that give their special flavour to the cheese made by the bachelor brother and spinster sister, Marcel and Marcelline. At the bottom of the ravines, the river water was as fresh and pure as ever.

Some years later, we revisited Saint-André one day in August. That used to be the busiest time of year. But now all was silence.

The square was deserted. The big old building which had housed the Estiennes' post office, the school where my wife learned to read and write, and the Mayor's office were boarded up. The walls were peeling, ugly amid so much natural beauty. The clock on the top floor from which the children had learned to tell the time had stopped long ago. The café had closed when the owner's wife left him and he went to a teaching job in the town down the hill. The school bus no longer came up the hill; there were no children to collect anymore.

As we stood in the shade of the trees in the square where le pickup once played and the men tossed boules outside the café, Marcel and Marcelline walked by, bent with age. Madame Roland still kept her café, but there was nobody to sit at her two tables. The earth mother, Madame Estienne, was in an old people's home in the Rhone Valley, said to be in poor health.

'The others?' my wife said. 'Dead—like my old village.'

Across France, there has also been a dramatic change in how rural people earn their living. A study published in 1998 by two official research institutes showed that only 20 per cent of their jobs are in agriculture. Back on the land, the nature of farming has changed as the balance of production shifted from animals to cereals—hence Hollande's promise in 2013 of a policy shift in favour of the latter.

The old image of France as a nation of small farmers eking out a living has been overtaken by intensive agriculture—just as rural backwardness has been punctured by consumer goods and one of the best rural road systems in Europe. In the north and the east, huge grain and beet fields are farmed as efficiently as anything in Britain or Germany. Agriculture is a compartmentalized business.

Once regions aimed to be self-sufficient, now they are part of a global market, and concentrate on what they do best. The west contains half of France's dairy farms. Brittany houses 60 per cent of the country's pig plants and grows most of the nation's cauliflowers. Paris is at the centre of a great grain belt. In the east, fortunes are made from sugar beet—France is one of the world's biggest producers with output of four million tons a year—not to mention champagne. One-third of southwestern farms concentrate on maize and oilseeds (and the poor uplands of the centre have made a speciality of living on

European subsidies). Winemaking has become a science as well as an art. The old regional languages of the land have been submerged in a common glossary of terms for agricultural machinery and scientific aids to greater productivity: a whole list of traditional names for farm implements no longer appear in the dictionaries of today. And, in a tiny village in the middle of the country, the gravediggers head to the churchyard in a Toyota four-wheel-drive Land Cruiser with a large Coca-Cola logo on the bonnet.

Off the three thousand miles of the French coast, farming at sea has run into rough weather. The fishing industry's production totals around 470,000 tons a year; France is the fourth country in the European Union in terms of catches. At the start of the second decade of this century, its fisheries provided 65,000 jobs, from 23,000 trawlermen to those engaged in production, preparation and processing of fish products, packaging and sales. Shellfish farming employs about 9,500 people, a number that doubles at peak harvesting time before Christmas and New Year, when three-quarters of the yearly output is sold.

But the trawler fleet has been halved since 1988, to around 5,000 boats in the Hexagon (another 2,500 are in overseas territories), under the impact of competition and rising operating costs. Most fishing units are small-scale, often family-owned, and have found it hard to stay in business in the face of larger fleets from abroad. Oyster producers have been hit by disease and lack of breeding space. It is not that demand is lacking—French fishermen provide only half the fresh fish France eats each year. The trouble is that domestic trawlers cannot compete on price with East European fleets. On top of which, the mark-ups along the wholesale and retail chain makes fish a relatively expensive dish without benefiting the fishermen too much.

A French magazine which priced a kilo of cod at the various stages between Brittany and a Paris fishmonger found that the fisherman got only 10 per cent of the final selling price. Trawlermen from north to south express their anger in the habitual way by blocking the entry to ports for foreign boats, pouring oil on imported mackerel and attacking lorries carrying rival catches. The government reacts by giving in. It doles out money and imposes health tests that ensure foreign fish goes rotten by the time it gets to market. None of this does any good. On sea as on land, the small harvesters of food face a future of decline.

Still, it is the old agricultural ways which loom large in the national mind, and the countryside still calls to the city dweller. Some follow the rural siren. An Air France executive gave up his career at the age of thirty-five, spent seven years moving from farm to farm to learn the ways of the land, and then set up in Normandy to raise goats and ducks, and make cheese, foie gras, sausages and paté. A fertilizer salesman from a big multinational bought a vineyard in the Rhône Valley and now sells 110,000 bottles a year. Such experiences warm the French heart. When there is good news from the depths of France, everyone cheers. So visit the small village of Calvinet, perched six hundred metres up in the very south of the Cantal department, between the blustery heights of the Massif Central and the sunny uplands to the south.

On the face of it, Calvinet should have had no more reason to survive than Saint-André-de-Rosans. It lies in a region known as 'chestnut country,' because the nuts used to be its main resource—they were the staple ingredient in the local flour. Today it remains much as described by a local carpenter, Joseph Lavigne, in a twenty-six-page memoir he wrote in a notebook discovered after his death in 1994 at the age of eighty-two:

'My parental home was by the pastures. The silence was broken only by the crow of the cockerel or the snorting of the cows. My commune stood on the rise of a hill and it got the first light of day. To the south were the big fields where the wheat rippled like a rough sea. To the east and west, there were chestnut trees under whose shade the cows passed by. To the north were the poor people, scratching a living from the soil. There, too, were sheep grazing amid swarms of bees sucking the honey from flower to flower. In the village, the houses were mostly white, low-standing and with slate roofs. They looked charming from a distance; a group of homes with a bell tower in the middle, a schoolhouse and the big lime tree on the square, known as the tree of liberty.'

Calvinet has gone through many changes since then. It was rent by a long and searing battle between reactionary Catholics and a pioneer of lay education: a Romeo and Juliet saga was played out between two young people from either side. In the 1930s, peddlers hawked their wares in patois at the market: '*Boutous de braguas, de comijias, de couls, de giletas, de broguetas.*' (Sixty years later, there were still vestiges of the local dialect. The nearby fifteenth-century village of Marcolès put up signs for visitors in both French and patois. Walking through a farmyard on the hills one spring day, my wife and I were surrounded by a pack of dogs. We implored them in French to leave us alone. They took no notice. Then the farmer came out of a barn and shouted at them in patois. The dogs turned tail and ran off into the woods.)

During the last war, a local inventor from these parts built a bicycle made of wood, but his plans to commercialiaze it came to nothing. The population declined, and the village became increasingly dependent on subsidies from Brussels. At the end of the twentieth century, several of the younger men decided to take its destiny into their hands. While they had no intention of demanding any less in the way of European funding, they believed that Calvinet should avoid becoming another rural basket case.

'It would have been easy to have sat back and done nothing and watched the young people leaving for the town, and their parents being reduced to watching the television because that was all there was to do,' said one of the younger generation. He, himself, works in the departmental capital of Aurillac, forty kilometres away— but the road has been widened and improved and the journey takes half the time it used to. Calvinet is part of the wider world: there was even talk of building a branch of the Auvergne motorway in the hills down towards the Lot River.

Louis-Bernard Puech, generally known as 'Loulou,' the son of the local charcutier, went off to learn to be a cook in Toulouse. He returned with a host of new ideas and ambitions, but was sage enough to draw on his mother's old recipes, especially her delicious duck in blood sauce (secret ingredient—dark chocolate) and his father's ham and sausages. He married the daughter of the local chemist, and they undertook the renovation of the hotel above the restaurant. Foreigners started coming for their holidays, and one day a fleet of bright red

Ferraris called by for lunch on a sponsored rally through the region. Soon his reputation spread as he won commendation from Michelin and the Gault-Millau guidebooks. He expanded his menu, but always retained his offerings of stuffed cabbage, potato cake with the local Cantal cheese, stuffed goose neck and dishes using chestnut flour.

The main square of the village has new curly lampposts and a wooden notice board with a large guide to the surrounding area. The main restaurant has won a Michelin rosette. There are two tennis courts in the woods by the camping site, a convenience store and a swimming pool of sorts in the reservoir. The baker still serves up good old-fashioned bread. Naturally, Calvinet is not free from complaints or concerns. The farmers worry not simply about the age-old uncertainties of the weather, but also about how well they are being defended in Brussels and what trickery the Americans are up to in world trade talks. A local producer of foie gras once told me that, if this delicacy were banned in the United States, it would not be because the Americans really thought force-feeding was cruel—who could imagine any such thing?—but as a non-tariff barrier aimed at France, which should ban McDonald's in retaliation.

If its rural roots stay strong in France despite all its urbanized modernization, the general mood of worry and self-absorption may be simply a translation of countryside concerns into the national bloodstream. Here in Calvinet, familiar national obsessions punctuate the conversation about falling beef prices and the grand wedding being held next Sunday on the street jokingly known as the Avenue de la Grande Armée because a couple of retired military officers live there. The restaurateur expostulates against the tax system which, he insists, makes it impossible for him to expand, and may encourage him to go back to his father's trade as a charcutier since VAT on cold meats is a quarter of the rate on cooked meals. Still, I say, he must be happy with his Michelin rosette. Yes, but his reply is complex. He reckons that he got the award for his traditional local dishes, like his mother's recipe for duck in thick sauce. Those are what the customers want when they drive up with the red guide in their cars. But what he'd like to be famous for is more adventurous recipes like his friend from the cookery school in Toulouse who heads one of the smartest restaurants in Paris. Yet, I insist, things are going quite well in Calvinet. In return, I get a grudging '*Oui, mais . . .'*—the undefined 'but,' which could mean that the weather may turn bad tomorrow, the crops may fail, the cattle may fall ill, the volcanoes may erupt, the world may come to an end.

On a ridge outside the village, a sharp-faced, weather-beaten farmer sits at a huge wooden table and keeps watch on the herd in his cowshed via closed-circuit television. He went to Paris once, but found the city so dirty and airless that he had to get home fast. His farmhouse has walls a metre thick. In the courtyard outside, there is a hundred-year-old drinking trough hewn from a solid block of volcanic rock. In the big, stone-floored main room, a stuffed fox stands on a ledge, copper cooking utensils hang on the wall, a grandfather clock reaches to the ceiling, three hunting rifles are racked over the huge fireplace and a big old television set sits on a dresser. By the door, a pair of horns has been mounted on the wall. The farmer's strongly built, smiling wife explains that they belonged to a cow which was a treasure at the farm, never caused any trouble, but which went berserk when taken to the slaughterhouse. The farmer and his wife shake their heads at the memory, as though the cow was an inexplicably wayward child.

We had telephoned that morning for a couple of rabbits for dinner. The farmer's wife couldn't supply them immediately because her husband was out harvesting, and she had nobody to hold the animals while she killed them. By afternoon, she had found help, and she brought the cut-up meat in on a plate from the pantry. Over our protests, she added a large chunk of stuffed cabbage—layers of vegetable and minced meat with herbs—and half a dozen eggs. Then her husband led us out into the kitchen garden, looking out on to a horseshoe-shaped wood and an endless vista of countryside all the way down to Rodez. He gave us a handful of cucumbers and a couple of big courgettes and told us that what he really needed was a good downpour. On the way back to the house, we passed the rabbit hutches, two of them empty and with their doors open.

Down the road, the local nobleman showed me round the wood-panelled rooms of his château one evening and then sat and sipped whisky as he talked about his daughter's wedding and told of the young man from the village who went to Paris after the Revolution and made a fortune out of floating brothels on the Seine before becoming a banker to the First Empire and developing the big park

on the Buttes Chaumont in the north of the capital. A century or
more ago, the nobleman's family held aloft the clerical standard; they
boycotted the village council when their lay opponents replaced the
cross in the main square with a statue representing the Republic.

After peace had broken out, the Baron became Mayor of the village, and used his social and political contacts to ensure that Calvinet
got a bite at any financial cake on offer from the region. He gave up
the post as he grew old, but his presence was still felt in the village,
standing in the queue for the checkout desk at the local self-service
store with a roll of kitchen paper towels under his arm or sitting
at a window table in the restaurant for Sunday lunch, a bottle of
Bordeaux on the table in front of him. 'Oh, Calvinet will always be
here,' he said at the end of our evening conversation. 'We just have
to make sure it is in as good shape as possible.' He accompanied
me to the door of his château. As I motored up the long driveway
to the road, I saw the Baron in my rearview mirror, urinating against
the wall of his ancestral home. It was an image from a book of
clichés about rural France, but a cliché that seems alive and well.

There may be a hundred reawakened Calvinets across France; still,
the waning of country customs cannot be denied. The annual killing
of the pig and the use of every morsel down to the ears and tail for
food has been supplanted by preserved cold cuts in cellophane from
the local supermarket. A professor remembers how, in her childhood
in the Vendée region, a rope was traditionally hung between two
houses after church weddings with a jar of sweets attached to it; the
mother of the bride then took a long pole and broke the jar with
heavy symbolism for her virginal daughter as the children ran forward to scoop up the bonbons; today, in the same area, old church
confessionals are being sold as big birdcages.

In an ultimate heresy from a native of a nation where rural
tradition died long ago, one might even wonder if the French
countryside really deserves special treatment and over-representation
in the National Assembly, when so many industrial areas have felt
such pain over the past three decades. It may be hard for young
people to find jobs in the Auvergne, but it is even tougher for late
teenagers in housing estates and projects around big cities, particularly if they are from immigrant families. Whatever the rigours of
their daily lives in some areas, the farmers, in general, remain a

protected class. Their social security payments have gone up more slowly than those of the rest of the population, and taxes on their production have fallen.

The special treatment is particularly rewarding for the big players, and relatively unfair for the small farmers of Calvinet or Saint-André-de-Rosans. European subsidies go mainly to large grain farms which have grown even bigger by taking over neighbouring small holdings, especially in northern France. A wheat or barley enterprise in the Oise department outside Paris can rake in subsidies nearly three times the national average, while a dairy farmer may get only half the general level. Agriculture has produced its share of boutique farmers, grafting together wild and cultivated strawberries for a new fruit called the *mara des bois*, pressing exotic vegetable oils or raising silkworm cocoons in the Cévennes.

There will always be a market for increasingly expensive fine fish, and France has become a big producer of kiwi fruit. Some four thousand 'bio' farmers cultivate their vegetables and raise their cattle without using any chemicals. Down south, in the Hérault department, the 430-inhabitant village of Avenge-les-Bains sells two million sprays made from its local waters in Japan each year. In Le Puy in the Auvergne, the number of lentil growers exploiting the unique combination of volcanic soil, altitude and climate has doubled in a decade, and, down by the Lot River at Port d'Agres, a market gardener does a nice line in Asian vegetables for adventurous restaurants. Breeders of free-range poultry in the Gers do good business not only from supplying starred restaurants but also with sales to locals who are willing to pay more for chickens that stay firm after roasting rather than disintegrating as battery-raised fowl do.

Still, the clear trend is for the big boys to grow bigger and the small folk to go to the old people's homes or to be bought off active farming by a hand out from Brussels. In one quintessentially rural village, a plump farmer's wife with tree-trunk arms who used to drive the fly-infested cattle to and from the fields lived placidly for years with her hard-drinking husband until he died, at which point, by coincidence, the European Union decided that it had too many cows, and would pay her and others like her to get rid of her beasts. This she duly did, using the money to refashion her house, buy a smart little car, have her hair done, and generally appear happier than she had ever been, free at last from the tyranny of the land.

As the average size of French agricultural holdings has doubled in the past thirty years, banks have taken to arranging seminars for their urban customers on the attractions of putting spare cash into the soil. Financial institutions buy up agricultural land as a good investment for themselves or their clients. Some farmers who rent their land have never seen the owner. The nature of farming changes year by year to meet the requirements of the bottom line and maximize the return on capital for owners who would not know wheat from barley. The agricultural trade union is controlled by the big operators in the north who make sure that they reap a double benefit from high prices and rising productivity.

Intensive farming and mechanized agriculture have spread steadily, requiring investment small farmers cannot afford. Ducks now provide far more livers for foie gras than geese because they are easier to force-feed with machines. Proclaiming that scientific advances did not always bear 'the mark of the devil,' the government lifted a ban on growing genetically modified maize, boosting France's position as the European Union's biggest producer of the plant. Increasingly, farmhouses are sold separately from the land to city dwellers or foreigners, and then the fields are amalgamated into larger holdings. It is difficult to wax sentimental over a grain baron from the Beauce, southwest of Paris, who runs his fields with a computer, buys genetic crop strains from a Swiss drugs firm and flies off to an exotic holiday twice a year. And equally difficult to expect a twenty-year-old son of a hill farmer to remain on the land. 'I can't wait to move to the town,' a youth in Calvinet said at the football pitch one afternoon. 'Except that I won't find a job there, will I?'

Some resist. Deep in a forest off a main north–south route, but light years from the world of motorways and high-speed trains, a farmer in his thirties lives in a muddy, fly-infested hovel at the end of a track. He ekes out a living with his wife and three children, tilling a small plot of earth and tending a herd of goats which produce fine cheese. It looks a miserable existence, but, he says, 'I am from the earth. I live with my beasts. This is my life.'

As the rural world meets the twenty-first century, that life becomes rarer. The identification between the countryside, agriculture, tradition and the nation is breaking down into an economic bargain. One demographer has worked out that active farmers make up only one-fifth of the fifteen million people who live outside towns and cities. Farmers, one of their leaders remarked, have believed for too long that the countryside belonged to them alone.

Now, if they want to survive and prosper, they have to jump on the latest bandwagon, drawing the maximum in European subsidies and convincing the banks that they are a step ahead of the market. The new race of rural entrepreneurs approaches the countryside with the logic of modern business. One year they grow grain; the next, maize. One year they raise battery poultry; the next, they go for calves. Behind them, they leave cinder blocks and corrugated iron, drained fields and an abandoned workforce, and are blamed for pollution in regions such as Brittany where the run-off from their fertilizers and the waste from their intensive breeding plants for chickens and pigs pollutes rivers and leaches out the soil. 'Farmers are their own worst enemy,' remarked a landowner whose locality had been devastated in this manner. Tradition fades, breeding resentment among many of those left behind as another divorce develops between a vital element of national life and the way the French actually live now. And as the icon of the small farmer at the heart of France dissolves, we should turn to look at the condition of the other pea in the national pod.

6

MODERN TIMES

The country which invented the modern popular revolution naturally gave its working class and its urban life a historic place in society. Now, as with the traditional rural world, the rush of present-day realities cuts deeply into the fabric of town and city life, while the industrial transformations of the past decades have eaten into the cherished old ways.

The Great Revolution may have been directed by the bourgeoisie and petty nobles and resulted, in part, from politics at the court of Louis XVI, but the storming of the Bastille has gone down in history as a defining moment of popular passion, and historians would point to the price of bread for the French people as a major cause of the anger fuelling the upheaval. Through five manifestations, from the late eighteenth century to the current system, France's Republics have claimed legitimacy as representing the nation and its people. But there have been significant interruptions of the story since the end of the eighteenth century, which raises the question of what kind of regime really suits the French people. Is it the citizens' regime bequeathed by the revolution, or a more authoritarian administration with a strong executive in the tradition of the two best-known French leaders of the past modern two centuries, Napoleon Bonaparte and Charles de Gaulle?

After all, the initial republic of 1792 was taken over after only three years by the corrupt Directorate, and was then dominated by Napoleon Bonaparte's Consulate after his coup of 1799 before he proclaimed his empire in 1804. The Bourbon monarchy was restored in 1815 after a short interruption when its installation the previous year was disrupted by Bonaparte's Hundred Days return from exile before his defeat at Waterloo. A popular rising in the streets of Paris in 1830 placed another king, Louis-Philippe, on the throne at the head of a regime that catered to the bourgeoisie, the aristocracy and Bonapartists who knew how to cut their cloth to changing times. A more serious revolution in 1848 drove out the monarch but soon ushered in Napoleon III, first as President of the Second Republic but then, after a coup, as Emperor from 1852 to his defeat in the Franco-Prussian war of 1870. Thereafter, republican government prevailed, with the exception of the Vichy collaborationist interlude between 1940 and 1944, but, as we have seen, the current regime was put in place by a man determined to replace legislative power with executive authority, using the Bonapartist device of the referendum to appeal directly to the people over the heads of their elected representatives.

Throughout, one leitmotif of French political life has been the power of the street, or, in the case of farmers, of direct action in the shape of attacks on châteaux or, more recently, the blocking of roads and the dumping of surplus produce, perpetuating the heritage of the first revolution. The first half of the nineteenth century was punctuated by violent insurrections, particularly in Paris and among the silk workers of Lyons. The defeat of 1870 brought the Commune in the capital and its bloody suppression. Demonstrations by industrial workers, wine growers and then right-wing 'leagues' inveighing against the system punctuated the Third Republic. In the 1940s and 1950s, the Communist Party was a major force, able to mobilize huge protests. In 1968, France was rocked by student demonstrations accompanying a general strike led by Communist trade unionists. Street protests, be it against government economic policy, in favour of Catholic schools or to condemn same-sex marriage, have rolled in through the subsequent decades.

Some French commentators extol this tradition as a sign of national health—'we get it off our chests whereas you British bottle it up,' as a journalist put it to me in 2010 during mass marches against Sarkozy's proposals to reform the pension system to moderate the privileges enjoyed by public sector workers. The drama of division is celebrated as part of the essence of France, in contrast to consensus in Germany or British hypocrisy.

Meetings of the hard-left Parti de gauche, founded in 2009 and including the Communists, resonated with calls for a Sixth Republic true to the nation's revolutionary heritage—its candidate, the pugnacious Jean-Luc Mélenchon, showed that this was not simply nostalgia when he got 11 per cent of the vote in the first round of the 2012 presidential election. On the other side of the spectrum, the National Front keeps up a constant barrage against insecurity, immigrants, the European Union, capitalism and any other targets likely to win votes among the disaffected—and saw its candidate, Marine Le Pen, taking 18 per cent of the first round in 2012 and enjoying 24 per cent positive ratings in the polls the following year, five points ahead of Hollande's dutiful socialists.

In hard times, in particular, extremism and tub-thumping can pay handsome political dividends, nowhere more so than in a nation in which compromise is viewed with disdain and principles are paraded as sacrosanct, however malleable they may turn out to be when put to the test, as in Mitterrand's U-turn after the economic disasters of 1981–2, Sarkozy's more recent failure to deliver on his 2007 campaign promises of reform and Hollande's awkward juggling of pledges of economic expansion and rejection of austerity on the one hand, and the grim reality of state debts, low growth and the German-led European consensus on the other.

The demonstrations may succeed, creating peace, as in Mitterrand's decision to shelve legislation to limit state subsidies for religious schools. Others may fail, as in the protests by millions against the regularization of same-sex marriage in 2013. Yet others may bring just the kind of compromise that might have been achieved by negotiations in the first place, as in the watering down of Sarkozy's planned changes. For purists of the revolutionary tradition, the outcome is less important than the fact that citizens make their voices heard; the act of going out onto the street with banners and slogans is an affirmation in itself. For others, the revolutionary tradition may risk opening the path to anarchy or, at least, the replacement of duly elected governments by a mob which may feel good in basking in the inheritance of 1789 and the claim to be representing the great mass of the people—or France's Catholic tradition—but which contributes little to the greater good once the banners have been rolled up and everybody has gone home.

Still, the importance of *le peuple* to France's view of itself cannot be denied. In the last century, the nation's greatest sacrifice of lives was by millions of working-class men from both urban and rural France in the trenches of the First World War. In the 1920s and 1930s, mass culture celebrated the workers; the icons of the age were not just popular but populist—the actor Jean Gabin in his vest; the actress Arletty making the most of her Parisian street accent; the songs of husky-voiced women bewailing the loss of their men; Marcel Pagnol's moving plays and films about life in Provence and around the port of Marseille; Jean Renoir's cinematic celebrations of everyday existence; and the imperishable photographs of cafés with accordion players, of a family picnicking on a riverbank, of a narrow suburban street under a railway viaduct. The Parti Communiste Français (PCF), which split with the Socialists in 1920, won nearly 9 per cent of the vote at parliamentary elections in 1924 and increased this to 11 per cent in 1928 and 15 per cent in 1936 as unemployment and recession bit and France looked beyond the parliamentary manoeuvres of the centre-right to install a left-wing government under the intellectual Socialist Léon Blum.

The granting of social rights by the Popular Front administration of 1936–8 was a landmark in French history as it brought together Socialists, progressive Radicals and the Communists, who did not, however, take any ministerial posts. Measures which left a heritage evident to this day included a reduction of the working week to forty hours, guaranteed welfare benefits, paid holidays, and nationalization of the central bank which had previously been in the hands of a hundred 'regents.' The government of Blum and his successor, the Radical Camille Chautemps, showed that France did not always have to be ruled from the right or the comfortable bourgeois centre. But it was all too much too fast on an unstable economic foundation and was fervently opposed by the vested interests of the right, coloured by anti-Semitism aimed at the Jewish Prime Minister Blum.

The right to holidays with pay for workers—the *congés payés*— has a particular historic resonance which may seem strange beyond French borders. The arrival of crowds of city workers and their families on hitherto middle-class beaches symbolized a social revolution.

If the trains from Paris to the coast of Normandy were not quite a new storming of the Bastille, they came close in their way. As the eminent British historian of France, Douglas Johnson, has put it, 'It was dramatic. There were those who saw the sea for the first time. There were children who at last met their grandparents. Men whose families had come to Paris to find work visited the countryside their forefathers had cultivated. And there are other memories. Bourgeois families who had enjoyed the privilege of using certain beaches . . . were invaded by "louts wearing caps" and their followers.'

The experience of the Popular Front certainly scared a lot of proper-thinking people. But, despite its domestic reforms, the left lacked a true cutting edge. It let down its Republican peers in Spain and quailed before the rampant slanders of the right. It did not mobilize the Communist workers' battalions as the right feared it would. But it bequeathed an imperishable mark on society which France would not forget and which would be taken up after the Liberation in 1944. When Blum was released from imprisonment in Germany, he took a suit to the cleaner. When he collected it, he found a handwritten note in one pocket: 'Thank you for the *congés payés*.'

Though there were important networks of right-wingers who opposed the German occupation of 1940, it was in the French Resistance that the left found its next vocation. The military importance of the movement is open to debate: Hitler's architect, Albert Speer, once responded to a question on the subject with a scornful 'What Resistance?' But standing up to the Nazis was essential to the salving of national pride after the Liberation and, once Hitler had invaded Russia in 1941, the Communists were free to take a leading role, some of their chiefs expecting that they could render de Gaulle a figurehead when he returned to his country in 1944 and create a People's Republic in France.

Their hopes were not so far from a possible reality. The left's role in fighting the occupiers—and the widespread collaboration or inaction by the bourgeoisie—gave the working class a special badge of respectability after 1944. In some cities, Communist Resistance leaders seemed poised to take power. But de Gaulle implemented a ruthless amalgamation of the Resistance with the regular army, forcing the Communists to disband their militia as he pursued his vision of a united state marching to his beat.

The General, a man who said that the 'forces of money' were the biggest threat to the nation, took a distinct lurch to the left in 1944 in line with the agreement reached before the Liberation to extend welfare and the scope of the state and to eradicate the moral failures of the 1930s which had culminated in the Vichy regime. Drawing on the 'social Catholicism' of his parents, de Gaulle preached the virtues of the public interest, of using national wealth for the benefit of all, and of the right of everybody to live, work and bring up their children in security and dignity while his government implemented a far-reaching programme to extend state power drawn up by the leaders of the Resistance during the war.

Between 1944 and 1946, the coal, gas and electricity industries, banks, insurance businesses and some major companies such as Renault were nationalized. Family allowances were introduced, together with unemployment and sickness pay, and women finally got the vote. Soon afterwards, long-term state planning was instituted at the behest of the future Father of Europe, Jean Monnet. The Communist leader, Maurice Thorez, who had fled to Moscow during the war after being condemned as a deserter, became a Minister of State. His party took 26 per cent of the vote in 1945 and 28 per cent two years later.

After de Gaulle walked out of government in 1946, the Communists joined in a tripartite coalition with the Socialists and the Christian Democrats of the new centrist MRP party, usually holding the ministries for public health, armaments, reconstruction, industrial production and labour, before being expelled from office in May 1947 amid growing tensions over the Cold War, strikes which fuelled fears among its coalition partners, colonial policy and France's acceptance of Marshal Plan aid.

The Fourth Republic, which came into being with the Liberation, would, as we have seen, degenerate into a regime far more splintered and impotent than its predecessor, but the bright dawn of 1944 gave it a socialist-statist base which became entrenched in national life. Much as foreigners might scoff at France's political instability, and de Gaulle might rail at his successors after he lost power in 1946, the inflationary, state-cushioned economy that ushered in the Glorious Thirty Years represented a triumph for a system which catered to the desires of France's workers and middle class alike. Resolutely

Stalinist, the Communist Party might have appeared an aberration in this evolution of soft *capitalisme à la française*, which, however, never questioned the underpinning of the welfare state. Though it remained in political isolation, the PCF had a powerful instrument in its tight control of the Confédération Générale du Travail (CGT), the country's largest and most militant trade union federation, that brought together millions of workers from different branches of industry and services.

After Thorez fell ill in the 1950s, effective leadership of the party fell to the diminutive, sharp-tongued First World War veteran Jacques Duclos, who sidelined rivals and kept the party strictly loyal to Moscow, backing the invasion of Hungary in 1956. Despite the introduction of an electoral system which favoured the moderate centre and militated against them, the Communists still won a quarter of the vote at parliamentary elections in the mid-1950s, but their continued refusal to join governments contributed to the Fourth Republic's ever-growing instability.

When de Gaulle returned to office and changed the political system in 1958, the position of the working class altered little. Ministers might be Gaullists rather than members of the myriad small parties of the previous Republic, but managers and workers went on cutting easy deals in both private and public sectors. De Gaulle's Premier, Georges Pompidou, ended the nationwide strikes of 1968 with the simple expedient of a budget-busting pay agreement. Labour leaders were great national figures, and a former union official called Jacques Delors became a top-level governmental adviser with new-fangled ideas about industrial relations and worker participation in companies. Though Duclos attacked him as a proto-dictator, the General's hostility to US 'hegemony' was welcome to Moscow even if his efforts to form a relationship of mutual understanding with the Soviet Union did not get far given the way in which the Cold War kept intruding over issues such as Berlin and Cuba. In its early years, the Fifth Republic set out with the theory of binding French society together above party lines, incorporating the working class into a broad Gaullist vision of a united people, though, as we have seen, the nature of politics meant that this was always more aspiration than reality.

As Prime Minister under Georges Pompidou, Jacques Chaban-Delmas worked with Delors, Enarques and disciples of Pierre Mendès France such as Simon Nora to draw up the guidelines for a 'New Society' designed to break through the social blockages holding back France. They were to correct what the Premier called in his speech to the National Assembly presenting the proposals, 'the fragility of our economy, the often deficient functioning of the state, our archaic and conservative social structure.' There was to be a 'concertation' between employers and workers as they joined forces for the general good. It was not so far from the more idealistic opinions at the time of the Revolution.

But Pompidou, who received his copy of the programme only shortly before Chaban spoke to parliament, did not like what he read. He had earlier rejected the phrase 'New Society' as a stupid formulation that implied a rupture with the past, whereas he wanted to be seen as de Gaulle's heir, perpetuating the General's heritage. Though Chaban was popular and enjoyed a legislative majority, his days were numbered from then on; power in the Fifth Republic lay at the Élysée, not at the parliamentary building of the Palais Bourbon across the Seine. There was another snag. To have any chance of success, Chaban would have had to have enlisted the major force representing organized workers, the Communist Party. But the PCF wanted to have nothing do with him and his schemes—in part because the aim of men like Delors was to bridge the class divisions that helped to bolster its support among workers.

The politics of the 1980s changed all that. To celebrate Mitterrand's presidential victory in May 1981, crowds danced in the streets and a new era was proclaimed in which the workers would triumph. As frightened businessmen smuggled money across the border to Switzerland, the Social Security Minister announced that her job was to spend money without bothering about the accounts. The government decided on the most expensive and inefficient way of nationalizing a dozen key companies, followed by a deeply misguided attempt to build up standalone French production chains overseen by that Enarque of the left, Jean-Pierre Chevènement. It was all done in the name of the workers, even if there were more teachers than labourers among the Socialist Party faithful.

When three rapid devaluations of the franc, a bounding trade deficit and out-of-control inflation woke the President from his reverie, it was those workers who suffered in the end. After the Socialists were forced into their economic volte-face in 1983, redundancies ripped through coal-mining, textiles and shipbuilding. François Mitterrand returned from a visit to the United States and said how impressed he had been by the automated steel plants he had seen there: in the ensuing years, job cuts in the great mills of Lorraine ran at 8 per cent or more a year, and those thrown out of work could only look for employment across the German border.

Lorraine was only a start. Unemployment shot up in the industrial bastions of the north and centre and along the Mediterranean, where the presence of large numbers of immigrants and of former settlers from Algeria exacerbated social tensions and gave the far right its deepest wells of support. Parisians grew accustomed to seeing teenage beggars, '*les nouveaux pauvres*,' huddled in doorways. The solidarity proclaimed by the Socialists in 1981 gave way to selfishness: it was increasingly difficult to be a good Samaritan if your job might no longer be there when you got back from helping one of your less fortunate fellow men on the other side of the road.

As the crisis bit ever deeper, and poverty became a way of life among the one-time workers of the old industrial areas, a reporter for *Le Monde*, Corine Lesnes, travelled to the northern mining basin and brought back a telling piece of reportage from a typical town of brick houses and paved streets. In Fresnes-sur-Escaut, eight hundred were out of work and two hundred families lived on welfare. To save money, dozens had moved out of their homes and into old, abandoned caravans. One woman cooked for a community of fifteen living in a Second World War blockhouse.

'A woman of thirty-four died after her lungs were contaminated by toxic fumes: she burned rubbish and electric wires to recover the copper inside and sell it,' Lesnes wrote. 'The four children of last year's Father Christmas at the parish church are in care; Santa Claus spent five days in prison for a tax debt of 1,800 francs. Women get pregnant younger and younger—the children's allowances are like a wage for them.

'The most common way of making money is to collect scrap metal and sell it to the foundry for three francs a kilo. Anything goes—skeletons of cars, railway tracks, drain covers and even, last year, the railings of the bridge in the neighbouring town. Misery has a particularly black tone here.'

One woman, Nadine, divorced from a drunken husband, had seven children aged from one to seventeen, one of them a chronically ill truant of a teenager. The children did their homework by candlelight because it would take two years to pay off the debts to the electricity company. An older woman, Marcelle, lived on fifteen francs a day, dropping in at neighbouring houses at mealtimes and watching for the days when rotten apples were thrown on the local dump. 'All one can do is to share their worries as winter comes and applaud the government's ritual anti-poverty plan,' Lesnes wrote. 'Or re-read Zola and Dickens. And flee.'

The end of the Mitterrand era in 1995 and the election of the neo-Gaullist Jacques Chirac brought no solace. Under succeeding governments led by Socialists and Gaullists, things only got worse for the working class. With the number of jobs falling in three-quarters of France's regions, nine million people were unemployed or in part-time posts or 'precarious' jobs. Star industries stumbled. Household names took the shears to labour costs: the loss-making appliance firm which gave the world the vegetable mixer (under the slogan 'Moulinex frees women') shed a quarter of its full-time jobs. Even the smile of the pneumatic Michelin man couldn't save 15 per cent of the tire firm's workers from getting the chop. The French term for downsizing—*dégraissage* (defatting)—moved out of the kitchen and on to the factory floor. Four former homeless men marketed social problems with a board game in which players had to dodge dole queues, debt, alcoholism and the police to reach the ultimate prize of a job—it was packaged in the brown cardboard from which street sleepers make their shelters.

Moving to the upper end of the working class, the number of office staff and white-collar employees signing on for benefits doubled over five years. The slowdown in hiring meant there were fewer and fewer jobs for young people, and those who did get work found it mainly in small firms and on short-term contracts.

The process which started with a series of political decisions by an administration which had come to power supposedly to promote the interests of the working class rapidly took on a life of its own, arching beyond politicians. Because they could not control events, ministers could not explain what was happening to their voters— or, more painfully for the Socialists, to their own party members.

The language of the early 1980s became archaic as the habits of past generations were blown away. The working class was abruptly removed from its sentimental pinnacle and made to feel useless. The old notion of long-term relationships between workers, managers and owners evaporated in the face of the pursuit of survival, as the old anchors were pulled up and the ship of everyday existence was cast to the winds. Take three examples from urban life—shops, cars and the party which claimed to stand for the workers of France.

In the panoply of French working life, small shopkeepers, tradespeople and artisans have long been a key element in the nation's daily existence. They give many city streets an essential part of their character. In the countryside, they served a far-flung community out in the fields and villages. Before the Germans destroyed it in 1944, the small town of Ouradour in the middle of France counted around fifty family or one-man enterprises—hairdressers and butchers, shoe and dressmakers, bakers and iron merchants, carpenters and dealers in agricultural produce, a dentist, a tailor who also sold insurance, and a bunch of weavers—plus six cafés. In the capital, even the smartest districts have traditionally been alive with a variety of small shops that made them self-sufficient: a two-hundred-metre stretch of a street on the Left Bank of Paris where I lived in the 1980s contained three butchers, a stationer, a locksmith, a greengrocer, a dry cleaner, a cheese shop and an outlet from the Felix Potin chain of grocers.

Launched in 1844, the Potin chain made its reputation by promising honestly weighed goods, quality products bought by the founder in person and a low profit margin. The firm established the first French food processing factories owned by a retailer and pioneered home delivery. Its clients included the Élysée Palace. The main Potin factory in the north of Paris stretched over four hectares. The shops were a unique kind of enterprise. Though small in size, they used bulk buying and a standard range of goods to undercut standalone rivals. They were mini-supermarkets and, as such, overcame smaller competitors. Yet, being neighbourhood establishments, they carried with them none of the looming size and power of the hypermarkets which were to follow. They kept a local feel and a family atmosphere. They were often run by a couple whom customers knew by name; in the early days, employees had to obtain the firm's permission before getting married. Many of the managers lived in company flats above their shops. And there was a fine nostalgic resonance of their founder's first name: very few French baby boys are called Félix these days.

In 1956, self-service was introduced to the 1,200 Potin outlets. Soon after that, two revolutions shook up French retailing forever. The first saw a boom in the mail-order business; this had been around since a company called La Redoute was founded in the northern city of Roubaix in 1875, but it now flourished on the back of reduced prices and efficient national delivery systems. The second involved the huge growth of giant out-of-town shopping centres. France has more hypermarkets per head of population than any other European country. Municipal authorities made the most of the planning powers devolved to them under decentralization measures to attract shopping centres. Consumers are estimated to buy 90 per cent of their groceries from such places. In services as well as retailing, big chains took more and more of the market.

From McDonald's to exhaust-pipe fitters, franchises spread across the nation. Five per cent of small hairdressers go out of business each year. Faced with competition from Asia, the famous piano maker Pleyel, set up in 1807 and once patronized and promoted by Chopin, dwindled to an enterprise employing just fourteen staff and producing twenty instruments a year from a workshop in the northern Paris suburbs. It sold its celebrated concert hall in the centre of the capital and announced the end of manufacturing at the close of 2013, marking an end to piano making in the Hexagon.

To track the decline of small shops, look at the town of Avallon in Burgundy, famous as a town where Napoleon spent a night on his way to Paris from his first exile on Elba. In the past two decades, the number of butchers in the town has dropped from twelve to two for a simple reason—a shopping complex run by the appropriately named Mammouth chain which opened just outside the town. As well as offering cut-price goods, the complex has become a focus of social activity, in a reversal of the old image of shoppers hailing one another and chatting as they move from one small shop to another. 'Mammouth has become the town centre,' says an Avallon fishmonger. 'People go there to meet their friends as well as to do their shopping.'

Social intercourse apart, shops like the Félix Potin chain simply could not compete on price; and if there was one thing that ruled in France from the 1990s, it was price. 'Bargain hunting has become a way of life,' *L'Express* concluded in a cover story on the wave of discounting sweeping the country. A new Anglicism even emerged: *'les hard discounters.'* It was not just the poor who flocked to them; plenty of middle-class mothers sorted through the cheap clothes, cut-price food and do-it-yourself gear on offer. A sociologist from the College of Political Science in Paris, Denis Stocklet, dubbed bargain-hunting a national sport, and an author has compiled a 564-page guide to factory outlets which sell brand-name goods cheap, complete with restaurant-style star ratings.

Though volumes increased in the first dozen years of the twenty-first century, the sector was under severe competitive pressure as 'hard discount' rivals piled in alongside the existing groups. The downturn of 2008 affected business and an upturn in 2010–11 soon petered out. People complained about having to dip into their saving for everyday consumption and having spent the whole of their wage by mid-month. They stocked up on cheap goods when supermarkets staged promotional price cuts and chose basic cuts of meat.

There had, of course, always been stores which piled the goods high and sold them cheap. The Tati chain, set up by an immigrant from Tunisia in a former brothel in the down-at-heel Barbès area of Paris, had the atmosphere of an Arab market as their customers, many of them immigrants themselves, sorted through goods heaped on counters before taking them away in the chain's distinctive pink gingham-pattern shopping bags. 'Keep the thieves out of my shops, and you'll take away part of my clientele,' the founder once remarked.

He knew how humiliating it could be for poor people to ask superior shop assistants for the price of goods which they might not be able to afford, so he did away with the assistants and let his customers check the prices themselves before taking them to the cash tills. At its height, the chain attracted some twenty-five million customers a year in nine cities. Then other retailers noticed how keen the French had become to save money on clothes. By 1996, one-third of garments were being bought at discount houses or in sales. Smarter stores, which had once let Tati have their unsold stock at knock-down prices, began to sell it cheap themselves. Turnover slumped in Tati's souks.

To restore its fortunes the chain looked overseas and cashed in on its kitsch image with disposable cameras in shades of its trademark pink, a Fifth Avenue store in New York and a jewellery outlet on the smart Rue de la Paix. Everybody was in the cut-price game now, and, as the lines of hypermarkets grew for kilometre after kilometre on the edge of provincial cities, Denis Stocklet reflected that, without realizing it, the French had gone back to nineteenth-century Catholic ways of parsimony and economy. That made a few people very rich indeed: three of the country's half-dozen largest fortunes belong to big retailers.

Governments tried to check the megastores, but with scant suc- cess. The bottom line rules, and the bigger the store, the greater the profit—takings per square metre in the country's 1,100 hypermarkets are double those in the 7,300 supermarkets. When predatory pric- ing was banned to try to protect small shops, one supermarket boss reacted with glee to the news that he would not have to offer bread at below cost price to lure customers. Jacques Chirac thundered about the 'extraordinarily negative' effect of supermarkets in draw- ing people to 'unfriendly' suburban centres; but his Prime Minister promptly presented a business award to the head of one of the mon- ster chains. A move to make planning permission more difficult for new hypermarkets only set off takeover battles as the bigger chains sought to grow ever larger by acquiring their weaker brethren. For all the rhetoric of regret for the cosy past and the place of small shops in the social blanket, the die was cast. Even if they shudder at its social cost, one thing successive governments have pursued with success is low inflation, and the discounters help to achieve that—the harder the better.

Some cut-price retailers see themselves as playing a positively crusading role in forging a better way of life for their compatriots. One such pioneer, Édouard Leclerc, was deeply hurt by official crit- icism. 'We're attacked like the Jews once were,' he said. 'They used to be held responsible for everything that went wrong. Now it's us.' Leclerc was a phenomenon of postwar France. Born into a poor family of thirteen children, he opened his first shop after the war in the west of Brittany, selling chocolates, biscuits and sweets at half the artificially high wartime rates still charged by other stores. The secret of his success was simple: 'I sold retail at wholesale prices.'

As Centres Leclerc sprouted throughout the country, small shop-keepers demonstrated against him and his methods. Local farmers refused to sell him milk or vegetables. Leclerc, a man who loved to upset established ways, relished the battle. Sometimes things turned violent. Lorries were stopped by force; a leader of protesting shop-keepers was hit in the face by a rock and lost two teeth. Then Leclerc had the idea of selling discount petrol to attract car-owners to his stores. Once there in their Renaults and Peugeots, what could be more convenient than to load up with goods from the adjoining store? A believer in astrology, Leclerc, who died in 2012, adopted a quasi-religious approach to retailing. 'He taught us that the only thing that counts is our intellectual capital,' one of his sons says. His local managers are known as disciples or adherents.

Though the founder had never taken much money out of the business, his followers do very nicely. Leclerc often gave his managers an ownership stake in their enterprises, and insisted that they share the takings with the staff. They were invited to conferences to listen to his vision of the future. 'As the years have gone by, one has seen them turning up in thicker and thicker furs, with bigger and bigger rings and in more and more powerful cars,' one observer of the Leclerc phenomenon told *L'Express*. 'Edouard is their god. It isn't a limited company he set up, but a movement. A man who lets you build up such a business for yourself without asking for anything in return except that you follow certain moral rules (don't rob the customer, sell as cheaply as possible and distribute a quarter of the profits to the staff) is unique.'

Growing prosperity following years of hard times bucked up retailing, though it was too late for the Potin group, whose founding family sold out to owners who saw that inner-city property prices meant the real-estate value of their assets was greater than the revenue to be earned from retailing. Little by little, the stores were hived off for development. At the end of 1995, the remaining four hundred Potin shops received a terse note from the central manage-ment: 'You can stay open until December 31 at 20:30.' Given that

New Year is a more important occasion for celebration than Christmas in France, it was a Christmas carol from a Gallic Scrooge, a death knell for an institution.

The commercial and social changes which had brought down Potin and other traditional retailers were augmented by the expansion of e-commerce. In 2013, the Kering company, owner of la Redoute, announced that France's biggest mail-order firm would undergo a massive exercise in *dégraissage*. Seven hundred of its 1,200 employees were to be made redundant. Staff journeyed from the firm's base in northeast France to demonstrate outside the Paris offices of the Kering boss, François-Henri Pinault, one of the country's top businessmen; he was also lobbied by the Socialist former Labour Minister, Martine Aubry, the leading politician in the region. Kering, which changed its name from PPR (Pinault-Printemps-Redoute) earlier in the year, replied that la Redoute had dragged down its group profits, that it had unsuccessfully sought a buyer for the enterprise and that its strategy was to focus on luxury goods—it owns top brands such as Gucci, Saint Laurent Paris, Boucheron and Bottega Veneta; against such names there was little room for a mail order business selling everyday goods with an offer of a 50 per cent discount on first orders of thirty euros.

In keeping with tighter times, the automobile market fell off, affecting domestic marques in particular, which both posed an industrial problem and provided a further dent in a national self-image. Car sales dropped in 2005–9 and never picked up properly; in the first ten months of 2013, registrations of new cars fell 7.4 per cent on the previous year. The French love affair with the motorcar has been charted by writers, lyricists, photographers and academics. The greatest modern French novelist, Albert Camus, died in a road crash; a far poorer writer, Roger Limier, won fame as 'the French James Dean' for dicing with death—which finally caught up with him—in fast cars. The revolt of shopkeepers and small businessmen led by Pierre Poujade in the 1950s would not have been possible had its leader not been able to drive about the country from one village meeting to another. The reputation of the novelist Françoise Sagan as a symbol of modernity was inflated by the way she ignored speed limits in her sports cars.

Despite the efficiency of French public transport, 82 per cent of local trips were still made by car in the late twentieth century, when France had more motor dealers than any other European nation. In 1973, a French sociologist was moved to write an article entitled 'Automobile Accidents and the Class Struggle.' The philosopher Roland Barthes devoted an essay to the semiology of the Citröen DS. An American academic, Kristin Ross, entitled a study of post-war French society 'Fast Cars, Clean Bodies,' noting that, after the 1950s, a revolution in attitudes towards mobility and displacement had permeated every aspect of life with 'the dismantling of all earlier spatial arrangements, the virtual end of the historic city, in a physical and social restructuring.' So it is not surprising that France's main car manufacturer should have played a key role in national life, going beyond the mere construction of vehicles, and that its history should tell a story about the evolution of French industry and those who worked in it.

For six decades, the Renault plant on the Ile Séguin on the Seine in the Boulogne-Billancourt suburb of Paris was France's greatest industrial citadel. Built in 1929 by Louis Renault, 'Fortress Billancourt' sprawled over sixty-five hectares. It brought major assembly line production to France, and was immortalized as an industrial monument and shrine to the French working class in photographs, books and even poetry. In the 1930s, the town of Boulogne-Billancourt became a treasure house of modernist buildings by the urban pioneer Le Corbusier and a dozen other leading French architects. During the German Occupation, the plant was turned over to the Nazis, who used it to produce military vehicles—Allied air-raids killed more than a thousand workers.

After the Liberation Louis Renault was arrested for collaboration, the company was nationalized and the Communists turned the factory into a union stronghold. Before she discovered silk stockings, Cyd Charisse's Ninotchka put a visit to Billancourt high on the list of things she had to do on her first visit to Paris. Edith Piaf moved into a villa across the river. Renault set the norms for pay and conditions—for a fourth week of paid holiday and for the wage rises that ended the 1968 strikes. When Sartre launched a revolutionary newspaper, he sold it at the factory gates. A line from one of his plays—'We mustn't make Billancourt lose hope'—became a catchphrase for the need to cater to the workers of France. When the left finally won power in 1981, a former chairman of the motor firm became the Minister for Industry. The company symbolized a society in which more than a quarter of the workforce looked to the state for employment. It was as solid as the nation itself.

With car ownership booming in the 1960s, Renault and other motor companies expanded production beyond their urban citadels, setting up new plants on greenfield sites in Normandy and importing cheap labour from Africa. Many of the immigrants moved to dormitory tower-block estates on the outskirts of neighbouring towns. One such place was Dreux, a market town west of Paris, which had once been a key frontier post between the Kingdom of France and the Duchy of Normandy. In the town itself, there are brick buildings with stucco facades, a Renaissance bell tower, a bridge over a slow-flowing river and an arrow-straight avenue which points up the hill to the railway station and the ride to the Gare Saint-Lazare in Paris.

Drive ten minutes out of the middle of Dreux and you land in a very different environment, where the local giveaway newspaper carries advertisements for witch doctors and the lifts in the tower-block are covered with Arabic graffiti. The flats are occupied by immigrants who came to work at the car plants and other factories in the area in the boom years. In the 1980s, robotization and downsizing threw many of them out of jobs, but they had no wish to go back to Africa. The town's left-wing Mayor devoted much money and effort to catering for the new arrivals. The French natives of Dreux resented this, and grew fearful of unemployed Arabs from the car plants and their teenage children. They wanted nothing to do with multicultural experiments. And so Dreux became the unexpected testing ground for France's National Front extremists whose anti-immigrant, law-and-order programme made such an impact that, in 1983, the orthodox conservatives in the town forged a pact with the devil. In return for his support, they appointed the local Front leader to the town council. After his death in a car accident, his wife went on to win the parliamentary seat for Dreux with 61.3 per cent of the vote.

Just as the National Front was exploiting the explosive seeds of unemployment, industrial mutation and racism unwittingly sown by the motor industry in Normandy, Renault was reflecting other changes in France as well. Amid an upsurge in extreme left-wing terrorism, the chairman was murdered in the street as an evil paragon of capitalism. A quarter of Renault's capital was opened to investors in France's privatization programme. Volvo took a stake in an ill-fated attempt at European co-operation. The management even summoned up the nerve to defy a twenty-two-day strike at one of its factories. And *dégraissage* hit Billancourt with a vengeance. When its workers had led the charge for more pay in 1968, the plant employed 24,000. By 1991, it had 1,230. At 2:30 p.m. on March 27, 1992, France's most famous assembly line came to a halt. Four days later, the Billancourt plant closed for good. The men went home, and the management looked for buyers for the land. It used to be said that 'when Billancourt sneezes, France catches a cold.' By 1992, France was already ill.

Three and a half months after its Paris plant closed, Renault got a new chairman, a former senior government official called Louis Schweitzer. His first year in office saw another 7,000 jobs cut. Renault had lost 37 per cent of its labour force in the dozen years since the left won power in 1981. Back then, Schweitzer had been the principal aide to the Socialist Budget Minister and reacted with cold irritation if one dared suggest that the government's plans for reflation and nationalization might be just a little unrealistic. As for France itself, the experience of the 1980s had been a steep learning curve for him. An Enarque who was distantly related to Sartre, he had dealt with ministerial problems over HIV-contaminated blood supplies and the blowing-up of the anti-nuclear Greenpeace ship *Rainbow Warrior* by French secret service agents. In the early 1980s, Schweitzer wore shoes with unusually thick soles; by the time he took over the partially privatized Renault, his footwear was a good deal more elegant. Once he was settled into the job, Renault announced that it was going to shed another couple of thousand workers in what the chairman described by the fashionable euphemism of a 'social plan.'

Like a number of his colleagues from the Socialist glory days, Schweitzer has gone through the 1990s with a deeply different ideology. As a member of the elite band of Inspecteurs des Finances, his prime loyalty must be to the state rather than to any political faction. But in his new incarnation, he faced the same question which hangs over his colleagues in boardrooms throughout the country. Whether renegades from the left or lifelong true believers of the right, France's business leaders have shown themselves as adept as anybody at sacking people. Now they have to prove that their slimmed-down companies can compete in a positive manner, selling as many cars as Fiat or Ford, prospering across the world in an open business economy, staying abreast of the changes bred by hardware and software, finding French equivalents to McDonald's and Coca-Cola, and mastering the byways of modern finance.

For all the cuts that closed Billancourt, cars remained a key industry—and a major employer. As sales stagnated in the 1990s, the government introduced schemes to give owners a financial incentive to sell their existing vehicles and buy new ones. This brought some temporary relief to the French manufacturers, but the overall trend was for sales of foreign models to rise more than those of domestic marques. Then the government-induced recovery faded away. In the late 1990s, car registrations fell to their lowest level for two decades and the pattern was to continue into the new century as we will see in the next chapter.

To return to political iconography, no political movement has caught the chill that emanated from Billancourt and other heavy industry plants more than the Parti Communiste Français. Its members made up the bulk of those who were laid off as Renault and its competitors modernized their operations and cut their workforces. For all the strikes and rhetoric, the Communist-led CGT trade union federation had been unable to prevent the onward march of the market and its impact on the long tradition of workers power. At the same time, it had been bested politically by the wily Mitterrand, who invited the Party's ministers into his first administration but then turned them into his prisoners to the point where survival as an independent force obliged them to quit and to see their electoral strength wither in a world to which they seemed to have no answers.

In 1981, the Communist leader Georges Marchais had been able to muster a respectable 15 per cent of the first round presidential vote. Seven years later, his successor got just under a fifth of Mitterrand's re-election score. The party had lost its way.

This was not simply a matter of the diminishing appeal of Communism. On the one hand, there was Mitterrand's superbly orchestrated long-term campaign to build up the Socialists as the major party of the left, taking the Communists into a one-way alliance which sapped their strength. Reformers might talk of forging a new brand of Marxism: a senior Communist civil servant spoke to me at length over a slab of pink calf's liver in a smart Left Bank restaurant of how the Communists could use the Socialists to broaden their appeal. But the party had been so dragooned into Moscow-directed orthodoxy over the decades that it could not get the worm out of its bud and establish itself as a real working-class party for modern times which would think for itself and stand apart from both the temporizing Socialists and the rampant forces of the far right. More than any other political group in this retrospective nation, the PCF was a prisoner of its past, to a degree which the vast majority of its members are unaware. That past laid hidden for a long time, and its effects on the French working class, which the PCF led for so long, remains opaque. But, for evidence of just how far the supposed spearhead of the revolution, French Marxist-style, subjected themselves to domination from the Big Brother from abroad, meet the still shadowy figures of Eugen Fried.

It was not until 1997 that two tireless chroniclers of French Communism, Annie Kriegel and Stephane Courtois, uncovered the extent of his role in ensuring that the supposed white knight of France's workers had been the slave of Moscow. As a young man, he had proved his worth to the Kremlin by organizing a campaign against Social Democrats in Czechoslovakia in the 1920s. Fluent in Slovak, Hungarian, Yiddish, Czech, German, English and French, Fried was sent clandestinely by Moscow to France in around 1930. Once installed, he promoted Maurice Thorez and other trusted figures in the trade unions and politics—and blocked the rise of a popular tribune, Jacques Doriot, who switched to the far right and ended up being executed as a Nazi collaborator. Fried made each senior party official fill up a seventy-four-part questionnaire covering everything from his education to his private life; the forms were immediately dispatched to Moscow. Fried himself regularly travelled to the USSR to report to the Kremlin, returning with Stalin's latest commands.

In 1934, Fried came back to France from one of these trips with an order that the PCF should set aside the rancours of the 1920 split and work with the Socialists again. The left was on a major upswing at the time, buttressed by the economic slump, fear of what was happening across the Rhine in Nazi Germany and the activities of fascist groups in France. But when the Popular Front won power two years later, there was another order from Moscow—the Communists were not to join the new government.

Instead, they must put bourgeois politics on one side and concentrate on building up industrial muscle through their labour federation, the CGT. The instruction was loyally followed by Thorez, his successor Duclos and the party's labour boss, Benoit Franchon. The loyalty to Moscow was not confined to politicians and unionists; a fair number of French intellectuals also made fools of themselves. 'Death to the saboteurs of the Five-Year Plan,' ran a line by the much-honoured poet Louis Aragon, who also confided later that his pain at Stalin's death was only equalled by the sense of sorrow and personal loss he had felt when his mother passed away.

Rewriting history is a futile exercise, but all the same: what if the PCF had been more independent of its puppet-master answering to Moscow? What if Thorez had grabbed the destiny which seemed to have been his to take at national level in 1936? What if the anti-fascist parties had formed a united bloc in government in the late 1930s? Would France have acted differently at Munich? Would Paris and London have been able to check Hitler sooner? And, if so, would Charles de Gaulle have retired to his country home as an obscure prophet of tank warfare? So much for speculation; the reality was that, after the Nazi invasion of 1940, Fried told the French Communists to collaborate with the occupying power. He himself moved to Belgium, but kept in touch over a clandestine radio linked with Moscow and with Jacques Duclos in Paris. He instructed Thorez to desert from his regiment, and Duclos to open political negotiations with the Germans. Hitler's invasion of Russia finally freed the Communists to join the Resistance, but Fried did not live to resume on-the-spot control after the Liberation: in 1943, the Gestapo killed him during a raid in Brussels. They had no idea who he was. Nor did any but a handful of the French.

After the Liberation, the control from Moscow continued, reinforced by the emotional strength which at least some of the resisters had drawn from news from the Eastern Front as they fought their lonely battle in the west. The first postwar elections gave it a quarter of the vote, but it remained aloof from the twisted manoeuvres of Fourth Republic Cabinet-making, and so could claim certain purity. It reacted with a famous court case when a former Resistance fighter revealed the nature of the Soviet Gulags in 1950. Though the Party lost, it could still count on the allegiance of Sartre and the intellectual left.

Still, the true nature of Communism in the East gradually seeped home, and the PCF's devotedly Stalinist leadership became increasingly isolated, though it again won credit for its opposition to the colonial war in Algeria. The advent of the Fifth Republic did the party no harm, since the Socialists were humbled and de Gaulle's independent foreign policy was welcome with Moscow. But the sands began to shift more decisively in the 1970s, when the Communists became epitomized by a man who hit a political nadir on their behalf.

Georges Marchais, Secretary-General of the PCF from 1972 to 1993, was a scary remnant from the caverns of Stalinism whose outbursts provided regular occasions for national mirth as he sought to defend the indefensible. Under his long rule, the survival of the least fittest became the be-all and end-all of leadership. A bushy-eyebrowed, potato-headed thug whose lack of style could make him almost endearing on occasion, Marchais supported the crackdown on Solidarity in Poland and the Soviet invasions of Czechoslovakia and Afghanistan (the latter in a television interview direct from Moscow), fully earning his nickname of 'Jojo' for his admiration for Stalin.

'What's a Gulag?' he once asked. 'What we call a prison, they call a Gulag.' When deportations and executions in the Soviet Union under Communist rule were mentioned, he retorted, 'I tell you, they didn't arrest enough! They didn't imprison enough! If they had been tougher and more vigilant, they wouldn't have got into this situation they're in now.' After pulling back from a tilt at Euro-Communist liberalism in the 1970s, he proclaimed the glories of 'democratic centralism' and made sure his party toed his line. Famously dogmatic, he told a television interviewer who cornered him that he was asking the wrong question. Communist Party membership fell by 70 per cent under his leadership.

Following the lines originally laid down by Eugen Fried, the PCF had always been an outsider. Marchais' pugnacious, unyielding leadership meant that, more than ever, it would not evolve into being seen as a natural party of government, in the way that the Socialists were from 1981 onwards. But then, contradictorily, Marchais allowed himself to be drawn into Mitterrand's web, ensuring that the PCF got the worst of all worlds. Most woundingly, the party found itself losing votes to the extreme right, which emerged as a powerful rival for protest votes in the south and in the old 'red belt' around Paris, where the turncoat tribune Jacques Doriot had set the rabble-rousing tradition in the late 1930s.

Revelations about financing from the KGB and the siphoning off of cash by Communist-run local councils further tarnished the image. Marchais himself could never explain away the fact that he had signed on as a wartime worker at a Messerschmidt plant before the Nazis introduced compulsory labour for young Frenchmen. But all this paled into insignificance beside the huge political failure of the would-be party of the masses to capitalize on the growing discontent with successive governments among its natural supporters.

The 1980s should have been the moment the PCF had been waiting for, with soaring unemployment showing up the harsh side of capitalism as administrations of left and right took ever more unpopular measures, and voters searched for new panaceas. Instead, the PCF's woes mounted, as did those of the nation. In the first round of the 1981 presidential election, Georges Marchais, for all his faults, had won 15 per cent of the vote to Mitterrand's 26 per cent. Seven years later, Mitterrand got about the same level of support, but the Communist candidate managed to muster only 5.4 per cent.

In 1993, the party eventually got a new leader, Robert Hue, a bearded, friendly-looking former nurse with an unusual wit who resembled a large garden gnome. At the National Assembly elections of that year, the Communists did so badly that the minimum requirement for a parliamentary group had to be changed to enable their deputies to sit together. In the 1995 presidential poll, Hue took

8.6 per cent of the first-round vote. Georges Marchais, who was to die at the end of 1997, said nothing in public, but sniped at his successor. Undeterred, Hue set out to bring the party into the modern world. Internal discipline remained tight, but reformers were no longer banished. Jacques Chirac's gamble in calling legislative elections in 1997 gave fresh reason for hope. United by pledges to slash unemployment and by scepticism about the demands of the Maastricht Treaty, the Communists and Socialists reached a broad policy agreement that, despite some decidedly grey areas, enabled them to campaign in the name of a united left.

Hue set a target of 10 per cent of the first-round vote; in the event, the PCF got 9.9 per cent on the first round and boosted its representation in the National Assembly from twenty-four to thirty-five seats. This meant the Socialists needed Communist support to achieve a parliamentary majority. Hue overcame opposition from some old hardliners, including Marchais, and agreed to join the new government; the central committee celebrated with a 1992 grand cru claret, cheese and strawberries. Still, the party was very much a junior partner in the Jospin coalition of the left. There was no doubting the decline of its once-mighty machine. The collapse of the Soviet Empire had dealt it a heavy blow. Industrial workers looked to the far right, not the PCF. Its past associations could not be easily shaken off—an 846-page account of the crimes of Communism around the world went to the top of the French bestseller list in the winter of 1997. The PCF won substantially fewer votes than the National Front, and its score was regularly less than one-third of the non-Communist left. Even the party's annual fete outside Paris began to lose money.

Hue asked an American reporter if he really looked like a frightening person; but that was not the point. When the PCF had been frightening, it was because of its disciplined mass following rather than its ideology. Now, the marchers in the street were a far more disparate lot, following different drums; Georges Marchais was heading for his grave; and it was the extreme right which inspired fear. The old certainties had ebbed even for the party which had once been sure that history was on its side. Appropriately, a guide taking visitors round the PCF's new headquarters remarked on how the building contained no angles, only curves. The party newspaper, *L'Humanité*, dropped the hammer and sickle from its masthead, relaunching its Sunday edition as a glossy magazine with advertisements from privatized companies. And, all the while, Hue proved to be Lionel Jospin's flexible friend: while the party remained sternly hostile to the European common currency, and asked for a referendum on the subject, it kept behind a government which was committed to a goal it opposed. Doctrinal certainty had been replaced by the basic need to survive.

The PCF retains some strength in suburban Paris, parts of the coal mining region of the Nord-Pas-de-Calais, the industrial harbours of Le Havre and Dieppe, in some departments of the 'Red Limousin' in Central France and in Mediterranean shipbuilding cities where no ships are built anymore. Some Communist Mayors can draw for support on a history of urban improvement. But the vote for Hue at the 2002 presidential election fell to 3.4 per cent, lower than the Trotsykites.

Five years later, despite efforts to form alliances with social movements and promote an 'anti-capitalist front,' the party's candidate got just 1.9 per cent. It sought succour in the hard left alliance of the Parti de Gauche headed by Mélenchon in 2012, but its contribution to his 11 per cent score was quite small. It won only ten seats in the National Assembly that year and, of the 138,000 members it claimed by then, just 70,000 had paid their membership dues. The battalions of union members have thinned out.

The party struggles on, its leaders mouthing brave words of defiance to capitalism and the European Community. But life has changed. For all its problems, the France of the twenty-first century is not the France of Thorez and Duclos, of Boulogne-Billancourt and the other faded symbols. That is hardly surprising given the social evolution of the Hexagon and the changes it has experienced and the fears they arouse.

7

ANOTHER FRANCE

The French city plays a key role in the development of the modern metropolis. The *bourg* gave its name to the middle class and, though the term refers to everybody, *citoyens* are linked primarily to urban areas. Despite repeated efforts to decentralize, the capital dominates; twelve million people live in Greater Paris and the surrounding region. France without Paris remains unthinkable, not only the political, administrative and business centre, and the scene of successive revolutions, but also home of the Louvre, Montmartre and Montparnasse, the Left and Right Banks, the quais of the Seine, the Arc de Triomphe and the Eiffel Tower. Many of the greatest works of French literature, art, cinema and song—not to mention the evocations of photography—have been set in the streets and apartments of the capital.

But people who term themselves Parisians are most likely to live outside the city's twenty *arrondissements* in the sprawling suburbs, some of which have built an identity of their own, from the genteel residential estate of the Yvelines in the south to Disneyland at Marne-la-Vallée to the east. Away from the capital, a score of conurbations are regional powerhouses in business, politics, culture and social life, from the second city of Lyons in the middle of France and Marseilles-Aix-en-Provence conurbation in the Midi to Lille in the north, Bordeaux, Rennes and Brest in the west, Strasbourg in the east and Toulouse in the southwest. Important as the countryside is, the city is central to France's self-image. For all the homogenization of

recent decades, smaller cities and large provincial towns have lives of
their own, too, a tradition of links with the surrounding countryside,
a specific character which sets a town in Brittany apart from one
in the Pyrenees, which distinguishes Toulon from Brest, Arles from
Dijon. It is not just a matter of geography and climate; though the
effect of television and mass food distribution is breaking down old
regional particularisms, the distinctions of attitudes, accents and ways
of life remain alive.

At the same time, there has also grown up an entirely different
urban culture, a source of concern and outright fear, which has
developed in ways that the orthodox society neither understands nor
is able to cope with. As such, it presents one of the biggest challenges to confront the nation today. Britain or the United States have
inner cities; France has the *banlieue*, and the people who live there.

Though it has become the accepted term, the word is, in fact, a
misnomer for what we are going to be talking about here. *Banlieue*
denotes, literally, the suburb. When a couple at a dinner party in
Paris say they live '*en banlieue*,' they probably mean that they are the
proud owners of a trim house surrounded by a garden in a place
with a genteel name like Fontenay-aux-Roses or Saint-Germain-
en-Laye, the neat town which gave its name to the main Paris
football team but is now well separated from the roar of the crowd
in the Parc des Princes stadium. However, when newspapers run
headlines about the problems of '*les banlieues*,' they do not mean
the suburbs to which many inner-city inhabitants have moved in
recent decades. They mean housing estates, often gaunt relics of
urban planning, which dehumanized the residents in concrete tower
blocks and where the population is usually mainly made of immigrant families of two generations.

France has attracted a large flow of immigrants from the continent,
starting with Polish mineworkers and Jews from Eastern Europe.
Immigration accounts for 40 per cent of the national population
growth since the Second World War. A quarter of the population has
immigrant family links. In the 1960s, 75 per cent of those who
came to live in France were from Europe, most of them Catholic

Spaniards and Portuguese. Generally, they looked like the natives and fitted into a comfortable pattern; the men worked in factories while their wives were concierges or cleaning women. They kept to the rules, and their children grew up in the French system. Manuel Valls, made Prime Minister in 2014 after two years as Interior Minister, and Anne Hidalgo, elected Mayor of Paris that year, are both from Spanish immigrant families. The National Front candidate whose success in the southern town of Brignoles in the fall of 2013 caused national excitement was called Lopez.

The extent of immigration is generally overstated. Polls in 2013 showed that people thought that it accounted for a quarter of the population; the actual number is half that, though the foreign-born population of Paris is around 25 per cent. The makeup of the immigrant community is changing as the expansion of the European Union brings increasing numbers of people from East Europe, with Romanies from Romania—known simply as 'Roms'—a particular source of hostility as they are accused of law infringement and a refusal to integrate with society. But the majority of immigrants are still from France's former colonies in North and West-Central Africa plus its remaining territories in the Caribbean.

The National Institute of Statistics (INSEE) puts the number of foreign-born immigrants in the country at 5.3 million. The European Statistics Agency, using somewhat different criteria, gives a figure of seven million, or 11 per cent of the total population. In addition, there are some 6.5 million direct descendants of immigrants born in France with at least one immigrant parent. This totals between twelve and 13.5 million, or 19 per cent of the total population in metropolitan France.

Though French law does not allow immigrants to be classified officially by ethnic origin, the European agency says five million, or nearly 8 per cent, come from outside the European Union. Unofficial estimates count 5.5 million of the overall total as being of European parentage, four million from the Maghreb of North Africa, one million from sub-Saharan Africa and 400,000 of Turkish origin. Among 802,000 newborn babies in metropolitan France in 2010, 27 per cent had at least one foreign-born parent, and 24 per cent had at least one parent born outside of Europe. Forty per cent of immigrants live in the Paris region of the Île-de-France, with other large concentrations in the Rhône-Alpes around Lyons and Provence-Alpes-Côte d'Azur around Marseilles.

The issue of immigration in France is an awkward affair. Initially, workers from North Africa were welcomed as cheap labour, especially in motor car factories. But, in general, they were not integrated—or did not want to integrate—into mainstream society and became prisoners of the virtual ghettos of the housing projects in the *banlieus*, or of rundown districts of towns. Their children grew up often feeling excluded and finding it hard to get a job, frequently lacking skills or motivation. Islam increasingly became a dividing line. While most clustered in the suburbs of cities, some smaller provincial towns also attracted foreigners. Guéret in the deeply rural department of the Creuse is home to well-established families originating from Italy and Portugal, and more recently from North Africa, Turkey and East Europe; unemployment reaches 40 per cent in some districts there, and one-fifth of families have only one parent present, compared with a national average of 13 per cent.

Hostility between communities has risen. The Interior Ministry reported 160 anti-Islamic acts in 2011 and 200 in 2012, which agencies that track them says is about half the real number. In the name of the principles of the lay state, the wearing of the veil and full head covering known under the general name of burqa was outlawed in public places, as were other 'ostentatious' religious symbols. As President, Nicolas Sarkozy declared in 2009 that the burqa was not welcome in France, calling it a symbol of subservience that suppressed women's identities and turned them into 'prisoners behind a screen.' Attempts to establish councils which would bring about reconciliation between Muslims and the French state foundered. The Muslim Council set up with Sarkozy's support to try to unite the Islamic community has been rent by internal rivalries, particularly between immigrant leaders of Algerian and Moroccan origin, and has found it difficult even to agree to name a president.

With unemployment rising, immigrants became a target for accusations that they were taking jobs from native French and were welfare recipients living off the state while their children dropped out and, in some cases, turned to a life of crime. Illegal immigration was reckoned by the Interior Ministry in 2006 to amount to anywhere between 200,000 and 400,000; it added that it expected 80,000–100,000 people to enter the country illegally each year, a number it hopes to reduce to 35,000.

The question of nationality is a recurrent cause for debate. Children born to immigrants who have spent five years in France automatically gain French citizenship at the age of eighteen, even if their families are living illegally in the country. The National Front naturally wants to end this and was joined in 2013 by Jean-François Coppé, at the head of the mainstream UMP party, who proposed that such children be barred from acquiring French nationality. The left-wing majority in parliament rose in opposition to Coppé's proposal as contrary to republican traditions, and Sarkozy himself had opposed any change in the law. As so often in such matters, the National Front was the only gainer as it could, at least, claim consistency and unity on the issue.

While the National Front profited from the anxiety and fanned it at the same time, mainstream politicians were at a loss as to how to reconcile France's traditions of brotherhood with the growing fears among a significant section of the population about the impact of immigration, first from Africa and then from Eastern Europe after enlargement of the European Union. Running for re-election in 2012, Sarkozy, whose father came from Hungary, said that there were too many foreigners in France and that the system for integrating them was 'working worse and worse.' While immigration could be a boon for the country, he added in a television debate, it needed to be controlled more tightly and some benefit payments to immigrants should be reduced. His Socialist opponent said that, at a time of economic crisis, 'limiting economic immigration is necessary and essential' and pledged that 'the numbers will be managed.'

The issue is made even more difficult by the changing make-up of the immigrant community as the expansion of the European Union brings increasing numbers of people from East Europe. The presence of the 'Roms,' who mainly live in caravans and camps dotted across France and are popularly accused of indulging in crime, became a major political issue under both Sarkozy and his successor. The Hollande administration was split between Interior Minister Manuel Valls, who wanted to send them home, and some of his colleagues, who cleaved to the tradition of offering a refugee haven, with the President trying to find a middle way.

In October 2013 the expulsion of Leonarda Dibrani, a fifteen-year-old girl immigrant from Kosovo, with her family showed how complex such issues could become and the perils Hollande ran when he got personally involved and tried to find a compromise that would satisfy both those who wanted the law to be applied and those who favoured flexibility in the name of 'republican values.'

The girl's family was expelled from France after having its asylum application refused several times; the girl herself had been a frequent truant from her school in eastern France. But there was an outcry when police picked her up during a school outing and bundled her out of the country with her parents and sister. Students staged protest demonstrations, encouraged by a parliamentarian from the Green Party, which is allied with the Socialists in the government. The Education Minister insisted that schools should be 'sanctuaries' from such police action. The Socialist Speaker of the National Assembly warned that the left was in danger of losing its soul. There was also a personal embarrassment for the President when his partner, journalist Valérie Trierweiler, who normally remained silent on policy matters, said publicly that there were some borders which should not be crossed, 'and the school door is one.'

Valls stood firm as he flew back from a trip to French territories in the Caribbean to handle the crisis. An official report found the expulsion in order but ruled that the police should not have detained the girl while she was on a school outing. As the storm engulfed the Socialist Party, President Hollande decided to intervene himself, going on television with what he thought would be a way out— Leonarda could return but not her family.

It was hardly a matter to which the head of state should have committed himself in such a public manner; the conservative newspaper, Le Figaro, quoted a member of the presidential team as saying that 'it was a complete grotesque show. It should have been dealt with by an official at a prefecture.' Hollande's intervention went horribly wrong. Television showed the family listening to his broadcast in Kosovo and

Leonarda refusing to take up the offer without her kin. It was as if the President was negotiating with the family, and being rebuffed. The right reacted with scorn, accusing Hollande of having undermined the law. The Secretary of the Socialist Party, Harlem Désir, called for the whole family to be readmitted. Hollande did not slap him down or react when the deputy from the Green Party, his coalition partner, suggested that students should resume their protests. What should have been a minor incident had mushroomed into another example of how awry Hollande's effort to rule by reason and reach a compromise could go. The left-wing newspaper, *Libération*, called the affair 'devastating' for him.

The long history of non-integration is summed up in the housing projects on the edges of France's big cities where the population of Arab and African origin is particularly large. These estates are part of a bad dream constructed from high unemployment, social and racial tension, brutalist architecture and decades of neglect. Once they were proud examples of modernity: 'Here, there was a field of beetroots; now I have planted a flag; thousands of flats will sprout,' as one of the first masters of urban development put it in the 1960s. They replaced the shanty towns—the *bidonvilles*—where immigrants once huddled. Now they have become known as rabbit-hutches, symbols of the plight of people who have been left behind by the economy. One former minister calls them places of despair; another urges 'an effort of solidarity from the nation equal to the one that set up the social security system after the war.' The former Premier, Michel Rocard, spoke of their crime-forming architecture, but when his government decided to paint such blocks in bright colours to cheer up the residents, only the outside walls got the treatment and the insides remained as drab as ever.

Rocard's initiative was one of a string of official schemes over the years to breathe fresh life into the *banlieues*. In 1996, the Prime Minister, Alain Juppé, unveiled a sixty-eight-part plan to grapple with the problem, but he had to admit that the real issue lay in unemployment. However many ideas the governments planners may dream up, the basic question is whether people can earn a living or are relegated to the margins where work no longer figures on the agenda. Estimates put the number of people living on the edge of society at three million: before his election in 1995, Jacques Chirac talked of almost double that number. Some beg in city streets; some hustle for euros in the Métro; some are the rural poor; many live in the *banlieues*. In a sign of its priorities, France devotes much more money and attention to its farmers than it does to those in need in the suburbs, but still expects them to feel solidarity with the Republic.

The *banlieues* have become the nexus of a new form of society which rejects the traditional integrationist dynamic of the French state—and which frightens those who would like everybody to live by the same rules in orderly fashion and to respect traditional European social norms. The world of the suburban estate is a universe which the average French person likes to steer clear of. But the more France passes by on the other side, the greater the challenge will be to its settled way of life in the rolling unrest and violence which has been termed the 'French intifada.' Take a series of snapshots from north to south over recent decades to plumb the depth of alienation.

Start in the northern city of Amiens, capital of Picardy. In distant sight of the cathedral, there are districts where nearly half the children aged under six live in families with no source of income other than welfare. A year after his election, Jacques Chirac visited a huge, sprawling complex housing 25,000 people on the edge of the city. He spoke of the need for a 'pragmatic' urban policy; he threw his arms around a group of young Africans; he climbed down to a basement to listen to a band called Bestial Overdrive. When he embraced a six-year-old daughter of immigrants, her brother shouted, 'Chirac, don't touch my sister!' From behind the barriers, another child noted the redness of the President's face as he glimpsed the underside of his country. Unemployment varied between 17 and 33 per cent from tower-block to tower-block. Among the residents were Arabs who had fought for France in colonial wars: half of them were out of work. One-third of residents were behind with the rent. The President's visit was punctuated by cries of 'Work! Work!' as police sharpshooters kept watch from the rooftops.

Turn southwards, to the Yvelines department west of Paris. This is, for the most part, an area of quiet villages and commuter towns. But in the town of Trappes, where violence broke out between second-generation immigrants and police in 2013, one-third of the 9,000 families living in the Merisiers estate receive help from social workers, and half are below the poverty line. Many of the local employers have closed down or cut their workforce. Unemployment is so high that people no longer bother to go to the labour exchange. Year by year, they slip down the social scale, from decent-sized flats to homes where four people sleep in a room. Most work that is going is in the black economy, where employers do not pay welfare contributions.

A couple of hours' drive to the south, the Loire Valley is one of France's great tourist attractions, with its châteaux, green, undulating countryside and its fine food and wine. The twenty-two buildings that make up the Croix-Chevalier estate in Blois are a long way from the picture-postcard image of the region. 'They've pissed by the letter boxes,' one of the caretakers told a reporter. 'They say it's the dogs, but . . .' She remembers the estate in the 1970s. 'You'd go out without bothering to lock up. We had parties. Now people call the police if they hear a drill in the afternoon . . . the kids hang about outside from morning to night . . . they break the lighting in the staircases . . . they steal bicycles and never get punished because they deny the evidence and take refuge in the protection of the law.' It goes without saying that she is referring to the young immigrants.

In the centre of France, Saint-Etienne was once a symbol of French heavy industry, with big factories and a triumphant football team. Now great regional firms have either closed their gates or reduced their workforce from several thousands to a few hundred. On the Montchovet estate, with its 971 flats, more than half the adults are out of work.

In the suburb towns around Lyons, such as Vaulx-en-Velin, Bron, Rillieux-la-Pape and Vénissieux, violence has rumbled on since the early 1970s with clashes between youths and security forces, car burnings, attacks on shops and official buildings and the deaths of young immigrants fleeing police. A local Mayor, who became a Socialist government minister, spoke of a 'breeding ground of delinquency.' A report from a local observer on one outbreak of violence went as follows:

'Barricades, sirens, skeletons of burned vehicles, masked groups looting shops, men in balaclavas sacking buildings, five hundred inhabitants of a rundown district facing squadrons of the forces of order. Such images are not from a far-away guerrilla war; this is what is happening right now, to the northeast of Lyons.

'Everything began at around three p.m. when police in a car decided to check on a motorbike carrying two people. A banal situation that turned brusquely into a drama; the motorbike hit the car and landed on the pavement. The passenger, Thomas Claudio, died immediately. He was twenty-one years old. The news spread and the estate at Vaulx-en-Velin was rocked by the first clashes between riot police and hundreds of furious youths letting out their hatred by implementing violence . . .

'Make no mistake, the riots now taking place in the suburbs of Lyons are evidence of the immense malaise in the "big ensembles" where the most unprivileged people in our society are gathered. Since the first unrest in 1981, nothing concrete has been done for the inhabitants of what are called dormitory communities; a very big immigrant population, the feeling of exclusion for those who live on the edge of large cities, the difficulty the forces of order have in establishing a dialogue and the absence of strong decisions on urban policies—all these reasons are the real causes of the violence we witness each evening.'

In Vaulx in 1995, police killed a young Arab, Khaled Kelkal, whose fingerprints had been found on a device used in an unsuccessful attempt to blow up a TGV high-speed train. His death was filmed by a television crew who accompanied the security forces. The drama made Khaled a martyr among the youths of the *banlieues*.

Dying 'in combat,' he became an icon of their exclusion from society, as well as a reminder of the thousands of young Algerians slain by the colonial army during France's last big war. In the two days after Khaled's death, as the violence spread through the sprawl of France's second-biggest urban area, fifty cars were set on fire, telephone kiosks and bus shelters were smashed, and shops set alight. The Mayor of Vaulx blamed the media for stressing the problems of his town, turning its 45,500 inhabitants into symbols of despair and depriving them of their dignity and identity. Touchingly, he argued that if a quarter of the adults are out of work, that means three-quarters are 'producing wealth and contributing to the development of the Lyon region.' He lamented how the *banlieues* were seen as another world, watched by the rest of France on television as though they were in a different country.

The government in Paris announced measures to try to contain the problem. But the violence was far from over, with the forces of law and order identified more and more as the enemy, a reputation that was heightened when a young man was shot point-blank in the skull while being questioned in handcuffs in a police station; riots followed. In the first half of 1999, there were 1,790 violent incidents in urban areas of the Rhône department round France's second-largest city.

Down on the Mediterranean, in a housing estate in the suburbs of Marseille, three-quarters of families get by on less than the official minimum wage. Two walls topped with barbed wire separate the crumbling estate from a smart development of individual houses.

Seventy thousand people live here. A third of the adults are unemployed. In another suburb of the port city, what is claimed to be France's biggest shopping centre was opened by the Mayor, Jean-Claude Gaudin, in the autumn of 1996. Before the inauguration, local youths attacked the site. The project had been due to create 3,000 jobs; in fact, it produced 1,200. In the north of the city, unemployment reached as high as 50 per cent.

Head east along the coast to the Ariane estate in Nice, which houses 20,000 people—old immigrants from Italy and French people who came from Algeria after that country gained independence in 1962 and their children, as well as more recent Arab arrivals. In one area of the estate, Spanish gypsies live beside an incineration plant. A passing reporter watched a woman grilling fish on a fire made out of plastic bags. Neither she nor her husband had a job. Their sons drove a turbo-charged car for which they did not have the registration documents. The nursery school nearby has been closed down. A local councillor set up a scheme for young people to earn some money cleaning up the estate. 'After three days, none of them came anymore,' he recalls. 'The desocialisation here is so great that it's difficult to get anything done.'

A family which beds down in an empty flat on the estate simply forced the door open and moved in. 'Everybody takes what they fancy,' a young Arab says. 'It's the same on the buses. Nobody's in charge. We young people would like some order. In summer, we dealt with the drug situation. When we caught a dealer, we gave him a hard time. We have to handle it because nobody else does.' Another group of youths took to holding up motorists at traffic lights and stealing their cash. 'We're the law,' they shouted as they ran off. A café was ram-raided, cars stolen. The Mayor's office has asked Paris to deploy a squad of riot police on the estate and wants the army to station troops on the frontier with Italy to stop illegal immigrants. As the priest from the estate remarks, 'Little by little, everybody feels caught up in this return to a savage state.'

The pattern of trouble from Les Tartarets to Nice has become all too familiar. A small incident between local youths and the police escalates into burning and looting, which sometimes spreads to neighbouring towns in a chain reaction. A gang society has emerged which naturally nurtures violence. 'If you go to a party now, you need your crew,' says a young man in the Parisian suburb of Chanteloupe-les-Vignes, where the raw ghetto film La Haine, on immigrant life and youthful crime, was shot. 'They come in a group of ten, somebody disrespects your girl, all of a sudden your ten have to fight their ten.' Casual violence has become commonplace. In a Marseille suburb, three youths who had been tormenting a handicapped boy stabbed his elder brother to death for daring to object; in Lyon, an eighteen-year-old died after four days in a coma from injuries inflicted by a gang after he refused to hand over his chain necklace.

The violence has spread well beyond the familiar areas of urban tension in France's biggest cities to Fontainebleau, Normandy and country towns. France's 'European capital' of Strasbourg became a centre for car burning—up to five hundred a year plus arson attacks on buses and municipal buildings. Younger and younger children became involved, both on the streets and in schools; according to the Education Ministry at the turn of the century, between 34 and 57 per cent of secondary schools reported violence from pupils. More than 60,000 youths were involved in crime each year, with people aged under eighteen, many from the banlieues, accounting for one-third of street crime and 20 per cent of all delinquency. A cartoon in Le Monde showed a schoolmistress teaching her pupils to decline their verbs: written on the blackboard was 'I want to burn a car; you want to burn a car; he, or she, wants to burn a car,' and the teacher is warning the class not to forget the circumflex accent on brûler.

At the start of 1999, the Interior Minister had set 'the republican reconquest of our suburbs' as a target for the year. But, in the first decade of the new century, the violence spread:

In Montauban in the southwest, after a house owner shot dead an immigrant robber who had broken into his home.

In Montbéliard in the east, following the arrest of a young man trying to rob a bank

In Strasbourg, also in the east, when a seventeen-year-old thief drowned in a canal while being chased by police.

In Nîmes in the south, after the death of a robber as he tried to escape from pursuit.

In Avignon on the Rhône, after an eighteen-year-old held for gang rape hanged himself in his prison cell.

In Paris in the largely immigrant district of the Goutte-d'Or, after police violence against young people.

On the housing estate outside Paris which was the setting for *La Haine*, a chubby seventeen-year-old called Imed Amri won a moment of fame when he appeared in the background in some scenes. One night, he went to a rap evening organized by a local Franco-Algerian solidarity organization to raise funds to pay for a skiing holiday for immigrant children. The youths from his estate and visitors from the nearby *banlieue* of Argenteuil got into an argument. Going outside the hall, they began to trade punches. Knives came out. The boys from Argenteuil went off to get a gun. When they returned, they shot Imed in the head. He died in hospital five hours later.

More than 28,000 vehicles were set on fire in the first ten months of 2005. In some cases, the rioters used Molotov cocktails and fired live rounds. There was a contagion effect. Riots in the Paris suburb of Clichy-sous-Bois after the deaths of two adolescents pursued by police as they returned from a football match set off unrest in immigrant housing estates across the country. More than ten thousand vehicles were burned in that outburst alone, and there were attacks on schools and community centres as well. It was the biggest and most sustained outbreak of violence France, or Europe, had seen. President Chirac took to the television to speak of 'a crisis of identity,' and a state of emergency was declared which lasted for three weeks before order was restored. Visiting the Paris suburb of La Courneuve which had been rent by war between two gangs, the Interior Minister, Nicolas Sarkozy, said he wanted to 'clean the place with a kärcher'—a high-pressure vacuum. When youths threw stones at him later that year in another suburb of the capital, Argenteuil, he called them 'scum.'

Despite Sarkozy's attempt to present himself as the man who could impose peace and order in contrast to the laxist left, things got no better. His election as President in May 2007 was followed by three nights of unrest in which 1,400 vehicles were burned in city streets, shop windows smashed and street fittings destroyed. Later that year, a wave of rioting spread through the Paris suburbs after two teenagers died when their motorcycle was hit by a police car in the town of Villiers-le-Bel. In all, 150 police and firemen were injured in two days of confrontations in Villiers itself, in which the rioters fired around eighty rounds of live ammunition and showed a sense of tactics that suggested organization. In the summer of 2009, the suicide of a twenty-one-year-old Arab in police custody in a suburb of the central city of Saint-Etienne set off three nights of car burning and attacks on shops. In the Alpine city of Grenoble, police were fired on during riots set off by the death of a local immigrant as he fled after robbing a casino.

François Hollande's promise of reasonable government that would seek to heal social wounds met with little success either. Three months after he was elected, seventeen police were injured in clashes on a deprived estate with youths who set fire to cars, a nursery school and a youth centre and fired buckshot. In July 2013, a police check on women wearing a complete face-covering veil in contravention of the law provoked fighting in Trappes, which necessitated the dispatch of sizeable police reinforcements. In Marseilles, insecurity reached such a pitch that summer that the Mayor of one district asked for the army to be sent in; the request was refused.

Despite the support they have received from Sarkozy and the Socialist Interior Minister, Manuel Valls, the police feel beleaguered, depicted by the left-wing media as brutal bullies with an animus against immigrants. The riot squads sit in their trucks, sinister in their padded uniforms and with tear gas guns at the ready. Police working the city streets tend to keep together and generally have little constructive contact with the people around them, especially on the housing estates. Take the example of Nathalie who came to Paris from the Mediterranean and spent a dozen years as a policewoman in the suburbs of the capital. She patrolled an estate in the Seine-Saint-Denis department outside Paris, checking cellars and lift shafts and the concrete alleyways between the tower blocks. When she joined the force, she thought her blue uniform would win her respect. Instead, 'the young people treat us like shit . . . the insults rain down on us.' Two of her colleagues have killed themselves in despair.

Nathalie dreamed of being posted back to her home region on the southern coast. Instead, hoods sidle up to her and tell her she could make much more money as a prostitute. Others set fire to a car and call the police; when they drive up, a dozen youths run out into the street and bombard their vehicle with stones and metal bolts. Her windscreen has been smashed several times; once it was broken by a flower pot dropped from ten floors up. 'You just hope that the doors are well-locked and the reverse gear doesn't jam,' she said

Her bus driver husband found her growing more bossy at home. 'I've lost all my sensibility as a woman,' she says. 'Seeing only the bad side of society means I trust nobody anymore. I feel as if the whole world reproaches me for being a cop. My only friends are in the police. At least they understand me.' Early on, she was shocked by the bad language of the streets, the petty crimes, the drug trafficking; then she absorbed the ultimate survival technique of the *banlieue* cops—the shrug of the shoulders. It is just as her husband no longer reacts when youths get on his bus without paying, kick the doors and horse around. But, still, there are moments which even a dozen years on the beat could not deaden. One evening, Nathalie was called out on an emergency. A man had fired his rifle by mistake while cleaning it. The bullet went through the floor into the flat below and hit a two-year-old baby in its cot. It died in her arms. When she got home at two in the morning, her uniform was still stained with blood.

The streets she patrolled are the parts of France where councils propose a nighttime curfew for children, or welfare withheld from parents of delinquents. In such suburbs, dogs are kept for protection or attack, not to be patted. A supermarket in the Paris suburb of Stains sells rottweilers in its pet section, and the authorities in the Hauts-de-Seine department had to ban pitbull terriers in public housing estates because there were so many. For many immigrants caught in the vice of the *banlieue* and rundown city areas, it is not surprising that France's second-biggest religion offers an increasingly attractive means of escape from the rejection so many feel in their daily lives.

Censuses that draw a distinction on the basis of race or religion have been banned in France since 1872, so establishing the number of Muslims in the country involves some degree of estimation. A study by the national statistics office in 2010 concluded that France had 2.1 million "declared Muslims" aged 18–50, including between 70,000 and 110,000 converts. Some five million inhabitants come from predominantly Muslim countries, with half from Algeria and Morocco, but polls indicate that only one-third practise the religion regularly.

For most Arabs and some Africans, Islam is above all a social and community glue in a foreign land; an assertion of their identity rather than any threat to those around them. For many non-Muslims, imams, mosques, veiled women and Halal butchers are a symbol of separation. Though France contains some 2,400 mosques, Muslims without easy access to one began to pray in the streets of Paris, Nice and Marseilles, disrupting traffic; the practice was banned in 2011 and the Interior Ministry offered alternatives, including a disused fire station in the capital. Muslim religious schools have been set up in back rooms. The Arabic graffiti on city walls shouts for itself. In prisons, warders keep watch on fundamentalist terrorists to prevent them from making converts.

A police association has warned of the religion's potent appeal to 'young delinquents who are seeking their identity and are ready to wage a struggle against the country's institutions, which is presented to them as legitimate.' However, efforts by fundamentalists to infiltrate mosques and other prayer places in France appear to have met with little success. Police say that they have made the effort in only seventy-five places of worship but were resisted in half the cases. Some thirty radicals have been expelled from French territory, and others monitored by the police.

Still, for the resentful youth of the *banlieues*, Islam meets a psychological need which all the anti-racist, integrationist movements of the 1980s never touched. 'Better to count yourself as a Muslim than as one of the unemployed,' as a saying goes. To which a minister responsible for towns and social integration under Chirac responded, 'They do not want mosques but jobs. They may not have the same roots, but they want the same payslips.' The trouble is that the jobs simply aren't there. A growing number of *banlieue* families have two generations without work. Islam, whether actively practised or not, is a counter to what its followers see as the indifference of French society to their plight. The evident suspicion that officialdom shows towards the religion only increases its appeal to those who already regard mainstream society as being biased against them and who harbour both hostility and resentment dating back to France's colonial legacy in North Africa and the support Paris gave to the repressive, anti-fundamentalist regime during the long and very bloody civil war in its former possession of Algeria. Militant Islamists proclaim that their holy war will continue until the whole world is conquered; France is their first foreign target and Jewish targets figure prominently. The record stretches back for three decades.

In the early 1980s, four people were killed and more than forty injured in an attack on a synagogue in the rue Copernic in central Paris. A bombing and shooting assault on the celebrated Jo Goldenberg restaurant in the old Jewish district of the Marais killed six, including two American tourists, and injured twenty-two. In Algeria, five people died in an attack on French diplomatic quarters, a French bishop was blown up and seven French Trappist monks had their throats slit after being kidnapped by fundamentalists. In the 1990s, a French airliner was hijacked across the Mediterranean. In 1995, the national and Paris rail networks, a school, public places and famous landmarks became targets after the assassination in Paris of Abdelbaki Sahraoui, a co-founder of the Islamic Salvation Front (FIS) in Algeria, who had opposed the extension to France of the *jihad* against the Algerian government.

The worst attack, on July 25, caused eight deaths and eighty injuries when a gas bottle was set off at the Saint-Michel station in the capital. Three gas bottles that went off at Métro stations in Paris wounded forty-two people. One alleged ringleader who had fled to Britain was extradited and sentenced to life imprisonment. A bomb at the Arc de Triomphe wounded seventeen. A large explosive charge was discovered on the rail track of a high-speed rail line near Lyon and Khaled Kekal, who has already been mentioned in connection with the riots sparked by his death, was identified after his fingerprints were discovered. A bomb in a Paris square injured four people and another explosion wounded fourteen at a Jewish school in Lyons.

At the start of the new century, al-Qaeda planned a bomb attack on Strasbourg Cathedral during the Christmas market of 2000 but was foiled by French and German police. The trial of four suspects in Germany heard that they intended to use pressure cookers packed with explosives, a technique they were said to have learned in camps in Afghanistan. The following year, the US embassy in Paris was the target of another unsuccessful bomb plot and then, in 2005, a French-Algerian, Kamel Daoudi, who had graduated as a computer engineer in Paris and trained with al-Qaeda in Afghanistan, was convicted of having tried to blow up the diplomatic mission.

In March 2012, another French-Algerian, Mohammed Merah, went on a rampage during which he shot seven soldiers and Jewish schoolchildren In Toulouse and Montauban. His brother later wrote a book to denounce an 'atmosphere of racism and hatred' in their family that led to Mohammed's radicalization; he said that his family supported banned terrorist groups and that their mother told them Arabs were born to hate Jews. Denouncing the way some fellow immigrants hero-worshipped his brother's memory, he remembered them congratulating his mother saying, 'Be proud. Your son brought France to its knees,' and filmed his sister declaring, 'Mohammed had the courage to act. I am proud, proud, proud . . . Jews, and all those who massacre Muslims, I detest them.'

Two months later, three days after a British soldier was killed in the street in London by two converts to Islam, another convert, an unemployed twenty-one-year-old, stabbed a French soldier in the Défense district of Paris but did not kill him; the investigation revealed that the attacker, who was spotted on surveillance cameras praying before his act, had refused to wait for a bus in a queue with women and would not take a job that involved working with women. Interior Minister Manuel Valls warned of growing radicalization of young French Muslims online and by extremist imams.

The combination of terrorist bombs and the threatening cloud of violence in suburban housing estates made it easy for the far right to warn of France being swept by a murderous horde from the Maghreb, poised to cross the Mediterranean and join up with their brothers in Corbeil, Vaulx-en-Velin or Marseille. One of France's most famous names, Brigitte Bardot, who married a National Front supporter as her fourth husband, said she might have to emigrate because of the overpopulation of foreigners, especially 'manic throat-cutter' Muslims, with their ritual slaughter of sheep. 'We have to submit against our will to this overflow,' the actress turned animal-rights fanatic declared. 'Year by year, we see mosques flourish across France while our church bells fall silent because of the lack of priests.' Such language earned her a fine for inciting racial hatred, by which time she had publicly pledged support for the Front in an election in southern France.

The perceived Islamic threat was given a new edge by an emerging link with organized crime. Over the last two decades, police have reported involvement of Islamic groups in hold-ups, explosions, gun-running and forged documents linked not only to North Africa but also to Bosnia, Chechnya and Afghanistan. One gang, based west of Paris, raised millions of francs for Algerian fundamentalists by selling forged documents to immigrants. There was also the case of convert to Islam, Christophe Caze, the son of a cleaning woman and an unemployed worker. He became a Muslim while a medical student in the northern city of Lille, changing his name to Walid, growing a beard and attending a fundamentalist mosque. After fighting on the Muslim side in Bosnia, he returned to France and led a gang which held up a supermarket, killing a motorist, attacked a Brinks security truck with a rocket launcher and made an unsuccessful gas attack on a police station. Police attacked the group's headquarters in a red brick house in the industrial city of Roubaix, firing rounds from a rocket launcher which set the whole building alight. Four burned bodies were recovered. Caze was not among them—he had been away for the night. With another member of the gang, he drove towards the Belgian frontier. Police were waiting for him.

Their fusillade killed Caze outright. His companion, wounded, took two women hostage before giving himself up.

Five months later, journalist Sara Daniel visited the Alma-Gare district of Roubaix where the gang had established itself. She reported:

'In summer here, nobody goes on holiday. But round rue Henri-Carrette, the silence of the dead reigns. A silence of mourning. Approaching Number 59, a woman draws the edge of her veil across to cover her face. So as not to see the little charred house with its windows covered with planks. Between the Alma district and Christophe Caze, a kind of love affair has come to life. A strange alchemy. Here the problems of living bring people closer. Everybody knows each other. Here, the young man who had converted to Islam found a new family. Christophe was something of the favourite son of the district. The kids in the street speak of him with respect. "He tried to persuade us to go to the mosque. He was intelligent, educated, but not haughty. We talked about football, anything and everything. He was tolerant. As for religion, he said it was up to us to make the decision, nobody could force us."'

In the once bustling textile centre of Tourcoing to the west of Roubaix, a different tone was to be heard. Tourcoing has also fallen on hard times. Racism, fear, unemployment and extremist politics meld into a sour brew on a run-down estate. 'My father told me, Arabs are worse than mice,' a thirty-one-year-old mother of five told a visiting reporter from *Le Monde*, pointing at a little Arab boy. 'What we need is a boat to put them in, or a good bomb.' People in places like this tell of young Arabs attacking old French people in the cemetery, of police who either turn a blind eye or suggest that they take the law into their own hands. Fifty per cent of respondents in one survey in 2013 said they thought immigrant children integrated badly into society, a 17 per cent jump from 2011.

Racism and unemployment feed off one another. A former trade union official complained how, in the old days, you could break off from work to have a cigarette; now, he said, there will always be an Arab standing in line to grab work, while an army of illegal immigrants is pouring into the country in search of jobs and the shop floor manager will remind you that there were two thousand people waiting to take your place. A retired Frenchman with a Socialist Party card who keeps several guns in his flat said he votes for the far right in local elections 'to stop the wogs getting above themselves.' In the southern town of Brignoles, an elderly man going to vote for the National Front in a local election in 2013 described immigrants as unfriendly folk who never spoke to people outside their community. One poll at the time showed that nearly two-thirds of the French thought the country had 'too many Arabs' and 'too many Muslims.'

The inevitable gulf between a North African family in a *banlieue* tower block and an orthodox French family has become immeasurably deeper because the feeling of non-acceptance is mutual. Increasingly, immigrants are asking what France is going to do for them. The jobs that brought them north are drying up, but they do not want to leave. Religion is the only rallying point in which they can have confidence, but, by its nature, it sets them even further apart. When a right-wing Interior Minister spoke of developing 'a French Islam,' an imam from northern Paris countered that this meant 'leaving our identity behind . . . the arrival in France of Protestants and Jews required changes in French society; now it is the time of the Muslims.' Before he embarked on his brief career as a terrorist, the would-be train bomber Khaled Kelkal said he was 'neither Arab nor French. I am Muslim.'

That frightens a lot of people. They regard the Arabs and Africans as outsiders who can only be a threat to the cohesion of their country and their own lives. Racism against black and brown people thus takes on a wider resonance and draws on the image France has had of its own social fabric for two centuries. The French do not see themselves as living in a land of separate ethnic communities: Islamists, as an Interior Minister said, should be French. The country may receive people from different nations and cultures, but it requires them to conform to the unity and values of the Republic.

The education system and the authority of the state are meant to impose a uniformity which ensures that the melting pot produces a single national stew. There are exceptions, but, as a general rule, multi-culturalism and the right of different ethnic groups to be treated on an equal plane with the native French are new, and often uncomfortable, concepts.

A report commissioned by the Ayrault government in 2013 met with a highly critical reception when it proposed a radical overhaul of the assimilation model requiring immigrants to adopt French culture, including an end to the ban on Muslim headscarves in schools and an emphasis on the 'Arab-Oriental' dimension of national identity. Leading the charge against the recommendations, Jean-François Coppé of the UMP party objected that '[i]t will no longer be up to immigrants to adopt French culture but up to France to abandon its culture, its values and its history to adapt to the culture of others.' Going into conspiracy mode, the newspaper *Le Figaro* accused the Prime Minister of a political manouevre in using the report to 'wave a red rag' at voters that would weaken the UMP by encouraging them to vote for the National Front—Marine Le Pen called the recommendations a 'declaration of war on the French.' The spokesman for the Socialist parliamentary group called some of the proposals 'hazardous,' and the Prime Minister back-pedalled, saying he did not plan to overturn the headscarf ban but insisting on the need to fight discrimination and inequality to 'get the republican model of integration working again because it has broken down.'

The base line remained, as defined at the turn of the century by the Comte de Paris, the Pretender to the French throne, 'If immigrants, no matter where they are from, settle in our country, then they must adopt our civilisation and bend to our rules, habits and lifestyles.' But the reality was that, despite inter-ethnic marriages and the emergence of a middle class of entrepreneurs from immigrant families, fewer were ready to follow such a path among the disaffected youth of the suburbs, as the alienation between them and mainstream society increased.

Such a message takes no account of places like the Lyons suburb of Vaulx-en-Velin, with its thirty-eight different nationalities, or the tower-block suburbs outside Paris in La Courneuve, Aubervilliers and Saint-Denis, where a rebellious youth declines to live in the traditional French mainstream. In another Parisian suburb, Sarcelles, sixty different nationalities have been counted among its 58,000 people. As well as Arabs from North Africa, many *banlieues* are home to substantial numbers from black Africa, who bring their cultures and traditions with them. In the suburb of Montreuil, where 5,000 immigrants from Mali live, the Mayor's office has fought an uphill battle against their polygamy. More than a hundred African religious sects have set up in the hinterland of France's cities. A bare, neon-lit hall in La Plaine-Saint-Denis, north of Paris, resounds at weekends to Zaïrois bands of electric guitarists and singers laying down the path to salvation. After a lengthy study of the Paris *banlieue*, publisher and author François Maspero observed that, if a plan for ethnic separation was viable for the former Yugoslavia, 'one day, we must expect such a plan, in the name of the same logic, to be set out for a just ethnic division of the people of Aubervilliers and La Courneuve.'

France's difficulty in coming to terms with the dysfunction between the old, all-encompassing idea of the nation and the ethnic separations that it cannot ignore is heightened by the high profile in media reporting of Arabs born in France—known as *beurs*, from a slang term for Arabs. The first generation of immigrants were overwhelmingly single men recruited from North Africa to work in factories and mines. According to an oral historian, Yamina Benguigui, their minds were set on returning home one day; at first, they kept their belongings packed, ready to make the journey back. But the longer they stayed in France and the more their families joined them, the further that prospect receded. 'If you go to Algeria, you will see the houses the immigrants had built for them,' Benguigui notes. 'Often there is no more than the first storey: the building stopped at that.'

For their children, the idea of returning to Africa was a non-starter, but, at the same time, France was not a real home. 'We were neither from here nor from there,' as Benguigui puts it. For teenage *beurs*, the process is complete. No question of crossing the Mediterranean, but little question of adopting traditional French ways either. They see themselves as a community—the second-most numerous in France—which has the right to live in its fashion by its own rules.

Amid such dark shadows of separatism, few immigrants or children of immigrants appear outside entertainment programmes on television; it was not until 2006 that the main channel, TF1, appointed a non-white news presenter, Harry Roselmack, born in Tours to immigrant parents. Zinedine Zidane established himself as probably the best soccer player in the world at a time when France's World Cup–winning team of 1998 awakened brief hopes for a '*bleu, blanc, beur*' nation, but the impact was fleeting. The Sarkozy and Hollande administrations included women of immigrant origins while the Socialist Party elected Harlem Désir, son of a father from Martinique and a mother from Alsace, as its Secretary in 2012. But the black Socialist Justice Minister, Christiane Taubira, was racially abused, with children at a protest against same-sex marriage filmed waving banana skins at her as they shouted, 'Who is the banana for? It is for the monkey.'

After denigrating her legal qualifications for the ministerial post and accusing her of being anti-French, Jean-Marie Le Pen told an interviewer that Taubira had got her government job because 'they thought her colour would be a shield when she proposed absolutely unacceptable things.' A National Front mayoral candidate in the Ardennes put a photomontage on her Facebook page of picture of a baby monkey with the caption, 'At eighteen months' next to one of Taubira with the caption, 'Now.' The party subsequently suspended her but said it would sue the Minister for having reacted by branding it as racist. The far right-wing weekly *Minute* returned to the fray at the end of 2013 with a cover line reading, 'Crafty as a monkey, Taubira finds the banana'—the government announced that it was taking legal action against the magazine.

Roselmark declared in an article in *Le Monde* at the time that 'Racist France is back.' He attacked 'deep-seated racism . . . not just within the National Front but in the deepest parts of French society.' There have been changes in some respects. Until recently, for instance, stardom in French cinema failed to reflect the multiethnic composition of the post-colonial population. Major stars were white. Those with non-white parentage, such as Isabelle Adjani, subsumed it under a colour-blind national identity. Conversely, actors of visibly non-white origins were confined to stereotypical roles, such as drug dealers in crime films.

Over the last ten years or so, however, a remarkable change has taken place. Increasing numbers of actors from immigrant back-grounds—many from the Maghreb—have reached the pinnacle of the star system through massive box-office hits: Samy Naceri (the *Taxi* series), Jamel Debbouze (*Astérix et Obélix: Mission Cléopâtre*), Gad Elmaleh (*Chouchou*), Dany Boon and Kad Merad (*Bienvenue chez les Ch'tis*) and Omar Sy (*The Intouchables*), to name the most successful. Most come from stand-up and television comedy, and their films play on ethnic stereotypes in what can be called 'comedies of ethnic

integration.' These men of modest origins now represent the aristocracy of the French star system.

Another outcome of *beur* pride was the emergence of a vibrant
alternative street culture, expressed mainly in rap music, which bred an
international star in the singer MC Solaar and claimed a transatlan-
tic brotherhood with a lexicon of terms like 'gangsta' and 'homeboy'
(no Académie Française gurus here). But, despite sometimes high record
sales to a wider public, this was essentially an outsider culture which lost
its edge if it allowed itself to be embraced by the mainstream. The *banlieue*
slang can be virtually impenetrable and can act as a wall in both directions. 'We are not like them, the words we use are not the same as them
because they speak old French, we talk our slang,' as a twelve-year-old
from the suburbs said about white children from inside Paris.

To those not in tune with ghetto life, it was a considerable step
further when the slang for 'leave me alone' became 'fuck your mother.'
And when a rap band of that name—Nique Ta Mère—performed a
song urging 'kill the cops,' the liberal establishment was in a quandary.
Condemnation meant lining up with the racists who waxed indignant
when the band was booked for subsidized music festivals. But to shut
one's eyes and ears in the name of racial harmony was, as the journalist Elisabeth Schemla pointed out, to renounce moral values needed
to stand up to the extremism which threatened civil society. If NTM
could get away with it, how about a band that sings a ditty entitled,
'Kill the Jews?'

The law eventually stepped in: two members of NTM—one
from white Portuguese parents, the other a West Indian black, both
French citizens—got suspended prison sentences for singing a song
which declared, 'I piss on the courts . . . Our enemies are the
men in blue and we piss on them.' Soon afterwards, two other rap
singers were fined for another cop-baiting song entitled, 'Sacrifice
de Poulets'—*poulet*, or chicken, being the slang term for the police.

The exact degree of racism is impossible to define, but there is
clearly a lot of it about. A report to the United Nations Human
Rights Commission depicted a country being shaken by 'a wave of
xenophobia and racism.' Nearly two-thirds of those questioned in
another survey acknowledged that they harboured racist attitudes.
Some people react with denial. A prominent university professor
banned the use of the word 'immigration' among his students because

it might encourage racism. A Christian group called on all public organizations to remove the word 'race' from official texts. Some newspapers do not run the names of criminals if they have a Muslim connotation. Others try to walk a fine line but fall from the tightrope. Though an enemy of racism and the National Front, Chirac spoke of understanding what ordinary French people feel about the noise and odours of immigrant neighbours.

'We're not at home here,' said one of the women on the estate in Tourcoing, 'They spit in our faces.' On the other side of the divide, a North African community worker in Khaled Kelkal's hometown of Vaulx-en-Velin recalled that ten years ago, young Arabs wanted to become French. 'Today, it is exactly the opposite. Whatever we do to adapt, it will never be enough to get us accepted. White people can get out of the *banlieues* if they make the effort. We'd have to move the whole Earth to do that. We are the slaves of the new century.'

A study by the national statistics agency in 2007 found that the jobless rate was twice as high among immigrants as among non-immigrants. Jobs that are available tend to be at the bottom of the pile—70 per cent of employees of cleaning companies in the Paris region were immigrants. Unemployment among qualified and skilled immigrants from Africa was even higher than the average, their foreign degrees not recognized and the way ahead sometimes barred by discrimination; jobs for similar people from Portugal, Spain and Italy tend to be on par with the French. As Chirac said in a television address during the urban riots in 2005, 'We are all aware of discrimination. How many CVs are thrown in the wastepaper basket just because of the name or the address of the applicant?' A 2010 study found that 'Muslims sending out resumes in hopes of a job interview had 2.5 times less chance than Christians' with similar credentials. In this context in the land of enlightenment, liberty, equality and fraternity, there is only one winner.

8

SPECTRE AT THE FEAST

Jacques Chirac was in the 'red carpet' office in the Élysée when aides brought him the first news. He had been forewarned by his wife, who was close to the grassroots as a local councillor in the Corrèze. Now it was his chief of staff, Dominique de Villepin, who came with early signs from ten constituencies that were thought to provide a good indication of the outcome of the voting in the first round of the presidential election of 2002. A few moments later, another member of the staff entered the room with confirmatory evidence.

The head of state refused to believe what they told him and instructed them to leave while he discussed with leaders of his government their television appearances that night. The conversation became ragged as they all thought about what they had been told. 'I sensed that they were bewildered, stupefied,' Chirac recalled. 'While forcing myself to appear imperturbable, I had, in fact, just as much trouble in concentrating on the subjects we were discussing. As the minutes passed, the atmosphere became strange and as if we were insisting on talking about a situation which had already been overtaken in order to shut out what seemed to us more and more probable. The shock was rough for me as for most of us.'

When the television news programmes put up the faces of the two front runners in the voting at 8 p.m. that night, the shock spread across France. Beside the head of the incumbent President was that of Jean-Marie Le Pen, who scored 16.8 per cent of the vote to the

Socialist Lionel Jospin's 16.1 (and the President's 19.8). Chirac recalled that he felt 'sad, first of all for France, for what it was and what it stood for.'

It was the moment the leader of the National Front (FN) had been waiting for ever since he launched his career on the extreme right as a National Assembly deputy for Paris in 1957. His success was facilitated by the lacklustre, complacent Socialist campaign and the fragmentation of the left-wing vote among half a dozen candidates. Nor was Chirac exactly the people's choice, since he did not expand his support beyond his usual 20 per cent base. Though he was assured of re-election, he recalled, 'I did not have the heart to rejoice at that. In my view, it was not only the Socialist candidate who had just been sanctioned, but the whole political class.'

The fact that the outcome of the first round was such an 'électro-choc' as the French call it, was, in itself, confirmation of how out of touch that class had become. Having taken the pulse of the electorate in the preceding weeks, I forecast in a press article that Le Pen might finish second, with votes from the discontented populist left as well as well as the muscular right. Editors at the newspaper for which I wrote that piece asked me if I could be serious, and French political journalists dismissed such notions as typical scaremongering by a foreign observer.

But, for me, the result that spring day was the culmination of a long process which showed all too clearly the divide between the establishment and the grassroots in a country where the long-standing habit of grousing had mutated into readiness to vote in large numbers—4.8 million to Chirac's 5.6 million—for the country's leading snake oil salesman, a politician who would have felt at home in Dixie and with unmatched skill at touching the darker parts of the national soul. Yes, this was the first round and so not binding (except to those like Jospin who were eliminated). Yes, Le Pen's vote increased by only 700,000 in the run-off two weeks later, whereas the incumbent gained twenty million adherents. Yes, Chirac sought to delegitimize his opponent by refusing the debate with him. Yes, Le Pen united all the correct-thinking French against him as hundreds of thousands turned out in hostile demonstrations. Yes, left-wingers went to the second round poll to vote for Chirac with clothes pegs on their noses declaring, 'Vote for the crook, not the Fascist.'

But something basic had changed as a new dynamic started to unroll. Ten years on, Le Pen's daughter, now leading the FN, forecast confidently at a gathering of the Front faithful in the summer of 2013 that the movement would win power within ten years. 'My obsession,' she added, 'is to make sure that the FN is ready.' This may be dismissed as a politician's bravado, but the boast had an uncomfortable ring to it. So sure was Marine Le Pen of herself that she rejected suggestions of accepting support from wavering members of the mainstream right, calling then 'corpses' and bracketing them with the Socialists under the dismissive tag of the 'UMPS.'

The course she set herself was to win the Élysée on her own at the head of a party which had its own policies across the board and could no longer be dismissed as a passing protest movement. If elected, she vowed in her speech to the meeting in Marseilles, she would be tough 'with self-proclaimed minorities which want to wreck the republican order,' 'with those who defraud the social security system,' 'with speculators who want to enrich themselves on the backs of the workers and enterprises,' 'with fanatics who want to impose their laws in the public space,' 'with all those who do not play the game,' 'all so that the will of the people is finally heard and respected.'

By then, the FN scared the establishment to a degree of which Jean-Marie could only have dreamed. With 6.4 million votes and 17.9 per cent of the poll in the 2012 presidential battle, the daughter outdid her father. The next year, she topped Hollande in some surveys. The Front's victory in a local election in October 2013 for a single cantonal seat in the southern French town of Brignoles (population: 17,000) was headline news, especially since the previous occupant had been a Communist, confirming how it was attracting votes from the left. Television stations sent teams to analyze what was happening and follow the Front candidate canvassing elsewhere.

The movement racked up a series of by-election performances in which it eliminated the Socialist candidates, even if it could not beat the mainstream right at the run-off ballot. It had become the main party for industrial workers and was expanding its support in rural areas. It was as if the 2002 result was proving to be a rehearsal for a chapter in French history that would make real the greatest fear of the political establishment.

After the Liberation, that fear had been concentrated on the Communist Party, whose candidate in the 1969 presidential poll had presaged the NF leader by describing his opponents as '*bonnet blanc, blanc bonnet*,' depicting no difference between the Gaullist Georges Pompidou and the centrist Alain Poher, just as Marine Le Pen would bundle Hollande, Sarkozy and all the other mainstream politicians into the same bag forty-five years later. But, as we have seen, the Communist political machine party imploded in the 1980s and dwindled to electoral insignificance. Now the menace came from the far right with a set of complaints that sprang from the way France had evolved under Mitterrand, Chirac, Sarkozy and Hollande. A party which had always seen itself as being outside the orthodox confines of French politics and which had been written off many times was suddenly at the centre of the nation's concerns.

The fear of those who had run the country for so long was that it would march on not as a simple protest movement whose fortunes would surely ebb, but as a durable element in the landscape of France, adapting its message to appear more reasonable, less thuggish, almost reassuring as it told ordinary people that somebody was listening to their worries about living standards, unemployment, law and order, Islam, immigration—and, free from the shackles of political correctness, said it would do something about it.

No matter that its solutions, when it advanced them, often made little sense or were so extreme as to be impracticable. No matter that its attacks on welfare reforms and Europe and its defence of the big state could have come from the hard left. Marine Le Pen had given the movement what the French call '*un relookage*,' complete with the recruitment of three Énarques to her team, and the combination of this sleek, rejuvenated image with the underlying message of fear of change put a wind in its sails which other parties could only envy. The main state television station ran a report after the Brignoles result showing a pert young woman, daughter of a former Socialist; she was running for the Front in a local election in the Paris suburbs and sounded the model of moderation. Her canvassing party consisted of equally unthreatening, fluent young people; one was an Arab. The winner in Brignoles, a well-mannered young man, had the family name of Lopez. A survey reported that 55 per cent of students say they would consider voting for the Front. Ms. Le Pen says she is in 'no hurry.' She reckons that time is on her side and adds with a smile that she will be in the Élysée in ten years.

As preceding chapters have shown, France has undergone a great mutation that has removed the bulwarks of traditional life for many people. For all its superficiality, implausibility, contradictions and knee-jerk reactions, the Front may seem to them to offer a safe haven for their fears. It may not be ready to be a party of government, but that is beside the point; it is getting to parts of the French pysche other parties do not.

This would have seemed a strange prospect when the Front, after its foundation by Jean-Marie Le Pen in the early 1970s, was able to win no more than 1 per cent of the national legislative vote. It has followed a long, testing road since then, but the roots of the success of the old man in 2002 and of his daughter ten years later lie uncomfortably deep, and one needs to go back to see how it evolved. For example, take a mass meeting held seven years before the shock of April 2002, which Jacques Chirac and Lionel Jospin would have done well to attend incognito.

The lights go out. The recording of Verdi's 'Chorus of the Slaves' rises to a deafening pitch. Two thousand people jump up on the rows of red plastic chairs set across the exhibition hall, craning their necks to catch a sight of the conquering hero. Outside the big utilitarian building, they had been a collection of individual groups—farmers slapping one another on the back, shopkeepers joshing with their customers, a white-haired priest darting through the throng to pay his respects to an elderly woman in pearls. The smell of grilling meat and sizzling chips was heavy in the spring air. Men drank beer from the bottle and chewed spicy merguez sausages stuffed inside chunks of bread; some bought their companions *cuvée spéciale champagne* at ten francs per plastic goblet. Once inside the hall, having paid a forty-franc entrance fee, they milled around, picked their seats, waved to acquaintances and chatted through the warm-up speeches. Stalls were selling reprints of newspaper front pages detailing great colonial humiliations—Indochina, the Suez expedition, Algeria—as if the organizers wanted to remind the audience of what France had lost. A small bar of soap with an evocative label lay on each chair.

As the star of the evening bursts through the back door of the hall, the individuals become a single, cheering mass. Surrounded by television cameras, Jean-Marie Le Pen marches towards the platform. The cheering drowns the Verdi choir. Placards bob in the air—'*Vas-y Jean-Marie*,' and one held aloft by a touchingly solitary young woman, '*Jean-Marie, our only friend*.' The priest stands in front of his chair, his eyes staring straight ahead. The elderly lady beside him holds her hands to her mouth, like a reincarnation of a bobby-soxer seeing Frank Sinatra for the first time. In a side aisle, three young men with shaved skulls punch one another playfully on the shoulder. As the leader reaches the platform, the roar from the hall grows even louder. Plump and sleek in a dark blue double-breasted suit, his one good eye glistening in the spotlight, his chest stuck out like a pigeon, the boss of France's National Front punches the air with both fists and waits for the din to subside. Then he tells a story.

He had arrived late that evening in Toulouse, and he apologizes for keeping the good people of the southwest waiting. But it had not been his fault. On the way down from Paris the good French pilot had told him why the Airbus—made in the great city of Toulouse— was running behind schedule. It was all because control of French skies was now based—guess where? The crowd didn't have the faintest idea. So their friend Jean-Marie told them: French air-space was controlled from Maastricht. That's right, Maastricht—the Dutch town where European governments signed a treaty to promote greater unity, much to the Front's horror. Drawing out the long first double vowel with a grimace, he snarls the final 'icht.' And what had happened when the air control centre at Maastricht had been given authority over the skies above our country? Why, the French air traffic controllers who worked there had been sacked. Their places had been taken by the Dutch, the Germans and the British who were delaying French aircraft on purpose in order to give their own national lines an unfair advantage. This was why Jean-Marie Le Pen's Airbus had been delayed on its way down to Toulouse that April evening.

Before the crowd can quite digest this revelation, the man who speaks for all that is irrational, extremist and xenophobic in the nation of liberty, equality and fraternity is off and running. If the national madeleines are crumbling around them, the man on the platform tells his audience why. For two hours, he paces from side to side of the wide stage, pausing occasionally to grin at one of his own jokes, halting to stand to attention when he invokes the memory of those who died to preserve France over the centuries. In a horribly great stand-up act, he plumbs every depth of national insecurity. Immigration and law and order flow like poisoned streams, sometimes apart, sometimes intertwined.

He tells of Arab families living on welfare who bring in their second and third cousins to squat in municipal housing estates: the bailiffs dare not evict them because they would be found later with their severed heads tucked under their arms. Ministries in Paris are trying to create a mongrel nation by making it easier to adopt an African or South American baby than to adopt a French child. And, as always, the mantra: three million immigrants sent home—three million jobs for the French—the social security system saved—public order restored—pensions safeguarded.

The mood of the crowd swings as violently as the orator's language: these farmers and townspeople are alternately moved to indignation at the perils facing them and to elation at Le Pen's evocation of France's greatness. 'France is beautiful!' he cries. 'Let us show ourselves worthy of her. Defend her! Rebuild her!' Joan of Arc and the heroic defence of Verdun crop up in every Le Pen speech; so do the traitors and enemies conspiring to bring the nation to its knees. After four decades in politics, his persona is set in rancid aspic—but he still aspires to be the great patriotic leader who will tear down the temple in order to rebuild it. He is waiting for the ultimate big bang which will open the gates of power.

The next morning, his audience would wake up in a more humdrum world. They would not go out on an anti-Arab pogrom or be mugged by drug-smoking children of immigrants when they travel home from work in Montauban, Albi or Castres. But they might read in their morning newspaper that the photofit of a serial killer in the Bastille area of Paris is of a 'North African type,' and, as they cast their minds back to the previous night, they could recall the clues offered by the portly man in the double-breasted suit as to why they felt a lot less happy than they should about being French in a rapidly changing age.

Every country has its dark side. It is, however, difficult to imagine a politician in another major Western democracy spouting quite the same degree of wild hogwash as Jean-Marie Le Pen and surviving as a significant national figure for more than a decade. At the turn of the century, 70 per cent of those polled recognized him as a danger to democracy, but approval for his ideas jumped by 50 per cent in just two years to 28 per cent of those questioned, and that backing rose to one-third when it came to immigration and law and order.

While Marine Le Pen remains true to her father's basic tenets, her repackaging of the Front as a less overtly menacing movement that addresses people's everyday concerns is clearly working—she threatens legal action against anybody who calls it 'extreme right.' Appeals to 'Republic solidarity,' in which the orthodox right and left would unite as a matter of principle against the FN, carry diminishing weight, especially after the statement by the former UMP Prime Minister François Fillon in 2013 that conservative voters faced with a choice between a left-winger and a Front candidate should simply chose the one they thought best.

The mainstream still finds it extremely difficult to confront the Front on its own grounds. After it won control of three big towns in municipal elections in 1995, and a former member had been installed as mayor of the nation's fifth-biggest city, the political editor of Le Monde declared that the party only prospered in conditions of backstairs intrigues and was rejected whenever the full light of day was shone upon it. Others played with words. For years, many French commentators preferred to call the Front a movement rather than grace it with recognition as a political party. Some of its opponents simply counted the days until Le Pen quit the scene, believing that the Front would wither after he went. His daughter has shown just how short-sighted a view that was and how demeaning towards people who are far from fascist but say, as one elderly man did at Brignoles, 'There is nobody else left to vote for.'

Successful as Marine has been in broadening her party's appeal, there would have been no Front without her father. Throughout his long career, Jean-Marie Le Pen was incorrigible and undaunted, the eternal bad boy who did not give a damn what anybody thinks. When he set off a storm by declaring that he believed the races are unequal, he quickly added that he was only saying in public what most French people thought in private. When he inveighed against the corruption and self-interest of the political class, he tilled fertile soil after the tide of scandals in high places under Mitterrand. The slogan on the wrappers on the bars of soap placed on each chair at his presidential rallies in 1995 went straight to the point: 'Head up high and hands clean: Le Pen, the great washer.' No matter that most of his personal fortune was inherited from an eccentric alcoholic and psychiatric patient who died of liver failure at the age of forty-two. Or that members of the Front ran into trouble over election financing in southern constituencies.

His position was strengthened by the evident appeal that part of the Front's rhetoric had for some orthodox conservatives, especially when they faced a strong electoral challenge from extremists. A conservative deputy from a southern constituency where Le Pen won a third of the vote in 1995 proposed banning immigrants from his department. A Gaullist member of parliament from the Paris suburbs called for mayors to be allowed to refuse municipal housing to foreigners. Another spoke of an invasion by 'ten million Muslims.'

The repeated proposals on immigration from governments and parliamentarians, which are clearly designed to meet the grassroots pressure they feel is being whipped up by the Front, have only served to reinforce the party's perceived influence. Sometimes such measures stick; sometimes they are dropped in the face of protests from those who fear France is slipping on to a racist path. During the period of cohabitation between the Socialists and the right in 1993–95, harsh immigration legislation was introduced by the tough Interior Minister, Charles Pasqua. Three years later, a parliamentary committee brought forward an even more draconian set of regulations against immigrants without valid papers, suggesting that they be deprived of health care, that they could be detained for questioning for forty-five days pending deportation, and that people who had put them up should be listed by the police.

The government stepped back from such steps, but the legislators felt they were reflecting what their native-born voters wanted. Alain Juppé's government introduced legislation requiring non-Europeans to hand in a 'departure tab' when they leave France, to ensure that they do not overstay their welcome—a more severe measure requiring their French hosts to report to the authorities when visitors left was abandoned after protests led by artists and intellectuals. One of the early acts of the new Socialist government in 2012 was to commission a report on immigration which, tellingly, left many of the measures introduced by its predecessors in place. Under Hollande, left-wingers accused the tough Interior Minister, Manuel Valls, of seeking to counter the NF with Frontist policies; hence the row within the ruling party over his decision to expel the 'Roms' and the schoolgirl from Kosovo and her family, though both were popular with the public at large.

There is no doubt that public attitudes have shifted, with the Front both propelling the movement and profiting from it. By legitimizing the fear and resentment aroused by dark-skinned youths on street corners or late-night Métro platforms, some of the upstanding members of the National Assembly bestow a fresh lick of respectability on the Front and hand the movement a major argument. Why be satisfied with their half-measures when the real medicine was waiting in its cabinet?

Jean-Marie Le Pen's electoral record had been a switchback of contrasting fortunes. The youngest member of the National Assembly when elected for a Paris constituency at the age of twenty-eight in 1956, his campaigns were marked by bare-knuckle politics from the start. Controversy always surrounded him—had he been a party to the use of torture in Algeria? Had he lost his left eye as he said, when he was beaten by opponents in a 1958 electoral battle, or had it been the other eye and the result of illness? How had he inherited his luxurious home outside Paris? In the 1960s, he headed a record company with an eclectic catalogue that included both Communist union songs and Nazi marches. In 1965, he organized the campaign of the far-right presidential candidate, Jean-Louis Tixier-Vignancourt, who wanted to rehabilitate wartime collaborationists—was de Gaulle braver than Marshal Pétain, Le Pen asked, adding a typical pungent phrase aimed at his gallery, 'It was much easier to resist in London than to resist in France.'

Tixier got 5.2 per cent on the first round, which was a big achievement compared with Le Pen's score at his first presidential outing in 1974, when he got 0.74 of the vote. Seven years later he could not obtain even the five hundred signatures of elected officials needed to run. Interviewing him shortly after that, I asked him if he envisaged any circumstances in which he might stage a political comeback. Sipping Chivas Regal Scotch in the salon of his villa in Saint-Cloud, known as the 'ocean liner,' he painted a scenario.

Imagine, he said as he stroked his chin with his index finger, a fight between a group of Frenchmen and Algerian immigrants in which 'one of our compatriots' was killed. Algerian immigrants stage a protest march down the Champs-Élysées. Things get out of hand. Shop windows are broken, stores looted and policemen injured. That, said Le Pen, would give him the fuel he needed for electoral ascent, even to as much as 10 per cent of the vote. He grinned, downed his whisky and left for a fundraising dinner after saying goodbye to his first wife, who later sought to embarrass him by posing semi-nude for *Playboy* in a skimpy maid's pinafore. Perhaps not surprisingly given his electoral fortunes at the time, the British newspaper for which I wrote up the interview spiked it on the grounds that Le Pen was a never-had-been who was not worth reporting on.

As it turned out, confrontations between police and immigrants took a more dramatic turn, as we have seen, even if they were not on the most famous avenue in France. The rising tension brought the Front growing support shown in European elections in the mid-1980s. Then Mitterrand introduced proportional representation for legislative elections in 1986; that helped the Front, which found it easier to get deputies elected under the new system, taking National Assembly seats away from the mainstream right as the wily President had intended. In all, thirty-four FN members sat in parliament, though they disappeared when the electoral system was changed back to the orthodox two-round winner takes all. But the FN made gains at the regional level, and Le Pen won a seat in the European Parliament in 1984 and marked his revival by taking 15 per cent, or 4.5 million votes, in the presidential race of 1996, opening the way for the shock of 2002.

By then the Front's organizers had established a wide-ranging party machine with groups to cater for young people, women, pensioners, ex-servicemen and farmers. There was a Front union for prison officers and, in professional elections in the Paris police, it took 13 per cent of the vote: in six police units charged with pre-serving order in the capital, its score shot up to 48 per cent. There were well-attended summer teach-ins, an annual march in central Paris on Joan of Arc Day and a 'Blue, White and Red' festival on the outskirts of Paris each year; at one at the turn of the century an effigy of Chirac was put up as a target in the shooting gallery.

But there were setbacks ahead. The 2002 result led to the gov-ernment introducing a new electoral system that halved the number of Front councillors in France's regions and weakened it in the European Parliament. The party ran into financial problems—Le Pen sold his headquarters in Saint-Cloud and his personal armour-plated car. Le Pen's score fell to 11 per cent in the next presidential race while his movement won no seats in the legislative election that year with only 4 per cent of the vote. He split with his principal lieutenant, Bruno Mégret, an intense ideologue who had grown tired of the old man. Above all, Jean-Marie was approaching his eightieth birthday. In September 2008, Le Pen announced that he would retire two years later.

Mégret thought he was the dauphin, but his worsening relations with the leader ruled him out, and he went off to found his own splinter movement. That left two people in the contest to head what had been largely a one-man band for all its existence. One was Bruno Gollnisch, the party's Executive Vice President, the other, Marine Le Pen, who had scored the FN's best performance in the 2007 legis-lative elections by getting to the second round in a constituency in northern France. The father backed his daughter against a backdrop of improved election results as the Front took almost 12 per cent of the vote at local elections in 2010. In January 2011, Marine took two-thirds of the vote in a party primary to win the leadership.

She set to work to modernize the Front's image (like Hollande, she lives outside marriage with her partner, who is a Front party official, as were her two ex-husbands). A vital attribute was that she was not her bully boy, out-of-date father. Her reward was rising opinion poll support and a 15 per cent vote in cantonal elections and going on to her 17.9 per cent score in the first round of the 2012 presidential poll, the FN's best-ever result to that date. In the ensuing legislative election, the party won two National Assembly seats in southern France, one taken by Marion Maréchal-Le Pen, Jean-Marie's granddaughter, who became the youngest ever French deputy at the age of twenty-two. Marine lost the race in her constituency in the Pas-de-Calais by just a hundred votes.

The presidential voting showed how widespread support for the Front had become geographically and how it had won backing in traditional industrial regions while retaining its appeal in southern areas. The highest regional score was in the northern rustbelt of Picardy, where it took 25 per cent, and its biggest departmental success was in the Vaucluse in the south with 27 per cent. Marine Le Pen took more than a fifth of the vote in ten other regions, including Corsica, Champagne-Ardennes, Provence-Alpes-Côte d'Azur, Lorraine, Languedoc-Roussillon and Nord-Pas-de-Calais. In municipal elections in 2014, the Front took control of eleven towns, including Béziers and Fréjus in its old stamping ground in the south, but also one in a depressed mining area of the north which would once have belonged to the left. It scored well in Avignon and Perpignan without winning a majority, and had clearly become a national political fixture.

A lawyer by training who has been on the hustings with her father since her early teens, Le Pen has policies on every subject under the sun and shows considerable dexterity in switching from energy to agriculture, from bimetallism to the need to recover the 'geo-political independence' her country enjoyed under de Gaulle. She has widened the agenda to economic and social issues as well as her father's hobbyhorses of immigration, law and order and strident nationalism, which she prefers to call simple patriotism in the line of Joan of Arc, whose birthday the Front celebrates with a procession in central Paris each year. Under her leadership, the Front is trying to establish links with teachers, lawyers, business people, economists, the military—and even Freemasons, whom her father regarded as a sinister force plotting against the nation.

Making the most of the disillusion with the EU reflected in polls in 2013 and with concern about the rise of Germany and its 'headmistress' Chancellor, Le Pen warns against Berlin dominating Europe, and wants closer relations with Russia—she says she admires Vladimir Putin and was given a red carpet welcome when she visited Moscow, St Petersburg and the Crimea in 2013. Her attempts to forge links with right-wing politicians in Israel has had little success—hardly surprising given her backing for the Assad regime in Syria and her father's dismissal of Nazi concentration camps as a 'detail' of history. A trip to the United States produced few dividends beyond a meeting with Ron Paul and hard-line conservative Congressman Joe Walsh—Israel described a meeting with its United Nations representative, at which she was photographed sporting her best smile for the cameras while the diplomat appeared more reserved, as 'a misunderstanding.'

However, closer to home she has forged an alliance with the far right PVV party in the Netherlands and said she hoped for associations with other like-minded groups across the continent. 'The day when patriotic movements were divided sometimes for fear of being demonised is long gone. A new era has begun,' she said as she smiled at the cameras in The Hague with the PVV's leader Geert Wilders in November 2013. 'Our old European nations are being forced to ask the authorisation of Brussels in all circumstances, forced to submit their budgets to the headmistress . . . forced to stick to a currency that has shown its ineffectiveness. . . . We want to give freedom back to our people.'

She embraces the tradition of French protectionism with her denunciation of the imposition of 'the destructive principles of ultra-liberalism and Free trade, at the expense of public utilities, employment, social equity and even our economic growth.' Reacting to criticism from the French employers' federation, she defined her beliefs as 'the construction of a strong, protective and strategist state, reasoned protections at the boundaries, support for small and medium enterprises, and recovering monetary sovereignty to assure France's recovery.'

The Front remains populist, nationalistic and authoritarian—and short of money. Its annual budget is only some eight million euros, and it has always depended on contributions from members and a few rich benefactors, but it has run into problems recently with an apparent reluctance of its main bank, the Société Générale, to advance funds as it faces a series of expensive election contests.

For all Marine's efforts to 'de-demonize' her movement and her insistence that it is not extremist, its basic policies which win the votes remain hard-line and based on antagonisms likely to appeal to people fearful of the epoch in which they live—cutting immigration to 5 per cent of its current level and creating a ministry to control this, quitting the eurozone and restoring the franc, a referendum on re-introducing capital punishment and opposition to same-sex marriage. As for the core element in the Front's appeal, she backs a 'French first' policy for jobs, welfare and accommodation. French citizenship, she says, 'should be either inherited or merited,' as she has warned repeatedly of the 'Islamization' of France—comparing the now illegal blocking of streets and squares for Muslim prayers to the wartime occupation of France.

She never lets a hot-button issue pass. In 2012, she seized on a television report that most slaughterhouses in the Paris region were killing animals by the halal method of slitting their throats while they are still alive because it was cheaper than stunning them first and because they wanted to sell meat to Muslims. Butchers, it added, did not tell clients how the animals were being killed. She held this up as evidence of how the country is being crushed by immigrants. 'I have the right as a citizen to know if I'm buying meat where the animal is slaughtered in horrible cruelty, taking sometimes fifteen minutes to die,' Le Pen said. 'This is a moral point. Don't French people who don't want to eat halal have the same rights as Muslims who do?' Sarkozy, facing an uphill re-election fight, promptly called for stricter meat labelling and said serving halal meat in school cafeterias was a contradiction of French secular values. The debate escalated when Prime Minister François Fillon told a radio interviewer that Muslim and Jewish ritual slaughter traditions should be re-examined if they 'do not have much in common with today's state of science or hygiene.' He then had to meet rabbis and Muslim leaders to try to explain away his remark. As her father had done so often in similar cases, Marine could only chuckle with satisfaction.

But her ambition for her movement stretches well beyond the party of protest embodied by her father as she rejects the label of 'extremist.' She has clearly set herself the goal of making the FN the rallying point for those unhappy with the state of France wherever they stand on the political spectrum. The true difference, she says, is not between left and right but between those who stand up for the nation and those who have sold out to globalism. She depicts the mainstream parties as moribund as she promises to create a 'large popular party that addresses itself not only to the electorate on the right but to all the French people.'

Her personality is essential to achieving that objective. Mother of three children from two husbands from whom she separated, the youngest of Jean-Marie's three daughters puts herself across as somebody who has experienced the problems of everyday life in contrast to politicians who live in a cocoon. At the age of eight, she was sleeping during a bomb attack on the family flat in Paris; nobody was hurt. When she was sixteen, her mother left home with another man. She is a fluent performer on television and mistress of the stage at Front meetings. Her voice, roughened by cigarette smoking, is less strident than her father's but still sways audiences. She knows how to make sharp debating points while deploying her femininity to reassure.

All this has enabled her to move the Front into a new dimension and to appeal to younger voters and women. While its anti-immigrant message remains at the heart of its appeal, it is far more than a party sounding racial warnings. It reaches out to all those who feel that they have been left behind by the evolution of France—industrial workers, small farmers, shopkeepers, the unemployed—and who are out of tune with the way the country appears to live now. It plumbs the concern about law and order and the decline in values. It caters for all those who see the mainstream politicians of left and right as having failed, or, even worse, as being incompetent, self-serving and corrupt. But, at the same time, Ms. Le Pen has sought to move the party upmarket, with a youngish Énarque as her deputy and neatly suited candidates to burnish the Front's image.

The more the establishment attacks her, the more she can claim to be the only politician who dares to speak the uncomfortable truth. It is a potent mix in a country with generally low tolerance level for successive governments. Hence the alarm generated in the fall of 2013 by a Front victory in a single local election in one of its southern strongholds; national politicians could all too easily see an expanding pool of NF voters which would challenge the establishment in ways it had found impossible to check ever since 2002.

* * *

Marine Le Pen's re-orientation of the Front has included softening her father's stance on the Holocaust. Most notorious was his statement that 'I'm not saying the gas chambers didn't exist. I haven't seen them myself. I haven't particularly studied the question. But I believe it's just a detail in the history of World War Two.' At a press conference in Germany, he then stated, 'If you take a thousand-page book on World War Two, the concentration camps take up only two pages and the gas chambers ten to fifteen lines. This is what one calls a detail.' A court in Munich found him guilty of 'minimizing the Holocaust' and handed down a fine. Jean-Marie denies being anti-Semitic, but he treads a fine line. At an election rally in Corsica in the 1980s, I heard him denouncing Simone Veil, a concentration camp survivor who was then a leading minister. Wasn't it unfair, he mused as he strolled the stage, that he came in for criticism every time he attacked her. 'If I'm not allowed to criticise her because she's a woman [pause], or because she's [another pause] ugly, or because she's [after a longer and more pregnant pause] a Jew, where's our freedom of speech?' he asked in mock indignation. The audience laughed and clapped.

In a truly awful pun in a later interview, he elided the last syllable of the name of a Jewish minister, Michel Durafour, which means 'oven' in French, with the word for a crematorium. On another occasion, he observed of Simone Veil that 'when I speak of genocide, I always say that, in any case, they missed old woman Veil.' Beside such remarks, he seemed almost benign when he dubbed a leading television interviewer who is married to Dominique Strauss-Kahn 'a kosher butcher.'

Under the elder Le Pen, the Front adopted a declared neo-Nazi as an election candidate. One of its representatives in the European Parliament referred to the 'invented' Holocaust. One of its prominent members in southern France wore a swastika necklace and liked to sing Third Reich anthems. After one of Le Pen's long-standing companions-in-arms became mayor of the port city of Toulon, the authorities threatened to shut down the synagogue because its fire extinguishers were held to be below safety standards and tried to stop Jewish students attending a Holocaust anniversary ceremony. A Jewish boy was suspended from a Toulon school for having punched another boy who praised the gas chambers, and a bookshop opened in the city centre specializing in works commemorating Nazi Germany.

Another National Front Mayor evoked an unfortunate historical echo
when she told an interviewer from across the Rhine 'You're German,
so you must understand us.' Le Pen himself noted that 'big international groups, such as the Jewish International, play a not-negligible
role in creating an anti-national spirit.' It all draws on a wellspring
stretching back more than a century.

France was home to one of the most notorious outbreaks of
anti-Semitism in the Dreyfus Affair that erupted at the end of the
nineteenth century and had been preceded by virulent attacks on Jews
by the journalist Edmond Drumont after the collapse of a fraudulent
scheme to build a Panama Canal in which two of the associates
were Jewish. The record of the way in which the French authorities
collaborated with the Germans to persecute and deport Jews during
World War Two remained veiled for decades after the Liberation. De
Gaulle kept it under the carpet in the interest of postwar national
unity. Simone Veil recalls how wounded she was by the way in which
nobody wanted to know what had happened to those like her who
survived the concentration camps and returned to France in 1945:
'Resistance fighters who came back from imprisonment in Germany
were, quite legitimately, honoured, while Jewish deportees had the
feeling of being rejected, that their return bothered people.'

In the immediate postwar years, mention of anti-Semitism was
virtually taboo—the historian Léon Poliakov had to wait until 1951
before publishing the first of his seminal works on the subject. Police
archives were among official papers that were sealed for sixty years.
The state television service sat for years on a groundbreaking documentary, *Le Chagrin et la Pitié*, that showed the extent of collaboration,
and it took an American historian, Robert Paxton, to reveal how
the Vichy collaborationist regime had done the Nazis' job for them.
France, it was said, had 'the right to forget.'

De Gaulle had ensured that it emerged on the winning side,
so how could it be guilty of complicity in war crimes? Having
been among the 569 deputies who voted power to Marshal Pétain
in 1940 (with only eighty voting against) did not stop René Coty
from becoming President of the Fourth Republic in 1954. Successive
presidents sent wreaths to the Marshal's tomb on the anniversary of

his death, as though his leadership in the First World War blotted out his record as head of the Vichy collaborationist administration. François Mitterrand, who had himself worked for Vichy, long maintained a friendship with a wartime police chief, René Bousquet, who had overseen the 1942 round-up in Paris that sent thousands of Jews to their deaths.

Mitterrand insisted half a century later that the state bore no responsibility for what happened to the Jews in France during the war. 'If the French nation had been involved in the unfortunate Vichy undertaking, then an apology would be due,' he said. 'But the French nation was never involved in that matter; nor was the French Republic.' He was among those who sent a wreath to Petain's grave. It was not until 1995 that Chirac acknowledged the French role in deporting tens of thousands of Jews to concentration camps.

Despite all the evidence, France has a tiny but active school of Holocaust deniers known as 'negationists.' In 1964, historian Paul Rassinier, who had himself been held in Buchenwald concentration camp for having helped French Jews escape, published a book that posited a Zionist-Allied-Soviet conspiracy to fake the Holocaust. Robert Faurisson, a literature professor at Lyons University, then wrote articles and letters to newspapers claiming that the gas chambers did not exist and became the leading negationist. 'Hitler never ordered nor permitted that anyone be killed by reason of his race or religion,' he wrote; one of his books was entitled *The Diary of Anne Frank—A Forgery*.

After legislation was introduced in 1990 against Holocaust denial, Faurisson was fined and dismissed from his post—President Mahmoud Ahmadinejad of Iran presented him with an award for 'courage' in 2012 after he had been handed new fines and had paraded his view on Iranian television and at a conference there. A magazine editor was fined 30,000 francs for publishing articles denying that the only concentration camp on French territory, at Struthof in Alsace, was used to kill Jews. Putting aside such people, what was still striking as late as the 1990s, given the tragedy that gripped the nation between 1940 and 1944, is the proportions which more innocent insensitivity can reach.

It took a storm of last-minute protests to get France's synchronized swimming team to drop a water ballet based on the concentration camps from its programme for the Atlanta Olympics. In 1996, a physics teacher in a town outside Paris gave her teenage pupils a test to calculate the volume of carbon gas required to kill Jews in a death chamber: when a scandal broke, she said she was trying to show the children the evils of the Holocaust. The following year, a maths teacher in Normandy set a problem involving counting the number of people killed in the Dachau concentration camp. At around the same time, it emerged that millions of dollars' worth of jewels, gold, stocks, bonds and cash confiscated from Jews during the war had ended up in a state-run financial institution. The newspaper *Libération* found that banks had still been selling plundered Jewish stocks two weeks after the Allied invasion of 1944. *Le Monde* reported that French banks had held on to the contents of Jewish accounts which had been blocked on Nazi orders, while nearly two thousand works of art stolen from Jews during the Second World War were still housed in national museums, most of them in the Louvre.

When the leading French historian of the Holocaust, Serge Klarsfeld, calculated that some 80,000 Jews had been deported from France, he was met with a mixture of indignation and disbelief. The feeling was that the French could not have participated in such an atrocity, and, if it turned out that they had, the less said the better. So Klarsfeld produced the names and birthplaces of 75,721 of the dead.

In the northern Paris suburb of Drancy, a drab housing estate was used as the main transit camp to which Jews were taken before being sent to their deaths in Eastern Europe. There were twenty water taps for up to 5,000 inmates. Many slept on the concrete floors. Meals sometimes consisted of bowls of warm water, with a daily ration of two lumps of sugar. The deportations started in March 1942 and speeded up to three convoys a week that summer. On arrival at the camp, mothers and children were forcibly separated. Some of the mothers went mad with despair, and some threw themselves to their deaths from the tops of buildings. A witness told of seeing one convoy which consisted entirely of children.

The memorial plaque commemorates those 'of Jewish religion or descendence, who were interned by the Hitlerian occupiers, then deported to Nazi extermination camps where the immense majority met their deaths.' There is a nagging problem in those words 'interned by the Hitlerian occupiers.' True, Drancy came under the overall command of the SS officer who supervised all Jewish affairs in France. But for most of its existence as a transit camp for Auschwitz, only a few of its staff were German. The day-by-day running of the camp was the responsibility of the Paris police, following a decree signed by the head of state of occupied France. French officers framed the rules governing the camp. For two years, all the guards were French. The files for the 2,000 children who passed through the camp were drawn up by French bureaucrats. Even after SS men moved in at Drancy during the summer of 1943, many local police remained. French gendarmes loaded Jews into the wagons on the 'sheep platform' at the nearby station. The French remained responsible for them until the trains crossed the frontier in the East, and the guards showed no compunction for those who passed through their hands.

In 2006, a court found the state SNCF railway company guilty of colluding in the deportation of Jews and ordered it to pay compensation in two test cases of victims who passed through Drancy. The judges ruled that the SNCF never voiced any objection to the transports in cattle trucks each containing around fifty people with no sanitation, a single air vent and water provided only once on the journey of more than thirty hours. The railway charged third-class fares.

Or consider the case of a woman known to history as 'Mlle B.,' who arrived at Drancy on June 20, 1944. She was twenty-two years old. The French police told her to bring her valuables with her when they arrested her. On arrival, the camp staff noted her possessions in their ledger—three gold bracelets, diamond rings, a strand of pearls, two watches, two diamond brooches, stock certificates, bonds, cash and a collection of seventy-five English books. Mlle B. died in Birkenau concentration camp on January 27, 1945. By then, her jewels had been stolen by the French staff at Drancy, and her stocks and bonds had been lodged with the French state in the official Caisse des Dépôts et Consignations.

Such matters were not mentioned in official memorials even half a century later. How could they be? The mythology of the Liberation needed to believe that, with a few wild exceptions, the French people had been anti-German during the Occupation. To say anything else until fairly recently was close to treason.

Symbolic of the ambivalence of the past half century towards this substantial period of history were the stories of the only two Frenchmen to have been convicted of crimes against humanity for their wartime activities. Brought up in an extreme right-wing Catholic family, where it was taken for granted that twentieth-century Jews bore the responsibility for the death of Christ, Paul Touvier became head of the wartime collaborationist militia, the Milice, in Lyon. He may have been primarily a legman for Klaus Barbie, the Gestapo chief in the region, but he also undertook some freelance activities— kidnapping and killing an elderly Jewish couple; flinging grenades at Jews as they left a synagogue; murdering seven Jews on Nazi orders in retaliation for the Resistance's killing of a Vichy official (the eighth of his captives was allowed to escape because he was gentile).

So far, so bad. But the Touvier story becomes more than the story of an evil man making the most of his wartime opportunities because of what happened to him after the Nazis were driven from France. Summary execution as the Allied tanks rolled into Lyon? Arrest, trial and sentencing? None of it. By the time Touvier was sentenced to death in absentia, he had disappeared into the inner sanctums of a Catholic order which hid him from his pursuers. In 1947, Touvier ventured out and was arrested—for armed robbery. He escaped before being tried and went back into his high church refuge. Twenty years later the statute of limitations expired, and Touvier was able to move about more easily, portrayed by his supporters as an old man who deserved charity.

In 1971, President Pompidou granted him a pardon, declaring that 'the time has come to throw a veil over the period when the French people were caught up in hatred, civil strife and even murder.' As more evidence surfaced of Touvier's crimes, he fled back to his Catholic friends, but, in 1989, he was finally arrested at a Benedictine priory in the southeast, echoing Edith Piaf to tell the police, *'Je ne regrette rien.'* He was duly sentenced and died in a Paris prison in 1996, after going through a civil wedding to a woman he had married in church while in hiding half a century earlier. A Gaullist member of parliament raised eyebrows by attending his funeral.

The trial of Touvier was the trial of the Milice; of the Frenchmen who had actively co-operated in the attempt to liquidate democracy, Gaullists and Jews forever. The trial of Barbie, in 1987, had been the trial of the Nazi occupiers. Ten years later, after interminable delays, the third aspect of the Occupation years finally came to court, and it raised questions which reached beyond those evoked by Touvier or Barbie.

From 1942 to 1944, Maurice Papon had been a senior civil servant at the regional prefecture in Bordeaux. Visiting the city after the Liberation, de Gaulle decided that, for the sake of keeping the French state functioning, he had to overlook the wartime record of such men. Later Papon became chief of the Paris police under de Gaulle, at a time when they killed scores of Algerians in the capital, and then a Cabinet minister under Giscard d'Estaing. For six months through the winter and spring of 1997–98, at the age of eighty-seven, he sat behind a protective screen in a courtroom in Bordeaux accused of complicity in the deportation to Drancy of more than 1,500 Jews, including 200 children, in his official functions between 1942 and 1944.

As a stream of witnesses, some even older than him, told how relatives had been rounded up and sent to their deaths, Papon remained unrepentant, insisting that he had tried to save Jews and portraying himself as a scapegoat for a nation's guilt. His arrogance was astounding: in the apt description of Robert Graham of the *Financial Times*, he exuded 'the irritation of a self-important man interrupting a weekend in the country to attend an unwelcome business meeting.' Still, his cause was bolstered by the rambling proceedings with 764 separate charges, and by the counterproductive histrionics of a showy young lawyer representing the families of the dead. But, little by little, the truth emerged. Appropriately for the trial of a consummate bureaucrat like Papon, it was often the documents which delivered the most chilling evidence: when a round-up at a hospital ran into problems because one victim was too ill to move, a handwritten annotation on the order simply instructed: 'Must be dragged.'

On April 2, 1998, after deliberating for eighteen hours through the night, the jury found Maurice Papon guilty. The old man in the dock cupped his ear to hear the verdict better and then covered his face with his hands. He looked totally alone: his wife of sixty-six years had died a few days earlier—Papon blamed her death on the prosecution. The sentence was ten years' imprisonment and payment of 4.6 million francs in damages and costs. Jean-Marie Le Pen dismissed the case as an example of 'Judeo-centrism' by which 'history must compulsorily order itself by events which affect the Jewish community.'

Despite all that had been written on the Occupation, an opinion poll at the time reported that 42 per cent of people still regarded Vichy as a period like any other in national history. Not for those who suffered and were sent to their deaths amid widespread indifference.

Take, for instance, the story of Sarah Yalibez. She grew up in the Marais district of Paris, a strange mixture of streets from the Middle Ages, pre-Revolutionary mansions and the place where the Jews from Central Europe settled. For Sarah Yalibez, it was the *pletzl*— the village square. Her parents had arrived there in 1922 from Poland. Her father ran an antiques shop. Twenty years later, under the Occupation, the Marais was classified as Zone 16. Marshal Pétain planned to raze it to the ground and build a new district for his senior bureaucrats. Jews were banned from owning property there. Sarah's father joined the Resistance and was caught in 1944. He was deported to Auschwitz with his three sons. All died there. Two of the sons were teenager twins; they expired in the wing where medical experiments were conducted at the camp.

Sarah was also deported, but survived. And she campaigned for fifty years to get a memorial put up to her father. 'I wrote to Presidents, Prime Ministers, Prefects and all the Mayors of Paris. And I just kept doing it, even though no one replied.' Then, in 1995, she attended a ceremony at the memorial to the Unknown Jewish Martyr in Paris. Jacques Chirac was also there. 'I decided to stare at him,' she recalled. 'He asked what was wrong.' She told him. A couple of months later Chirac became the first President to admit the 'inescapable guilt' of the leaders of Vichy France. More personally, Sarah received an official letter which authorized her to put up a memorial plaque to her father and brothers on her father's old antiques shop in the Marais. It says, 'Here lived Mr. Elias Zajdner, who died for

France at the age of forty-one. A resistance fighter, he was deported to Auschwitz by the Nazis in May 1944 with his three sons, Albert, aged twenty-one, and Salomon and Bernard, aged fifteen, who died in the experiments wing. We shall never forget.'

In the chronicles of the persecution of the Jews in France, no event stirs more shame than the great round-up of 12,884 men, women and children on July 16, 1942, carried out by police under Mitterrand's friend, René Bousquet. Some 4,000 of the children and 3,000 adults were held in stifling summer heat under the glass roof of a Paris cycling stadium, the Vélodrome d'Hiver, generally known as the Vél d'Hiv, which gave the round-up its name for posterity. On that day, a French gentile from western France who was on holiday in Paris happened to go to pay a visit to the parents of a Jewish friend called Jacques at their home in the north of Paris. That night, Roger Galéron wrote in his diary:

'Go to the home of Jacques' parents, 38 rue Arthur-Rozier. Nobody there. Go opposite, 2B passage des Annelets, second floor. Knock at the door for five to ten minutes. No reply. However, I hear the sound of gas. Go up to the third floor. The neighbour questions me, and then takes me into the Schpeisers' place.

'I had realised that they dared not open the door because of the round-ups going on since morning. Plainclothes police inspectors arrive, give the unfortunates half an hour to put together their little bundles of possessions, and then cram them into a bus. Their destination? Forced labour in Germany or a concentration camp.

'I will long remember the little drama that played itself out in front of me. Monsieur and Madame Schpeiser are there, with their daughter Fanny and the two little ones: a boy of nine and a girl of four—both very good-looking. They gave me tea and delicious cakes cooked by Madame Schpeiser. I had trouble eating. Fanny and her mother were crying.

'Five times, there were knocks at the door. Minutes of anxiety. We had to keep quiet. The police? A friend? They checked, looking through the half-closed shutters, when the unknown person left. A stroke of luck in their unhappiness—the neighbour living below is humane and helps them as much as possible. For fear of being caught, they do not dare go outside, even to get milk for the little ones. Can this really be happening in our century and in France, blessed land of free spirits?

'In any case, the reprobation is general, even among a number of anti-Semites. Children of a certain age are separated from their parents. Jacques' sister, Sarah, and her son of eleven were taken this morning. Only Fanny knows. Happily, Jacques is not aware of this drama.

'I leave after embracing them and wishing them the strength to put up with their trials which, it must be hoped, will be halted one day by the victory of reason and humanity. The poor folk are convinced that they are victims of a new inquisition and that the extermination of the Jewish race is being planned. Fanny talks about suicide by gas. Facing this extreme ill fortune, I feel shameful, I who can move about freely and without fear.

'I leave, upset, my heart full of sadness and bitterness. In the street, a new warning (*Bekanntmachung*). Any person who harms the German army will be shot, as well as his brothers, brothers-in-law, cousins etc. (all the male members of the family over seventeen or eighteen years of age). I have to read it twice to believe it.'

There were many instances of French people saving Jews at the risk of their lives. More Jews survived the Occupation than died. Luck could play its part; one concierge might keep quiet while another tipped off the police or the Germans in the hope of stealing the family silver as the Jews were led away. The Deputy Director of France's Institute of International Relations tells how his mother was taken into hiding in a convent in the southwest on the very day that his father, who had been decorated with the military cross in 1940, was arrested by the Germans after having been denounced as a Jew by a Frenchman. A male cousin of the family whom Roger Galéron visited was picked out of the line at Auschwitz because he was carrying his violin, and musicians were needed for a camp orchestra: he died four decades later as a featured soloist in Hawaii.

The tragedy was all the greater because many of the adults who were deported to their deaths had fled pogroms from Central and Eastern Europe in the 1920s and 1930s; some had been specifically encouraged to come west to help make up for France's population losses during and after the First World War. There is no doubt that they aroused the kind of racial prejudice which new immigrants often suffer, with their foreign ways, their difficulty in speaking French and their clannishness born from generations of persecution. But they shared a general feeling of trust in the Republic, and could be reassured by the knowledge that many of their children were French citizens by dint of having been born on French soil. But, in the great 1942 round-up in Paris, it was French police who took thousands of those same children from their parents and sent them off in cattle trucks to die alone in the east. Mitterrand's police chief friend, Bousquet, played a leading role in the organization and was rewarded by the Germans with additional supplies for his force.

Some of those involved in such oppression complained about the job they were given to do, and they may have exercised their duty with less than full rigour. As one eyewitness of the raids in Paris noted of the French police, 'Some did not push it; others kicked down the doors,' A few families were tipped off by friends at police headquarters. But there were only a handful of resignations in the Paris police: at a similar round-up in Lyon, a local commander did refuse to let his forces be used to round up Jews, and was obliged to retire by his French superiors, not by the Nazis. At war crimes trials, Germans noted that the whole of the French police were at their disposal. The occupying forces drew up the plans; as loyal lackeys, the French executed them virtually without question. 'The French police have so far carried out a task worthy of praise,' a German security chief advised his masters one week after the Vél d'Hiv round-up.

Sometimes, indeed, the Pétain administration in Vichy went further than the Germans demanded. Even veterans who had been decorated in the First World War fighting for France were not spared. The French produced a definition of Jewishness which was wider than the one the Nazis proposed, and it was the Vichy Prime Minister, Pierre Laval, who decided that children should be deported with adults. If he could not quite deliver Jews like goods in a shop, he declared, he would do his best.

Tens of thousands of Parisians visited an anti-Jewish exhibition which equalled anything staged in Germany. Frenchmen who signed up with the collaborationist militia, the Milice, swore to fight against Jewish leprosy as well as combating democracy and Gaullist insurrection. Associations of lawyers and doctors purged Jewish members. French people took one hundred francs from the Germans for each

Jew they denounced. Bishops and priests kept their silence when not actively celebrating the values of Vichy. Members of the French SS division 'Charlemagne' were among the last defenders of the Reichstag before the Russians took Berlin.

Though historians have found that bureaucrats who resigned rather than carry out German orders were not punished by the occupiers, many officials preferred to fall under what the historian Marc-Olivier Baruch has dubbed 'the anaesthesia of the conscience of civil servants.' Jewish goods and assets were painstakingly listed. At the Prefecture of Police in Paris, an archive of 600,000 record cards was put together, listing Jews by name, nationality, address and profession. There were censuses of Jewish ex-servicemen, of Jews who owned wireless sets, of Jews with bicycles. In 1942, a Prefect in Normandy forbade Jews to travel more than five kilometres from their home, and the Vichy regime then banned them from leaving their commune of residence. In Bordeaux, the prefecture paid a taxi firm 350 francs to drive two Jewish girls to a railway yard to make sure they did not miss the train to Drancy. Even after the Allied landings in Normandy in 1944, some Prefects were drawing up new lists of Jews in their areas, and one official was planning a ration card which would enable him to keep track of where Jews shopped.

And as a post scriptum to the fate of tens of thousands who were deported to their deaths between 1940 and 1944, there was the simple observation from Sarah Yalibez as she told her story fifty years later: 'I never saw a single German uniform when they took us away.'

Brown and black immigrants are the main target for racism and the far right today, but Jews represent a deeply rooted source of fear and loathing among some French people. 'Better Hitler than Blum' was a motto for the hard right in the 1930s and, after the war, the great Jewish politician Pierre Mendès-France came in for racist abuse as he led decolonization in the 1950s. Going back to the Dreyfus Affair, as Prime Minister, Lionel Jospin tried to put all the anti-Dreyfus blame on the right, and claim that the left was for the wronged man, but the truth is that some prominent Socialists were initially all for condemning the Captain—the great tribune of the left, Jean Jaurès, even thought he should have been executed rather than sent to Devil's Island, while a less illustrious Socialist deputy hailed a fistfight on the matter in the National Assembly as being the beginning of revolution.

The 1998 centenary of the publication of the most famous French headline—'*J'ACCUSE*'—over Émile Zola's article on the Dreyfus Affair showed how alive the issue of anti-Semitism is today. President Chirac declared that it was a reminder that 'forces of darkness, intolerance and injustice can penetrate the highest levels of the state.' Clearly, nearly a century after the rehabilitation of Dreyfus, there is still a question about the rights of the individual as against the *raison d'État* invoked to maintain his condemnation long after the forgeries on which it had been based had been exposed for what they were. But, in this context at least, it is not so much the top of the state that one should be worrying about. Rather, it is the defiling of the statue of Dreyfus in Paris with anti-Semitic slogans, or the way in which a descendant of the family still gets racist digs simply because of her family name.

Some Jews worry about attacks by Arabs who cite the Israeli-Palestinian conflict as a reason for turning to violence. Education Minister Luc Ferry told parliament in 2003 that the Middle East conflict had 'entered our schools,' warning that a new form of anti-Semitism no longer came from the extreme right but was of Islamic origin. 'There is a new, dangerous phenomenon of the Nazification of Israel that justifies hatred of Israel and therefore of the Jews,' warned philosopher Alain Finkielkraut. To which Sarkozy, then the Interior Minister, riposted, 'All those who explain the resurgence of anti-Semitism by the conflict in the Middle East say something that is false. Anti-Semitism existed before the existence of Israel.'

France has the largest Jewish community in Western Europe, totalling some 600,000, but this does not make relationships as easy as they should be. Anti-Semitism still crops up in casual conversation in a way that would be rare in England or America. In the 1970s, my son was once warned by a hotel owner in deepest France that he should not admit to being half-Jewish for fear of what might befall him. A Jewish dentist who has practised in the west of France for many years still does not mention his race for fear of losing patients. In 2013, a comedian introduced a Jewish actor on a popular television show with the words 'You never plunged into [Jewish] communitari-anism . . . You could have posted yourself in the street selling jeans and diamonds from the back of a minivan saying, "Israel is always right, fuck Palestine." You show it is possible to be of the Jewish faith without being completely disgusting.' The presenter's intentions were far from clear but, when the Representative Council of Jewish Institutions protested at a dangerous trivialization of anti-Semitism, the head of the television channel replied that the Jewish community had no sense of humour.

This is a familiar response from those who deny an anti-Semitic intent in their negative treatment of Jews. The best-known exam-ple is a powerfully built stand-up comic called Dieudonné, son of a father from Cameroun and a white French painter. He made his name by performing as an African immigrant who spoke antiquated French and mocked a shorter, agitated friend, appearing in varied roles before becoming notorious for attacking Jews, campaigning for 'anti-Zionism' and calling the Holocaust 'memorial pornography.' He presented the negationist Robert Faurission with an award for being an 'insolent outcast' during his stage show, the medal presented by an assistant dressed in a concentration camp uniform with a yellow badge. Along the way he split with his comic partner, who is Jewish.

Dieudonné stirred outrage when he adopted what was called the 'quenelle' gesture he invented as his signature gesture; consisting of holding his left arm across his chest while pointing his right arm down, it appeared to be an inversion of the Nazi salute, though those who follow the comedian in giving it say it is 'anti-system' rather than anti-Semitic. 'I've been able to laugh at everything except Jews,' he says, 'I realized that it was forbidden to laugh about them,' add-ing as justification, 'When you are the son of a slave, you can laugh at everything.' He has been charged with violating anti-hate laws nearly forty times but generally escaped conviction or was only fined. His political efforts have met with no success; when he ran for a parliamentary seat, he got 1 per cent of the constituency vote. But he is undeterred and directed a film in 2012, titled *L'Antisémite*, which showed images of an American soldier inspecting a gas chamber at Auschwitz and mocking instruments used by the Nazis to kill Jews; a scheduled showing at the Cannes Film Festival was cancelled for jeopardizing public order and religious convictions. Finally, in early

2014, the government issued an order banning a national tour he had been due to put on. The top administrative court, the Conseil d'État, backed the measure since the content of his show was known 'to include anti-Semitic comments and remarks encouraging racial hatred.' A video he posted on the Web attacking the Interior Minister, Manuel Valls, attracted almost two million views in its first week. A French soccer player, Nicolas Anelka, celebrated a goal in the English Premier League by giving a quenelle and, in Bordeaux, a group of young people performed it outside a memorial to the 5,000 Jews deported to their deaths from the city during the occupation of France. Traffic on Dieudonné's social media sites soared.

The practical difficulty of teaching the Holocaust to pupils who know nothing of the deportation of Jews and have been polarized by events in the Middle East was shown by a book published by a group of teachers in 2002, entitled *The Lost Territories of the Republic*, who wrote that such instruction was impossible in some classes because students of Arab origin were so hostile toward the subject. There have been reports of Arab teenagers applauding when the concentration camps are mentioned. A *New York Times* report told of an Orthodox Jewish school in the Paris suburb of Gagny where one seventeen-year-old said that Muslims outside 'call the boys in yarmulkes "dirty Jew" and they tell us to go back to our country.' The school was firebombed in 2003, leading Israel's ambassador to France, Nissim Zvili, to say that French Jews were so afraid of anti-Semitic attacks that many were thinking of emigrating, a claim which Roger Cukierman, head of the council of Jewish organizations, called 'really exaggerated.'

Still, anti-Semitic outrages recur regularly—between 2010 and 2013 they included the stabbing of a rabbi and his son by an Iranian man who had escaped from a psychiatric hospital, street attacks on Jewish boys and girls, desecration of synagogues, swastikas scrawled on Jewish cemeteries and shops and firebombing of kosher stores, not to mention the killing of four Jews at the Ozar Hatorah school in Toulouse in 2012 by the terrorist Mohammed Merah. In 2006, a twenty-two-year-old Jewish man was lured by a seventeen-year-old girl to a Paris suburban apartment where he was held by a gang of twenty-four African immigrant youths known as Les Barbarians. He was beaten, especially on his testicles, wrapped in duct tape, burned with acid and cigarettes and left naked tied to a tree—he died while being taken to hospital. The gang leader, from Ivory Coast, was arrested after he fled to Africa and sentenced to life imprisonment. Though the number of French Jews emigrating to Israel in the first nine months of 2013 was limited—2,185—it was still 49 per cent above the number for the same period of the previous year.

Cukierman has remarked that 'traditional extreme-right anti-Semitism has not got worse in France—anti-Jewish acts committed for the last year have clearly been situated in areas where Muslim and Jewish communities are neighbours.' The annual tally of anti-Jewish attacks and threats collected by the human rights organization CNCDH showed big variations year by year, from 219 in 2001 to 936 the following year, falling to 508 in 2005, then rising to 815 in 2009 before dropping once more to 389 in 2011 and increasing to more than 600 the following year. Overall, the yearly average for the first decade of the century was 634.

Apart from the Israeli-Palestinian conflict, the 'Jewish conspiracy' always lurks around the corner. As a Gaullist deputy, Patrick Devedjian, remarked tartly, 'There is a general consensus that our problems always spring from elsewhere—Europe, the United States, foreigners, globalisation.' A poll at the start of the twenty-first century reported that, asked if they agreed with the statement that Jews had too much power, 34 per cent agreed partly and 10 per cent completely. In his New Year address to the nation for 2014, François Hollande felt he needed to make a specific condemnation of anti-Semitism.

Though most racism came traditionally from the right, left-wing opposition to Israel shaded into broader sentiment which could easily verge on anti-Semitism at least by implication. That shift in opinion was made for Le Pen senior who constantly warned that *la patrie* was the target of an evil international conspiracy. He fulminated about foreign finance, international organizations and, above all, 'cosmopolitans'—an old far-right code for Jews.

Thus, despite her modernization efforts, Marine Le Pen cannot escape a long and poisonous heritage stretching from Dreyfus through the fascist leagues that unsettled governments in the 1930s, Vichy and the Milice, the Poujadist small shopkeepers movement that rose in revolt against the Fourth Republic, the settlers of Algérie française and the OAS desperados who tried to keep alive France's empire in North Africa and on to the anti-immigrant swell of our time. When asked if he could work with the new-model FN, Nigel Farage, the frankly spoken leader of Britain's anti-European party UKIP, told the *Financial Times* in 2013, 'subjects like anti-Semitism are so deeply embedded in that party that I think it's difficult to change it.'

To a degree which the politically correct find hard to accept, the Front is no longer necessarily an outsider. In its often confused, often primitive manner, it goes to the heart of many of the concerns felt by ordinary French people today. After the local election result in Brignoles in 2013, *Libération* wrote that 'the FN poison contaminates the whole country and all its politics.'

But what if the poison, or at least its first traces, was already in the bloodstream and the Front was simply tapping into it? What if voters no longer wanted to be told by the headquarters of the orthodox parties of left and right in Paris what to think? What if respect for the whole political class had sunk so low that people thought it did not matter who sat in the Élysée and were ready to let their *ras-le-bol* take over even if that meant voting for a movement which had been on the margins for much of its existence, but now melded with national chord? What if the French were only too willing to seize on external reasons for their woes—immigrants, the Commission in Brussels, globalized finance—rather than facing their own weaknesses and examining why the Germans had done better in coming to grips with the twenty-first century? What if the equivocations and refusal to face reality by the established political class since Mitterrand had created the context in which the Front could put itself forward as the only political movement that addressed the true issues facing the nation?

Shocking as such questions may be to a land of reason and fraternity ruled by a superior elite, it is really not so surprising that the gamut of social, economic and existential problems comes together on the unlikely figure of a twice-divorced forty-year-old who has never held national office. But the roots of France's problems run much deeper and have a longer historical perspective in framing the national psyche. So let us now look back at the framework within which the nation has evolved before we explore the way in which half a dozen politicians fought a succession of civil wars which account significantly for the present difficulty in resolving the Hexagon's discontents.

9

DIVIDED WE STAND

It may be no accident that France was the Western country where the Manichaean heresy took deepest root, positing an absolute division between light and darkness, between the spirit and base matter, between an ultimate paradise for perfect followers of God and the irredeemably sinful world where the rest are damned. A tradition of dualism courses through French history, extending deep into everyday life before the homogenization of the age of mass-produced foods, television and the Internet.

Over the centuries since King Philip II of the Franks proclaimed himself 'King of France' in 1190 (following three centuries in which the land was known as Francia after its denomination under the empire established by Charlemagne), the Hexagon displayed a patchwork of the regional differences. There was a plethora of local tongues, which were partially submerged into the common national language by the centralizing Jacobins of the Revolution; but only partially, since patois dialects endured well into the twentieth century. The strong accent of the *pays d'Oc* in the south contrasted with the more precise *pays d'Oil* in the north, their names taken from the different pronunciation of the word for 'yes.' There was the extended social structure of the south as against the nuclear family of the north; the former cooked in vegetable oil, the later in butter and cream. There was wine down south, beer up north.

Old geographical traditions constantly assert themselves. Thus the medieval home of the Manichaean heresy in the southwest, which was

suppressed with ferocity by crusaders from the north at the beginning of the thirteenth century, later became a hotbed for Protestants
and then for left-wing politics. The plateau around Chambon-sur-
Lignon in the rugged Haute-Loire department, which had been
a Protestant bastion in France's religious wars, sheltered Jews and
others fleeing from the German occupiers in the early 1940s. The
Resistance stronghold of the Limousin in the centre of the country
France remained one of the last bulwarks of the Communist Party
fifty years after the Liberation. On the other side of the political
spectrum, the anti-Revolutionary lands of the Vendée in the west
gave birth to a family-values, anti-European party two hundred
years later, and two Mayors of stately Bordeaux became centre-right
Prime Ministers.

If such regional patterns pop up everywhere, history has given a
particular resonance to the divisions of France, often deepened by
violence. The country's territory was the target of invasions dating
back well beyond its existence as a nation. The Roman ruled the
territory that had been that of the Gauls in present-day France (as
well as North Italy, Western Germany, Luxembourg, Belgium, most
of Switzerland and the Netherlands) for five centuries before they
were defeated by the Franks at the battle of Soissons in 486. In
the eighth century, a Moorish army got as far as Poitiers, where it
was turned back by Frankish and Burgundian forces under Charles
Martel. The English gained the big territory of Aquitaine through
Henry II's marriage to Duchess Eleanor and then staged repeated
attacks in the Hundred Years War, occupying large swathes of land
after smashing victories at Crecy, Poitiers and Agincourt, where 40
per cent of the nobility of the defending army were slain.

The victor, Henry V, annexed Normandy, homeland of his distant
predecessor William the Conqueror, formed an alliance with the rich
and powerful Burgundians who had conquered Paris and married
the daughter of the king of France in 1420—their children were to
inherit both realms. Thirty years later, the English were gone except
for their remaining stronghold of Calais, defeated by their own
internal weakness and a revival of French fighting spirit, promoted by
the visionary influence and innovative tactics of Joan of Arc (before
she was captured by the Burgundians, sold to the English and burned
as a witch).

The Reformation brought violent wars in the sixteenth century between regional barons proclaiming different faiths, even if power and territorial gain was at least as important a stimulus. As well as pitched battles, there were repeated massacres of Protestants, the best known on St. Bartholomew's Day in 1572 in which the death toll in Paris and other cities probably exceeded 10,000. The strife was largely brought to an end by the victory of Henri IV, a Calvinist from Navarre in the Pyrenees who founded the Bourbon royal dynasty after converting to Catholicism in 1589 on the grounds that 'Paris is worth a Mass.' There was tolerance in some places—adepts of the two religions shared the nave of the fine sandstone church in Collonges-la-Rouge in the Corrèze, Protestants in the southern half, Catholics in the northern half. But, more broadly, discord rumbled on, and the Edict of Nantes, which granted freedoms to the Protestants, known as Huguenots— nobody knows quite why—was widely resented by Catholics.

Fresh fighting erupted in the early seventeenth century after Louis XIII launched a campaign against the Protestant heartland of the southwest. Royal victory reduced the autonomy of the Huguenot regions and the liberties of its inhabitants, though their freedom of worship was preserved. Louis XIV, the 'Sun King,' who claimed to embody the state, went a step further and, revoking the Edict, made Protestantism illegal; one effect was a stream of hundreds of thousands of Huguenot emigrants, who included some of the country's best and brightest, many of them artisans and businessmen whom France would sadly miss during its industrial revolution.

Most went to Britain, the Netherlands, Prussia and Switzerland. But some adventurous souls journeyed as far afield as Brazil, where they landed in the bay of Rio de Janeiro, and South Africa, taking with them vines and acorns to make wine which they stored in oak barrels. In North America, Huguenots travelled to the Dutch colony of New Amsterdam and established the settlement of New Paltz, where they laid down what is now the oldest street in the United States. They founded New Rochelle, calling it after one of the towns they had inhabited in France before royal troops took it after a long siege. Other Huguenots set up in Florida, Pennsylvania, Virginia and South Carolina, where their church remains active to this day.

Back in France, Protestants continued to follow their beliefs in the wild upland country of the Cévennes, where they staged a revolt at the start of the eighteenth century marked by ruthless fighting on both sides and which ended with the authorities tacitly tolerating the minority religion. It was not until 1764 that Protestants gained their religious freedom and only during the Revolution that they became full citizens of France along with Jews.

Though differences between strands of Christian religion is hardly a hot topic anymore, the old divisions peep through at the summit of politics—if he had had a religious role, François Mitterrand would surely have been a calculating Cardinal of the Ancien Régime (didn't he call his illegitimate daughter after one?), whereas his chief rival in the Socialist Party, Michel Rocard, was the epitome of Protestant reason; equally, Jacques Chirac characterized cavalier Catholicism, whereas Lionel Jospin radiated earnest Calvinism. Nicolas Sarkozy had something of the wild impulsive priest on a short fuse as he tries to convert others to his views, and his successor could have been a reasonable prelate who listened to all views before delivering somewhat unctuous sermons from the pulpit.

The eighteenth century saw the struggle of the Enlightenment against what Voltaire and his peers painted as obscurantism, setting up the long-running fight between reason and religion. The over-throw of the old régime in 1789 and the establishment of the First Republic three years later represented a deep fissure, which was widened by the flight of royalists who mustered armies to ally with foreign invaders of their homeland and then by the execution of Louis XVI in 1793. Not that the revolutionaries had been exactly a united force. No sooner had the Bastille fallen than Democratic royalists were at odds with the National Party and radicals led by Maximilien Robespierre. Then the Jacobins grouped around the 'incorruptible' lawyer and set on creating a new society, confronted by the more moderate Constitutional Monarchists and the Girondins.

As foreign and royalist armies invaded, Robespierre and his col-leagues plunged France into the Terror that took anywhere up to 250,000 lives, some by the guillotine but many others by drowning, beatings or being blown away by cannons. The rights of man were transmuted into a template for modern totalitarianism. 'The Republic consists of the extermination of all that oppose it,' they declared. The city of Lyons, which had shown its independence of the Committee of Public Safety in Paris, was ordered to be wiped off the map, its executioner, Joseph Fouché, declaring that 'Terror, salutary terror, is the order of the day. We are causing much impure blood to flow, but it is our duty to do so, it is for humanity's sake.' A bloody war against royalists in the Vendée in western France degenerated into something close to ethnic cleansing. A letter attributed to a revolutionary general, whose authenticity has been queried but which probably speaks truth about the nature of the campaign, read:

'There is no more Vendée. It died with its wives and its children by our free sabres. I have just buried it in the woods and the swamps of Savenay. According to the orders that you gave me, I crushed the children under the feet of the horses, massacred the women who, at least for these, will not give birth to any more brigands. I do not have a prisoner to reproach me. I have exterminated all. The roads are sown with corpses. At Savenay, brigands are arriving all the time claiming to surrender, and we are shooting them non-stop . . . Mercy is not a revolutionary sentiment.'

When the Committee's excesses and the parlous state of the economy brought down the Committee of Public Safety, Robespierre and his companions took their turn at the guillotine and a more moderate, if notably corrupt, series of governments took office. But it was not long before Napoleon Bonaparte stamped his authority on the regime at the very end of the century and inaugurated another tradition, that of the saviour on the white horse, the military genius who would forge a direct link with the people and lead the nation to greatness.

It was great while it lasted, though at the cost of so many lives. Victories won acquiesance for the Corsican until defeat and the strains of his empire began to tell, and, finally, he was vanquished at the 'close run' battle of Waterloo. This brought back the senior branch of the Bourbon royal house in the person of the obese, impotent, well-meaning Louis XVIII, and a fresh dividing line—not only between revolutionaries and royalists but with Bonapartists, too. Crafty survivors endured, headed by Fouché, who had shed his radicalism to become Napoleon's police chief and then played a similar role at the restoration, and Talleyrand, who served both the Emperor and the returning kings as a by-word for conforming with whatever regime happened to be in power.

After only fifteen years, the senior Bourbons were gone, their last king, the elegant but quite stupid Charles X, fleeing with his court to England and then finding final refuge in the Austro-Hungarian empire. After the mob in the streets of Paris had got rid of one set of royal rulers in the revolt of the 'July Days' of 1830, canny politicians installed the head of the junior Orleanist branch of the Bourbons, the eminently bourgeois Louis-Philippe. But he and his regime turned out to have limited vision, continuity and bourgeois prosperity being its watchwords. This left a lot of people increasingly dissatisfied, above all the radicals and street fighters of Paris, who, harking back to 1789, saw themselves as the arbiters of the nation's destiny.

So another rising in the capital in 1848 forced the Citizen King to follow his predecessor on the road to exile in Britain. He left behind him supporters of his upper middle-class system, and another division was added. There were now royalist-reactionaries lurking in their country châteaux and the grand hôtels particuliers on the Left Bank in Paris; revolutionaries fomenting in the poor quarters of the capital around the Bastille; Bonapartists gathering round Napoleon's adventurous nephew; and Orleanists who put their faith in rule by their elite group.

Three years of the increasingly incoherent Second Republic born from the uprising of 1848 gave way to Bonapartism as Louis Napoleon, nephew of the First Emperor, got himself elected president and then staged a coup to install himself as Napoleon III. A womanizer who encouraged business and incurred the undeserved disdain of figures ranging from Karl Marx to Victor Hugo via Charles Baudelaire, he began by persecuting the left but then ruled over a more centrist Second Empire. He experimented with democracy before being overthrown after France's defeat by German forces at the Battle of Sedan in 1870. After another outburst of violence between the proletariat of the capital's Commune and the Government of National Defence, it was time for the most enduring of French post-royal regimes, the Third Republic, which was ushered in by the deaths of hundreds of insurgents in the suppression of the Commune, subsequent executions and the deportation of four thousand people to the distant colony of New Caledonia.

Lasting until France's defeat in 1940, the Third Republic is usually seen as a time of moderate centrist politics in which men of good sense made deals with one another and moved seamlessly between successive governments, Yet it witnessed fresh divisions, some so deep that they seemed to threaten the republic. State was pitted against the Catholic Church, with education a primary battleground. The Dreyfus Affair split society and families. On the left, the Communists and Socialists divorced in 1920. Right-wing extremism rose in the 1930s with bloody clashes outside the parliament building in Paris and the emergence of anti-democratic 'leagues.' The Popular Front of 1936–8 engendered hatred from the right; de Gaulle's reactionary mother considered the Socialist Premier Léon Blum to be an agent of Satan, and one slogan stated simply, 'Better Hitler than Blum.' The Civil War in Spain divided not only left from right, but also the left itself between those who wanted to aid the Nationalists fighting the rebellion led by General Franco and those who preferred to stay out and put their faith in impotent international pressure. Throughout, the politicians who swapped ministerial posts were constrained by the need to maintain backing from parties which combined interest groups and saw their leaders as men who owed them fealty.

The historical switchback between 1815 and defeat in 1940 gave birth to national political and social camps that endure to this day. Charles de Gaulle, Jacques Chirac and Nicolas Sarkozy have embodied the Bonapartist touch. Georges Pompidou and Giscard d'Estaing incarnated the upper middle-class tradition of Louis-Philippe, and business with aristocratic trappings in the second case. Though his ideological commitment was open to doubt, Mitterrand reached back to the old traditions of the left to give some ballast to his long quest for the presidency, topped by a mammoth street party in Paris which greeted his success in 1981 as a peaceful re-run of the revolutions in the capital during the nineteenth century. Hollande is the heir to the reasonable, pragmatic men of the centre-left who tried to keep the national ship afloat but were constantly blown off course by more extreme forces around them, a leader subject in many ways to the political movement that backs him.

The traumatic divisions of the Occupation bred a further set of inheritances. The four years under the rule of the Nazis and the Vichy administration headed by Philippe Pétain set resisters against collaborators, in London, the General against his one-time mentor the Marshal, in France, partisans against the regime's militiamen. Each camp was factionalized under its supreme leader. The court around the First World War hero in Vichy was rent with jockeying for power and favours, while the rivalries in the Resistance were accentuated by the inevitable paranoia that dogs any clandestine movement.

At a grassroots level, take Saint-Amand in the middle of France as an illustration of the starkness of the Franco-French enmities of the war. The town contained both Resistance and collaborationist militia groups. Hearing of the Allied landings in Normandy in 1944, the Resistance partisans took control. They held some of their opponents hostage together with the wife of a militia leader, who responded by taking hostages of his own, threatening to slay them if his wife was not set free. As German troops moved in to re-establish control, the Resistance fighters killed thirteen of their captives. In retaliation, the militiamen turned on the local Jews. Thirty-eight were thrown down a well and then had bags of cement and rocks dropped on them until they perished.

Arriving back in France in August 1944, de Gaulle sought to impose national unity. He acted ruthlessly to disband the Resistance and accepted as necessary for the administration of the country the continued employment of some civil servants who had collaborated. For the General, the Vichy regime was illegitimate. The true republic had never ceased to function, carried by him to wartime exile in London and now restored by his return to France. It was a nice piece of fiction for its author's purposes. The fact was that most French people had not resisted. Not that many had been active collaborators, either. Most had simply sought to get on with life until Germany was defeated by other powers. But, whatever one had actually done—or not done—since 1940, it was politic in the summer of 1944 to claim to have been a member of the Resistance. As a literary historian remarked acidly of the country's most famous postwar couple, 'On 11 August 1944, Jean-Paul Sartre and Simone de Beauvoir entered the Resistance, at the same moment as the Paris police.'

Despite de Gaulle's quest for unity, vengeance was inevitably the order of the day. Some 4,000 collaborators were sentenced to death, and 767 were executed, among them the Vichy Prime Minister, Pierre Laval, who was shot after trying to poison himself while awaiting the firing squad. There were less official revenge killings—some estimates put the number of those who perished in the settling of scores in the tens of thousands. Another 25,000 went to jail, and Marshal Pétain ended his days in lifelong detention on an island off the Atlantic coast, where he died in 1951 at the age of eighty-nine.

Sometimes the punishment of those who had been too close to the occupiers was ideological, but often the cause was more human. When accused of collaboration for her affair with a German officer, the actress Arletty could be bold enough to tell the court, 'My heart is French but my cunt is international,' and get away with it. But many other less fortunate women, who were never more than sexual collaborators, had their heads shaved by kangaroo courts before being paraded in the streets in shame.

The war had left France 'ruined, decimated, torn apart,' as de Gaulle put it. The new regime, the Fourth Republic, had a difficult birth amid a three-way split between the Communists, the main force in the Resistance, the Socialists and a new Christian Democratic party, the MRP. The autocratic figure of the General sat atop the pile as Prime Minister until he stalked out at the beginning of 1946 in dudgeon at the bickering of the politicians around him and his inability to impose the executive authority he considered necessary. The Communists stayed on until being forced out of coalition by the Socialists in 1947. The revolving door system of governments that ensued encouraged the existence of small political parties whose leaders could bargain for a place in government in return for committing their members' votes to coalitions living on knife-edge majorities; Mitterrand exploited this element of the system to become a minister eleven times. The left-right division was vitiated by the way two major players stayed out of the game and acted as disruptive forces— de Gaulle pursuing his personal crusade to return to office at the head of a strong executive and the Moscow-aligned Communists presenting a constant challenge through their electoral strength among workers and their ability to deploy big trade union battalions in strikes.

The decolonization in the 1950s and 1960s produced bitter rancours, exacerbated at a crucial phase by virulent anti-Semitism directed at the austere Prime Minister, Pierre Mendès France. The traumatic defeat by the Vietnamese at Dien Bien Phu now belongs to the history books, but the end of France's colonization of Algeria is still a living memory to older French people; Jacques Chirac served across the Mediterranean as a sub-lieutenant. As national traumas go, the withdrawal from France's last major possession was about as searing as you could get for a modern European nation. Apart from the bloodshed, the repression and the violent demonstrations in Algeria itself, it is easy for foreigners to forget that, as comparatively recently as 1958, France faced the very real prospect of an army coup.

At a time when Dwight Eisenhower was presiding over bland Republican prosperity and Harold Macmillan was telling the British they'd never had it so good, generals in French Algeria were drawing up plans for Opération Résurrection, which was to drop paratroopers in Paris, send in tanks and surround the National Assembly, City Hall, police headquarters, broadcasting stations and the Eiffel Tower. A detachment of paratroopers actually landed in Corsica on a self-proclaimed mission of revolt against the elected leaders of the nation. Had the plan, which smacked of a Latin American coup rather than modern Europe, been implemented, it would have led to civil war, with the Communists playing a leading role in opposing the insurgents. But Charles de Gaulle was back in power after an exceedingly skilful juggling act in which he refused to throw his lot in with the army while leaving the threat of action in the air; his peaceful coup was naturally resented by some politicians, notably Mitterrand—he and the General would be bitter opponents for the remaining dozen years of de Gaulle's life.

For all his rhetoric about rallying the French into a single historic mass, the General's style was hardly calculated to avoid dispute; he had been a controversial figure for most of his life dating back to his unorthodox military views and his championing of tank warfare in the 1930s. Having returned to power in the most dramatic circumstances of any postwar West European leader, he invited controversy from the start with France's politicians, its allies and the Algerian settlers, who welcomed his arrival but soon realized he was not going to be their providential saviour. At the extreme, the nihilist Secret Army Organization (OAS) and the repeated assassination attempts against the General by the ultras of Algérie Française that lasted until 1962 showed the potent bitterness of the post-colonial resentment felt by some of the French.

The Gaullist process injected France with the new life it so badly needed, but, once the threat of military action had been lifted, nobody could pretend that the President acted as a balm to the country's divisions. A decade after the barricades of Algiers, the nation was again split beyond the realms of orthodox politics by the biggest combination of urban strikes and street revolts of the century. Contrary to the hopes of those who saw a fresh revolution in the making, the student riots and general strike of May–June 1968 fuelled conservative reaction and led to thirteen years of rule by the centre-right. But, as we will see in the next chapters, this did not put a cap on political infighting on both sides.

Today, after Sarkozy's defeat in 2012 ended another seventeen years of rule by the centre-right, the familiar internal jousting has resumed among leaders of his UMP party. Left and right are split by real dislike, rising above the usual jockeying between politicians. Moderate politicians complain at the rising degree of rhetoric violence. Extremist parties on both sides of the spectrum raise the temperature. Compromise is not in the air, whatever it would do to ease the nation's troubles.

It was par for the course that the present head of state of France and his predecessor took separate planes to attend the funeral of Nelson Mandela while George W. Bush travelled there on Air Force One with President Obama. Officials explained that it was cheaper for them to go separately in smaller private jets rather than travel in a big presidential plane. The two men could, of course, have shared a Falcon, but that would have brought them closer together than either could have borne. After all, when he went to the Élysée for his investiture as President, Hollande accompanied Sarkozy to the top of the palace steps after the ceremony but then left his predecessor to walk to his waiting car alone. All very much par for the course in a country where divisiveness is embedded in society as well as in history.

Take almost any element of French life, and it will almost certainly contain rival factions. The three main trade union federations carry on doctrinal disputes alongside the fight for members; each labour conflict is likely to produce a different line-up between them as they balance tactics and strategy. When Breton farmers, fishermen, shopkeepers and some bosses of factories due to be closed down donned red bonnets to protest against taxation in 2013, another group staged separate rallies on the grounds that the first had included members of the hated boss class.

There are competing associations of chess players and authors, filmmakers and anglers. The number of concierges may be falling by the year, but they still have no fewer than five unions to represent them. Two centuries after the execution of Louis XVI, the old royal family was badly split: the pretender to the throne, the Comte de Paris, disinherited his eldest son and denounced four other children for trying to stop him selling off family treasures. Not to be outdone, the Bonaparte clan has recurrent rows about who is the rightful claimant to the imperial succession.

There are two main national honours systems—the Légion d'Honneur and the Ordre National du Mérite (the two are not, admittedly, incompatible—the author has been awarded both, once under Mitterrand and then under Sarkozy). The cassoulet stew may be the quintessential dish of the southwest, but don't expect regional solidarity as you sit down at the table. In the town of Castelnaudary it comes with pork, in Carcassonne with roast shoulder of mutton, and in Toulouse with the local sausage; and each version has its fervent disciples. To avoid becoming entangled in the gastronomic civil war, the writer Anatole France opted for an all-around spiritual benediction, which hardly fits the temporal solidity of the dish—the cassoulet of Castelnaudary was God the Father, that of Carcassonne the Son and the Toulouse version the Holy Spirit.

Religious persecution may be long gone, but the 900,000 Protestants still remain in many ways a group apart, characterized by their seriousness and their perceived absence of social graces. We have seen how many immigrants are divided from mainstream society. Within the seemingly solid ranks of the middle class, a strain of anti-bourgeois thinking has been kept alive and kicking by critics from Gustave Flaubert to the filmmaker Claude Chabrol. In the country's top kitchens, civil war broke out in the 1990s between defenders of traditional French gastronomy and those whom they branded as being guilty of 'globalization.' There is always a good pretext to set up a new organization whose chairman will revel in the title of 'Monsieur le Président' until his dying day.

The main Islamic and Masonic organizations have each been upset by internal political rifts which overlie more basic battles for influence. There are rival organizations of hunters which put up competing lists at regional elections. Feelings in the world of former French settlers from Algeria grew so heated that the head of the main *pied noir* organization was murdered by three members of another group. In some places, one café is frequented by Socialists, and another by conservatives, perpetuating an old tradition—in the mid-nineteenth century, Balzac noted that 'in the provinces, trades-men had to profess a political opinion in order to attract customers.'

Both left and right claim a different historical inheritance—the first as guardians of the sense of progress which the Revolution is meant to have embodied despite its retrograde aspects, the second as the defenders of national grandeur and pride. That is the great fault line in which each side negates the other and invokes the val-ues of the past to down its opponents. In fact, both are on shaky ground, for modern France has hardly been a triumph of the forces of enlightenment and its grandeur has suffered plenty of knocks.

Most governments of the last two hundred years have come from the conservative side. Between the foundation of the Fifth Republic in 1958 and the election of François Hollande in 2012, the presidency was held for all but fifteen years by Gaullists and the centre-right. If conservatives keep their heads, they can usually be confident of returning to power and wealth. 'Society dreams of revolution but is, in fact, repelled by change,' as the former minister and historian Michel Poniatowski put it. The French, in the old truism, wear their hearts on the left, their wallets on the right.

It can well be argued that, behind the political slogans that carried Mitterrand to the Élysée, the revolution which the left held out in 1981 was really the last manifestation of postwar economic and social conservatism, promising to keep life as it was through massive intervention of the state just at the moment when computers, the decline of Communism and the economic rise of East Asia were changing the balance of the world. Rather than putting itself in shape to meet such fundamental international shifts, supposedly progressive modernist France reacted with outdated nostrums and flirted with isolationism. Even the widespread nationalizations of 1981 can be seen as part of a tradition of reactionary state power. Then, the government of Lionel Jospin in the period of cohabitation with Chirac's presidency saw the Socialists turning into primarily a party of management with aberrations, such as the introduction of the thirty-five-hour week, but also administering the biggest campaign of privatization of state assets that the country had seen.

Naturally, influences from each move to the left have not vanished completely, most notably with the persistence of the postwar welfare reforms. But, in terms of real power, the progressives get the write-ups and the realists govern. France needs to be able to think of itself as the cradle of revolution, a place of daring ideological innovation, a powerhouse of ideas—and, until very recently, those were seen as the property of the left. The notion of progress stemming from the right was, for the French, an oxymoron. Now this has changed as the system comes under criticism in the face of high unemployment, low growth and high government debt built up by successive administrations of right and left, but, at the same time, there is a reluctance to abandon the comfort blanket of the providential state. That creates a funda-mental division between what needs to be done and what people are ready to accept—a division that politicians flee from seeking to resolve.

The traditional reverence for the state stands in evident contradiction to the individualism and divisiveness of the French people, a con-tradiction that forms one of the great fault lines of France. Back in 1944, de Gaulle expressed the view that 'there can be no security, no freedom, no efficiency without the acceptance of great discipline under the guidance of a strong state and with the enthusiastic sup-port of a people rallied in unity.' Half a century later, Jacques Chirac made no bones about it: 'For a Frenchman, the notion of the public good is inseparable from that of the state.'

The state's servants exist to do its bidding without question, from the highest-placed Énarque to the gendarme on the beat. The tradition was set long ago and epitomized by Joseph Fouché, the ever-adaptable exponent of the Terror turned Bonapartist police chief and then royalist fixer, and by Charles-Maurice de Talleyrand, successively Catholic Bishop of Autun in Burgundy, servant of the revolutionary church, Foreign Minister for the first Emperor (who called Talleyrand a 'shit in silk stockings'), then plenipotentiary for the restored Bourbon monarchy, and finally Ambassador to London for their Orleanist successor.

Take, for instance, the story of Maurice Papon, who had belonged
as a young man to the moderate Radical Socialist Party, the main
political grouping of the Third Republic. In 1931, at the age of twenty,
he joined the staff of the Air Minister, a senior member of the party.
Five years later, he took a bigger job with another Radical Socialist
member of the Popular Front government. At the end of 1940, he
joined the Vichy administration, rising to become Secretary-General of
the Prefecture of the Gironde department, based in Bordeaux. There
were plenty of prefectorial jobs going since Vichy had sacked half the
old staff to ensure loyalty to its order. In his new post, Papon was
given responsibility for activities linked with the war and the Occupation, including Jewish affairs. Convoys of Jews left Bordeaux at regular
intervals, and Papon earned high marks from the Germans for his
'quick and trustworthy' work. In May 1943, there was a disagreeable
episode in which Gaullist graffiti was found scrawled in the toilets of
the Prefecture; Papon had the toilets watched, and a twenty-year-old
employee was duly caught and sent off to forced labour in Germany.

At the end of 1943, as the Allies were landing in North Africa,
Papon agreed to shelter a civil servant who had joined the Resistance
after being sacked because he was Jewish. In January 1944, he turned
down the offer of a prefecture of his own; at the same time he
signed a warrant for 228 Jews which even told the police how to deal
with the pets of those arrested—the servants of the state are sticklers
for detail even in the worst of times. That spring, he made contact
with a local Resistance leader and, when Bordeaux was liberated in
August, became his chief of staff. After a postwar career as a prefect
in France and its colonies, he worked as a senior official for the
Socialist Interior Minister and was then appointed chief of the Paris
police. Holding on to the job under the Fifth Republic, he was in
charge of the forces of order who killed hundreds of Algerians in the
capital in 1961. Elected to the National Assembly in 1968, he headed
the parliamentary finance commission and became Minister for the
Budget under Giscard d'Estaing. It was only in 1981 that, as a result
of an electoral manoeuvre which we will hear more about later, the
truth about his wartime career came into the spotlight.

Setting aside questions of morality, what is so striking about
Maurice Papon's career is how he worked for whoever was in power,
whatever their creed. It is one thing for a civil servant to regard

himself as being above politics, but still quite a feat to have laboured for the Radical Socialists in the 1930s, Vichy in the 1940s, the Socialists in the 1950s, de Gaulle in the 1960s and Giscard in the 1970s. And it is equally amazing that his successive bosses did not seem to care about his past affiliations, so long as he did the job. For sixty years, Papon was the embodiment of the administrative continuity which that state prizes so highly; as he himself wrote, 'There are no crises of conscience when one obeys the orders of the government.' Or, as the war criminal Paul Touvier pleaded when he was finally brought to trial, 'All I ever did was to serve the French state.'

The state's less elevated civil servants make up nearly a quarter of the national workforce, compared with an average of 15 per cent in OECD developed nations. Their salaries take up almost one-sixth of the national income. The 5.2 million *fonctionnaires* in 2013 represented a 36 per cent increase since 1983. A list of white elephants spawned by bureaucratic incompetence in recent decades has included a high-speed train station that handles only five hundred passengers a day, a museum in Nice which was still empty ten years after being commissioned, a projected road tunnel in Toulon which collapsed and was abandoned and a conference centre in Paris which remained unbuilt despite expensive planning work. The cost of the grand building for the Paris Philharmonic is, at the time of writing, three times over budget and the project is two years late.

Away from its apex in the central administration in Paris with huge ministries and the panoply of power, the state's wider presence lies at local level down through regions and departments to villages with their mayors and grassroots officials. In all, France has 60,000 separate local authorities, 85 per cent of its communes containing fewer than 2,000 people alongside the great city mayor-barons of Paris, Marseilles, Lyons, Toulouse and Bordeaux. The spending of local collectivités has risen two and a half times since 1990 to reach 240 billion euros a year. Between 1998 and 2009, the number of their employees doubled. To meet the cost, local taxes have gone up by between 72 and 96 per cent in this century. Much of the spending has been for the good of inhabitants, but there have been notorious examples of Pharaonic local government buildings, such as the huge expanse of monumental edifices in Montpellier. There is a shortage of magistrates to carry out checks on spending, which are done only every four or five years, often too late to have any real effect.

As long ago as the 1995 presidential campaign, Jacques Chirac spoke stirringly about the need to make the state less grand and more impartial. Successive administrations pledge to reduce the burden of bureaucracy. But, while they may sometimes resent its encroachment on their individual lives and fret at having to fill up yet another form, the French do not necessarily want any less pomp and circumstance or any less of a buffer against the cold world outside. They would probably like the state to be more impartial, less political—at least, when their own interests are not being advanced. But they know that the chances are slim of any president loosening the grip of his men and women on the levers of power. No politician to date has shown any real sign of taking a self-denying ordinance on pulling those levers, but the assumption that the people will follow obediently has been disproved time and again as the Hexagon displays its regional heritage.

Despite the standardization of life, with local customs swamped by the television culture and the connection of regions by modern transport, France remains the country of many parts it has been for more than two thousand years. Julius Caesar found Gaul divided into three parts; in fact the people the Romans conquered were split into dozens of warring tribes before they made the error of banding together into large armies that the legions could defeat. Under Charlemagne's empire around 800, the territory was divided along the Loire. The Vikings found the country so permeable that they sailed three times down rivers to Clermont-Ferrand in the heart of the Massif Central.

It is not surprising that, in reaction, since the unifying genius of Louis XI brought the modern nation together at the end of the fifteenth century, France has been obsessed by the idea of itself as a single entity bounded on three sides by the sea and on three others by its neighbours. But the legacy of regional power players runs through the ages and underpinned recurrent wars of religion stretching from the Manichean Cathar heresy of the thirteenth century to the reign of Louis XIV five hundred years later. Some were mightier than the king, who could be pushed back to his limited domain of the Île-de-France. A Duke of Normandy conquered England;

other Normans and then the Counts of Anjou reigned over Sicily; other Normans set up as rulers in the Holy Land. Marriage united the great duchy of Aquitaine with England and provided the pretext for a hundred years of invasion by the power on the other side of the Channel. Had they possessed greater willpower, the Counts of Toulouse might have established a separate kingdom in the south which, with neighbouring Provence, would have looked west and east along the Mediterranean coast, rather than northwards to Paris.

As France took shape, there was often a complex international and inter-regional dimension as warfare shifted frontiers of power. Take as an example the beautiful hilltop fortress township of Najac in the Aveyron department of the southwest. Probably a Roman oppidium in the first century after Christ, it gravitated into the orbit of the powerful Counts of Toulouse, but then passed to the English after Éléonore d'Aquitaine was repudiated by the King of France and married Henry II from across the water. The destinies of England, France, Toulouse and northern Spain collided there when Henry's son, Richard the Lionheart, met the ruler of Aragon at the castle of Najac to forge a pact against the Count of Toulouse. But then the Count's son married one of Henry II's daughters, which put Najac back under the authority of Toulouse. Najac was strategically important because it towered over a vital river route through a lush and fruitful area where four powers jockeyed for influence.

At the dawn of the thirteenth century, Anglo-Norman Crusaders swept down from the north to exterminate the followers of the Albigensian heresy in one of the most damnable expeditions of European history. After the Counts of Toulouse bent the knee to the invaders, the inhabitants of Najac were sentenced to build a large church atop the hill beside the castle to show their new loyalty to the Church of Rome. But when Count Raymond VII failed to produce a male heir, the fortress returned to the King of France, only to revert to the control of Toulouse five years later. Half a century after that, the English regained control of the region, but their rule provoked the people of Najac into a revolt in which they massacred the occupying garrison. Other English occupiers returned for a while, but Najac then became French for good. Such places show the complexities of history behind the facade of a single French identity. From the Rhine frontier to the Pyrenees, the Hexagon is made up of a complex of characteristic regions and localities within them which draw on their different pasts, and need to be woven together rather than taken as parts of a uniform whole by the centralizing heirs of the revolutionary Jacobins.

To add to the complexity, some regions, and their capital cities, look beyond France's frontiers to confirm their wider identities. Thus, Montpellier and Toulouse connect with Barcelona and Catalonia; Bordeaux retains links with Britain, some of its best vineyards being called Montrose, Talbot or Lynch; Nice has a strong Italian streak; and the towns of Alsace could be in Rhineland Germany. In the west, an organization called the Atlantic Arc, with its headquarters in the Breton capital of Rennes, is trying to stitch together the old Gaelic world of Ireland, Wales, Cornwall, western France and northern Spain.

Within France, regional groupings reach into the heart of the capital. Hard-working men and women from the Auvergne and Aveyron dominate the café trade in Paris: a parish priest who runs a hostel for young men up from the Cantal department reckons he can find them a job as a waiter within twenty-four hours of their arrival. There has long been a Corsican bond in the Paris police and the civil service—a 'Corsican clan' whose members were called Tiberi, Dominati and Romani helped Jacques Chirac to run the capital for many years. Associations linked to rural communes in far-flung parts of the country attract hundreds of diners to their annual banquets. The district around the Gare Montparnasse, where the trains from the west arrive, is stuffed with Breton restaurants—in one street alongside the station, there are restaurants and cafés named after the towns of Saint-Malo, Nantes and Morlaix, plus L'Atlantique, L'Océan and Au Rendez-Vous des Bretons. Some of the best *choucroute* in town is to be found by the Gare de l'Est at the end of the tracks from Alsace.

Layers of government enshrine the nation's diversity—22 regions, 96 departments and 36,500 communes, each with its own mayor and council. In Paris, the twenty arrondissements each has a mayor of its own. In the provinces, departments and regions of France, the local rulers have always been anxious to flex their muscles against the power of the capital and the mandarins in the ministries—and against one another, as seen in the long-running political contest between the power brokers of individual departments and the politicians running the larger regions to which they belong.

When France rises against the central administration's proposed changes to public sector working conditions, sociologists detect a strong element of revolt against Paris as the place which issues orders, another sign of the tension between the unitary state and the individualism of the people. Marches through the streets of the capital may catch the eye of foreign correspondents, but the real action is often in the provinces, as in the rolling demonstrations against taxation in Brittany in 2013.

While being capital to the nation, Paris is also a great regional city whose population has a historic role in rising up to deliver judgment on the national authorities which sit in the city. They were not allowed to have an elected mayor until 1976 because of the central government's fear of the authority he might wield. With the surrounding region of the Île-de-France, it houses one-sixth of France's population. As Mayor for eighteen years, Jacques Chirac made it his power base, using it to underwrite the political party he headed. The Prince of the City works in the biggest office in the whole country. The City Hall, rebuilt after being burned during the Commune uprising, has 1,290 windows and 142 Baccarat crystal chandeliers.

Among the people of Paris, some paid the price for the Chirac vision of the capital as more and more traditional labouring areas turned into middle-class developments. 'Simple people have been made to leave, the very character of parts of Paris has been destroyed,' lamented one opposition leader. The old pattern of property ownership was broken by taxation and inheritance duties. In 1950, 68 per cent of Paris buildings were owned by individuals; now, that has shrunk to around 20 per cent. The gentrification of the city was matched by an office construction spree, which led to a glut of new commercial property and the descent of foreign 'vulture fund' investors out to buy empty buildings for half their original price. On the edges of town, rows of charming two-storey houses have been remorselessly torn down to make way for apartment towers. The developers ruled, and the authorities made sure nobody got in their way.

Chirac was helped by abundant funding from the nation. Nearly 30 per cent of municipal revenue comes in grants from central government or from the surrounding Île-de-France. Farmers in the Jura or Languedoc help to keep Paris Métro tickets cheap by subsidies paid with their taxes. They do not complain because, wherever they are, the French regard Paris as a city that represents their country: they may not want to live there, but they wish it to shine.

After Chirac stepped down, a series of scandals came to light, with one earning his close associate Alain Juppé his suspended jail sentence before he bounced back to take a government post. A cloud spread over Jean Tiberi, who held the mayor's office from 1995 to 2001, and it was time for a change with the election of the efficient, moderate Socialist, Bertrand Delanoë, who became the first left-wing mayor since the Commune. Unlike Chirac, he did not use the post to further national ambitions, but was content with the job of running the city. Delanoë, the first openly gay politician to win such high office, struck popular chords, for instance by campaigns to improve the environment, by having sand spread on the quays of the Seine to create *Paris-Plages* (Paris-Beaches) for Parisians stuck in the city during the summer, and by inaugurating a widely copied system of bicycles for rent. He got a second term in 2008 with nearly 58 per cent of the vote and was that rare beast, a politician content with what he had and intent on making Paris work better. In 2014, one of his deputies, Anne Hildago, retained the capital for the Socialists, beating off a spirited UMP challenge and providing her party with a bit of good news amid its string of defeats in municipal elections that year.

Though it has made a religion out of centralization, France nurtures a multilayered structure of regional authority. Leading provincial nabobs are not content with their weight back home; they also want a national stage. So they become ministers, run parties, even head governments, and all the while remain at the head of their local power bases. Some leading politicians stay on in provincial cities and towns for an extraordinary length of time, a tradition set under earlier Republics when a figure like Edouard Herriot was Mayor of Lyons for thirty-seven years while serving as Prime Minister three times, and Edouard Daladier held sway as Mayor of the southern town of Carpentras from 1912 to 1958 while holding a succession of government posts in Paris.

The elder statesman of the postwar right, Antoine Pinay, outdid him in mayoral longevity, reigning in the town of Saint-Chamond in the middle of France from 1928 to 1977. Jacques Chaban-Delmas carried on the tradition as Mayor of Bordeaux for almost half a century, from 1947 to 1995. His successor there, Alain Juppé, has run the municipality on the Gironde River since 1995 (with a short break after his conviction of misuse of public funds for political purposes while working with Chirac in Paris).

There is a term for the way politicians combine local and national roles—the *cumul des mandats*. This has been reduced; members of the National Assembly are now permitted to occupy only one other significant elected post, and their total incomes have been capped. But when Lionel Jospin set out to reduce the accumulation further, he struggled against an entrenched tradition in which some 90 per cent of deputies also held a local government post. More than half were mayors. Eighteen ministers were among them. Governments in Paris come and go: provincial politics are for life.

Stretches as Prime Minister, Foreign Minister and Defence Minister did not stop Juppé continuing as mayor of Bordeaux, while Ségolène Royal remained President of the regional council of the Poitou-Charentes region while running for the Élysée in 2007, and another prominent Socialist politician, Martine Aubry, held on to her office as mayor of Lille during her four years as the party's First Secretary. In the fall of 2013, a proposal by the Hollande administration to limit the *cumul* so that legislators concentrate on their national jobs was once against blocked, with a third of the Socialists in the Senate joining the right in voting against it.

Other towns and cities were put on the national political map by their mayors. A slightly dotty defender of small businesses was emboldened by his record running Tours to mount a quixotic presidential bid. The moderate Mayor of La Rochelle became a symbol of the alliance of environmentalism and orthodox politics after turning his port into a green citadel. The undistinguished towns of Château-Chinon in the west of Burgundy and Conflans-Sainte-Honorine outside Paris acquired unwarranted fame through the presence of

Francois Mitterrand and Michel Rocard as their Mayors. In a different mode, Canon Félix Kir, Mayor of Dijon, became one of France's most celebrated names through his taste for mixing blackcurrant liquor and the local white wine.

Despite the media's concentration on national politics as played out in the republican palaces of Paris, political shifts in the regions often prefigure wider movements. In late 2013, the Breton tax protests were taken up in wider demonstrations of *ras-le-bol*. One key to the left's victory in 1981 was the way it had expanded its control of electoral bastions across the country in the previous years. A sweep of twenty of France's twenty-two regional councils by the right in 1992 foreshadowed its subsequent parliamentary and presidential victories. The left's recovery in regional polls six years later was a key element in the Socialist strategy of retaining the presidency. A death knell had sounded for the Communists when they began to lose their local government strongholds in the 1970s and 1980s—and were constrained by economics to close down the regional editions of their daily newspaper. Once they had got over the shock of defeat in 1981, the former President and Prime Minister each began their comeback bids in the middle of the country, not in national politics.

French big-city mayors can be the epitome of the place they run. Pierre Mauroy, the bluff friend of the workers who took coach trips to Portugal for his holiday, was Prime Minister for three years at the start of Mitterrand's presidency, but his true vocation was as the political master of the declining industrial region round Lille in the northeast of France. He was Mayor of the city for almost thirty years from 1973, president of the regional council and ended his political career as senator from the area. Stout and red-faced, his political concerns were rooted in the problems of his city and its hinterland. His heritage was carried on by his successor, Martine Aubry, the Labour Minister who introduced the thirty-five-hour working week and who established her provincial power base by becoming Mayor of Lille in 2001.

Chaban-Delmas and Alain Juppé both cut fitting figures as the suave representatives of their elegant city of Bordeaux on the Gironde. The rotund former Prime Minister Raymond Barre symbolized the sensible conservatism and gastronomic excellence of Lyon. The disgraced Mayor of Nice Jacques Médecin stood for the raffish high life of the Riviera. But, while underpinning the dichotomy between central and regional authority, the combination of powers which they exercise at local and national level reinforces the closed political society in which the same limited circle of politicians have their hands on the levers in Paris and the provinces, guiding the state in their chosen direction.

For four decades, Gaston Defferre was Marseille. An afternoon with him at the height of his power was a living illustration of how a big boss operated—a clique of courtiers bowing to his every whim, a ward boss explaining what favours he needed to keep key voters happy, a businessman coming in to talk about planning regulations, a boat builder submitting plans for the Mayor's new yacht, and the editor of the main local newspaper ringing to read out the leading article of the night. Defferre had grabbed the paper at the Liberation in the summer of 1944 by the simple expedient of walking into the building with two pistols stuck in his belt and taking control from its collaborationist proprietors. Four decades later, he tried to convince his friend the President of the Republic that his wartime background would enable him to persuade the terrorist Carlos not to attack French targets if only they could meet and talk as one resistance fighter to another.

Such romanticism goes to the heart of Marseille, France's oldest city. Defferre was the only French minister to have risked his life in a duel—not once but twice, with swords and pistols. That was the kind of exploit that the people of Marseilles loved, and the city founded by the Phoenicians has a special place in French hearts, with its buccaneering tradition, its flamboyant gangsters, its *bouillabaisse* fish stew and its equally pungent local accent. More than a century as the gateway to the colonies brought wealth from trade with overseas possessions. It was the door to adventure and fortune-seeking in Africa or the East, for the eventual return from exotic journey—the poet Rimbaud came home to die in a Marseilles hospital with his leg amputated after a decade of travels in Africa—and, in the other direction, for deportation of political prisoners to exile in Algeria.

The city thrived on melodrama and a belief in its special corner in southern folk wisdom. Its people like to think of themselves as being larger than life, personified by figures like the late pastis king, Paul Ricard, whose family name appears each year on ninety million bottles of the celebrated aperitif and who, though not a Catholic, took his entire workforce to Rome to be blessed by the Pope. It could also claim a notable part in modern urban architecture as the place where the modernist architectural pioneer Le Corbusier built his *Cité radieuse* (radiant city), one of the most influential twentieth-century huge apartment blocks, whose influence may be felt in the suburban projects that are the scene of so much unrest.

Throughout the twentieth century, Marseille provided a home for immigrants from all around the Mediterranean—Armenians fleeing Turkish massacres, Greeks from Asia Minor, Spanish Republicans, Jews and Christians expelled from Nasser's Egypt, and then tens of thousands of *pied noir* settlers from former colonies in North Africa. The city was both outward-looking and self-regarding. The old port was not unlike a stage. Music hall, operetta and popular theatre merged into everyday life and politics, epitomized in Marcel Pagnol's immortal fictional characters of Marius, Fanny and César. As played by the prodigious actor Raimu, the latter gave France an iconic father figure, a dominating presence swinging from pathos to humour and an unschooled fountain of native wit and cunning. As the cinema historian Ginette Vincendeau has noted, the Pagnol trilogy was a paean to archaic values, spreading the notion of a specifically southern culture to the rest of the nation through the cinema. If Marseille already believed itself to be special, Pagnol and millions of cinemagoers confirmed it in that belief.

It was an amenable place, ready to offer anything the visitor wanted. During the First World War, a British troopship filled with Indian soldiers being sent to die on the Western Front hove into view and sent a request for 1,000 'girls' to be waiting for them; the Mayor said he could summon up 300 young women immediately. The message was then corrected to call for 1,000 'goats.' If that's their pleasure, so be it, said the Mayor. Even the underworld was painted in romantic colours, as in the hit film *Borsalino*, which brought Jean-Paul Belmondo and Alain Delon together in a tale of men who did what they had to do under cover of their broad-brimmed hats. The reality was less glamorous: the two gangsters on whom the starring roles were modelled formed a compact with quasi-fascist officials in the 1930s which allowed them to ply their trade unhindered and to get into the drugs business.

During the war, the city became the base for an extraordinary American Scarlet Pimpernel, Varian Fry, who arrived in 1940 with a dress suit bought in his last hours in New York, $3,000 taped to one leg and a list of two hundred artists and writers he had come to spirit out of occupied France during what was meant to be a three-week mission. In the end, Fry, the son of a stockbroker with a red carnation in his buttonhole, stayed in Marseille for thirteen months. Working with false passports from the Czechoslovak consul and forged papers, he personally helped Marc Chagall, Hannah Arendt, Max Ernst, Wanda Landowska and 1,200 others leave France for the safety of America. His wider operation, run from Marseille, is estimated to have saved 4,000 in all. Evidently, the local police were impressionable: when they took Chagall away from his hotel in one of the early round-ups, Fry telephoned to warn them that the arrest of such a famous artist would embarrass Vichy. If Chagall wasn't freed within half an hour, Fry threatened to inform the *New York Times*. The artist was released, and, after bizarrely assuring himself that there were cows in America, crossed the Atlantic.

After the war, the hoods who had picked the winning side took control of France's biggest port. They helped the CIA by attacking the Communist dockers' union and, in return, got a free hand to export heroin across the Atlantic. Marseille became a major world narcotics centre. The heroin 'cooks' worked in remote houses in the countryside, in cellars, outhouses, garages and tenements. At the pinnacle of production in the mid-1960s, according to a historian of the opium trade, Martin Booth, there were about two dozen laboratories operating around the clock, producing high-grade heroin of a purity usually difficult to attain. The drugs went to America either direct or via France's overseas possessions in the Caribbean, where customs checks were minimal. In time, the American authorities hit back, arresting a top chemist involved and shutting down the main distribution point in New York—known as the Pleasant Avenue Connection. As exports to the United States became more difficult, some narcotics barons began selling heroin in their own country.

Through all this, the nominally Socialist Gaston Defferre held
the city in the palm of his weather-beaten yachtsman's hand. He was
invulnerable and did not need to be too scrupulous in his choice of
associates. A suppressed photograph showed the Mayor at the head
of a political procession arm-in-arm with a leading underworld figure.
This man helped to organize his campaigns, had an office in the
City Hall and told police who had the audacity to try to arrest him,
'Let me go or I'll talk.'

Defferre was a fixture in the national parliament and served as a
minister under the Fourth Republic. In 1969 he made an ill-advised
bid for the presidency, netting just 5 per cent of the vote. That
didn't dent his authority, however, for his passport to power was
down on the Mediterranean, where he ruled from City Hall behind
the Quai du Port, or by remote control from his large yachts. While
nobody suggested that he had anything to hide personally, the fact
was that Gaston could get away with just about anything he chose.
The Socialist Party needed the Marseille electorate, and Defferre
always delivered. It was an era when taxis were sent to pick up
elderly voters who could be counted on to vote as he wished.

This ensured that nobody on the non-Communist left in Paris
would raise any questions about how he ran things back home, and
would accord him proper deference when he travelled north. Successive governments of the centre-right saw him as a dependable
anti-Communist bulwark, and did not object if their local chieftains
allied themselves with City Hall. Defferre's system had room for every
shade of opinion, so long as it wasn't Communist. He maintained a
right-wing newspaper, *Le Méridional*, alongside his pale pink flagship,
Le Provençal. However, his forays into national electoral politics were
none too successful. As a minister during the Fourth Republic, he
oversaw decolonization in sub-Saharan Africa, but a campaign to
promote him as a presidential candidate against de Gaulle in 1965
fizzled out, and, when he did run in 1969, he got just 5 per cent of
the vote, the lowest ever for a Socialist.

When the left won power under Mitterrand in 1981, Defferre
became Interior Minister and the second-ranking member of the first
Socialist government of the Fifth Republic. But his authority was
fraying with time and age. A string of municipal scandals, which once
would have been hushed up, broke into the open. A local police

chief and five members of his family were murdered by three Gaullist toughs. One of the Mayor's more shady associates wound up in jail. With Communists sitting beside him in the government in Paris, Defferre was forced to call off an investigation he had authorized into the party's affairs in Marseilles; the civil servant in charge of the case was found dead—officially a case of suicide, but there were troubling inconsistencies. With the colonies gone and nothing much to replace it, local commerce slumped into the doldrums. Rising unemployment and a big immigrant population helped to raise social tension which was exploited by Jean-Marie Le Pen and the National Front.

Defferre died in 1986, and the once-powerful coalition through which he had ruled the city fell apart in a jungle of feuds: the old man's widow, a distinguished author known for her implacable hatreds, banned any mention of those she considered to have been disloyal to her husband from the pages of *Le Provençal*. Bernard Tapie tried to become the new prince of the city, peddling populist politics against the Front and taking over the Olympique de Marseille soccer club, which won the French Championship and the Europeans Champions League. But the flamboyant businessman and would-be politician was accused of fixing a match, and the club was stripped of its French league championship, though not of the European title, and was relegated to a lower division because of financial irregularities widely blamed on Tapie who, as we have seen, was subsequently sent to jail for complicity in corruption and subordination of witnesses.

A decade after Defferre's death, the city was in a bad way, with unemployment at 21 per cent. In 1995, the mayor's office passed to the mainstream right under Jean-Claude Gaudin, a leader of the main non-Gaullist party of the right—the Union pour la Démocratie Française (UDF). He showed a fine taste for *cumuls* by combining the mayoral office with ministerial office in charge of Regional Development, Towns and Integration, seats in either the Senate or the National Assembly, the presidency of the regional council and leader of his party's legislative group. He was re-elected Mayor of Marseilles in 2001 and 2008. A bachelor, he also found time to put his name to three books.

The city had reason for pride when it was named European Capital of Culture for 2013, but gang warfare, crime and drug traf- ficking got so bad in some area that one district administrator called for troops to be sent in. Gaudin says his goal is for everybody to live together as a united community. Unemployment has fallen from the catastrophic level when he took office, but still stands at 13 per cent. A report by the OECD in 2013 judged that the metropolitan region taking in Marseilles and Aix-en-Provence was one of the most unequal in France in incomes, education and access to employment. In some districts, it added, youth joblessness was 50 per cent, and more than a third of the inhabitants had no formal education.

The northern suburbs of Marseilles, inhabited largely by immigrants, are a wasteland of bleak tower blocks. A third of all murders recorded in France during 2012 occurred in the Marseilles region. The city's Socialists remain fragmented—in 2013 the local party rejected a mayoral candidate backed by the government in Paris and preferred a local who had called for the army to be sent in to deal with the drug-related killings. Emboldened, the seventy-four-year-old announced at the end of 2013 that he would run again for office. Tradition is not dead in some places.

Several chapters have passed without mention of food, so let us get back to that key subject and look at its contribution to the diversity of the nation. Nothing embodies French regionalism so much as what people consume. 'Tell me what you eat, and I'll tell you what you are,' said the gastronomic writer Brillat-Savarin. He might have added, 'and where you come from.' We have noted the link which food provides to the countryside as a whole. Now focus this on the regions. Yes, sales of mass-processed produce rise year by year. Yes, France likes to experiment with exotic fruit and vegetables. And, yes, chic new restaurants in Paris offer tamales, Caesar salads, sushi variations and even English grub. Still, the essentials of eating are rooted in the provincial diversity of the nation.

Dishes may be available across the country, but each has its home. If you can get a perfectly fine cassoulet or *sandre au beurre blanc* in Paris, the dishes should truly be eaten in restaurants in Toulouse or the Loire Valley. Tripe in Normandy is different from tripe in Nice or Lyon. How fish is treated in Brittany sets it apart from the Mediterranean. Wine from different regions not only tastes different, it is also put into differently shaped bottles—from the thin containers of Alsace and the elegance of Champagne to the wine pots of Lyon, with their thick glass bottoms designed to keep them upright in the gravel of *boulodromes*. Regional cuisine is a serious matter for the swelling ranks of food historians and academics. An ethnologist from the south has written a treatise on 'The Influence of the Sardine on the Mediterranean Imagination,' while a conference in the eastern city of Nancy heard papers dealing with subjects such as 'An Unusual Island of Stockfish-Eating in Rouergue-Quercy,' 'A Spatial Analysis of the Alimentary Habits in Lozère: Oil, Soup and Pig Meat' and 'Pork as a Cultural Determinant in the North-East of France.'

Though they have become less common as supermarkets peddle ready-made meals and people have less time to spend in the kitchen, an array of dishes links directly with towns and regions across the country—*Tourte de la Ville de Munster, Choucroute Alsacienne, Kougelhopf, Galette Charentaise, Cul de Veau à l'Angevine, Oie Farcie de Sègre, Boeuf aux Herbes de Massiac, Potée Auvergnate, Toro de Saint-Jean-de-Luz, Sauce Béarnaise, Homard à la Morbihannaise, Brochet Braisé au Champagne, Cou Farci du Quercy, Pommes Sarladaises, Confit d'Oie du Gers, Tête de Veau à la Parisienne, Poularde Demi-deuil de Lyon*—not to mention such world favourites as *Boeuf Bourguignon, Gratin Dauphinois* or *Salade Niçoise*.

France is, of course, home to the richest variety of wines to be found anywhere, but there is an even greater range when it comes to the 250-plus varieties of cheese. French cuisine and vineyards may face a growing challenge from cooking and wine grown in other countries, some quite close, such as Spain, Italy, Britain and Denmark, others far off, like Australia and the United States; even China is now producing drinkable wine. But the strong regional roots and variety which persist despite all the homogenization of products on offer in the deep freeze cabinets still constitute a central element in what makes France France (and long may that remain the case).

Regional pride has bred separatist movements in various parts of the country, but mostly their support has been small-scale, connected more to folklore and tradition than to any widespread desire to throw off the yoke of Paris. Brittany has had its autonomists, but after setting off a bomb or two they appeared to have been calmed by being given bilingual road signs and Breton language classes in school. Then, in 2013 the protests against factory closures and road taxes raised revolt which took a regional form, as the demonstrators in the red bonnets once worn by rebels against royal taxation insisted they were being particularly badly treated, a complaint that held little water given the depression elsewhere but which played effectively to local sentiment with the black and white Breton flag flying over their marches. The leader of the protests in 2013 called for devolution as he complained that 'we have no institutional power over our authority.'

Along the border with Spain, France's 250,000 Basques have proudly guarded their identity in less militant or violent manner than their counterparts across the mountain frontier in Spain—and have considerably less say in running their own affairs. Along Mediterranean coast, students can learn Provençal, but there is no movement to recreate the great fiefdoms which ruled southern France in the Middle Ages. So the nation seems pretty secure on most sides, but then, 180 kilometres off its southern coast, there lies a cancerous growth on the state of France.

On February 6, 1998, the Republic's leading representative in Corsica set out to walk to a classical music concert in the island's capital of Ajaccio. Claude Erignac, a no-nonsense administrator, had been appointed Prefect of Corsica by the government of Alain Juppé in January 1996 and kept in his post by the Socialists the following year. During his two years in the job, the sixty-year-old Erignac had not hesitated to use his authority to block a number of potentially lucrative projects backed by Corsican and Italian entrepreneurs, including a scheme to double the number of slot machines in the Ajaccio casino and another to turn the military barracks in the picturesque port of Bonifacio into a luxury hotel. He had launched probes into alleged fraud in the use of national and European subsidies and into contracts for waste disposal and public car parks. He also had in his files a police report recommending investigations of local banks and racketeering by two well-known gangs—and, most explosive politically, of the island's agriculture, which would involve some leading nationalists.

Although it has been under French rule since the eighteenth century, the island and its people stand apart from the mainland. Lying

in the Mediterranean between France and Italy, Corsica has a long
tradition of violence, clan politics, racketeering and poverty—and
a desire to affirm its own identity, if only it knew how. Recurrent
efforts by governments in Paris to get to grips with the Corsican
problem have met with little success. The island of 300,000 people
is famed for its beauty and is a tourist magnet, but it also has the
highest per capita murder rate in Europe. Since 2007 there have been
105 assassinations. In 2012 its best-known lawyer, Antoine Sollacaro,
was shot dead by two gunmen on a motorcycle as he filled up his
car with petrol at a gas station. Once the violence was by nationalists
seeking independence. Now it is carried out mainly by criminals who
often have links with local officials and who seem largely immune
from action by the national authorities; fewer than 10 per cent of
murders have led to conviction. Sollacaro's daughter has accused the
judicial authorities in mainland France of being afraid to make arrests.

The island is an economic basket case which could not live in
its accustomed style without cash from Paris. The devotion of the
inhabitants is open to considerable doubt. Very few of them avail
themselves of the possibility of taking the baccalauréat school-leaving
examination in the local language. There is a long history of economic dependence on the mainland stretching back at least to the
state pensions paid to the large number of men who died in World
War One. The island has no industry to speak of and its gross
domestic product is 30 per cent below that of France as a whole,
but it contains four airports and six harbours built with subsidies.
For generations, the young people have gone off in search of fortune
elsewhere. Corsicans have long formed the backbone of the civil
service on the mainland, and helped to bolster its security forces,
sometimes themselves only on the edges of legality.

Corsicans pop up in Venezuela and Indochina, Canada and Hong
Kong, in business and in the underworld. Men from the island ran
the Marseille 'Connection.' During the wars in Indochina, Bonaven-
ture 'Rock' Francisci headed an airline which flew morphine base
from Laos to Saigon on its way to Europe and America. Corsicans
smuggled gold, gems, currency and narcotics to Marseille from
Indochina long after the last French soldiers had left their former
colonies. At one restaurant by the main cemetery of Saigon, which

served excellent *steak au poivre*, I was assured in the mid-1960s that one was safe from Viet Cong attacks because '*le patron est Corse.*'

Back home, the island's politics have been riddled with infighting between clans defending their territory and income with endemic fraud at the voting booths. In southern Corsica, the Rocca-Serra family has held sway since the 1920s. When the father fell into disgrace for wartime collaboration, his son—known as 'the silver fox' for his cunning and his hair colouring—took up the reins. Mayor of the beautiful coastal town of Porto-Vecchio for forty-seven years and a member of the National Assembly for thirty-six until his death in 1998, he paid for funerals, gave free consultations in his medical practice and seemed to know everybody. Once, when a village mayor gambled away the communal funds, Rocca-Serra met the loss from his own pocket and kept the police quiet. His price was that he got the votes which maintained his influence whatever Paris said.

This was the kind of jungle which the Prefect, Claude Erignac, was trying to come to grips with. In one all-too-familiar incident amid the wave of attacks on the island and against mainland targets in the autumn of 1997, nationalist commandos raided a police barracks in the southern town of Pietrosella. They blew up the building and took two gendarmes hostage, later freeing them in the maquis scrubland. Five weeks later a nationalist group issued a statement pledging an uncompromising struggle against the French state.

A month later, two young men walked up to Claude Erignac as he made his way to the concert in Ajaccio. One was unshaven and fair-haired, the other dark and wearing a T-shirt. One of them shot the Prefect in the back of the head with the Beretta stolen at Pietrosella. He died immediately. The killer dropped the pistol and fled with his companion. Three days afterwards, a statement from the nationalist group claimed responsibility for the murder.

Erignac's assassination shocked even the blasé Corsicans. Almost a sixth of the island's population joined in silent protest marches. Jacques Chirac and Lionel Jospin flew south to condemn the deed. The Interior Ministry declared the discovery of the killers to be its number-one priority.

Police seized tonnes of documents from a local bank, went through the accounts of Corsica's development fund and looked at doubtful loans amounting to a billion francs. It then emerged that the explosive police report recommending a probe into the island's agricultural affairs had fallen into the hands of hard-line nationalists. Time passed, and the inquiry got nowhere until finally a separatist, Yvan Colonna, was caught in 2007 hiding in a shepherd's hut after spending four years on the run in the island's wild maquis country. He was given a life sentence for the Prefect's murder. But a retrial was ordered on procedural grounds which ended with confirmation of the sentence. However, Colonna continued to insist on his innocence and other militants who had testified against him retracted their accusations. The Corsican imbroglio continued with little sign of peace and harmony breaking out on the Isle of Beauty, where police felt obliged to don masks to hide their faces when they went to arrest hoodlums for whom easy money, illegality and nationalism had become inexorably entwined.

Look east now. One of Louis XIV's ministers may have dreamed of '*Germanis Gallia clausa*' (Gaul closed to the Germans), but the east is where France's identity is most porous, in land and people. The key events have been the three German invasions of 1870, which led to the loss of Alsace-Lorraine for nearly half a century, 1914, which produced an enormous bloodletting that undermined national morale despite victory, and 1940, which brought defeat and shameful abasement. In the 1980s, French officials worried that divided Germany was an unstable nation which needed France's guiding hand. Thirty years on, the concern in Paris focuses on the power of the reunited neighbour and the way in which its economic prowess is translating into geopolitical power.

The Franco-German Treaty, signed by de Gaulle and Chancellor Konrad Adenauer in 1963 when Germany was still divided, is Europe's most important bilateral agreement since the end of World War Two, and the fact that there has not been a fourth armed conflict between the two nations since 1945 has been a boon of immeasurable dimensions for the continent. Hundreds of thousands of young people have taken part in educational exchanges. A poll in late 2013 showed Germany as the European nation to which the French felt closest, with 37 per cent naming it, well ahead of the UK—though Germans ranked Austria, Switzerland and the Netherlands ahead of the Hexagon.

Yet there have been geopolitical reservations in Paris ever since the Berlin Wall came down in 1989. Seeing the danger of a united Germany for the status France had enjoyed since de Gaulle's presidency, Mitterrand was lukewarm about German unity. As the writer François Mauriac remarked while the Berlin Wall still stood, 'I like Germany so much that I'm happy there are two of them.' Today, the preeminence of Germany in Europe is indubitable, and France is the main victim. Even if Angela Merkel is a reluctant continental leader, economic reality puts her country on a rung above that of France.

In a world where invasion is more likely to come from currency dealers' terminals than from marching feet, the Hexagon is as vulnerable as any other medium-sized nation caught up in the globalization process. But it now also suffers from doubts about the European project of which it has been a central actor ever since it joined the early moves towards continental cooperation with the Coal and Steel Community established in 1951 following a proposal by Foreign Minister Robert Schuman. Another Frenchman, Jean Monnet, became 'the Father of the Common Market,' and the Treaty of Rome which institutionalized that six-nation association would have been unthinkable without France. But the same poll which showed national feelings at the ends of 2013 found that only 16 per cent of French respondents thought that the European Union delivered benefits, while 48 per cent saw it as bringing disadvantages, with the rest undecided. The negative proportion was three points more than in Britain, and the positive number was half that in Germany.

As well as such wider concerns, France is prey to internal tensions of its own springing from the conflict we have seen between the centralized state, even if it is less omnipotent than republican theory imagines, and an invigorating taste for individualism and rejection of authority fuelled by economic and social problems. Taken together, both sets of concerns raise troubling questions of national status and identity which, naturally, pose themselves just at the time when the rulers have fewest answers.

Like their ancestors, the Gauls, the French need chieftains who find a way of bringing cohesion out of these contrary strands in their nation and society. The Fifth Republic presidency was meant to achieve that, with the directly elected leader in the Élysée ™ drawing together all of the myriad groups, units, associations and factions which make up the mainstream of the nation and owe loyalty to national unity as represented by the state. Instead, France has found itself wounded by politicians who have fallen short of the task and who have exacerbated the nation's contradictions. This fault line dates back four decades, and it is now time to examine the way in which politicians have taken the country to the brink but have always managed to keep it from tipping over—so far.

10

THREE MEN AND A COUNTRY

As political conflicts go, France's Thirty Years' War had its deadly aspects: two spectacular suicides and many personal wounds. Men and women saw their careers destroyed and their lives diverted to serve the ambitions of François Mitterrand, Valéry Giscard d'Estaing and Jacques Chirac. Between them, these three men encapsulated France's political history from 1974 to 2007. When hostilities opened, Lyndon Johnson was in the White House, American troops were beginning their big build-up in Vietnam. China was in the throes of the Cultural Revolution and the Soviet Union's domination stretched from the middle of Germany to Siberia.

Other democracies renew their leadership at regular intervals, usually less than ten years, as new figures come to the fore, but as we have seen, France's politicians are masters at survival, even if victories are usually frittered away while defeats are rarely final. The script may be adapted to changing times but the same actors dominate the stage. Both Mitterrand and Chirac were beaten twice before finally winning the job, and each of them plummeted to the bottom of the opinion polls within a few years of seizing the ultimate prize. In France, politics is a game the top players never give up—and the only losers are the people.

The oldest of the three protagonists was in the north Burgundian town of which he was Mayor when he learned on December 19, 1965, that his first presidential bid had failed. With greater difficulty than expected, France's reigning monarch had repulsed the challenge to his throne from a collection of competing forces ranged against him from the far left of the battlefield to the far right. De Gaulle's final victory in the second round of France's first presidential election of the twentieth century by universal suffrage was no surprise, however, and François Mitterrand's 45 per cent of the vote was an honourable score which established him as the leader of the left, ready to mount a fresh challenge when the ageing patriarch finally stepped down.

That became increasingly likely as the 1960s drew to a close. After a decade of Gaullist pre-eminence, the ground was shifting. The General and his country were growing "out of touch with one another"—as a leading political commentator put it, France was getting bored. De Gaulle reflected that he should have ruled from the royal surroundings of the Palace of the Louvre rather than from the more modest and less historic surroundings of the Élysée, but voters were more interested in inflation and wages than in grandeur. It seemed that Mitterrand had only to wait patiently to claim his ultimate reward after more than twenty years in politics.

Three years later, everything fell to bits for the challenger. The General's hour of greatest danger, during the strikes and student riots of 1968, should have been a time of maximum opportunity for the opposition and its chief. But the upheaval caught the orthodox left as much by surprise as the Gaullist administration. Mitterrand resorted to history, imagining himself on the barricades of 1848 or 1870, and proposing a Government of National Salvation. The Gaullists easily turned that into an attempted coup. Spectacular as the unrest was, most of the French soon came to want salvation from disorder. If they entertained doubts about de Gaulle, it was because they wondered if, nearing eighty, he really was in charge anymore. So they rallied behind the reassuring Prime Minister, Georges Pompidou, who bought off the unions, made concessions to the students, and ended the revolt without a life lost on either side.

When de Gaulle sacked the Prime Minister, who had become too powerful for his master's taste, France had an alternative head of state from the Gaullist ranks for the first time under the Fifth Republic, a man of experience who, vitally, was now a free agent. Scheming against him by Gaullist diehards goaded the phlegmatic

Pompidou into action and, on a visit to Rome, he made it plain that he would stand for the presidency if De Gaulle left the Élysée. When the head of state responded by asserting his intention to serve out his seven-year term, his former Premier spoke to a Swiss television interviewer of his own 'national destiny'—a phrase that could have only one meaning.

That helped to propel the enfeebled founder of the Fifth Republic into a last bid to regain the initiative and restore the link between himself and the people. He opted for the old Bonapartist device of a plebiscite in the form of a referendum on the unexciting subject of regional and Senate reform. Pompidou's presence made it impossible for the General to play his habitual trump card of warning France that it faced a choice between him and chaos. So he was committing political suicide, choosing to go out on a defeat at the ballot box rather than simply resigning in mid-term, not a palatable course for a leader who had never shirked a battle. On Sunday, April 27, the General went to mass in the morning at the parish church of the country village of Colombey-les-deux-Eglises, where he had maintained a country home for thirty years, voted and then shut himself away in his austere house. The referendum proposal was lost by 47 per cent to 53. At ten minutes past midnight on April 28, 1969, the French news agency put out the terse statement from the head of state: 'I am ceasing to exercise my functions as President of the Republic. This decision takes effect at noon today.'

François Mitterrand decided not to stand in the 1969 presidential election that followed De Gaulle's departure; nobody asked him to, anyway. Pompidou won an overwhelming victory. Gaston Defferre and Pierre Mendès-France ran in tandem for the Socialists and received 5 per cent of the vote.

After the heroic founding epoch of the Fifth Republic, with its reassertion of national glory, the ending of the Algerian war and the development of the nuclear force, the Pompidou presidency ushered in a more businesslike era characterized by the construction of industrial empires rather than great international ambitions. It was a time of respite during which the left licked its wounds while the ambitious men of the centre and right planned their future. Things changed sooner than any of them had expected. Pompidou's face ballooned, and he increasingly had difficulty walking. He died of cancer on April 2, 1974, at the age of sixty-three.

His death precipitated an era of treason. The prime Gaullist candidate for the presidency was Jacques Chaban-Delmas, a resistance leader who had been Pompidou's Prime Minister before being sacked for being too liberal. Popular, attractive and fit—an accomplished golfer and fine tennis player who ran up stairs four at a time at the age of sixty—he should have been a natural winner, but he was distrusted by many Gaullists on two counts.

The first was that he had swung too far to the left, listening to siren voices like that of his adviser on social affairs, Jacques Delors, as he sought to craft his 'New Society' for France. While Pompidou was preaching unadventurous corporatism, Chaban-Delmas promoted employees' involvement in running the companies they worked for. His second problem was more personal. He had run into difficulties over revelations about his tax affairs; he was a lacklustre campaigner with an unpleasantly metallic voice; and he seemed to many not to possess a true hunger for the job. In short, for the hard wing of the Gaullist party, Chaban-Delmas was not nearly tough enough to hold the most important post in France.

Nobody harboured such doubts more strongly than two of Pompidou's close advisers, Pierre Juillet and Marie-France Garaud, who had achieved near-mythic status as forces behind the throne. Garaud, originally a lawyer from Poitiers, had a dominating manner that seduced and subjugated the men around her; Juillet was a man of the shadows who walked with a cane and kept a sheep farm in the Limousin. In 1974, their main aim in life was to prevent the Socialists and their allies from winning the presidency. To do that, they were convinced they had to stop Chaban-Delmas being the Gaullist candidate.

There was no doubting the task that the centre-right faced in retaining power. In one of the extraordinary recoveries which marked his political career, François Mitterrand had established himself as the single candidate for the main parties of the opposition as he launched into his decade-long exercise of drawing the Communist Party into his tent in order to strangle it. In 1969, the Communist Jacques Duclos had won 21 per cent of the vote—four times as much as the Socialist. Now, Mitterrand had got the whole of the left to line up behind him. Parliamentary elections had brought big gains for the opposition and the loss of a hundred constituencies for the governing parties. The Gaullist crown was under serious threat. If Chaban could not defend the castle, it was time to find another standard-bearer against Mitterrand (even if he came from outside the orthodox Gaullist ranks) and to infiltrate his army in preparation for an eventual restoration.

Valéry Giscard d'Estaing looked and acted like a highly intelligent aristocrat from the great days of the court at Versailles, though his family was actually only authorized to use the d' in 1922. Born four years later in Germany, where his father was a civil servant with the occupation forces after the First World War, Giscard was one of those brilliant individuals who shoot through the upper reaches of France's education system to run the country. He joined the Prime Minister's staff at the age of twenty-eight, won election to the National Assembly by the time he was thirty and was a junior member of the government at thirty-three. De Gaulle found the young man too clever by half, and there were doubts about the Algerie Française affiliations of some members of the right-wing political group he led. But nothing could stop Giscard. He became Finance Minister a month before his thirty-sixth birthday.

The post ranks just behind that of Prime Minister in terms of power, since its occupant controls so much of what his colleagues can afford to do. Giscard held the job in grand offices at the Louvre Palace for nine years, during which he and the job became synonymous. When I told a taxi driver I wanted to go to the Finance Ministry one Saturday morning, he nodded and replied, 'Ah, chez Giscard!'

The Minister had style to spare. He spoke for hours in parliament without notes. Tall and self-assured, he looked perfect in formal dress, but he also met me that Saturday in his ornate office in the Louvre wearing a cardigan and no tie. Touching the populist bases, he played the accordion and turned out for football in his native Auvergne—photographs taken in the changing room showed that he carried not an ounce of surplus fat, in striking contrast to his well-padded Cabinet colleagues. Giscard had ambition by the kilometre. After a dozen years at the top of government, he was ready to make his bid for the summit in 1974, and the time was right. France was ready for a change from Gaullism. Giscard knew he could capture that national mood, without frightening the conservative middle classes. He presented himself as the thoroughly modern leader his country needed, a French Kennedy—he had visited JFK in 1962 and a magazine resurrected the photograph of the two of them together at the White House. In terms of personal ambition, he was well aware that if he did not grab the opportunity in 1974 he might never have another chance: either Mitterrand would win, possibly going on to a second term, or a failure by the left would ensure Gaullist rule into the next century.

The snag was that, for all his attributes, the young man lacked one essential element—a mass political movement. However much de Gaulle may have despised parties and aspired to rule above them, the election of the president by universal suffrage, which he introduced in 1962, meant that the head of state needed a big political organization to get out the voters and maintain electoral discipline. Giscard had his followers, organized by a much more truly aristocratic friend, Prince Michel Poniatowski. But there were not enough of them; his Independent Republican party had only 55 of the 488 seats in the National Assembly, compared with 183 Gaullists. Giscard's followers tended to be local bigwigs, notables who ran French country towns, men and women at home in upper bourgeois houses and small châteaux, where the food was excellent, the service discreet and money not mentioned as deals were made in a quiet corner of the salon after a day's shooting. However highly they might prize themselves, such folk were simply not numerous and well-organized enough to withstand the challenge from Mitterrand backed by the still formidable battalions of the Communist Party. Rattling pearls at the peasants and workers wasn't going to repel the populist hordes.

Juillet and Garaud had no great liking for the Finance Minister: in many ways, he was the antithesis of their idea of a leader and his centrist friends were even worse. Still, they needed him, as he needed them. Pompidou's death had come two years too early for the backroom pair. They were grooming their presidential candidate; but, like a classic racehorse being trained for the Prix de l'Arc de Triomphe, timing was everything. If Pompidou had lived to the end of his term in 1976, it would have been a different matter. But this was 1974, and there was an inescapable symmetry. The anti-Chaban Gaullists had the troops to put into the field but no general to lead them; Giscard had few troops but was the ideal man to head the charge.

So a deal emerged. A breakaway group of forty-three Gaullist members of the National Assembly distanced themselves from Chaban-Delmas and lined up behind Giscard, who ran a smooth campaign under the slogan 'change in continuity.' He offered modernization without upsets in contrast to the collectivist programme Mitterrand had adopted as the price of gaining Communist support. In the first round of the two-stage presidential voting, Mitterrand easily topped the poll with 43 per cent. That had been expected. The vital thing was that he had fallen well short of the outright majority needed for election and had no reservoir of new votes for the run-off. The important figures were Giscard's 32.6 per cent plus Chaban-Delmas's mere 15.1. Although the left's man had finished first, the electoral arithmetic was stacked against him. A dozen candidates had run in the first round, and most of the votes for those who were eliminated would go to the right. Mitterrand could count on far smaller reserves of new support than Giscard. Even the Gaullists who had backed Chaban-Delmas reconciled themselves to the treason which had knocked their candidate out of the race.

At fifty-seven, Mitterrand looked decidedly dowdy compared with the cool young intelligence opposite him. Though Giscard had first entered government fifteen years earlier, he had no trouble presenting himself as a force for new thinking and casting his opponent as an old stager who had been around for three decades and had experienced more failures than successes. In many people's mind, the older man was still identified with the discredited Fourth Republic, and he had not held ministerial office for sixteen years. When his opponent asked him a direct question about international finance in France's first televised presidential debate, Mitterrand couldn't reply. Responding to the left's portrayal of him as a hard-hearted technocrat, Giscard told his rival that he did not have a monopoly on feelings of the heart. It was no shock when, on May 19, Valéry Giscard d'Estaing became the third President of the Fifth Republic with 50.81 per cent of the vote. The only surprise was that the margin had not been larger. Much as Giscard wanted to lead France into a new era, the electorate did not seem entirely convinced it wanted him or the change he sought to epitomize.

Mitterrand had come much closer to victory than in his first bid for the top job nine years earlier. But the seven-year length of the term in the Élysée Palace and the awesome power of the office make opposition a lonely, ill-defined job: France does not recognize a Leader of the Opposition as Britain does, which is sensible since there are nearly always several oppositions. As a man who knew the value of time, Mitterrand devoted the rest of the 1970s to building up a new Socialist Party and to his long-term campaign to snare the Communists in his web as he prepared for what would be a third tilt at the Élysée. For the moment, the field belonged to the new alliance which had defeated both the left and the old-style Gaullists. Giscard, the presiding general of the victorious forces, moved in to the Élysée on May 27. His first action was to appoint as Prime Minister the man who had made victory possible.

Jacques Chirac was Georges Pompidou's political son. After a flirtation with the left during his late teens, when he sold the Communist newspaper *L'Humanité* in the street and signed a Moscow-inspired anti-nuclear petition, he had turned into a dyed-in-the-wool Gaullist. Pompidou had taken the young Enarque on to his staff while he was de Gaulle's Prime Minister. The product of a comfortable upper middle-class family, Chirac had had a full life already: he had trained as a cavalry officer, had gone to sea and spent a summer in America where he studied at Harvard, won a certificate from a Howard Johnson ice cream parlour for his skill in making banana splits and gave a southern belle Latin lessons—and her first kiss, which she said she remembered forty years later.

To blood him politically, Pompidou sent the young man off to the Corrèze department in France's agricultural heartland to conquer it for the Gaullists: Chirac and his wife drove through the night from Paris each Friday or took the train that arrived at 4:10 a.m. to campaign through the weekend in the markets and *charcuteries* whose produce he particularly relished. He became a municipal councillor, and, in 1967, went on to win the parliamentary constituency he still held when he became president two decades later. After Pompidou moved into the Élysée in 1969, he promoted his protégé to be Minister for Relations with Parliament (where he was a disaster), then

Agriculture Minister (where he ferociously defended French interests) and finally to the Interior Ministry (where he took office a month before Pompidou died). The President's death was a huge blow. 'I had the feeling of suddenly being an orphan,' he wrote. At the memorial mass for Pompidou, he sobbed.

Had Pompidou lived through his presidential term and then been prevented by bad health from running for re-election, Chirac might well have been the Gaullist candidate in 1976. That was what Juillet and Garaud had planned. They had taken Chirac to their bosom as their hope for the future. On his way home in the evening from his various ministries, the young man would drop in to see them. If Pompidou was his political father, Pierre and Marie-France were his uncle and aunt. An only child, Chirac hid an unexpected need for mentors behind his straight-ahead style. With a grasshopper attention span, he required advisers who could ensure he kept at least a degree of focus and would supply confirmatory approval.

Since 1974 was too early for a presidential bid, Chirac and his two promoters decided that, if he could not be in the Élysée himself, he should at least become the power centre in another man's reign. As Interior Minister, he organized the election, and Fifth Republic tradition did not require ministerial impartiality. Chirac had access to police polls which showed Chaban-Delmas losing to Mitterrand. With Juillet and Garaud orchestrating every move, the forty-three eminent anti-Chaban Gaullists published a joint text saying there should be just one representative of the governing majority in the coming election. The signatories included four members of the government, headed by the Interior Minister. Their message was clear: they would swing a significant section of Gaullist support away from Chaban-Delmas and behind the Minister of Finance and the Economy. 'Chirac is a falcon placed on the gloved fist of Marie-France,' Chaban-Delmas wrote later. 'From time to time, Juillet slips the chain so that Chirac flies for an hour. And kills.'

In one of the recurrent ironies of French elite politics, Chirac delivered the eulogy at Chaban's funeral in Paris twenty-six years later. He lauded the former Premier as a 'precursor' who had understood the need to get away from the old divisions of France to construct a society which was more just and more united. 'Jacques Chaban-Delmas showed us the way,' he concluded of the politician he had betrayed and destroyed. It was, an old Gaullist remarked, 'the first time that Jesus had managed to have his funeral oration delivered by Judas.'

Nine days after being elected President, Valéry Giscard d'Estaing appointed the leader of the Gaullist as the sixth Prime Minister of the Fifth Republic. The two men were strikingly young for a country which generally liked its leaders to show their age. Giscard was forty-eight, Chirac forty-one. They had first worked together when Chirac held a junior post at the Finance Ministry. They had been in endless Cabinet meetings since then. They seemed the perfect team to move their country to the forefront of the modern age. They may even have believed it themselves: winning battles can provoke dangerous illusions. The truth was that victory opened up a steadily widening war between two men pursuing the same prize. At the memorial for Chaban, Giscard left the church when Chirac began to speak, as if he could not bear to hear the hypocrisy of his one-time partner.

Valéry Marie René Georges Giscard d'Estaing set out to be a great president. He introduced a flood of social reforms, with particular attention to women's rights. His administration liberalized the abortion laws. He modernized France's telecommunications and sought to free up the financial system. With Helmut Schmidt, Germany's equally brainy Chancellor, Giscard set up the European Monetary System. He improved relations with the United States and pressed ahead with the construction of Europe. He established the Group of Six, or G-6 (now the G-8), bringing together the heads of government from the United States, West Germany, Italy, Japan and the United Kingdom to discuss global issues and try to forge a common response.

But, as his presidency wore on, much of what he did could be summed up by Marie-France Garaud's dismissive phrase—'*des gadgets.*' Whether because he was, at heart, more conservative than he seemed or because he was too removed from the realities of daily life, Giscard's reforms changed things less than he thought. The President was like one of those eighteenth-century aristocrats who played with all the most advanced ideas about changing society, who set up model farms and chatted with Voltaire and felt good envisaging a new enlightenment—but who were never really ready to challenge the society which had bred them.

There was another problem with Giscard. The exorbitant powers of the presidency were irresistible. The opportunities to put his finger in every pie could not be passed by. De Gaulle and Pompidou had known that the President needed to leave the Prime Minister room to breathe while his gaze rested on loftier horizons: if France had been a business, the Fifth Republic gave it a Chairman and a Chief Executive Officer. De Gaulle told the Americans to get out of Vietnam; his Prime Minister dealt with public sector wage negotiations. Pompidou let Britain into the Common Market; his Prime Minister worried about workers' rights.

Giscard relished the world horizon, but, like Nicolas Sarkozy three decades later, he found it hard to delegate at home. This was partly a personal trait. He wanted to be Chairman of the Board, Company President, CEO, CFO (he kept the Finance Ministry under close watch) and any other O around. He also had ambitions to replace Gaullism with Giscardianism, establishing his centre-right followers as France's main political movement. His anti-Gaullism was no new development—in 1967 he had spoken openly about preparing 'France for her future,' and his party had discreetly advised its members to vote against the General in the 1969 referendum.

Had he seized the moment in 1974 and called legislative elections, Giscard might have taken a big step towards his dream of a dominant centre-conservative party. Instead, with a Gaullist as Prime Minister, he made the mistake of contenting himself with the parliamentary majority bequeathed by Pompidou with its big Gaullist group in the National Assembly. At the same time, he kept a tight hand on the government, paying scant attention to the constitutional nicety that it should have been run by the man who had made his victory possible. Giscard telephoned ministers directly, by-passing Chirac. He appointed his close friend, Michel Poniatowski, as Interior Minister with the job of building up their Independent Republican party and cutting the ground from beneath Chirac's troops. But, as the President's men sought ways to change the face of French politics, the soldiers who had crossed the lines to win him victory in 1974 were preparing to move in a different direction.

For Marie-France Garaud and Pierre Juillet, Giscard's presidency was an unfortunate, if necessary, period whose only virtue was that it had stopped François Mitterrand becoming head of state. France, they calculated, would tire of this hollow neo-aristocrat and be ready for the return of dyed-in-the-wool Gaullism. Though Giscard would remain in office until 1981, preparations had to be made for the return of their man when the next election eventually came around. In the interim, the President could be reduced to a puppet by draining off his power towards his Prime Minister. So while Giscard sought to undermine the Gaullists, they were out to do exactly the same to him. It was a recipe for disaster, exacerbated by the basic differences of temperament between the men leading the two groups.

The new head of state was desperately eager to find the common touch. He made regular television appearances to tell the nation what he was doing. He shared a barbecue at his Mediterranean presidential retreat with North African soldiers who had fought for the French and invited dustmen to breakfast at the Élysée. He ventured out from time to time to dine with ordinary citizens—a lorry driver, a picture framer, a gamekeeper and a young couple in Garaud's home city of Poitiers. Sometimes, the President would abandon his official car and walk to official appointments through the streets of Paris. There were stories about him having crashed into the back of a milk delivery van while driving himself back to the Élysée in the early hours after a romantic assignation.

Still, away from the public-relations machine, the head of state had a strikingly lordly style for a supposedly modern man. He instructed his Prime Minister to walk three paces behind him on official occasions. His wife, Anne-Aymone Sauvage de Brantes, daughter of a marquis and a princess, was said to have been flummoxed when a magazine photographer doing a feature on their home life asked her to put a pot on the stove; she did not know where the utensils were kept or the way to the kitchen at the Élysée. Even if the stories were fiction, they fitted their personalities so well that everybody believed it.

After their initial honeymoon, life with Giscard became steadily less pleasant for Jacques Chirac. If he did not exactly condescend to the younger man, Giscard revelled in his own superiority. The Presi-dent's broad intellectual approach sat ill with the hyperactive Chirac, who found himself frozen out of decision-making and reduced to jiggling his long legs beneath the Cabinet table in frustration. Their taste in food betrayed the essential gap between the two men. Chirac liked nothing better than large meals of solid country fare; his favourite dish was calf's head with a piquant sauce. Giscard preferred truffles—either with scrambled eggs or in a soup under a pastry shell created in his honour by Paul Bocuse. The President savoured fine wines; the Prime Minister preferred beer. As the gastronome Brillat-Savarin observed, 'Tell me what you eat and I'll tell you what kind of man you are.'

Not that Giscard's sense of superiority could not be punctured, even if nobody dared to notice it. His reign included a prime example of *farce a la française.* When OPEC sent oil prices soaring, Giscard produced a reassuring phrase. France might not have oil, he intoned, but it had ideas (an alternative was to call French agriculture 'green oil'). All very well, but when he was offered a revolutionary key to oil wealth and military security, he reacted like a child in a candy shop and thereby became the most eminent figure in the cast of a farce that also involved two Gaullist bosses of the Elf oil company, the state Audit Court, intelligence agents, a vanishing Italian inventor, a Belgian count and the doyen of French conservatives, Antoine Pinay. Jacques Chirac was kept in the dark. He would have been furious had he known of his exclusion at the time. But, when the affair came to light seven years later, he must have blessed his stars that he could plead complete ignorance.

A self-styled inventor Aldo Bonassoli claimed to have two electronic devices, code-named 'Delta' and 'Omega,' which could shoot a newly discovered particle into the earth. This particle would play back images or sound waves revealing the existence of oil deposits. By mounting the equipment on aircraft known as 'sniffer planes,' an oil company could avoid the high costs of exploratory drilling and would be able to buy cheap leases in the precise sites where the devices detected big reserves.

Bonassoli had an associate, a Belgian count who brought the invention to the attention of a well-connected French lawyer who also happened to be a reserve officer in France's counter-espionage service. The lawyer told Pinay, a former Premier who was something of a political father-figure to Giscard. Pinay informed the President and the Chairman of Elf, Pierre Guillaumat, himself a former Gaullist intelligence chief. The President and the Chairman leaped at the chance of giving France the jump on its rivals; Giscard also observed that the technique had military significance, since it could be used to detect deep-diving nuclear submarines.

The head of state insisted that the project be developed in the utmost secrecy. When he gave Elf Aquitaine approval for a first investment in June 1976, the board of the oil group's holding company was not told and the expenditure did not figure in the accounts. Secret official clearance was given for the transfer of funds to the scheme's promoters in Switzerland. The Italian inventor and the Belgian count told the French that they were putting large sums in the project, installing computers in their laboratory and equipping the sniffer planes. They would not allow staff at Elf to get a proper look at the equipment for safety reasons, warning that the boxes were dangerously radioactive. Tests were held. Giscard attended one. Although the results were poor, Elf decided to buy the process. Soon afterwards, the Industry Ministry, which was on bad terms with the oil company, took an initiative which somebody might have thought of a bit earlier. An independent expert, Professor Jules Horowitz, was called in to sniff out the sniffers.

The professor went to see the Omega device, which was said to be able to show images from the other side of a wall on a screen as proof of its power. On his first visit to the laboratory, Horowitz placed a test card behind a wall opposite the Omega box. Nothing happened. Then the machine minders gave him a metal ruler and suggested he take it behind the wall. When the professor did so, an image of a straight ruler appeared on Omega's screen. Good enough—except that, on his way to the back of the wall, the professor had bent the ruler into a V-shape.

On a later visit, Horowitz repeated the test card experiment. This time, two vertical bars came up on the screen. Excellent, except that they appeared before the professor had put his cards in place. When Omega was eventually dismantled, it was found to contain sheets of photocopied images and cheap components. Elf broke off the agreement. The Belgian count and the Italian inventor vanished. The whole affair remained secret. When the Audit Court looked into the oil company's accounts at the end of 1979, it was told that any mention of the oil-sniffing scheme should be kept confidential. Three copies of the report were sent to the government; the head of the Audit Court kept three others in his desk and destroyed them when he stepped down from his job in 1982.

The story of the sniffer-plane project eventually surfaced the following summer in the whistle-blowing weekly *Le Canard Enchaîné*. Initially, it produced smiles but little reaction. Then, just before Christmas 1983, the *Canard* reported that the Audit Court copies of the report had been destroyed. An indignant Giscard went on television to show that he had a copy and that it was still intact. He insisted that secrecy had been essential in view of the sensitive nature of the project. Elf's expenditure, estimated at up to 790 million francs, was, he argued, small by the standards of the oil industry. But the supposedly superior man in the Élysée had been gulled in a way that showed he was only human, and as Max Gallo, the Socialist writer and politician, observed, it was irresistibly reminiscent of the hare-brained inventor of the Tintin comic strip, Professor Calculus. Not the kind of association the superior Giscard would relish.

A few months before he was told of the sniffer scheme, Giscard reshuffled the government. He told the Prime Minister only after he had drawn up the new list of ministers, summoning him back from the country at a moment's notice on a Sunday morning to tell him what he had decided. That might have been grounds for resignation, but Chirac soldiered on.

The Whitsun holiday of 1976 brought him a ray of hope. He and his wife were invited to spend the weekend at the presidential retreat at Brégançon on the Mediterranean coast. It was meant to be a simple occasion—Le Président and Madame Giscard d'Estaing invite Monsieur et Madame Chirac to a weekend by the sea. The Prime Minister, a man in whom hope sprang eternal, thought this might be an opportunity to sort things out. It turned out to be a Weekend from Hell.

Chirac flew south expecting meaningful discussions. As soon as he arrived, he was disabused about the nature of the event. One other guest was present—Giscard's ski instructor. That set the tone. As Chirac later recounted it, the President and his wife sat down for meals in armchairs while their guests were relegated to straight-backed seats. Things went from bad to worse. On a joint visit to review the fleet off Nice, Chirac became so annoyed with a television interview the head of state was giving that he grabbed a pair of binoculars and scanned the sea as a diversion, not noticing in his rage that he was holding the glasses the wrong way round.

On August 25, the Cabinet assembled at the Élysée following the summer holiday. After a ninety-minute trot through the agenda, Giscard regaled his ministers with a lengthy account of a recent trip to Gabon, where he had enjoyed big-game hunting laid on by the friendly dictator, Omar Bongo. Eventually, he looked across the table.

'Monsieur the Prime Minister,' he said, 'I believe you have something to say.'

'Mr. President,' Chirac replied, 'I have the honour to present you with the resignation of my government.'

It was a first in the history of the Fifth Republic. Previously, presidents had thanked prime ministers and sent them on their way. Now, the head of government was declaring his independence of the head of state. This was the in-your-face Gaullism of 1940 and 1958. Nobody was better suited to that than Chirac. A new civil war had erupted. Whatever his brilliance, Giscard was condemned to eventual ruin by the Faustian deal he had done in 1974 and by the nature of the partner he had chosen so mistakenly—the squire who ended up destroying his master.

Jacques Chirac's drive could be positively alarming, particularly for those who have crossed him. For all his smiles and hand-clasping, he was a political killer with a singular ability to go for the jugular. Four days after leaving government, he travelled to the Creuse department in the centre of France to spend Sunday at the country home of Pierre Juillet. Also present were Marie-France Garaud and two other Chirac loyalists; she was cutting, telling Chirac, 'It is not that you were a bad Prime Minister—you weren't a Prime Minister at all.'

At lunch, Mme. Juillet placed four-leaf clovers on each plate. By the time night fell on the calm countryside, the quintet had mapped out plans for a new political party. It would be headed by the recently departed head of government. It would have mass appeal, with an army of political militants based on the existing Gaullist movement but reaching out more widely with a message of national rebirth and dynamism.

The new party's strengths would be incarnated by its chief, personifying all that was strong and true about France, safeguarding the unity of the state and its leading role in the world, bringing together the disparate threads of the nation in a single great popular movement. The setting that day was symbolic: not a château or a Parisian apartment, but a farmhouse deep in the true heart of the land they would lift to new heights. The new party was to come from the real France, and the potency of the rural myth underpinned that day at the farm. Though its progenitors had actually spun their partisan webs on either side of the Seine for almost a decade, the new force they envisaged was to stand above and beyond selfish, sectional Parisian concerns. The people around the table believed in the recurring Gaullist mantra: They, and they alone, knew what was best for France. A fly on the wall might have been a trifle concerned at the quasi-fascist superman tone that hung in the air, and a realist might have wondered about the white knight at the head of the army; Gaullism had worked under its progenitor, but Chirac was not the General.

To underline its freedom from the political salons of Paris, the campaign began with a speech calling on the nation to rally to its basic values, delivered by the departed Prime Minister in the gymnasium at Egletons in his electoral home department of the Corrèze, a town celebrated for the excellence of its sausages. In December 1976, at a great meeting in a Paris exhibition hall, the ex-Premier launched the Rassemblement Pour la République (Rally for the Republic) to take Gaullism into the next millennium and prove that ideologically led populism had a future. The name had a vital historical echo: De Gaulle had called his postwar political movement the Rassemblement du Peuple Francais. Such was the Chiracian surge that the existing Gaullist party agreed to be swallowed up; it helped that most of its barons were promised important posts in the new enterprise.

From the start, the RPR had one over-riding aim—the election of its leader as head of state in 1981. That meant there were now two competing presidential candidates on the right, for an election where they would face a candidate of the left who was busy turning the Socialist Party into a vehicle to get him to power at long last. The long wait until the next presidential election was no problem for Giscard while Mitterrand needed time to consolidate and build his strength at the head of a united left. For Jacques Chirac, on the other hand, no time could be wasted. Leading a big new party was a necessary platform for his ambitions. But he needed a means to asserting his electoral appeal. He did not have to wait long for a chance to get back from the wilderness.

Among the reforms Giscard cherished was the idea of giving Paris an elected mayor in place of the officials who ruled it at the behest of central government. As Prime Minister, Chirac had not been convinced; a real boss of the capital might become a thorn in the side of the national authorities. He was not alone in such thinking: it was why there had been no elected mayor of the city for so long. But Giscard had his way, and the poll was set for March 1977. The head of state took personal charge. Ensuring that a friendly figure ran Paris would further enhance his own power. So, at a luncheon at the Élysée Palace in November 1976, the President picked one of his most faithful lieutenants, the Industry Minister Michel d'Ornano, as the Mayor of Paris-to-be. Two days later, Juillet and Garaud had an idea: why didn't Chirac run against d'Ornano? Another front opened in the battle between the companions-in-arms of 1974 as a classic duel emerged between the Orleanist and Bonapartist strains in French politics.

Once the RPR leader had announced his candidacy, the idea seemed the most inevitable thing in the world. The Gaullists were strong in the city: a Chirac follower had just won a smashing by-election victory in the 5th arrondissement, while two Giscardians had lost seats elsewhere in the capital. A plump-cheeked Norman count, d'Ornano, did not fit naturally into campaigning in city streets. Chirac, on the other hand, relished the endless round of glad-handing and small talk in the shops, markets and cafés; it was said that his palms became so sore that he had to wrap them in soothing bandages at night. There was a challenge from the left to be fought as well, but the opponent who mattered for Chirac was not on the list of candidates. The RPR leader might be crossing swords with d'Ornano day by day, but his real target was the man in the Élysée.

On March 25, 1977, seven months to the day since he had resigned as Prime Minister, Chirac was elected Mayor of Paris. He and his RPR were triumphant. The ex-Premier now had a mighty double power base, made up of a mass party and control of France's greatest city, and he was ready for the ultimate challenge. Giscard was humiliated. His plight increased by successes for the left whose candidates ran under a joint programme in 155 of the 221 cities with over 30,000 inhabitants. Mitterrand had forged his machine for the presidential election of 1981. But recurrent revolts against his policies by the RPR served warning on the incumbent of the Élysée that he faced not the straight fight he might have expected but a triangular contest stemming from the way he had managed, or mismanaged, his alliance of seven years earlier.

The presidential battle brought together themes which had run through French politics since 1965. In the left-hand corner, François Mitterrand had the solid backing of a resurgent Socialist Party which had extended its electoral influence, especially in Brittany, and had done markedly better than the Communists at legislative elections in 1979; this caused some friction between the two parties, but they still managed to agree that they would unite for the run-off behind whichever candidate did best at the first round. There was no ideological re-thinking among the Socialists on the lines undertaken by the Social Democrats in West Germany. Mitterrand offered dreams that harped on the providential, all-providing state and a refusal to accept economic logic. The united left had failed to win a victory many predicted at the 1979 election, but it could only profit from the division on the centre-right and Giscard's continuing reliance on the parliamentary support of an increasingly hostile RPR whose deputies constituted 150 of the 287 administrations supporters in the National Assembly, most of them Chiracians who would have preferred their leader in the Élysée.

As well as guerrilla warfare from Chirac's troops, the presidency was bogged down in low growth, rising unemployment, uncertainty about France's international standing and rumours that the President had accepted diamonds from the self-proclaimed Emperor Jean Bedel Bokassa in Central Africa. Social tension was rising: far from seeing their country becoming a fairer place, as Giscard had pledged, the

French watched as inequalities rose and growth fell after the oil price crisis. The Prime Minister, former economics professor Raymond Barre, spoke a lot of sense about the need for belt-tightening in reaction to the oil price shock of the late 1970s. But his language did not go down well with the public, and Giscard refused to replace him with a more pliant figure. Though it won the 1979 legislative election, the margin in the national popular vote had been only 2,284.

Mitterrand turned his longevity to his advantage, presenting himself as a reassuring figure who understood France. Even if he needed their backing, he had the experience and cunning to handle the Communists. Though the left's big electoral successes had been in cities, his posters, dreamed up by a smart advertising guru, Jacques Séguela, depicted him standing against a background of an idyllic rural scene with a mediaeval church on a hill and the slogan, '*La force tranquille*' (Calm strength). There was no doubt that he would finish ahead of Georges Marchais of the Communist Party in the first round, so he could be sure of the backing of the big battalions of industrial workers in the run-off. He had an impressive group of potential ministers, headed by the experienced Mayor of Lille, Pierre Mauroy, and including Chaban's one-time adviser, Jacques Delors.

The smoothly aloof man in the Élysée was easily characterized as epitomizing the haves to the growing ranks of have-nots. When he attempted a reprise of his triumphal 1974 television debate with Mitterrand and asked about currency rates, the Socialist sat back and smiled; the next day, one of his staff told journalists that his boss had thought of asking whether Giscard knew the market rate for diamonds, but had held back out of respect for his office. The unspoken remark shot around town. Seven years of power had not been kind to Giscard; the unstoppably bright young man of 1974 had become the brittle autocrat of 1981. Eight months before the election, he held a 61–39 lead over Mitterrand in the polls. By the following March, the gap had narrowed to 51–49. The President was unable to refute the allegations about having accepted diamonds from Bokassa, and there was fresh embarrassment when, just before the first round of voting, *le Canard Enchaîné* revealed the wartime role of Maurice Papon, the Budget Minister, in deporting Jews from Bordeaux.

More serious politically was the challenge Giscard faced from his former Prime Minister. Three years earlier, in the 1978 European elections, Chirac had shown his wild side with a Le Pen–like attack on the Giscardians as 'the party of the foreigners.' His only excuse was that he was in hospital after a car crash which may have affected his judgement. Chirac was unabashed. He was also more alone than he had ever been, having lost the counsel of his two guides as the initial common purposes dissolved under the weight of policy and political differences. It was said that his wife, Bernadette, had issued an 'it's them or me' ultimatum. So Pierre Juillet went off to tend his sheep while Marie-France Garaud stood as an independent presidential candidate.

Chirac's 1981 campaign fell well short of his ambitions to succeed Giscard. In the first round of voting, he won 18 per cent to Giscard's 28, Mitterrand's 26 and Marchais's 15 (Garaud scored 1.3). But the crude result was not the point. The RPR's leader was a killer force, a Clint Eastwood figure on a trail of vengeance.

In public, he had to say that he would vote for Giscard in the run-off fight with Mitterrand. But there was a deafening lack of any rallying call from Gaullist ranks to back the incumbent. A minister recalled hearing Chirac say he would do all he could to ensure that the President was not re-elected. As for the RPR rank and file, five years of infighting had turned them against Giscard and his clan to the point at which some might let their hostility overcome their desire to keep Mitterrand out of the Élysée. The prospect of staying at home or going fishing rather than voting on Sunday, May 10, 1981, held a large appeal for Chirac's supporters. On the other side, Marchais and the Communist leadership were quite ambivalent about backing Mitterrand, but their voters sensed a chance to install a government of the left at long last and voted with their hearts. Taking into account the fringe parties, left and right had been very evenly balanced in the first round. So, strong support from RPR voters was essential for Giscard's re-election.

As France's preeminent electoral strategist, François Mitterrand knew that he had to exploit the cancerous split between the President and his former Premier. Accordingly, he arranged to meet Chirac over a secret dinner at the home of one of his most devoted supporters, Edith Cresson. As the evening ended, Mitterrand told the Mayor of Paris, 'If I am not elected President of the Republic this time, it will be a bore for me but, in the end, not too serious. I would go down as the man who took Socialism to 49 per cent of the vote. My place in history is already assured. I have left my mark. On the other hand, if Giscard wins again, you will have problems. I would not like to be in your shoes. He won't do you any favours, eh?'

The old fox knew who he was dealing with. Back in 1977, Chirac had been quoted as saying during a dinner at the flat of a gadfly publisher, politician and short-lived Giscardian minister, Jean-Jacques Servan-Schreiber, 'You may perhaps be surprised that I would allow— or even cause—the election of Mitterrand, but it's the only way to get rid of Giscard. And we can't go on letting him sink France.' As for Mitterrand, before the first round of the election, he confided to a businessman friend: 'God save me from facing Jacques Chirac in the second round. If he is the candidate of the united right, I don't think I'll win.'

Before the second round of voting in 1981, the champion of the united left sent a trusted friend, François de Grossouvre, to see the Mayor of Paris. De Grossouvre, an intriguer who spun schemes in the shadows for Mitterrand, had a special message to deliver. The left's electoral programme promised to introduce proportional representation to give smaller political groups seats in the National Assembly. This was acutely worrying for Chirac's RPR, which gained greatly from the winner-take-all system. De Grossouvre told Chirac that, whatever his programme proclaimed, Mitterrand would keep the existing electoral system—if he said anything else in public, it was only to keep in with his Communist allies, who would benefit from a change in the voting method. Chirac appeared content. It was said that his visitor reminded him, pleasurably, of Pierre Juillet.

As the campaign reached its peak, François Mitterrand took to quoting the Paris Mayor's public criticisms of Giscard in the late 1970s. Chirac did not rebut any of them. In a crucial television debate with the President, Mitterrand cited Chirac ten times. The Socialist and Gaullist might be on different sides of the political fence, but their mutual enmity towards Giscard brought them together. 'You have always been wrong,' Mitterrand told the head of state in their television duel. He might have been speaking for Jacques Chirac, whose attitude and desire for revenge was a major element in giving the left victory with 51.76 per cent of the vote.

The first defeat of his life was traumatic for Valéry Giscard d'Estaing. President before he was fifty, he found himself rejected at fifty-five. In 1969, Charles de Gaulle resigned with a one-sentence communiqué and remained in seclusion in his country home. In 1974, Georges Pompidou died in office. In 1981, the third President of the Fifth Republic delivered a televised farewell message to the nation. When he had finished speaking, he rose from his seat and walked off the set while the camera stayed symbolically focused on the empty chair. The implication that France had a vacuum at the very pinnacle of the state was yet another sign of Giscard's self-regard, a maudlin exercise by a man whose main public relations failure had been that, after their first honeymoon, he had related less and less to the public.

The ex-President suffered the indignity of an abusive Socialist demonstration as he drove out of the Élysée for the last time. He did not read newspapers for months to avoid hurtful criticism and said he found it hard to look at his own reflection in a mirror. He had banked so much on his own brilliance that he could not duck personal blame for defeat and the sweeping Socialist gains in ensuing parliamentary elections. At a private dinner the following year, Mitterrand told Giscard that history had been unfair to him. 'You are the best,' the new President added, 'I am sure we will meet again.' Soothing words, but little balm. By then, Jacques Chirac was rising in the opinion polls and Giscard's second Prime Minister, Raymond Barre, had emerged as the true incarnation of reliable conservative values. In the new trinity of opposition, Giscard ranked only third to his two former heads of government. No wonder he spoke of wearing widow's weeds.

Three years later, the ex-President was driving a bright green Peugeot through the narrow, winding roads of the central Auvergne to modest meeting places where he chewed over the problems of milk prices with farmers, sipped an aperitif in country cafés and showed a remarkable ability to remember the names of the pettiest of rural dignitaries. He told me that he had seen 7,300 people in his by-election campaign for a rural constituency in his home department of the Puy-de-Dome. Giscard had come out of purdah: he spoke to small groups in villages and town halls facing the official portrait of his successor. This was where he had entered politics at the age of twenty-nine, displacing a very old member of his mother's family back in 1956. The setting might be modest for a man who had founded the European Monetary System and sat at summits with superpower leaders, but Giscard showed an unexpected common touch as he discussed agricultural subsidies and the water supply. In one café, he sat at a Formica-topped table and recalled what he had done for the mountain farmers during his years in power. I'm no longer President,' he told the thirty people in the room. 'I'm picking up life again, and so should you. Your purchasing power is falling, so are your livestock prices. You haven't been defended.' To make the farmers feel important, he pulled rabbits from the hat. One morning, seeing me at the back of a quarter-filled village hall, he veered away from rural matters and told the assembled audience that the eyes of the world were upon them. 'How you vote will be noted in Great Britain, in the United States. The *Economist* (for which I was working at the time) is here, watching you,' he informed the old men in caps and clogs. Nobody but Giscard could bring such attention to a village lost among the volcanic peaks of central France.

The ex-President was relaxed that autumn day. He won the by-election easily, and later wrote a book expounding the notion that, if only the sectarian political barriers could be surmounted, two-thirds of the French could agree on a programme of national consensus—whose natural leader needed no identification. He had, he told me, drawn fresh inner strength from his reflections in the heart of the countryside. He was now involved with real life, real problems. 'I am taking the heartbeat of France,' he said as he piloted his green Peugeot on the upland roads. Then I asked him what he thought of the resurgent Jacques Chirac and the rising star of his other Prime Minister, Raymond Barre. Giscard replied with a pleasantry, but his gloved hands tightened sharply on the steering wheel and the car almost lurched off the road. The war was not over.

11

FRIENDS OF FRANÇOIS

As the face of the new President of Republic scrolled up on television screens across France at precisely 8 p.m. on May 10, 1981, the left erupted in joy. Crowds danced in the streets to celebrate the end of twenty-three years of rule from the right and centre. In the suburban Paris flat where I was having dinner, my host rushed into his kitchen and re-emerged with a bottle of champagne and a sheaf of Socialist red roses. Millions who had supported the left through decades of Gaullism and Giscardianism suddenly saw their impossible dream come true. François Mitterrand had proved that power at the summit could change hands. Driving home late that night to our flat near Socialist Party headquarters beside the Seine, I had to abandon the car because of the crush of people celebrating in the street.

No presidential victory had ever been so feted by the winners or feared by the losers. The Manichaean strain in French life was quickly apparent. While joyous crowds milled through the night on the site where the revolutionaries of 1789 had stormed the Bastille, alarmists on the right warned that political police would soon be knocking on doors. As businessmen smuggled their money over the Swiss border in suitcases, the head of the French Rothschilds went into exile in New York with the bitter phrase about being 'a traitor under Vichy, a pariah under Mitterrand.' A Socialist congress compared such people to the Royalist émigrés of 1789. A writer from the losing side reviled France for having the stupidest right wing in the world.

Having shown that an alternance of power was possible, the left went on to win an absolute majority in parliamentary elections the following month. Four Communists joined the government headed by Pierre Mauroy. In their first year in office, the Socialists brought in changes which equalled Roosevelt's New Deal or the British Labour reforms of 1945. A dozen major firms were nationalized. The death penalty was abolished, the working week was cut to thirty-nine hours, and everybody got the right to a fifth week's annual holiday. A wealth tax was instituted. The minimum wage was raised and welfare payments increased substantially. The regions of France were promised decentralization by the new Interior Minister, Gaston Defferre.

When the Finance Minister, Jacques Delors, suggested after six months that it might be time for a pause in the pace of reform, nobody took any notice. But intimations of reality soon rose to the surface. In the first thirteen months of François Mitterrand's presidency, the franc was devalued twice, and inflation rose to 18 per cent. Despite all the reflationary measures, unemployment hit two million. The boom in purchasing power sent imports spiralling upwards. France was forced to raise billions of dollars in international loans to cover its soaring debts.

In June 1982, the first knockings of what came to be known as the policy of *rigueur* were introduced with an evident incoherence as ideology met necessity: state spending was cut but the minimum wage was raised again. Economics and politics had rarely made such uneasy bedfellows. But then the President took no interest in the former and seemed to float above the second, saying that, for all his past criticisms of the Gaullist system, he found the accoutrements of presidential power fitted him well.

Amid all these great events, it was not surprising that few people paid any attention to the affairs of a shock absorber company called Vibrachoc. The firm had an array of foreign subsidiaries and a murky web of cross holdings through the financial haven of Liechtenstein. At the start of the 1980s, it was not in the best of health. One big industrial group which looked at it as a possible takeover target estimated that it was worth a maximum of sixty-five million francs, and warned that a purchaser would need to pump in capital to keep it afloat.

Three months later, that same industrial group and the subsidiaries of two large banks paid 110 million francs for the struggling shock absorber manufacturer. Part of the payment went to Liechtenstein; part was transferred to a company operating under Luxembourg law from the capital of Liberia. It was just the kind of transaction which the new President denounced in his fulminations against 'money which corrupts, money which kills, which rots consciences.' This made it all the more striking that the man who had sold Vibrachoc to such personal advantage was the President's oldest friend.

'Tell me who you frequent,' as a French proverb goes, 'and I will tell you who you are.' By that measure, François Mitterrand does not emerge with flying colours. The Bernard Tapie saga and the string of scandals linked to the Elf oil empire have already been set out. But the story of Roger-Patrice Pelat takes the tale of moral decay a step further. It shows how the rot set in from the start of the Mitterrand era, and was not—as the President's defenders would have it—simply a function of old age in the last years of his reign. And, in its way, it provides another illustration of how little those at the pinnacle of power are even aware of the gulf separating them from the proper standards of everyday life.

Pelat had fought for the Republicans in the International Brigade during the Spanish Civil War. He met Mitterrand when they were prisoners of war of the Germans. Later, they were colleagues in the Resistance. It was in Pelat's Paris flat that Mitterrand first saw a photograph of his wife to be. Half a century later, Danielle Mitterrand told an interviewer that the friends who had never disappointed her and the President were people they had met during the war, such as Roger-Patrice. He was certainly most helpful to the Mitterrands over the decades. One of the future President's brothers worked as a manager of Vibrachoc in its early years. Between 1972 and 1980, the firm paid the politician an annual fee for advice. After 1981, the payments were directed to one of Mitterrand's sons, a Socialist deputy in the National Assembly. Asked what the firm got in return, Vibrachoc's finance director said that the payments were simply a means of assuring the younger Mitterrand of 'a friendly annuity.'

The thick-set businessman was one of the few people allowed to call Mitterrand '*tu*.' Danielle spoke of his 'intoxication' when he was with François. On one occasion in 1988, he made out a cheque for 150,000 francs to Mitterrand: questioned about it later, the Élysée explained that the money was reimbursement for old books which the President had bought for his friend on his foreign travels. Although the head of state had a perfectly good home in the narrow Rue de Bièvre on the Left Bank, Pelat contributed 300,000 francs to a fund established to help him buy a new flat in case a right-wing electoral victory deprived him of a second term in the Élysée. On a visit to Paris, Mikhail Gorbachev was surprised when a large man walked calmly into the salon at the Élysée where he was conferring with Mitterrand. As recounted by a French journalist, the head of state smiled and said, 'Let me introduce Patrice Pelat. He's an old friend.' Some came to call the former maker of shock absorbers France's Vice President. He was said to keep a dinner jacket in the President's wardrobe.

Whatever Mitterrand might say in public about the awful power of money, his old pal liked getting it and spending it—and avoiding as much taxation as possible. He acquired a company yacht in the Mediterranean; he and his sons drove Rolls-Royces; he owned a hunting estate and racehorses. Vibrachoc was Pelat's biggest killing, though Mitterrand's wife sought to put a different gloss on things, saying that Pelat had 'relinquished his main business in order to be more available and closer to his friend (the President).' There was no mystery about how he managed to get such a good price for his stumbling firm. The main buyer was the Alstom industrial group, and Alstom's parent company had just been nationalized by the Socialists. The two banks which bought smaller stakes were also under state control. At the same time, Pelat had also built up a relationship with a couple of men he called the 'two Bs.' One was Alain Boublil, an adviser on industrial policy at the Élysée. The other was Pierre Bérégovoy, Mitterrand's Chief of Staff before becoming Minister for Social Affairs. Both were ready to do whatever might please their master.

A couple of months later, after he had become Minister for Social Affairs, I was interviewing Bérégovoy in his office. The telephone rang. He motioned for me to stay. May I say, he breathed into the mouthpiece, that your funeral address today was one of the most brilliant speeches I have ever heard? Then the Minister humbly suggested that the speech might be reprinted and distributed to every school in France for the edification of the nation's youth. With that, he ended his conversation with the President of the Republic and went back to outlining his plans to get to grips with France's welfare system, where even Mitterrand had to admit that spending needed to be brought under control.

While 'Béré' was drawing up plans to slim down the social security budget, Pelat went on trying to add to his fortune. His closeness to Mitterrand got him a seat on the board of Air France, meaning unlimited first class travel to any destination he liked, including a home he had bought in the Caribbean. In the summer of 1982, he tried to muscle in on a deal to sell uranium to India, but was repulsed. Six months later, he invited a select group of guests to spend Christmas with him at a luxury hotel in an oasis in Morocco. Among the guests were Boublil and Bérégovoy, who had his fortune told by a local wizard.

Back in France, away from the delights of Yuletide in the desert, the government was fast falling out of favour. In municipal elections in March 1983, the left lost major cities, including Grenoble, Saint-Étienne and Rheims, and only held Marseilles narrowly due to the power of the Defferre machine. Chirac's supporters swept all twenty arrondissements of Paris. Later that month, Mitterrand spent a long weekend debating whether France should remain a full member of the European Community or should sheer off in pursuit of Socialism in one country. Jacques Delors negotiated the European course in Brussels while some prominent Socialists in Paris, including Bérégovoy, urged the President to go it alone.

The President took the tough but inevitable course. The franc was devalued again. Returning from Brussels, Delors introduced a full austerity plan. With German help, France got a huge European loan, The Communists quit the government. Mitterrand concentrated on strengthening relations with the European partner across the Rhine, going to the World War One battlefield of Verdun to link hands with Chancellor Helmut Kohl to provide an image iconic of Franco-German friendship.

France needed all the support it could muster. Job cuts were being decreed in the newly nationalized industries which had been hailed as guarantors of employment and national prosperity a couple of years earlier. Delors was the man of the moment, but when he was offered the premiership, he overstepped the mark by making it clear that he would insist on retaining control of the Finance Ministry, which would have made him as powerful as the President. Instead, he was lined up to head the European Commission when the job became vacant in 1985. By then, Mitterrand had replaced Mauroy with the thirty-seven-year-old Laurent Fabius, who set out to reconcile Socialism with the market, and Pierre Bérégovoy moved to the Finance Ministry.

Amid all this turmoil, the President found solace in long, reflective walks around Paris with Roger-Patrice. The two elderly men called at antiquarian bookshops and strolled by the Seine, Mitterrand wearing his characteristic big black hat, Pelat in a cap. When his friend turned back to affairs of state, the businessman devoted himself to seeking out fresh avenues of profit. France's economic policy might have gone austere, but that did not mean a man could not use his contacts to good effect, even if it involved one of the more bizarre enterprises France has ever undertaken. The story was fully unveiled by the journalist Jean Montaldo in a book stuffed with revelations about doubtful members of Mitterrand's entourage.

Shortly before his election to the Élysée in 1981, Mitterrand had paid an unpublicized visit to the Stalinist outpost of North Korea. After his victory, the North Koreans pressed for an improvement in relations with Paris, and the idea emerged of France building a prestige hotel development in their country. A French company took up the idea, but wanted export credit guarantees from the government in case anything went wrong. Given the nature of the North Korean regime and the country's dubious attractions as a tourist centre, French ministers were wary—among them, the new chief of the nation's finances.

Bérégovoy advised Fabius against the state underwriting the North Korean project. But the contract for a forty-six-storey hotel with 879 rooms and 123 suites was signed with export credits guaranteed up to 95 per cent. Pelat had used his influence at the highest levels to get the state to step in. In return, according to Montaldo, a subsidiary of the French company involved in the project showed its gratitude by carrying out work on Pelat's country estate to the precise value of 24,655,462 francs and 60 centimes.

Soon after he moved into the Finance Ministry, Bérégovoy invited three foreign journalists to lunch. His new seat of power was housed in part of the Louvre palace, where elegant salons and corridors stretched further than the eye could see. We sat with the Minister at a round table in his ornate private dining room and waited for him to lecture us about the economy. Instead, he picked up the plate set before him—it was probably Sèvres porcelain.

Who could have thought, he said, that the son of a Norman café owner and a Ukrainian immigrant, a man who had gone from school to work in a textile factory at the age of sixteen, would now be sitting in the splendour of the Louvre eating off the finest of antique plates? And now could we three journalists give him, the newly appointed Finance Minister of one of the world's major economies, some tips on how he should behave at a meeting with his peers in Washington the following week? In anybody else, it would have been sickeningly insincere. But Bérégovoy really meant it. Throughout his life, he was so genuinely and touchingly struck by what he had achieved that he found it impossible to hide his delight and not to invite others to be equally impressed. But he also always seemed in need of a helping hand, a reassuring word.

The dining room in the Louvre was indeed a long way from the world into which Bérégovoy had been born in Normandy two days before Christmas in 1925. His mother ran a small café-cum-grocery shop in a suburb of Rouen. The original Ukrainian family name meant 'down by the riverside,' and Pierre was nicknamed '*le petit russe*' at school. The four children were brought up by their grandmother in the countryside. Once he had earned his school proficiency certificate, Pierre went to work as a fitter and turner. Then he moved to the railways and, while training to be an engine driver at the age of seventeen, joined the Resistance, derailing German trains during the invasion of Normandy. After the Liberation, he joined the state gas board and took out membership of the main Socialist party of the time, the SFIO. He attended night school classes and was promoted to increasingly important posts at the gas company, but quit the SFIO in protest at its support for repression in Algeria and gravitated into Mitterrand's orbit, negotiating electoral agreements with the Communists and rising to the number-two position in the new Socialist Party.

Bérégovoy's modus operandi was clear and honourable, unlike the ways of many around him. He got a foothold with a modest position in a company or political party and then, by dint of hard work and intelligence, rose steadily. Some of Mitterrand's more urbane companions sneered at his earnestly upward mobility. But he got things done. Just as Jacques Chirac had been Pompidou's bulldozer, so Pierre Bérégovoy was Mitterrand's earthmover, and he readily shouldered responsibility for policies that won the government growing unpopularity at home but which made him a pin-up boy of international finance as French inflation dipped down to 5 per cent in 1985—less than a third of its level in the left's go-go years. There was one prize waiting to be won, but Mitterrand held back, appointing Fabius to the Hôtel Matignon and letting Bérégovoy know that, at fifty-eight, he was too old for the job.

The Finance Minister's tight policies contributed powerfully to the triumph of the right at National Assembly elections in 1986, when the combined forces of Chirac's RPR and the Centrist headed by Jean-Claude Gaudin won 129 new seats, for a total of 276 deputies to 206 for the Socialists and only 35 for the Communists. Mitterrand had introduced proportional representation for the poll. This had been among the proposals advanced by the left in 1981 but had been largely forgotten since then. However, it now seemed a useful means of boosting the chances of the National Front, which had insufficient members in individual constituencies to win parliamentary seats but was able to amass nearly 10 per cent of the national vote. Mitterrand calculated that this would make life harder for the mainstream right, and Le Pen's party won thirty-five seats, but this was not enough to prevent an RPR-UDF majority. So Mitterrand was forced to usher in the first cohabitation between a president and a prime minister from different side of the political divide.

Both Chirac and Mitterrand had their eyes fixed on the next presidential election in 1988, and the older man showed himself expert at combining the gravitas of his position as head of state and his control of foreign and defence policy, with occasional exercises in more basic politics, refusing to go along with some economic liberalization measures and taking a benign view of student resistance to university reform. Chirac did his best, but he was no match for the Florentine in the Élysée. Adopting a moderate programme that promised 'neither nationalization nor privatization,' and stressing national unity in contrast to Chirac's divisiveness, Mitterrand sailed to re-election with 54 per cent of the vote, only one point less than de Gaulle's margin over him in 1965; he even beat Chirac in the Corrèze. After moderately successful National Assembly elections, the President was now free to pick a new Prime Minister from among his own followers again.

For the second time, Mitterrand told Bérégovoy he was too old. The man he was forced to appoint by the balance of power on the centre-left, Michel Rocard, was only five years younger and had been around since the mid-1960s. The President's visceral and well-known dislike for Rocard—'He's just about good enough to be a junior minister for the Post Office,' he once said—made the appointment all the more galling for Bérégovoy. The Finance Minister received some consolation in being ranked as a Minister of State.

The new Prime Minister, who had been Mitterrand's main challenger in the Socialist ranks for a decade, was a reasonable man who believed in dialogue and wanted to establish a broad Social Democratic party on West German lines. But few from outside the ranks of the left agreed to join the experiment, and France grew bored with Rocard's painstakingly sensible approach, his Protestant earnestness and respect for numbers and facts. The Socialists did very badly at European elections and tore themselves apart at a fratricidal party congress. And all the while, money stayed tight, unemployment rose, taxes remained high, the National Front stirred up rancour and the President played favourites with his courtiers.

Still, France's state companies could cut a dash on the world stage. In November 1988, three months of negotiations ended with an agreement for the big nationalized metals company Péchiney to buy a US firm, American National Can, for $1.2 billion. On November 14, Péchiney informed the government of the deal, which was made public a week later amid official celebration that French enterprises were still international players. Within a few weeks, the takeover had set off one of the great scandals of the Mitterrand era, involving a rich cast: a Middle East arms dealer; a senior Finance Ministry official; banks in Switzerland, Luxembourg and Anguilla; sharp-eyed investigators from the Securities and Exchange Commission in the United States—and some of the President's men.

The Securities and Exchange Commission was intrigued by the pattern of trading in the shares of Triangle, the company which controlled American National Can, before the deal was announced. The value of Triangle stock had increased significantly when the sale was made public. Anybody who bought Triangle shares in the weeks before the deal had got a nice bargain. The US investigation prodded the control commission at the Paris Bourse into a similar probe. Joint inquiries revealed large buying of shares in Triangle before the announcement by French and Middle Eastern investors, partly through Swiss banks.

As the scandal became known, Mitterrand went on television to denounce speculators, go-betweens and well-connected financiers. The snag was that the two main buyers of Triangle shares turned out to be his good friend, Roger-Patrice Pelat, and another businessman with close Socialist connections. Pelat was reported to have acquired 10,000 shares just one day after the government in Paris got its first confidential notice of the takeover agreement—and a full six days before the announcement. Then *Le Monde* revealed that Pelat, or one of his sons, had bought another 40,000 Triangle shares through a bank in Lausanne. Their profit totalled $1.8 million.

The Péchiney affair was not the only such case of financial legerde-main. A group of businessmen linked to the government was alleged to have used insider information in a bid to take a strategic stake in a big bank during a takeover bid. There was also the matter of a sheaf of documents which various journalists were shown at the time. They indicated that France had tried to raise a $20 billion loan as the initial Socialist experiment went off the rails. It was never evident if the papers were real or forged, and, if genuine, whether they documented real negotiations or were an attempt to wring a large commission out of the government for a deal that never was. What made them tantalizing was that one of those named in the documents was referred to as 'M. Patrick'—a name just one letter away from Patrice. Even if it was all a hoax, it was intriguing that the perpetrators had chosen to point in the direction of the President's best friend.

In the Péchiney case there were no such uncertainties. Pelat had clearly indulged in insider dealing before the takeover was made public. The question was where he and his associates got their information. The answer led to the less illustrious of Pelat's 'two Bs,' Alain Boublil.

The short, tubby and cocky adviser at the Élysée, Boublil was not a popular man. He exuded self-esteem and, as industrial adviser at the presidency in 1982, had contemptuously waved aside any suggestion that the subsidies and corporate engineering which the Socialists were implementing might not work. As losses in the state sector rose and jobs began to be cut, he showed not the slightest trace of self-doubt, switching seamlessly to the new orthodoxy like any good apparatchik. Moving to Bérégovoy's Finance Ministry, he strutted his stuff clear of the norms of mere mortals. He saw no problem, for instance, in accepting hospitality from a Lebanese wheeler-dealer, Samir Traboulsi, who was an intermediary between Péchiney and Triangle, and who gained the nickname of the 'Vizier of pleasures'—in 1998 he was named in a court case as having organized an evening with five or six high-class prostitutes for a Saudi Arabian prince, allegedly receiving $400,000 for his services. Boublil's defence was simple: he was being got at because he was 'neither a practising Jew, nor a freemason, nor a provincial, nor a member of the upper bourgeoisie, nor a member of the top civil service.'

When this insider-outsider and Traboulsi were sentenced to jail terms in connection with the Péchiney affair, nobody grieved. What was piquant, however, was that some of the insider information on which Pelat capitalized so avidly was divulged to him at Pierre Bérégovoy's fortieth wedding anniversary party in a restaurant off the Champs-Élysées, which Boublil and Traboulsi attended. Told of the guest list, Mitterrand exclaimed, 'He shouldn't have done it.' The Lebanese fixer was said to have put his private plane at Bérégovoy's disposal for election trips. A month before the anniversary party, the Finance Minister had presented Traboulsi with the Legion d'Honneur for his help in freeing French hostages in the Middle East: once again, Pelat had been present at the reception. Mitterrand had warned Bérégovoy against appearing in such company. But some things seemed to override even his master's voice for the Minister who had found it so impressive to be eating off fine porcelain.

By the time Boublil went to jail for his involvement in the Péchiney affair, Roger-Patrice Pelat was dead. He had a weak heart and died while awaiting trial. In conversation with his aide, Jacques Attali, François Mitterrand struck a self-pitying tone. 'It's endless,' he said. 'Those people who are accused have no electoral mandate, no public job. They do not work with me. One cannot sanction them or sack them. I'm told I should do something, but I'm not going to put out a statement saying: "Tom is no longer my friend; I won't lunch with Dick anymore; and I'm not going to go for walks with Harry."'

It was time for another change of Prime Minister. Yet again the President ignored the claims of Pierre Bérégovoy. He turned first to Jacques Delors, who spent a sleepless night considering whether to return to Paris but decided he preferred to continue running the European Commission. Rebuffed by France's most popular politician-in-exile, Mitterrand appointed France's first woman premier, Edith Cresson. Bérégovoy promptly submitted his resignation from the Finance Ministry, where he had maintained the parity of the national currency through thick and thin. Mitterrand's reaction was typical: 'You'll get used to Cresson, and you can hold the franc firm in the meantime,' he told his faithful servant, sweetening the pill by expanding Bérégovoy's empire to take in industry, trade and telecommunications. When asked how he was bearing up, the Minister replied darkly, 'I just do what I'm told, but I'm keeping my own records about everything.'

Powerful though he was, Bérégovoy showed signs of insecurity. He was always pulling opinion polls from his pocket to consult. The Finance Ministry moved to a huge new building down the Seine, where Bérégovoy delighted in showing foreign colleagues the extent of his domain. The defender of the franc, whose notepaper was headed 'Former Mechanic, Minister of the Economy and Finance,' grew testy when it was suggested that he had known little about economics before 1981 and had been forced to take a quick lesson from the Governor of the Bank of France. He hated being the butt of the jokes which, as a politician, he should have learned to endure long before. The Interior Minister, Pierre Joxe—a superior fellow whose father had been a Gaullist luminary—once remarked that it

was obvious Bérégovoy was an honest man because of the cheap red
socks he wore. The story immediately did the Parisian rounds. It
was said that his wife bought them at the low-cost Prisunic chain.
Bérégovoy was furiously touchy about this: his staff was reported to
have complained to *Le Monde* because its cartoonist, Plantu, always
showed him with crumpled socks under baggy trousers.

When Cresson was sacked after a short and unhappy spell in
power in 1992, it was obvious that whoever took over from her
would be inheriting a rotten job. The National Assembly elections
the following year were being written off in advance. Poll approval
for the President was down to 26 per cent. It was lamb-to-the-
slaughter time and so the perfect moment to summon the final
kamikaze. With Bérégovoy as Prime Minister at last, the Socialists
slumped to 18 per cent in regional elections; unemployment rose to
one-tenth of the labour force; and the European Maastricht Treaty
only barely scraped through a referendum despite being backed by
almost the entire political establishment. On top of everything else,
the spectre of Roger-Patrice Pelat fell across the Prime Minister's
path from beyond the grave.

Bérégovoy was not a rich man, but his years in office had bred
a taste for what the French, in one of their linguistic adoptions,
call '*le standing*.' When he was given the job of bringing welfare
spending under control, Bérégovoy insisted on having a private lift
installed in his ministry. Later, he demanded a personal helicopter. He also bought a one-hundred-square-metre flat in the smart
16th arrondissement of Paris. How was he going to pay for it? No
problem: the President's pal stepped in. On September 18, 1986, a
notary registered a loan for one million francs to Pierre Bérégovoy
from Roger-Patrice Pelat. That covered nearly half the price of the
apartment. And Pelat went even further—the loan was interest-free.

On February 3, 1993, seven weeks before the National Assembly
elections, *le Canard Enchaîné* reported the Pelat loan. Bérégovoy was
immediately pursued by questions. Instead of coming clean, he gave
ambiguous and halting replies. *Le Monde* recalled the existence of an
anti-corruption code which insisted that officials must be clear and
open about any loans they were granted; the code had been drawn
up by a commission appointed by Pierre Bérégovoy.

When the second round election results were announced, the Socialists had lost 203 of their 258 seats in the National Assembly. The RPR took 246 and the UDF, back under Giscard's leadership, 207. Fifteen ministers were beaten. It was one of the greatest thrashings any major French political party had ever undergone, the price of sustained austerity, scandal and boredom with the same gang of men and women in government. If anybody carried responsibility for that, it was François Mitterrand, but, in his aloof way and with only two more years of his second term to run, he managed to position himself above the crude political battle, leaving Bérégovoy to take the blame.

Since Chirac did not want to become Prime Minister again and preferred to conserve himself for the 1995 presidential election, he passed the baton to his close colleague, Edouard Balladur, who, like him, had begun his political career in the service of Pompidou. On a sunny afternoon on March 30, 1993, Balladur was driven to the Matignon. After conferring inside, he and Bérégovoy emerged at the top of the steps in the courtyard. They smiled for the photographers and walked down the steps, arm in arm. The staff crowded to the windows to clap their departing boss. Bérégovoy turned to raise his hand in a final greeting.

Watching the scene, Balladur's press secretary saw it as a perfect illustration of the continuity of the republican state as government swung from one party to another—'On the two men's faces one read something like mutual respect, a common faith in national institutions, and a quasi-certitude that the story would not stop there for these two men who recognised one another's mutual value, even if the fortunes of public life had placed them in opposing camps.' As he drove out into the Rue de Varenne, the outgoing Prime Minister looked remarkably serene.

Six weeks later, Pierre Bérégovoy bought flowers for his wife and went through routine duties as Mayor of Nevers. It was the ultimately symbolic left-wing day of May 1, and Bérégovoy had a meeting with trade unionists as well as giving out prizes at a cycling race. He had not heard from the head of state since the election, though at least a word of comfort from on high might have been appropriate. At the end of April, Bérégovoy had placed telephone calls to the President who had dictated so much of his life. But there was only silence from Paris. François Mitterrand had spoken publicly of his esteem for Roger-Patrice Pelat when his friend was caught insider dealing; in the spring of 1993, there was not a word for Bérégovoy.

So the son of a Norman café owner, one-time gas fitter, negotiator with the Communists, former Chief of Staff to the President, Social Affairs Minister, Finance Minister and Prime Minister of France got into his official car and asked the driver to take him to a canal outside Nevers. When they arrived, he instructed his driver and bodyguard to get out and to leave him alone. Unseen by them, he took his guard's pistol from the glove compartment of the car and walked to the side of the canal. There, he shot himself in the temple.

Bérégovoy was flown to Paris in a critical state. Mitterrand and Balladur rushed to the hospital. Bérégovoy was dead on arrival.

In an interview recorded shortly before his death, the former Premier had spoken of the 'unpleasant political climate,' and of his share of responsibility. As a loyal servant of the President, he gave no hint of the depths of his despair, though there were reports that he had written to another leading Socialist in terms that could have presaged suicide. For all his devotion, Pierre Bérégovoy never quite fitted into what one senior presidential aide described as 'a luxuriant jungle with some very beautiful aspects to it, but a jungle all the same.' He was always just a little too literal, a bit too ponderous on his feet and never as amusing as the bright stars and con men who rose and fell at the Élysée, a victim of the system that enabled him to move from obscurity to the uplands of power but that, in the end, left him with nowhere to go. It was entirely in character that Mitterrand should use his suicide for his own purposes, attacking the press for investigating the tide of scandals lapping around the regime. The President's voice choked when he lambasted the media as dogs who had hounded an honest man to his grave.

Bérégovoy would have sounded a similar note. Shortly before he killed himself, he told a group of journalists that he couldn't help feeling angry about the fuss over the Pelat loan. 'I'm sixty-seven and

I cannot even have a one-hundred-square-metre flat,' he said. 'You know in France, no one likes people who climb up the social ladder.'

The Mitterrand presidency saw the emergence of a bright younger class of Socialists. Some, like Lionel Jospin, remained resolutely serious and middle-class, intent on improving themselves and the people they ruled over. Others—*la gauche caviare*—went for the high life, and were ready to make the most of their positions. But behind both these groups was a small cohort of men who had been with Mitterrand over the long years out of power, and who formed his praetorian guard. If Roger-Patrice Pelat was one of the more unusual of these, and Pierre Bérégovoy the most stoic, others fitted more readily into the traditional image of a political cabal. None more so than a man who combined a career as one of France's smartest lawyers with a long history as a key Mitterrandist.

On a snowy morning in 1956, Roland Dumas had taken the train from Limoges to Paris. A former Resistance fighter whose father was shot by the Germans, Dumas had just been elected to the National Assembly as a deputy for the Democratic and Social Union of the Resistance for the Haute-Vienne department. He was met at the Gare d'Austerlitz by an emissary who took him to meet a leading figure of the soft centre-left of the Fourth Republic in a two-room office on the Champs-Élysées. 'Your election was a surprise,' François Mitterrand told the younger man. They soon became companions-in-arms, with the ultimate aim of winning power for the older man.

Away from politics, the elegant, silver-tongued and well-connected Dumas made a fair fortune as a lawyer for the Picasso estate, Marc Chagall and Herbert von Karajan. From time to time, he showed that his heart was still in the right (that is to say, left) place by appearing in major political cases, including one involving Mitterrand. His legal office was in the narrow street off the Boulevard Saint-Germain where his leader had a duplex apartment. As a 'tenor' of the bar and part of the President's 'first circle,' his standing was not diminished by not being included in the initial Socialist governments. Meeting him in the early 1980s, you knew he was a man with a direct line to the top.

When he did become Minister for European Affairs and government spokesman in 1984, one felt that the job was not quite up to him. Once, during lunch looking out over the Seine on the Quai d'Or-say, Dumas excused himself after the main course by explaining that he was required 'on the other bank'—that is, at the Élysée. He dropped references to what *le Président* was thinking into the conversation like truffles. When the Socialists returned to government in 1988, Roland Dumas became Foreign Minister, dealing directly with Mitterrand.

Naturally, such a man liked to live high on the hog and felt lit-tle need for the reserve which might have cramped a less confident fellow. He lamented how his income had dropped when he joined the government. But he also claimed another side to his character; explaining why he kept large amounts of cash in his office, he said that it was out of 'a peasant's mentality.' A renowned ladies' man, he entertained close relations with the daughter of the Defence Minister of Syria and with a Frenchwoman employed mysteriously by the Elf oil firm and who said later that her job was to use her influence with the Foreign Minister on the firm's behalf. Despite their friendship and the incident when she bought a pair of 11,000-franc shoes for him on her company credit card, Dumas denied having been swayed in any way. In particular, he denied most vehemently having anything to do with an intriguing U-turn in the mid-Mitterrand years.

Ever since de Gaulle established diplomatic relations with Beijing in 1964, France had been anxious to maintain a special link with China. But at the end of the 1980s this foreign policy objective was threatened by another strand in the Gaullist legacy. Since the 1960s, arms exports had been one of the driving forces of France's economy. Mirage jets helped to win the Six-Day War for Israel; French arms were sold covertly to South Africa; Exocet missiles equipped the Argentine forces (though details of how they worked were slipped to Britain during the 1982 Falklands War). At a time of high unemployment, making weapons to sell abroad brought social as well as industrial benefits. So it was not surprising that the state-owned Thomson embarked on a big sales drive in 1989 for its new generation of high-technology frigates. The salesmen soon hit gold dust on the other side of the globe when Taiwan, which remained separate from mainland China under the Kuomintang, undertook to buy six of the ships for sixteen billion francs.

The French Foreign Ministry vetoed the sale for fear of a hostile reaction from Beijing. Dumas was unequivocal: 'From start to finish, throughout the decision-making process, I gave an unfavourable opinion,' he insisted later. Still, the sale went ahead, with Elf getting involved for reasons that were not clear. Dumas's woman friend from the oil company was alleged to have been paid a large sum for her attempts to get the Minister to approve the contract. An investigation by an examining magistrate revealed regular cash deposits in his bank account totalling fourteen million francs. Dumas, who had been made President of the Constitutional Council at the end of Mitterrand's rule, said the money came from the sale of artworks and insisted that the whole affair was an attempt to get at the memory of his late friend at the Élysée. But *Le Figaro* then ran a report of bribes paid in connection with the frigates deal amounting to no less than $500 million—with Mitterrand's approval. Mystery continued to surround the whole affair and how much had stuck to whose fingers; what was abundantly clear, however, was the disjunction between the distaste the first Socialist President of the Fifth Republic affected for money and its attraction for some of those closest to him, especially those who moved in the murkier areas of Mitterrandism.

François de Grossouvre had been as close to Mitterrand's secrets as anybody over the years; even Roger-Patrice Pelat probably did not know as much. The two François were both educated by Catholics. Each had participated in extreme right-wing groups in the 1930s, though they did not meet. Both had relations with both the Vichy regime and the Resistance and said their collaborationist links were undertaken to aid the Resistance. In the early 1960s, however, they seemed to have nothing in common. Mitterrand was a politician with a long past and an uncertain future; de Grossouvre was a doctor, a farmer, a former company chairman and Coca-Cola's bottler in Lyon. But when they met, the two men fell for one another.

Though never a man of the left, de Grossouvre helped to organize Mitterrand's 1965 campaign against de Gaulle and took an interest in the Socialist Party's finances throughout the 1970s. Wherever Mitterrand went, De Grossouvre was there, an elegant figure with beautifully cut suits and spade beard: he could have stepped from a late Renaissance Italian picture. De Grossouvre hated to see his name in the newspapers and carried over a love for secrecy and intrigue from his days in the Resistance. He maintained discreet contact with wartime buddies who had moved into the covert shadows of Gaullism. For a while, he worked for France's espionage service under the code name of 'Monsieur Leduc.' He saw himself as a man of hidden spheres who got the business done, whether settling his chief's financial problems, warding off trouble, establishing deniable contacts—or just making sure the leader's overcoat was ready for him when he left a meeting. 'A well-informed, silent and secret man of business,' a police report said of him.

Like Mitterrand, de Grossouvre was fascinated by the mechanics of power and the manipulation of people. Each operated on a need-to-know basis towards the rest of the world, including those who put their trust in them. Neither saw any need to tell third parties what they were doing. As they aged, the two men also discussed ways of staying young: De Grossouvre favoured ginseng from the Far East while Mitterrand preferred borage. The politician did not share his friend's love of hunting and riding, but de Grossouvre turned his passion to other ends—he used hunting pavilions for secret meetings between Mitterrand and his opponents. So it was no surprise that, when the Socialists won ultimate power, François de Grossouvre moved in to a corner office at the Élysée with the duties of looking after the intelligence service 'and various matters.' He also secured for himself an apartment on the Quai Branly by the Seine in a building which was the residence of Mitterrand's mistress, Anne Pingeot, and their daughter, Mazarine.

He was also a man who knew the value of his position—Pelat was not the only friend of François to cash in on his contacts. In one case, he received more than 300,000 francs for his services as intermediary between a French company and Middle Eastern interests. He was said to have acted as a go-between with African dictators who supplied funds for French political parties. He made secret trips to the Middle East, while his discreet visit to Jacques Chirac on behalf of his master at the time of the 1981 election was the kind of mission he was cut out to perform. It was all highly deniable: from 1988, his salary was paid by the Dassault aircraft firm and not by the presidency.

By 1994, however, according to another of Jean Montaldo's insider accounts of the Mitterrand years, something had gone terribly wrong between the two François. He nurtured a hatred for Pelat and Tapie and had warned Mitterrand that he was surrounded by bandits.

'You cannot say that,' was the President's reply, according to the account he gave Montaldo.

'Not only can I say it, but I can prove it.'

'I forbid you,' Mitterrand commanded.

So, said de Grossouvre, 'I slammed the door on him.'

A colleague reported that de Grossouvre was suffering from some kind of hallucination, and believed he was being tailed. Another said he felt as though he was being treated like a dog. Once, it was said, he burst into the office of the Élysée Chief of Staff without knowing where he was. He was reported to have told the President that he was losing his mind. 'If something terrible happens to me, it will be that they have killed me,' de Grossouvre told Montaldo. 'They'll get me.' The former head of Mitterrand's secret 'black box' cell at the Élysée, Paul Barril, recalls him saying in 1993, 'They're going to gun me down. I know everything now. They're afraid.'

Either de Grossouvre was becoming paranoid, or he had reason to feel a net tightening around him. On April 7, 1994, he lunched with one of his sons, put in a spot of hunting outside Paris and then drove to his office. He took with him a heavy revolver from the collection of almost two hundred guns he kept in his official apartment. At around 6:00 p.m., he had a visit from his doctor. Seemingly mentally and physically disturbed, de Grossouvre turned the conversation to suicide and firearms, and referred to the buzzing in his ears. His doctor, an old friend, spoke of God and of the importance of keeping up one's spirits. De Grossouvre produced a small hunting badge and gave it to his guest, saying, 'Keep this in memory of me.' Then they talked of other things.

At 6:30 p.m., according to Captain Barril, de Grossouvre sent flowers to a former African Prime Minister with whom he was due to dine, saying that he would arrive two hours later. He let his secretary leave, and spent half an hour alone. His doctor, meanwhile, had sent a message to Mitterrand warning him of de Grossouvre's state of mind. By then, however, the President's once-faithful servant had put the .357 Magnum pistol to his head and pulled the trigger. Blood splattered the walls, but the thick doors muffled the sound of the shot. His chauffeur discovered the body an hour later.

Barril declared himself unconvinced by the official account. The message that had gone out with the 6:30 flowers hardly indicated a man who was about to end his life, he observed. There was no suicide letter. 'If he had, indeed, killed himself, the man I knew would have left a delayed-action bomb, files, the hundreds of notes he had sent to the President,' the Captain added in an interview given as he promoted his own memoirs. In the halls of mirrors of the late Mitterrand era, it is impossible to separate truth from conjecture, book promotion from genuine questions.

It was raining on the morning of April 11 as the President of the Republic arrived at the church of Saint-Pierre in Moulins, capital of the agricultural Allier department in central France. A couple of Socialist former ministers waited for him. An ex-President of Lebanon stood to one side. Four hundred people filled the church for the funeral mass. After the service, a cortege of thirty vehicles drove with the coffin to the village of Lusigny, fifteen kilometres away, where François Mitterrand had sometimes stayed in the dead man's manor house set in a large estate. At the cemetery on top of a small hill, the coffin was carried down a sandy path to the family tomb. There, François de Grossouvre was laid to rest under the gaze of his former friend who stood holding an umbrella. For a brief moment, his eyes met those of the widow, standing surrounded by her children and grandchildren. Not a word was spoken. Accompanied by one of his ex-ministers, Mitterrand turned and walked away.

A close friend gone from a heart attack in the midst of financial scandal, a former head of government committing suicide, an associate of three decades shooting himself in his office at the presidential palace; flying too close to Mitterrand's flame was a dangerous business. Particularly so because of the emotional power which the man was able to exercise over even strong-minded, successful individuals. The self-interest of a Bernard Tapie was understandable, but the depths of feeling which rejection by Mitterrand evoked in de Grossouvre or Bérégovoy was out of the ordinary. Politicians who came across him in his early provincial campaigns in the 1940s remembered his powers of attraction fifty years later. As his actor brother-in-law observed: 'Mitterrand aroused even more loving feeling among men than among women.' Which, given his sexual conquests, was saying quite something; he could, it was said, have seduced a stone.

12

A FRENCH LIFE

The French were intrigued more than shocked when the existence of François Mitterrand's mistress and illegitimate daughter became public knowledge late in his second term. His wife had known about them for a long time, but accepted the situation. 'So, yes, I was married to a seducer. I had to make do,' Danielle Mitterrand said later. 'She's his daughter, and François loved her enormously. They resemble one another like peas in a pod.' Asked about the young Mazarine towards the end of his life, Mitterrand shrugged the matter off. His widow was philosophical. 'We must accept that a human being is capable of loving, passionately loving somebody—and then, as the years go by, he loves in a different way, perhaps more deeply, and then he can fall in love with someone else. It is absolute hypocrisy to want to pass judgement on that.'

Such honesty spoke volumes about France. It was fitting from the widow of a man who, in so many things, personified his nation's history over more than half a century. By the time he became President, Mitterrand had already spent nearly four decades in politics. He was Europe's last ruler who had been in office in pre-nuclear days, holding his first government job when Truman, Attlee and Stalin were meeting to fix the shape of the postwar world. For most of his presidency he was known affectionately as '*Tonton*' ('Uncle'). By the end, some followers had taken to calling him '*Dieu*' ('God'), if only for his seeming immortality. In everything from his childhood to the secrecy about his health, from his private life to the equivocations

297

about his wartime years, from the twists of his career to his last New Year's dinner, François Mitterrand's odyssey was a parable of modern France. Beginning as a true Catholic believer, he ended up, in the words of one of his Prime Ministers, as a pure cynic. The man and his country moved in parallel from traditional roots to end-of-century malaise.

'My childhood, which was happy, has illuminated my life. When one is a child, when one arrives on this planet of which one knows nothing, everything is to be learnt, everything to be felt. The first sensations are so strong and dominant. They make their mark on a virgin canvas. I draw the largest part of my reserves of strength from my childhood. I have the impression that what I had at that moment, and the little of it I have preserved (and I have kept some of it), represents the purest and cleanest part of my personality.'

Jarnac is an ordinary town of some five thousand inhabitants surrounded by open countryside and rivers in the Charente department of western France. It is best known for having given its name to the expression for a stab in the back, '*un coup de Jarnac*,' from a sixteenth-century incident in which one nobleman struck another from behind in a duel. François Maurice Adrien Marie Mitterrand was born there on October 26, 1916. His father was a stationmaster who later changed profession and became head of the vinegar makers of the region. With four sons and four daughters, the Mitterrands were a close-knit family into which, François recalled, 'guests entered as if they were burglars.' Austere and devout Catholics, they distrusted moneymaking and rarely displayed emotion, in all respects akin to de Gaulle's father and mother.

François was sent to boarding school in the nearby big town of Angoulême. A withdrawn child, he had trouble communicating with others and made few friends. One lifelong character trait was established at an early age. 'I have never tended to confide in others,' Mitterrand remarked much later, 'In a big family, one has to develop zones of solitude.'

As a loner, the young Mitterrand enjoyed going for long country walks. He nurtured a taste for strolls along riverbanks and wrote poems about their waters, starting with the Charente and the Gironde of his native region and going on to take the Rhine, the Rhone, the Nile and the Niger as inspiration. Seventy years later, he recalled with pleasure the sound of the wind blowing at night through the riverside trees. On his walks, the shy boy from the Catholic school spoke to imaginary crowds, haranguing them with rhetoric inspired by the revolutionaries of 1789 and 1848. Back at home, he climbed up to the attic, littered with maize husks, and launched vibrant speeches through the window overlooking the garden, 'changing the course of history according to my choices.'

If he looked back with happy nostalgia to his childhood in the Charente, he was less forthcoming for many years about his early life in Paris. Arriving by train from Angoulême just before his eighteenth birthday to study politics and law, he felt lost and small in the big city—'at the foot of a mountain that was to be climbed. I was without an identity.' Living in a religious *pension* in the Rue de Vaugirard on the Left Bank, he soon gravitated into reactionary politics.

This was hardly surprising for somebody of his background in the fevered climate of the mid-1930s, when some dreamed of a Socialist-Communist revolution and others looked at Mussolini and Hitler as role models. He joined a group called the National Volunteers, the youth wing of a big extremist movement, the Croix-de-Feu, and took part in his first demonstration within a month of arriving in the capital. A photograph taken in February 1935 shows him at a march against foreign students: a banner beside him proclaims, 'Go on strike against the wogs.' He wrote for a newspaper which admired Mussolini, travelled to Belgium to visit the pretender to the throne of France, gave 500 francs to a campaign against the Socialist leader Leon Blum, and became head of a right-wing student group. At the age of twenty-one, he also fell in love.

'One Saturday, I had the blues,' he recalled. 'I went back to my room. On the table, I came across an invitation I had forgotten about. It was to a dance at the teachers' training college. I went. I saw a blonde with her back to me. She turned towards me. My feet were riveted to the ground . . . Then I asked her to dance . . . I was mad about her!'

Women were always important to François Mitterrand. Over the years there was as much speculation about his love life as about his real political beliefs. He was said to have had a string of celebrated journalists as mistresses and a love nest in Venice. He was reported to take particular pleasure in caressing the insteps of his lady friends. 'He was fascinated by Casanova,' according to a journalist whom Mitterrand picked to chronicle his last days. 'He couldn't go into a bar or a restaurant without seeking out the face of a woman and giving his famous wink.' When he met the actress Juliette Binoche by chance in a bookshop, he asked her to give him a call. With undue modesty, she found the prospect too intimidating: 'How does one call the President of the Republic?' she wondered, 'It's like picking up the phone and asking for Father Christmas.'

Others were not so reticent. Any attractive woman who rose to a high position in the Socialist ranks was suspected of having slept with him on the way up. When he told one of them that she might become a party secretary as a reward, she is said to have replied on the pillow that she didn't know how to type. A roman-à-clef in the 1980s intimated that he had an illegitimate child as well as the three sons born to his wife. The rumours were confirmed in 1994 when *Paris-Match* magazine printed photographs of the President stepping out to a twentieth-birthday lunch at a celebrated fish restaurant with his daughter, Mazarine, who had been conceived as he embarked on his second unsuccessful presidential campaign in 1974, and who bore a striking resemblance to her father.

Her mother was an archivist whom Mitterrand had met near his home on the southwestern Atlantic coast. In *Premier Roman*, a thin novel that was scoured for autobiographical fragments when it became a bestseller in 1998, Mazarine wrote of her heroine's parents as 'longtime lovers, unmarried, leading their own lives, even while loving each other more than anything. They taught her that love was the only tie that triumphs over looks and judgements, convention and taboos.'

There was never any secret about Mitterrand's first love, even if the blonde Marie-Louise Terrasse had not been as struck by him as he was by her when his eye fell on her at the student ball. She did not give him her name because her mother forbade her to identify herself to unknown young men. In his mind, Mitterrand dubbed her 'Beatrice,' as in Dante. He spoke incessantly about her to friends and watched her as she travelled between home and school. Finally, he accosted her. Defying her mother's command, she joined him at a café table, and they shared a pancake. In the spring of 1940, when Mitterrand was called up to the army, they got engaged. In his letters to her from his army post, he referred to Marie-Louise as VM, for '*visage merveilleux*' (marvellous face).

As a sergeant during the Phoney War before the Nazis attacked, Mitterrand must have found the time slow. So, when not writing to VM, he turned his hand to a spot of fiction, with a short story entitled 'First Chord,' about a young couple, Philippe and Elsa. She was 'supple and gay, sparkling as she awoke, a Persian at the sword, her pink curves like a jar of hair cream.' The prose slurped on: 'Every day of their brief love, she leaped from bed. As he lay about, she walked round the room dressed in her blue dream [sic]. She loved this hour of daydreams . . . Elsa never dared to parade naked in their room, for Philippe had a curious degree of modesty for a flirtatious man: odd habits, delights that remained ever elusive.' He was, after all, only twenty-three years old, and, if only he had known it, was following in the footsteps of de Gaulle, who had penned romantic fiction (equally unpublished) while convalescing from a war wound in 1914.

After France's defeat, the sergeant was taken prisoner of war together with thousands of French soldiers. As the months dragged by in his Stalag, VM's letters became rarer and rarer. Friends attributed Mitterrand's three escape attempts to his desire to get back to her. Again, there was a parallel with de Gaulle, who repeatedly escaped from German prison camps in the First World War, only to be recaptured each time. Mitterrand was more successful; his third breakout succeeded, and he returned to France, entering a controversial period of his life which will be dealt with later.

But he found that the girl with the marvellous face no longer fancied the idea of marrying him. Early in 1942, the engagement was broken off. Many years later, as Catherine Langeais, Marie-Louise became more famous for a time than her former fiancé as an early television announcer. Some amateur psychologists believe that rejection hardened the young man's character and contributed to the growth of his pervasive cynicism. At the time, he spoke of the 'dryness of my feelings.' Decades later, he still sent Langeais flowers on her birthday.

Two years after being dropped by Marie-Louise, Mitterrand was in love again, this time with a photograph. In March 1944, when he headed a Resistance network, Mitterrand attended a party at the Paris home of his friend, Roger-Patrice Pelat. On the piano in the flat was a photograph of the sister of Pelat's partner at the time. 'I want to meet her, I will marry her,' Mitterrand said. A blind date was duly arranged at a restaurant on the Boulevard Saint-Germain. As with Marie-Louise, Mitterrand was not an immediate hit. Wearing an off-white raincoat and the large hat which became his trademark in later years, he also sported a pencil moustache. The overall effect made him look like a caricature of a tango dancer.

The young woman, Danielle Gouze, was in her last year at school. She found his acid tone irritating: Mitterrand only fell more deeply in love with her. He deployed to the full his persuasion and seduction, and, within a couple of months, she agreed to marry him. There then followed a series of wartime adventures, including a train trip to her native Burgundy during which a friendly German soldier unknowingly ushered the young man through a police control that had him on its wanted list.

They married in October 1944, after the Liberation of France (during which Mitterrand claimed to have saved de Gaulle's life by grabbing his legs as the General was about to be swept out of a window by an enthusiastic crowd in Paris). Over the wedding lunch, the groom announced that he was going off to a political meeting with former prisoners of war. The bride said she would accompany him. If you want to, Mitterrand replied. That was the moment at which she discovered her 'first and main rival: politics.'

Nobody outside the couple knows how much Danielle influenced her husband. Her own reflections on the subject indicate that she was content to watch him go his own way while she dedicated herself to good works and Third World causes. What she thought of her husband's decision to maintain close relations with some of Africa's worst dictators can be imagined; she, herself, showed lasting concern for human rights and stayed true to her old beliefs. She organized demonstrations for prisoners of conscience and remained a fan of Fidel Castro to the end, urging her husband to invite him on a state visit to France. She persuaded the shyster businessman Armand

Hammer to agree to contribute $300,000 to her good works, though she never got her hands on the money.

Danielle Mitterrand could have become an object of pity; instead, she remained dignified. After his death, she wrote, 'I see now how my husband excelled in the art of seduction towards the young girls who passed by. He was François the seducer.' That was part of life. A striking photograph taken at the Cannes film festival in 1956 shows a dark-suited Mitterrand gazing with more than passing interest at Brigitte Bardot while Danielle, in matelot jersey and sunglasses with her hands clasped behind her back, stares at the twenty-two-year-old starlet as though at an anthropological specimen. 'Which woman can say, "I've never been cheated on," or that she never cheated in her own love life?' Danielle Mitterrand once reflected. 'I stayed with him because he was different. With him life was never boring.' It was the matter-of-fact voice of the woman who, as a high school girl, had hidden Resistance fighters at ultimate risk to herself. When warned by a friend that she should flee Paris because her photograph had been seized in a Gestapo raid on a Resistance hideout, Danielle had replied, 'But what about my exams?'

'I could have devoted my life to refection, to have lived in the country in the company of trees, animals and a few loved ones,' Mitterrand wrote. 'Perhaps that is a bucolic dream; still, I think I could have done it. But the stimulus of action was doubtless stronger than that of reflection, so in the end I launched myself into politics!'

In October 1946, after an unsuccessful attempt to get elected in the Paris region, the thirty-year-old aspiring politician set off for the rural Nièvre department in central France to seek a seat in the National Assembly of the Fourth Republic. His first campaign in the department which was to become his electoral base for the next thirty-five years had its share of ironies given what was to happen three and a half decades later. The politician who would lead the Socialists and their Communist allies to the greatest power they have ever enjoyed in modern France first won his way to the National Assembly with the active backing of a network of conservative local notables. His speeches denounced the government of the left and moderate Catholics that ruled France after de Gaulle stalked out of the premiership. The man who was to give the Communists their only taste of ministerial power under the Fifth Republic was particularly strident in his attacks on the Moscow-aligned party in his speeches to audiences in country halls.

The Nièvre, where the faithful Bérégovoy was to kill himself half a century later, went on electing Mitterrand throughout the Fourth Republic as he moved smoothly between ministerial posts—from ex-servicemen's affairs to the Information Ministry, then on to super-intend France's Overseas Territories before taking the powerful post of Interior Minister in 1954–55 and ending up as Justice Minister in 1956–57, at the time of the Suez expedition and France's war to hold on to its last big overseas possession. He left no public doubt of his belief that Algeria must remain French. Heading a series of small parties and political combinations, he never had a strong popular following and was eclipsed in intellectual ability by Pierre Mendès-France and in clout by the Socialist boss, Guy Mollet.

Though never getting to the Hôtel Matignon, Mitterrand still proved to be one of the most skilful exponents of the Fourth Republic game of ministerial musical chairs. The ever-shifting, un-ideological backroom world of French politics in the 1940s and 1950s suited him to perfection and shaped his style. Still, not everybody was impressed. A US ambassador, Douglas Dillon, wrote of the Interior Minister of the time in a classified despatch in 1954 as 'very competent but dangerous . . . intensely ambitious and will do anything to reach his goals.' The failure of the Fourth Republic was, above all, a failure of its politicians to provide leadership and take hard decisions, Mit-terrand epitomized such people.

When de Gaulle swept away the Fourth Republic in 1958, he was a lonely voice of opposition, refusing to vote for the General's inves-titure. He paid the price in the first parliamentary elections of the new Republic when he was defeated. He denounced de Gaulle for having mounted a coup d'état and set out to re-invent himself. 'For a long time, I have said "no" to complicated party combinations, to immobility, to colonial wars,' this archetype of the Fourth Republic and defender of French Algeria suddenly declared. If one constant ran through Mitterrand's long career, it was the readiness to disown his beliefs of yesterday for the benefits of today.

Such a man did not stay politically unemployed for long, and, in 1959, he won election to the Senate, a body whose members are picked by local dignitaries. Mitterrand dramatically announced that he had been the target of an assassination attempt, which appeared to have been a put-up job engineered to win sympathy. The episode earned him ridicule and reinforced the widespread belief that he was a man without scruples who would stop at nothing to advance his political career.

He stayed in the Senate for three years, writing biting anti-Gaullist tracts before winning his way back to the more important National Assembly. At the same time, he strengthened his roots in the Nièvre by becoming Mayor of Château-Chinon in the hilly, wooded Morvan area of the department. On election days, he put up at the old-fashioned Hôtel du Morvan in the middle of the town to await the results. He would frequently eat lunch with the hotel's owners and always slept in the same room on the first floor. Lit by a single weak light bulb, it was sparsely furnished with a lumpy bed, a straight-backed chair and a plastic-topped table on which Mitterrand wrote late into the night. There was a wash basin, but the lavatory was on the landing. A window looked out on to the surrounding hills—the latter-day equivalent of the attic window from which Mitterrand had once imagined himself addressing the nation as a boy.

During the long years of waiting for supreme power while the right fought its fratricidal battles, François Mitterrand collected an odd bunch of friends and associates, some of whom we met in the last chapter. But there was one acquaintance who would stand out as an especially strange man for the first President of the left to have entertained. A jovial rogue like Roger-Patrice Pelat might be explained away on the basis of wartime comradeship. René Bousquet was a different matter, and Mitterrand's relationship with him over more than three decades reflected another aspect of France which still stirs deep emotions half a century after the 1940 parliament voted full powers to Pétain and Vichy agreed to collaborate with the Nazis.

The question of collaboration and complicity in genocide has, as we have seen, been so uncomfortable that France has often preferred to ignore it. Few of those who went along with Vichy and the

German occupiers could have imagined the existence of extermination camps as such: they preferred vague formulae about work camps in Eastern Europe. Yet, even if they did not know of the extermination camps, anybody with eyes in their head could see that Jews were being forced to wear yellow stars on the streets of France before being rounded up and taken away. Later, even those who owned up to working for Vichy or the Germans denied that they had known about the more unpleasant things going on around them. A fair number insisted that their collaboration had, in fact, been a cover for clandestine Resistance work, leading the press baron Robert Hersant, who made no bones about his collaborationist record, to give himself the ironic badge of 'the only Frenchman of my generation not to have been a hero of the Resistance.'

In much later years, nobody's war record was more subject to debate than that of François Mitterrand. Not only did he seem to have played a double game, but he also appeared unable to shake off the negative elements of the past or even to admit that there might be anything questionable about them. Sometimes he grew indignant that anybody should presume to raise the subject, or else he put on a poker face and muttered a dismissive 'So what?' If France preferred to blot out the memory of its equivocations about the years between 1940 and 1944, François Mitterrand stood as an example for the nation.

His role during those years reflected both sides of the country under occupation. There was no doubt that the future President had faced great personal danger as a member of the Resistance. He helped to organize underground networks among ex-servicemen, travelled to England for a frosty meeting with General de Gaulle and was on the wanted list under his pseudonym of Morland. At the same time, he worked for the Vichy government as a civil servant dealing with prisoners of war, which enabled him to save some French servicemen from concentration camps.

Mitterrand said later that he did this with the blessing of the Resistance, which certainly found it useful to keep some of its people as moles inside the collaborationist regime. 'I was not part of the Vichy system,' he said in his posthumously published memoirs. 'I was not a functionary but a contract worker.' He used the word 'press-ganged' to describe his employment and added, as if it had some relevance, that he had filled a high-level post for less than today's minimum wage. The young man must have been good at his job because he was awarded the Francisque, one of the regime's top decorations, and was presented to Pétain. As President, Mitterrand continued the tradition of sending a wreath to the Marshal's grave each Armistice Day in honour of his military leadership in the First World War.

If he was to be believed, Mitterrand, who prided himself on being a great humanist, managed to keep his eyes shut to some of the things going on around him. 'I didn't think about anti-Semitism at Vichy,' he once insisted. 'I knew that, unfortunately, there were anti-Semites who filled senior positions around Marshal Pétain, but I didn't follow the laws of the time and the measures that were being taken.' The 'unfortunately' jars, and Mitterrand's memoirs struck a somewhat different tone. 'Vichy was a weak regime, shapeless and lacking in soul, inspired by fascists, anti-Semites and determined ideologues,' he told a journalist who worked with him on his last reburnishing of history.

Still, as head of state, he steadfastly refused to accept that there was anything amiss in his long relationship with a man who had signed the agreement with the Germans pledging the French police to round up foreign Jews and who was the main organizer of the Vél d'Hiv atrocity in Paris in 1942. When it came to René Bousquet, Mitterrand said simply that he found the man to be a brilliant individual with whom he had interesting conversations. The President went on meeting the former police chief until 1986, five years into his rule and after well-publicized moves were made to get Bousquet tried for crimes against humanity. Despite having access to the full panoply of official French records, Mitterrand insisted that he had not been aware of Bousquet s wartime activities.

This was simply unbelievable. It was no secret that from April 1942 to December 1943 Bousquet had been Secretary-General of the police. As such, he was in charge of the national police, of economic policing and of 'supplementary police,' which meant the anti-Jewish, anti-Masonic and anti-Communist crusade. He, too, claimed to have been involved with the Resistance and was indeed arrested by the Germans in 1944, by which time any sensible collaborator would have sought a lifeline on the other side. After the Liberation, Bousquet was sentenced to five years of 'national degradation,' but was later amnestied. Whatever his Resistance activities may or may not have been, there was no doubting Bousquet's key role in rounding up Jews. It was not as if Mitterrand needed access to official papers to know what Bousquet had been up to during the Occupation. His responsibilities had been outlined at the Nuremberg war crimes trials in 1946 by the lawyer and politician Edgar Faure, another friend of Mitterrand.

Every time the President denied that there was anything wrong in his links with Bousquet, new information emerged. There is no evidence that the two men actually met while serving Vichy, but Mitterrand's evasions inevitably fuelled speculation. It was widely believed that his Resistance group, based on ex-prisoners of war, had unofficial contacts with the Vichy Ministry of the Interior and the police—and his membership of a far-right organization was only a decade behind him. Whether Mitterrand found Vichy ideologically objectionable is a question which is unlikely ever to be answered, just as the true extent of his commitment to Socialism will always remain uncertain. No doubt he deplored Vichy's treatment of those it persecuted; but as a cool-eyed realist, his engagement in the Resistance may have been as much a matter of pragmatism as of political conviction, just as he could see clearly from 1965 onwards that the only way to win the presidency was to come at it from the left.

The links with the collaborationist right continued after the Liberation. When Mitterrand found himself briefly out of a job, he was taken under the wing of a cosmetics group founded by a tycoon who had financed pre-war terrorists of the far right and who gave him a job running a beauty care magazine. Back in politics after winning his place in parliament from the Nièvre, Mitterrand pushed an amnesty bill for collaborators, which was said to have weighed on the judges' decision not to punish Bousquet more severely for his wartime activities. At that time, the former policeman was on the board of the Banque d'Indochine, which financed anti-Gaullist politicians after the General's return to power in 1958. That year, Bousquet ran unsuccessfully for parliament—with the backing of a small political party headed by Mitterrand. Another of his associates was Robert Hersant, who had also been found guilty of collaborationist crimes.

During Mitterrand's first presidential bid in 1965, the Toulouse newspaper *La Dépêche du Midi* printed his leaflets for free, contributed half a million francs to his campaign funds and ran an appeal by former Petainists and extreme right-wingers to vote for the anti-Gaullist candidate. Bousquet was on the board of the newspaper. The two men met again during Mitterrand's second presidential campaign in 1974. A magazine photographer snapped a lunch party at the candidate's country home in the southwest. Bousquet and his wife sat opposite Mitterrand: the caption did not identify the guests.

Research by a tenacious British journalist, Paul Webster, uncovered other links. Around the time Bousquet was being tried by the High Court of Justice, the rising politician named one of the former police chief's wartime staff as his press officer. At the Interior Ministry in 1954, with access to all the files, Mitterrand appointed three members of Bousquet's old entourage to his team. In 1965, he engaged as his parliamentary aide another of Bousquet's former subordinates—a man called Pierre Saury, who had worked on the deportation of Jews from Paris. Saury also acted as Mitterrand's link with former Petainists. When he died in 1973, his wartime and peacetime employers both attended his funeral. As President, Mitterrand did not break off contact with Bousquet until 1988. That was five years after France's leading hunter of Nazis and collaborators, Serge Klarsfeld, had published documents detailing Bousquet's eagerness to deport Jews. But still, the head of state was unable to snap the link completely. After being booed by young Jews at a commemoration of the 1942 roundup in Paris, Mitterrand appointed his own lawyer, Georges Kiejman, whose father died in Auschwitz, as junior Justice Minister. Kiejman blocked legal proceedings against Bousquet in the name of national unity.

Towards the end of Mitterrand's rule, the Nobel Prize-winner Elie Wiesel was commissioned to write up a series of conversations with him. It was to be the President's philosophical apotheosis. When Wiesel, a Jew and a great admirer of Mitterrand at the time, raised the matter of Bousquet, the head of state replied that he felt he had made no mistake.

'None?' Wiesel asked.

'None,' Mitterrand insisted.

'So,' wrote Wiesel some years later, 'there was no remorse, nor regrets.'

Trying to delve more deeply, Wiesel asked about Pétain, the wreath sent to the Marshal's tomb, Bousquet and Mitterrand's Vichy medal. The President did not deign to reply, and then, unbelievably, insisted that he had been the one who had wanted to deal with the subject of Bousquet. All Wiesel could say was, 'I feel bad about that man.'

It was not even as if Bousquet was an isolated example. His wartime deputy was charged, but was never brought to trial, and died in peace in 1989. Another senior official who oversaw all the prefects in the Vichy zone ended his days untroubled at his Riviera villa in 1992. And when it came to Maurice Papon, irony was added to neglect on the President's part. If the story told by the Jew who escaped death by hiding in a cupboard in Bordeaux in 1942 is true, Mitterrand owed part of his election against Giscard in 1981 to the revelation of Papon's wartime role. But, when the case came up in Cabinet, the President made it plain on several occasions that he was not in favour of reopening the case against a man he described as being 'of outstanding stature.'

The fact that Mitterrand felt so little compunction about befriending Bousquet and protecting Papon was both a reminder of the extent of his own self-centred amorality and—once again—a sign of how accurately he reflected the inner feelings of so many of his compatriots. There was also an obvious personal parallel between these two Vichy-Resistants and his own wartime career. When Bousquet was murdered in his Paris apartment in 1993, conspiracy theories flared up, but the truth seemed to be that the killer was simply deranged. As he was sentenced to ten years in jail for the shooting, he said he sought pardon from God for breaking the commitment not to kill, from the Jews for having prevented Bousquet appearing in court and from the dead man's family for having removed their father. A crazy gunman had also deprived France of a chance to purge part of a dark stain on its history, and the first elected President of the left ended his rule under the shadow of the collaboration his country longed to put behind it without going through the pain of exorcism.

It was a sunny day in September 1994, and the President of the Republic was talking to a guest at his home among the pine trees of the Landes department on the southwestern coast, where he felt 'the ocean in the forest.' They ate foie gras, lobster and grapes and drank white wine. Mitterrand was in aphoristic mood, speaking of 'Nationalism, the opium of imbeciles,' or producing the none-too-profound observation that 'Socialism and Communism are branches of the same tree—like Christianity and Islam.' He felt free to criticize his opponents and his successor as leader of the Socialist Party, Lionel Jospin, with impunity as birds whirled above and a bluebottle swooped on to his forehead.

Three months later, the man whom some referred to as God was asked what he expected the Father in Heaven to say to him when he reached paradise. Terminally ill, Mitterrand sat stiffly in his chair as he pondered his response. He had difficulty speaking; from time to time, his right hand darted to the pocket of his jacket as if he needed to touch a talisman. A confirmed agnostic who had rejected his Catholic upbringing, he showed a shaft of wit as he answered the question: 'Now you know,' God would say, 'And I hope that He would add—"Welcome."'

By then, the President had been living under the shadow of death for more than a dozen years. In his 1981 election campaign, he had pledged transparency on the state of his health. There would be none of the secrecy which had surrounded the last months of Georges Pompidou's life, he promised. His doctor, Claude Gubler, issued two bulletins a year, giving his patient a good bill of health. They were, to say the least, highly economical with the truth. Every day for eleven years, the head of state received secret medical attention. When he travelled abroad, he had treatment at night wherever he was: the needles and bottles of liquid were sealed in special suitcases and sent back to France in diplomatic bags for destruction. On trips to Communist countries, the injections were conducted in total silence for fear that the room might be bugged.

In 1992, the President was operated on for a decade-old cancer of the prostate, and the secret was out—or rather, in true Mitterrand fashion, part of it. Gubler had diagnosed the illness six months after Mitterrand moved into the Élysée; the new President insisted that it must remain a state secret. After the first diagnosis, he asked how long he had to live. Told that the prognosis was three years, he muttered under his breath, 'I'm done for.' But the treatment appeared to be working, and Mitterrand began to believe he had beaten the cancer. He did not consult Gubler before announcing that he would stand for re-election in 1988. France duly gave another seven years in power to a cancer patient in his seventies.

Only he and his doctor knew the truth; the government and the electorate were kept in the dark. If it had known, would France have voted differently? Jacques Chirac ran a terrible campaign, but the facts about Mitterrand's state of health might have swung the balance or, even worse from the President's viewpoint, have encouraged the centre-left to throw its support behind his long-time antagonist, Michel Rocard. But Mitterrand played the sphinx; he did not even tell his wife of his condition until 1991. In her usual understanding fashion, she said she did not regard this as untoward: 'He simply preserved our tranquillity of spirit.'

Even when the operation in 1992 destroyed the secrecy, the fact that the cancer had already spread was still kept quiet from the public. But radiotherapy, chemotherapy and a second operation diminished the man physically. In a book published immediately after Mitterrand's death, which was later banned and earned him a four-month suspended prison sentence, Gubler reported that Mitterrand was so weakened that he was incapable of doing the job for the last six months of his time in the Élysée. His Gaullist Prime Minister of the time did not object, since he was left to get on with running the country. The President apparently went straight to bed when he arrived at the Palace from his private home on the Left Bank at 9:30 a.m., and rested for most of the day. Nothing interested him except his illness and some of his grand projects, particularly the controversial new national library in Paris, which was on its way to running six times over budget.

François Mitterrand spent the 237 days that would remain to him after he left the Élysée revisiting what he had most enjoyed in life— Venice and the booksellers of Paris, the countryside of Burgundy and political gossip with his old associates. Dying, he stayed in control. He saw out 1995 at separate Christmas and New Year celebrations with his wife and his mistress and their respective offspring. On his return from a trip to the Nile Valley with his second family, he told Danielle that he had decided to end his life by stopping eating. He asked his doctor what would happen if he ceased his medication. He would die three days later, he was told. Before that, he took a last delight in food.

At a dinner over New Year, he started by consuming thirty oysters. He then ate an ortolan. This rare small bird is an officially protected species, but it is still caught while flying over the southwest and fattened on grain in a darkened barn for three weeks before being killed by a big shot of Armagnac liqueur. By tradition, the ortolan is eaten whole—wings, beak, innards and all. To ensure that not a whiff of the bird's unique aroma is lost, it should be consumed under a large napkin. At the end of the main course of the New Year dinner, one ortolan remained on the platter. Mitterrand took it and disappeared beneath his napkin for the second time that evening. After chewing the little bird, he lay back in his chair, beaming in ecstasy.

Then the man who had fought a solitary combat for half a century got ready to perish. He wrote out the instructions for his funeral—one grand state affair in Paris and a simpler ceremony in his native Charente department. He completed his memoirs. He wrote a letter to a long-time crony. And then, on January 9, 1996, at the age of seventy-nine, François Mitterrand died. A joke which did the rounds a few months later had the President arriving at the gates of heaven: 'You can't come in,' says God, 'you are an adulterer—even worse than that, you think you are God, and in this kingdom there is only one God.' To which Mitterrand replies, 'When's the next election?'

His death was the occasion for a great outpouring of national reverence. A monument had gone; the Fifth Republic had lost its second great figure. His hometown of Jarnac became a pilgrimage centre (though local tradespeople were disappointed when they tried to cash in on the Mitterrand legacy—a confectioner sold only forty of one thousand boxes of chocolates with the President's face stamped on them). Even a strident anti-Socialist like the former Gaullist minister Alain Peyrefitte opined that it was no time for polemics since Mitterrand had been France for fourteen years. There were bizarre touches; in Bulgaria, Mitterrand was hailed as the first foreign leader to draw attention to that country, and in China it was recalled that the transliteration of his name was said by the paramount leader Deng Xiaoping to mean 'Enigma, all is clear.' Two months after his death, five of the ten best-selling books in France were about him: in all, at least four million books about him are reckoned to have been sold. Two were spoof memoirs in the name of his Labrador dog, Baltique.

A Swedish journalist wrote a book about her 'loving friendship' with the late President and their conversations on the Middle East, but she drew a veil over whether he was the father of her son. A woman who helped people to die peacefully told how she had eased the President through the last stage of his life and how he had asked her to place a small stone for him near a Celtic cross below her house in the South of France. A former head of the secret service went into print to show that Mitterrand had personally approved the project to stop the Greenpeace boat *Rainbow Warrior* from sailing to protest against French nuclear tests in 1985, leading to an operation by French agents which cost a Portuguese photographer his life.

A member of his intimate court unveiled Mitterrand's views on the great and the good: Margaret Thatcher had the lips of Marilyn Monroe and the eyes of the Roman Emperor Caligula, while Ronald Reagan 'has only a few records going round and round in his head.' In keeping with the paranormal tenor of the times, France's leading popular astrologer revealed that the late President had consulted her before making important decisions, greeting her with the query 'How am I doing, and how is France doing?'

The manuscript of Mitterrand's gooey wartime short story about Philippe and Elsa fetched 38,000 francs at auction. His family successfully sued Dr. Gubler over the revelations about the President's illness, though they got less than half the damages they sought. In December 1996, Jacques Chirac inaugurated the huge new national library building by the Seine. When he had been asked if he wanted the building to be named after him, Mitterrand had replied, 'If you had to take the decision and you asked me to take that decision, I would say "no."' Which most people took for a yes. So the huge thirty-billion-franc building was called the Bibliothèque François Mitterrand. A poll carried out for *Le Figaro* at the same time showed that he was the second most popular President of the Fifth Republic. Despite all the woes and stress they had suffered under him, 65 per cent of those questioned said they had good memories of the Mitterrand years. As the newspaper remarked, 'He is greater dead than alive.'

Nobody had reflected the contradictions of the people he ruled more clearly. Nobody had done more to turn the Socialist movement into a party of government. Nobody had been more removed from the everyday world but more intimately involved in human affairs. Nobody had contained more contradictions—Vichyite and Resister; the visceral enemy of the Fifth Republic who became its longest-serving head of state and pronounced its presidential vestments greatly to his liking; intellectual and base schemer; a seemingly unworldly figure who never carried money but who presided over a scandal-ridden administration; a chronically unpunctual character who was one of the greatest experts on the minutiae of French electoral geography. A man who liked to present himself as a great humanist and champion of freedom in the Third World, he had presided over a government which armed the genocide in Rwanda and propped up crude dictators in its former colonies. A driving force in the construction of Europe, he had proved unable to craft a role for Paris beyond the shadow of Bonn. A man who prided himself on his grasp of history, he had failed to visualize the breakup of Yugoslavia or the unification of Germany, which he saw primarily as a threat to France's position in Europe. In the end, François Mitterrand was everything and, at the same time, nothing: his own greatest promoter and his own worst enemy, a solitary figure whose self-esteem and contempt for those around him seemed to know no limits as he proclaimed that the greatest political quality was indifference. He was, he told his aide Jacques Attali, surrounded by dwarfs. 'What an artist!' was the verdict of Jacques Chirac, who called his predecessor in the Élysée 'the reflection of his century.'

In the end, two things were plain: France's longest-serving President was not nearly as clever as he thought he was, and he had sacrificed the good of his country at his own altar. Commentators and those who had been seduced and abandoned by François Mitterrand wondered at his lack of any ethical dimension. In opposition, his amorality could be excused as necessary in the pursuit of power. But once he had reached the summit, it got even worse. He simply did not seem to care about any real values, be it in domestic politics or in support for the genocidal regime in Rwanda. If a manipulation of the electoral system would help the National Front, so be it, provided that his opponents were damaged in the process. If the electorate was likely to go for economic promises which would cripple the country, that was fine. The trouble was that, while he held the Élysée for fourteen years, his lack of coherent, sustainable policies not only damaged the country but also set a pattern with deeply unfortunate results. Yet his power of seduction from beyond the grave is such that he can still be hailed as the most successful left-wing leader Europe has known in recent decades, even if he was neither of the left nor successful except in terms of personal ambition, and unscrupulousness.

His ultimate cynicism in power may have had a very simple root: from the end of 1981 onwards he knew that every additional day was a medical miracle. He was on the way out physically from virtually the moment he finally achieved supreme power. Life, in existential terms, held no promise, and so he would amuse himself by playing with power until the end came. The sadness for France as a nation was that the game lasted so long.

To the very end, there were two sides to the man. Asked late in life if he had any regrets, Mitterrand replied, 'None. Not everything was perfect in my life; who can claim that it was? But everything I did, I can be proud of. I mean to say, as a man. I never bowed the knee in front of anything or anybody.'

But there was also another side.

A traveller comes across a group of men in his path.

'What are you doing?' he asks them.

'We are piling up stones,' they reply.

Further on, he meets another group, doing the same thing.

'What are you doing?' he asks them.

'We are building a cathedral,' comes the response.

'Well,' added François Mitterrand as he recounted the story to visitors before his death, 'I ought to have, and could have, built cathedrals. Often, all I did was to make piles of stones.'

13

THE JAWS OF VICTORY

L a Rochelle, in the Charente-Maritime department of western
France, is a pleasant place, with excellent fish restaurants, pedes-
trian zones and a fine yachting harbour. An English expedition sailed
there in 1627 in a vain attempt to relieve the siege of the Protestant
Huguenots, an episode immortalized by Alexandre Dumas and his
musketeers. Three and a half centuries later, two of France's leading
politicians flew to La Rochelle for a party congress to confirm who
would become the next President of the Republic. The meeting was
meant to be another step towards an effortless Gaullist restoration
after François Mitterrand's fourteen years in the Élysée Palace. The
discredit he had brought on the left was such that victory seemed
assured. As things turned out, the weekend on the Atlantic coast set
off the final battle in the Thirty Years' War of French politics.

The period since the left won power in 1981 had been a frustrating,
unsettled time for the Gaullists under Jacques Chirac and the centre–
conservative coalition headed by Valéry Giscard d'Estaing. Frustrating,
because the right was not accustomed to being out of power; its leaders
had been brought up to assume that the Fifth Republic belonged to
them and, though they had won two major parliamentary elections
in 1986 and 1993, they had been unable to best the schemer in the
Elysée. Unsettled, because it was never quite clear who was in charge
of the opposition to the so-called Socialist presiding over France.

After 1981, Jacques Chirac had rushed into the vacuum on his side of politics. Alone of Mitterrand's opponents, he had a real power base as Mayor of Paris. Then the man who had succeeded him as Prime Minister back in 1976, Raymond Barre, emerged as the incarnation of true French values, too. Watching him tucking into a meal at Paul Bocuse's celebrated restaurant outside Lyon one stormy night in the mid-1980s gave one the impression that this was a man made to lead the traditional forces of France.

On the menu that night was the truffle soup which Bocuse had named in honour of Giscard. The coolness that had set in since one man lost the presidency and the other the premiership did not affect Barre's appetite. As always, he acted as though he had time on his side. During the dinner, he mentioned a piece I had written in the *Economist* which contrasted his deliberate style with the livewire Chirac. He appeared quite content to have been portrayed as the tortoise moving at his own pace behind the Gaullist hare. Once described by Giscard as the best economist in France, his conservative manner disguised a sharp appreciation of the realities of modern finance. The portly Barre was never in a hurry, feeling no need to run, confident that he will get there in the end. He was certainly not lacking in self-assurance. Once, when a journalist queried the rightness of one of his policies, he simply told the man not to be so silly.

That approach struck a chord in the increasingly rudderless right of the mid-1980s, and the notion of both his former Prime Ministers moving to the front of the opposition ranks was enough to spur the deposed head of state into action. Giscard thought he could outflank the impetuous Chirac without difficulty. But the idea that Raymond Barre might become president was a goad that could not be tolerated. Stirring the pot, Mitterrand promoted the ludicrous idea that Giscard might agree to become his prime minister. A short time afterwards, he spoke approvingly of Barre as the kind of man with whom he could easily work. The right was in a mess, and Mitterrand knew how to make the most of it, adding the extra pepper of his electoral help to the National Front.

Though it was Chirac who was appointed to run the government after the left lost its parliamentary majority in 1986, Barre insisted on standing in the presidential election two years later. He was the best man in the race, but he lacked an electoral machine to get out the votes and was eliminated with only 16.5 per cent in the first round. As one of his aides later said with a sigh, 'In France, the best never win.' Mitterrand's heavy victory despite the woes he had brought France was fresh evidence of the right's continuing ability to auto-destruct through internal rivalries.

Some drew the inevitable conclusion that Chirac was not the man to wrest power back at the summit of the state. For others, it was time to leave the battlefield. Raymond Barre moved to the sidelines to become a sage and happy Mayor of Lyons. As he put it to me on a trip to Asia, having operated at a national and international level, it was good to get down to earth. He seemed that rare animal, a one-time prime minister who was actually content with his born-again role in the centre of France, and chuckled with genuine pleasure as we talked in a Hong Kong hotel of *quenelles de brochet* and *poularde demi-deuil* and the dinner at Paul Bocuse's restaurant.

So the civil war on the centre-right narrowed to the two companions-in-arms of 1974. It was an unequal conflict. Giscard's day was clearly passing. Recovering from a period of depression after his presidential defeat, Chirac consolidated his power by building up the Gaullist party. By the time of the left's collapse at the 1993 parliamentary election, the one-time protégé of Georges Pompidou was king of the heap. He had wobbled from time to time, notably during France's referendum on the Maastricht Treaty, but he and his cohorts were now on a roll, and the future seemed assured. No more internal wars, no Giscard, no Barre, no concern about the National Front. Having twice suffered as Prime Minister, Jacques Chirac was only too happy to leave his good friend and former Finance Minister, Edouard Balladur, to head the government while he concentrated on the apparently easy campaign to get to the Élysée. Two decades after knifing Chaban-Delmas in the back, life seemed to be simple at last. Blood simple, as it turned out.

Chirac and Balladur met when the first was Pompidou's dashing lieutenant and the second the President's Chief of Staff. They stayed together through the years. From 1986 to 1988, Finance Minister Balladur implemented privatizations and financial liberalization for Prime Minister Chirac. The Gaullist leader regularly sent drafts of his speeches to his friend for comment and approval. Just as he had taken guidance from Pierre Juillet and Marie-France Garaud in the 1970s, two decades on, Jacques sought another source of benediction. For a man who lived for the roar of the crowd and who washed down his favourite dish of calf's head with Mexican beer, his choice was a strange one. Pierre and Marie-France spoke from the roots of France; Edouard floated free of terrestrial attachments.

Son of a rich trading family living in the Turkish city of Smyrna, he had pursued a career as discreet as that of his Gaullist friend had been public. Balladur was a born-again chamberlain of the Ancien Régime, a man of silk and velvet who could glide across a gravel courtyard without leaving the trace of a footstep. The Prime Minister hated loud noise and liked the company of soft-voiced noble ladies. He ate steamed sole and answered his telephone with a strange, fluting 'alloooo.'

As Finance Minister, he had insisted on moving his offices from a modern building down the Seine back to the Louvre, where major-domos walked backwards in front of him. The flashier members of the Mitterrand entourage were known as the 'caviar left'; there was no doubt that Edouard Balladur belonged firmly in the ranks of the caviar right. As President-in-waiting from 1993 onwards, Jacques Chirac waded through a hundred banquets, pumping hands, promising everything under the sun, a man seemingly with no aim in life except to campaign. As Prime Minister, Balladur lulled the nation into a comatose sense of peace and watched with hooded eyes while his popularity soared. Everybody knew Chirac's latest opinion before his brain had fully formulated it; nobody had much idea of what went on behind the Premier's opaque exterior.

After the Gaullist triumph at the general election of March 1993, the deal had been clear: Balladur for Prime Minister, Chirac for President. Apart from freeing Chirac from the day-to-day business of government, which he was convinced had harmed his previous presidential bid, the arrangement gave him time to tour the country, drum up support, think and seek campaign themes. The two men might be very different, particularly in their public personae. But if each kept to his appointed role, they could make a perfect team.

When he spoke to his Gaullist party congress at La Rochelle six months later, Chirac referred to their pact. As his eyes swept the hall, he saw Balladur looking up at the ceiling, avoiding his gaze. From a man as subtle as the Prime Minister, it was more than a signal. So the two companions-in-arms decided to take a stroll around the harbour. After that, Chirac later recalled, he 'understood that the presidential election might well not turn out as planned.' Balladur flew off in his official jet while the man who had headed his party for twenty years was left standing on the tarmac, waiting for his hired plane. At that moment, Jacques Chirac could be in no doubt that power had gone to his friend's head.

This was hardly surprising. Anybody with a surer strategic sense would have seen the danger coming; most French prime ministers nurture presidential ambitions. Still, the rise of Edouard Balladur had something unreal about it, as if he was touched by divine providence. Platitudinous and self-satisfied, he rose from peak to peak in the polls. He gave in to the threat of strikes and won more plaudits. He avoided decisions and became a hero. The *Financial Times* made him its man of the year. With Balladur, it was time to look forward to the past. Like his first patron, Georges Pompidou, two decades earlier, he epitomized a settled national existence. After the tremors of the Socialist years, his deliberate, courtly style struck a reassuring note. He seemed within reach of forging a new conservative consensus which would go beyond Gaullism and give France a single big centre-right party as a rampart against the Socialists.

The Prime Minister personified the rule of the state, with pre-revolution echoes: *Le Monde's* cartoonist showed him being carried in a sedan chair. Let them eat cake, he might have said as he sought to keep the populace happy by taking the easy way out. Adopting a phrase invented by Marie-France Garaud, satirists altered the last syllable of his name to dub him '*Ballamou*' (*Balla-dur* = Balla-hard; *Balla-mou* = Balla-soft). But his hauteur created an illusion of living on a thoroughly superior plane, in which the nation could share—at least for a while.

As the Prime Minister soared in the polls, ambitious young conservatives also looked back at recent history. If Balladur was a second Pompidou, they could not help calculating, his presidency might spawn bright younger protégés. So they lined up to be a second

Giscard d'Estaing. Nicolas Sarkozy deserted his RPR party leader to the side of '*cher Edouard.*' It was, after all, only what Jacques Chirac had done in 1974. More surprisingly, the Interior Minister, Charles Pasqua, switched camps. In his ministerial job, Pasqua had access to political intelligence reports from around the country; so, some reasoned, if he had jumped ship, Chirac must really be done for. The Prime Minister's people began to talk of '*pauvre Chirac*' who had been outrun by the seemingly effortless rise of his former friend.

This was a battle between two strands of politics, between straight-on, no-nonsense populism and genteel conservatism—calf's head versus caviar. While Chirac championed republican values, Balladur once told a lunch party that, overall, he thought that the 1789 Revolution had been a bad thing for France. Had there been a serious chance of the left winning, Balladur's ecumenical appeal might well have been irresistible. His base was broader, and he could easily have painted Chirac into a corner, accusing him of opening the door to another seven years of Socialism in a repeat of his performance in 1981. But once the only heavyweight from the opposite corner, Jacques Delors, decided not to run, the way was open for Chirac to stamp around the ring, facing Balladur with an impossible task in broadening his coalition.

It was as if the imminence of the return to presidential power had infected the neo-Gaullist movement with the virus of division. The Socialists appeared terminally discredited; the centrists could not find a candidate. So the RPR had only to push the door, and the Élysée was its for the taking. But they nearly blew it. Another strange tale of the ways of the men who presume to run France.

As the election came over the political horizon, Balladur was ready to move from his official residence at the Matignon to a much grander residence across the Seine, where he could have as many major-domos as he wished waiting on him morning, noon and night. International finance and the French establishment knew whom they backed. 'Chirac's fun, but Balladur's serious,' one major fund manager told me. 'Chirac's time has passed; we're ready for a time of real management,' echoed a French business tycoon. 'It's simple,' said an international businessman, 'Chirac's mad.' Given the later disclosures about Mitterrand's parlous state of health and preoccupation with day-to-day survival, the Prime Minister's authority was even greater than it appeared at the time. So much so that Chirac showed uncharacteristic signs of hesitation about declaring his own candidacy—and, by one account, had to be encouraged into making the announcement by none other than the old man in the Élysée, who may have calculated that a wild performance from the right could be the only faint hope left to the Socialists.

In fact, Chirac enjoyed strengths of which Balladur could not even dream. He controlled France's strongest political party machine, and had a thousand debts to call in. His praetorian guard was loyal, and he had Paris. The Prime Minister might be the darling of the establishment, but elections are decided by voters—and, when it came to the hustings, there was only one show in France in the spring of 1995.

Jacques Chirac hurled himself into his third presidential campaign with all the brio of a man who knew that this was his last chance to win the prize he had sought all his adult life. Incoherence incarnate, he promised both wage rises and a decline in inflation. One day, he swore his European fidelity; then he talked of a fresh referendum on the Maastricht Treaty. He pledged tax cuts, but predicted an increase in the value-added levy if elected. He was for modern business, but sent an emissary to ensure the latter-day support of the leader of the rioting small shopkeepers of the 1950s, Pierre Poujade. It was great theatre, with policy made on the hoof, arms in the air, rictus smiles freezing his face, a hundred hands pumped every hour. In contrast, Balladur was an also-ran, and some key figures read the way the wind was really blowing.

France's greatest political proponent of free-market economics, the Minister for Business Alain Madelin, stayed loyal to Chirac. As an exponent of *libéralisme avancé*, he saw Balladur was the reincarnation of a consensus-corporatist spirit which even the born-again left rejected. The government's best cutting edge, Foreign Minister Alain Juppé, also remained true to the man he had first served in 1983 in the Paris city government. And the main Gaullist Eurosceptic, the bloodhound-faced President of the National Assembly, Philippe Séguin, decided that, whatever their differences, Chirac was the man who should win the election. This trio, and the party machine, constituted such a formidable force that Balladur's chances ought to have been discounted as the election campaign got under way. But his bromide appeal was so great that the media went on promoting him as the next head of state—which only spurred the Mayor of Paris to greater activity.

As the election battle moved into top gear, one of the main protagonists of the Thirty Years' War considered his options from the sidelines. The last non-Socialist President had every reason to hate Chirac for his tepid attitude in the 1981 presidential poll. But Mr. Ex, as Valéry Giscard d'Estaing had come to be known, still had hopes for the future; if the European Union ever had a real president, who was better suited to fill the post than himself? At the same time, he wanted to preserve a domestic power base, and he knew that Balladur was going for his natural constituency: the local notables who had kept him at the forefront of French politics through good times and bad. If the Premier won the election, Giscard might as well retire to his memoirs. Under Chirac, there might still be a role for him. So it was time to put aside old rancours for the sake of mutual survival.

As spring blossomed on the hillside behind his elegant country home in the Massif Central, Valéry Giscard d'Estaing announced his support for the man whose rivalry had cost him the presidency fourteen years earlier. His hopes for the future were not to be fulfilled, however. He failed in a bid to become Mayor of the Auvergnat capital of Clermont-Ferrand, up the road from one of his châteaux, and family pride was dented when a nephew was fined for involvement in a corruption scandal. Eventually, in a meeting hall in Lyon, the seventy-year-old Wunderkind of the 1960s and 1970s was forced to pass the leadership of the UDF to a former Defence Minister, François Leotard. He was not the successor Giscard would have chosen; the two men had long crossed swords. But the ex-President's days of party political influence were waning. He could settle old scores by influencing the choice of ministers on the right, entertain dreams of becoming Europe's world spokesman and turn his hand to a volume of soapy romantic fiction. He could rouse himself to indignation at the design of the British architect Richard Rogers for a great motorway viaduct over the Tarn River, caress a project for a volcanic theme park in his native Auvergne and speculate about the benefits of devaluing the franc. But Giscard's time as a frontline general had passed. The war on the right had narrowed down to the Gaullist ranks.

On the hustings, the Prime Minister cut an increasingly poor figure. But who could have asked for anything more? Whatever one might think of Edouard Balladur, he was always true to himself, and his self did not include being at ease with the people. So when he accosted teenagers in the street and tried to talk to them about basketball, he clearly didn't have a clue what their replies meant. Electioneering in a café, he was visibly ill at ease if he had to touch anybody. Down in the Rouergue, a lamb urinated on his jacket, and the farmers laughed among themselves.

A satirical television show which shaped public perceptions had great fun with skits in which His Smugness the Prime Minister washed his hands after each electoral handshake and told his wife that he had discovered some charming new words—'tu' and 'le peuple' Such invention went down so well because everybody believed it to be true, and the Prime Minister's behaviour seemed to confirm it each and every day. As his press secretary put it later, Balladur had a problem with 'those French who are called ordinary when one doesn't want to have too much to do with them but who are the real people of France, those whose virtues one praises as a group but whom one ignores as individuals.'

Suddenly, the man who had done so well seemed incapable of getting anything right as his poll ratings went into free fall. When low clouds forced his helicopter to land in southern France, the newspapers were fed a folksy story about how the Prime Minister had been picked up by a passing motorist, with two big dogs on the back seat, and how he had shown the common touch by chatting to the driver as she took him to the next stage of his trip. Some even reported the unlikely spectacle of Balladur standing by the road with his thumb in the air, hitching a lift from the lady. A couple of days later, he sent her a bunch of roses and a visiting card with his handwritten thanks. Unfortunately, it later turned out that the woman was the cousin by marriage of a Balladur adviser who was on the trip—and that he had telephoned to ask her to come to pick up the Premier. When the press learned of the spin that had been put on the tale, it reacted with a belly laugh and a fresh dose of satire about the hitchhike that never was. Things got even worse when it emerged that the supposedly ordinary motorist had been driving a large white Mercedes.

The first round of the election duly gave Chirac 20.8 per cent to 18.6 for Balladur, eliminating him from two-person run-off. Lionel Jospin, the last-minute candidate of the supposedly down-and-out Socialists, took 23.3 per cent of the vote, but if the scores of the two Gaullists were combined and some of Le Pen's 15 per cent were added in, Chirac was well ahead for the run-off.

'This is the ultimate combat of his whole life, and he will not let himself fail,' one of his advisers said as we sat at a pavement café between the two rounds of voting. 'Anyway, the country wants a change. But it will be a hollow victory. We should have blown both Balladur and the left out of the water; we should have humbled Le Pen. We have the best candidate, the man to lead the nation, but we have to struggle to win over voters. They don't believe in us. They don't believe in anybody anymore.'

As the second-round campaign unfurled, Chirac became somewhat more presidential; he even relaxed from time to time. His press office disclosed that in the afternoon of the Saturday before the final voting he went into the garden of the Paris City Hall to read a volume of Japanese poetry. Not everybody believed the tale, but it was a sign of how his staff was trying to spin an image of a mature, thoughtful politician with wide horizons. Balladur rallied more loyally to the flag than Chirac had done to the colours of Giscard in 1981. Some 85 per cent of the Prime Minister's first-round voters backed Chirac in the second round. So did a few from the left who had been alienated by the Mitterrand record. As for the National Front, its leader told his supporters they might as well go hunting snails as vote; and 60 per cent of them did not support Chirac in the run-off, but that left him with the rest. However one analysed the figures, there were a lot of non-Socialists who felt disassociated from the new President.

If France was still a chauvinist nation when it comes to the sexes, imagine it as a woman in an old-fashioned tale. In 1974, she fell for the undeniable seduction of a brilliant, tall and slim young semi-aristocrat who promised so much but delivered a lot less and ended up spending too much time away on safari. In 1981, she collapsed into the arms of an old political roué who offered to lift her to better and brighter horizons. Despite his broken promises and self-absorption, she found herself unable to turn her back on him when the occasion came in 1988, given her doubts about his young rival. Seven years on, she had become terminally disenchanted with the decaying and dying man and wanted a complete change of partner. For a while, she was seduced by the notion of a platonic, pursed-lip relationship with an unctuous eater of steamed sole. But, in her heart, she still believed that each advent of the seven-year itch should bring a fresh outburst of passion. The prospect of slipping into bed with Edouard Balladur was hardly calculated to give her a new lease of life.

So she went for a former cavalry officer who had been trying to sweep her off her feet for fourteen years. He was hardly a dashing new figure, but consider the alternatives. The professorial Socialist Jospin would give lectures and was hardly calculated to stir the juices. She might engage in a quick flirtation with the one-eyed rascal on her far right-hand side. But, in the end, she let her most assiduous suitor have his way with her at last, though not with any great joy. The groom grimaced in crazed excitement as he fought his way through the crowd to the wedding party on the Avenue d'Iena on election night. A kilometre away, a clutch of political experts gathered round an early-morning dinner table in a restaurant off the Champs-Élysées gave the marriage two months before it would begin to run into the ground.

They were right. After an initial honeymoon, troubles mounted. Fury abroad at the new President's decision to resume nuclear testing suspended under Mitterrand was followed by a wave of protests at home against proposed reforms in the welfare system. A month of strikes led the re-elected President to abandon plans to introduce provisions to maintain basic public services in the event of work stoppages in the state sector. The concentration on beating Balladur had been so intense that Chirac's men and women came to office without having been able to give sufficient time or thought to the job ahead. As the political editor of *Le Monde* put it, Chirac's only real election programme had been 'no to Balladur.' His promise to heal the 'social fracture' remained vague in the extreme.

'Our economy is good and healthy, our inflation is one of the lowest in the world, and our foreign trade is in strong surplus,' the new President declared, 'What is not working is our public finances.' 'Now our difficulties start,' the new Prime Minister, Alain Juppé, told his staff. His government made it known that the budget deficit was some fifty billion francs greater than it had been led to believe (a charge indignantly denied by Balladur). Privatization revenue was a good deal less than expected. Alain Madelin was sacked from the Finance Ministry after a running fight with the Prime Minister. The President's ideas man, Emmanuel Todd, rounded on Chirac at the Élysée one day and accused him of having slammed the door on his electorate. As if to confirm Todd's suspicions, Juppé drew up his programme to reform welfare and state spending without any of the traditional consultations with bodies representing those who would be affected. When he unveiled his proposals, two million demonstrators took to the streets and crippling strikes spread across the nation.

What was a month of strikes when the administration had seven years ahead of it to reform the country, mused Chirac. But the administration's unpopularity made it difficult to get anything done, let alone push through the deep changes it had in mind. The President's standing in the polls dropped as he alternately scolded the French for falling short of his expectations and then told them how wonderful they really were. His one-time companion-in-arms Charles Pasqua compared him to 'an unstable husband who beats his wife one day, then apologises the next day by showering her with compliments.' Such unions, Pasqua noted, usually go off the rails—'the wife gets fed up, finds a lover and the marriage collapses.'

Or else, the husband turns his weary eyes from problems at home and thinks about going abroad. Chirac plunged into incessant international journeys acting as France's top travelling salesman. He also made some sensible decisions to set relations on a more realistic basis for the post-Cold War world. France brought itself to admit, 'without acrimony,' that the United States was the sole superpower, and that Paris ranked only as one of the seven or eight most influential world capitals. A closer relationship with NATO was developed. Missiles aimed at Russia were dismantled. After the nuclear tests were completed, the Pacific explosion site at Mururoa was run down. To restrict government spending, plans were announced to reduce the overall strength of the military forces by more than 20 per cent, with an end to conscription. Most of the troops stationed in Germany would be withdrawn and the nuclear missile base on the Plateau d'Albion in southeast France shut.

By the end of his reign, Europe had become François Mitterrand's overriding concern. That meant reciting the mantra of the Maastricht Treaty designed to further the project launched by France and its partners four decades earlier and nurturing relations with Germany, even if the former president had been less than enthusiastic about the effects of reunification on France. Jacques Chirac set out to reassert a broader and specifically Gaullist and French approach to international affairs, aspiring to rekindle the glory years of the 1960s. But the overarching question which he studiously avoided was whether France could—or should—play its old role in a post-Cold War world.

By balancing membership of the Western alliance with independence from Washington, Charles de Gaulle had been able to carve out a national niche in a bipolar world. Now the globe was a much more fractured place and there was only one superpower. Chirac wanted to build up stronger relations with Washington; at the same time, he could not resist the temptation to try to ape the old Gaullist pretensions. Yet, with united Germany the dominant continental power, any attempt to run a freelance foreign policy on behalf of Europe could only irritate other EU states and make a less than convincing impression in Washington. Economic policy was shaped in Germany, and world policy across the Atlantic; where did that leave France? As the second most important member of the European Union, certainly. But on a wider world scale, as little more than a power which might or might not decide to join ad hoc alliances and might be welcomed or barracked according to its decisions.

While the economic criteria of the Maastricht Treaty snapped at France's heels, the vicious circle of economic policy remained as tight as ever and took its political toll. The price of continuing low inflation and Euro-orthodoxy was poor growth. That kept down government revenue, made the deficit reduction required by Maastricht more difficult to achieve, and turned promised tax cuts into a chimera.

To try to boost its income, the Juppé government put up the VAT sales levy, which hit the poor and the unemployed whom Chirac had promised to defend to reduce the 'social fracture.' The number of firms going bust rose, with almost 6,000 businesses shutting down each month. Unemployment edged up again to the record levels of the worst days of the Mitterrand era. The President went on television with a marathon programme whose audience dropped embarrassingly low as viewers turned to a sexy film on the other channel.

'The truth is that we live in a profoundly conservative country and that it is very difficult to change things,' he lamented. Perfectly true, but he was in a fix of his own making. He had won the presidency by promising a new economic and social deal at home, and he wasn't delivering. Or, rather, what he was serving up through his Prime Minister was not the dish the nation had ordered. It had asked for a rich stew; Chirac and Juppé were giving it gruel. No wonder that a lot of people saw attractions in *l'autre politique*, a code word for reflation. Senior officials might speak proudly of the strong franc and sneer at the floating pound, but the economic situation across the Channel could look quite attractive to a long-term unemployed steelworker or a former Felix Potin manager searching for bargains at the local discount store.

Le Monde compared the President to an unidentified flying object— 'one no longer knows quite who he is, where he is, what he wants.' But Juppé kept an iron grip on the business of government, omnipresent and putting his imprint on everything—in the midst of the strikes of 1995 he put in an urgent telephone call to the head of the Communist trade union federation to ask about the staff situation on one Paris Métro line.

A trusted aide moved across the Seine to become Chief of Staff at the Élysée; other acolytes were put in to run ministries, often showing more loyalty to the Juppé machine than to their nominal bosses. The Minister of Justice, Jacques Toubon, was moved to remark that there was a difference between a conductor and a one-man band. All this might have been fine if the government was doing well, but

Juppé actually achieved very little in the way of concrete results given the vested interests with which he was dealing while hitting new records for unpopularity. Matters were made more even complicated by the sizeable bloc of Balladur supporters in the National Assembly who could not get over the defeat of their leaders and proved less than enthusiastic backers of the new administration.

The President established a four-man 'crisis cell' at the Élysée, consisting of himself, the Prime Minister and their two closest officials. 'Act without talking,' was their watchword. But the results were meagre, and senior politicians warned that the long grind of reform risked undermining the administration and encouraging anti-European sentiment. Gloomy forecasts were piling up about even higher unemployment, plus the need for further tax rises and spending cuts. Loyalty to Juppé ruled out the traditional presidential escape route of sacking the Prime Minister.

Eventually, Chirac concluded that it was time to go back into battle. Dominique de Villepin, the Chief of Staff at the Élysée, proposed the old Gaullist recipe of a referendum, this time on Europe. That idea was rejected since it entailed the risk of provoking a hostile line-up, ranging from the left to the National Front and taking in a fair number of Eurosceptic Gaullists along the way. The idea of a crisis government of the great and good, to include Giscard and Barre, was soon dropped. On April 21, 1997, the President announced the dissolution of the National Assembly and two rounds of elections for May 25 and June 1 to give France 'a fresh impetus' for the challenges that lay ahead. On a visit to Beijing soon afterwards, he told the Prime Minister, Li Peng, that he had called the election because his majority was too large and uncontrollable. 'I will lose a hundred deputies, but they will be easier to handle,' he added, 'And Juppé will put everything in order.'

There was no denying the problem Chirac and his men faced. But the way they attacked it was like the old joke—'How do you get to the Eiffel Tower,' asks a tourist. 'If I were you I wouldn't start from here,' responds the Parisian. As often happens with politicians who hunker in the bunker, the men in the crisis cell were starting from the wrong point in several ways. They assumed that France was still set in the political environment of 1993–95, in the crushing defeat for the left at the last parliamentary election and the pre-eminent position of the Gaullists at the presidential poll. The debacle of the late Mitterrand years seemed too close for the French to be ready to put their faith in the left under the leadership of the well-meaning but uninspiring Lionel Jospin.

If the President and his men had lifted their eyes from their dossiers, they might have noticed how Mitterrand was not faring so badly in posthumous opinion polls, seen the way in which Jospin had revived the spirits of the left in 1995, and even recognized how his shadow team looked a good deal more attractive than the apparatchiks of the right. And some fearless aide might have pointed to a poll which showed that 59 per cent of those who had voted for Chirac two years earlier now thought that he talked a lot but that nothing concrete followed.

He and his head of government had nothing new to offer except fresh spoonfuls of Dr. Juppé's purge. So why was he holding an election at all? If he won, it was more of the same. The only logical conclusion was that he was offering voters a chance to change policies. And then there was a difficulty which went to the heart of the political system: however low his popularity, a president of France has to appear to be in charge. At the depths of his fortunes, François Mitterrand always seemed capable of manipulating events. But Chirac appeared to be in thrall to his Prime Minister. Even worse, he looked like a man who was running scared on behalf of his government.

And scared of what? Surely not Jospin. The Prime Minister had summed up the administration's contemptuous view of him when, a cigarillo between his lips, he asked a group of journalists at the start of the campaign what they thought of the Socialist chief and, before they could reply, supplied his own answer: 'He's really very bad, isn't he?' No, the demon at Chirac's back was the French people. He had won their highly conditional love in 1995, but now it was seeping away by the week. He had to regain it, haunted by a terrible frustration at having been unable to capitalize on winning the greatest prize of his life and by the fear of what might lie down the road. For the ultimate macho performer of French politics, this could only be a sign of failure foretold.

Now pause for a paragraph of what the French call *la psychologie de concierge*. Throughout his career, as we have seen, Chirac has sought guidance from others. Having won the supreme prize, he should have been his own man. But he still felt the need for a bond, and he chose Alain Juppé as the mast for his ship of state. The two men had worked together for more than a decade at the Hotel de Ville in Paris. According to one account, they had another bond. Chirac's elder daughter was prey to suicidal depression. Reports of her death swept Paris from time to time; on one occasion, the Chiracs received thousands of condolence messages for a death which had not taken place. Juppé's youngest daughter fell victim to the same illness, and Chirac moved in to comfort and give advice. She survived in much better shape than Chirac's daughter. That gave a depth to their relationship which went beyond politics, and contained an echo of the way in which Georges Pompidou had run a foundation in memory of de Gaulle's Down's syndrome daughter. In a sense, the policies which Chirac and Juppé were jointly defending could be seen as being irrelevant. This fragile President had put faith in his Prime Minister in a way that went beyond the usual relationship between the Élysée and the Hotel Matignon. In human terms, it was admirable. Politically, it paved the way for ruin.

The worst duly came to pass. The Socialists mounted a campaign which made some of their more thoughtful leaders blush in private—a little, at least. Under the slogan 'Dare to return to the left,' they pledged to create hundreds of thousands of jobs without upsetting public finances, to cut the working week to thirty-five hours without any reduction in pay, to stop privatizations and to meet the requirements of the Communists, the Greens and any other allies they could find. Jospin emerged as the head of government France was able to think it had had been looking for—modest, determined, approachable and honest, the embodiment of serious values that should underpin the Republic. Though an Enarque himself, he struck a welcome contrast to the superior technocracy of Juppé, De Villepin and their ilk.

As a power in the land under Mitterrand, Jospin had been as obnoxiously full of himself as the average French minister, a man who had undergone a charisma bypass somewhere along the path from his first career as a diplomat to the heights of the Socialist Party. I recall meeting him once at a 'summer university' outside Bordeaux and being taken aback by his condescension towards those he was introduced to. When the Prime Minister of the time, Michel Rocard, suggested that they might call one another *tu*, Jospin was reported to have replied that the head of the government should remember that he was speaking to *Monsieur le Ministre de l'Education Nationale* and ought to address him as such or by his even grander title of *Ministre d'Etat*.

But a new marriage, and his unexpectedly good showing in the presidential poll, produced a definite change. His smarter colleagues complained that Jospin still dressed badly; however, he made the effort of buying some glad rags and a dinner suit from Armani—apparently he had a model figure, because the only alterations that had to be made were to the length of the trousers. He also learned how to smile. The nickname of 'Yo-Yo' given to him by a satirical television programme became rather endearing. He bought new glasses and a car with a convertible roof. Pictures of him smiling behind the wheel made Jospin look like a man who had discovered pleasure in life somewhat late in the day.

Showing the requisite degree of steel, he sidelined the political dinosaurs of the Mitterrand era and brought forward a new team, including Jacques Delors' tough-minded daughter, Martine Aubry, whose job would be to get to grips with unemployment if the left won. He kept the usual voluble Socialists quiet and disciplined during the month-long campaign, calculating correctly that their best chance of success lay in creating as few waves as possible and leaving their opponents to lose. Shedding their downbeat image of the early 1990s, the main opposition party held out the comfort blanket of promises the French wanted to hear, their unity contrasting with the divisions on the right between Chiracians and the unrepentant Balladurians. Even if their sums did not add up, they radiated an impression of managerial competence and of relative youth. In keeping with the times, Jospin declared himself to be a man of ideas, not ideology. On examination, those ideas sometimes looked less than realistic, and the move to a thirty-five-hour week by the dawn of the twenty-first century promised by Aubry seemed distinctly ideological, but they were sold by men and women who spoke the language of modernity. And, unlike their opponents, they offered some of the dreams the French always cherish.

However well the Socialists fought, this was an election waiting to be lost by a centre-right which appeared to have acquired a death wish. Chirac recalled in his memoirs the 'execrable' atmosphere on the centre-right fuelled by the continuing rancour of Balladur's supporters who had not accepted the result of the presidential election. Public opinion, he added, was 'in the grip of pessimism and morosity,' A saying from the 1980s that France had the stupidest right wing in the world suddenly came back into vogue. Travelling through France during the campaign that spring, I was struck by how many of those who rejected Alain Juppé retained a degree of respect for his fortitude and how even those who backed the left raised their eyebrows when the talk turned to its economic programme. What people couldn't fathom was why those in power had given the country the chance to reject them.

That questioning became even more pointed when Juppé proclaimed that he would unveil his programme for the future within forty days of the poll if his supporters won the legislative election. Why not do it straight away without needing an election? There was only one answer: what the Gaullists had up their sleeve must be so dreadful that they did not dare to reveal it before the voters went to the polls. In such circumstances, the prospect of flopping down at an oasis with Lionel Jospin rather than undertaking another forced march across the desert behind the unrelenting Prime Minister was all too alluring. So, at the first round of voting on Sunday, May 25, the orthodox right got its lowest score under the Fifth Republic, at 36.5 per cent to the left's 45.6. Almost one-third of voters stayed away from the polls and the National Front saw its score rise to 15 per cent.

It was the greatest political shock Alain Juppé had ever suffered, his first major defeat. What made the awakening even worse was that he had ignored the storm signals. Such was the blindness at the top that, as France voted, the chief of staff at the Hotel Matignon had been working on the inauguration speech for the Prime Minister's second government. The normally imperturbable Juppé was reported to have been unable to string more than a couple of sentences together when he met right-wing leaders on the Sunday evening. Later, he drove to the Élysée and mentioned the possibility of resignation. Chirac brushed aside the suggestion with a gesture of his hand.

The following morning, the climate changed. Jacques Pilhan, the President's adviser on public relations, and Chirac's daughter, Claude, insisted that Juppé had to go. The Prime Minister's champion at the palace, Dominique de Villepin, was powerless to protect his man. Within ninety minutes the decision was taken. Some of the Prime Minister's faithful technocrats burst into tears when they learned the news. On Monday night, Juppé went on television to announce that, whatever happened at the decisive second round six days later, he would step down. The President was alone in the front line.

The following Sunday, June 1, the left duly won its majority. The Socialists doubled their representation in almost half the departments of France. Rejected in his constituency near Toulouse in 1993, Lionel Jospin was returned this time with 63 per cent of the vote. In Bordeaux, Juppé, who later acknowledged how mistaken he had been not to have called a legislative election in 1995, won his seat—but with a much reduced vote. Jospin became the new head of government, and France entered a new era in its politics with a humiliated head of state who still had five years of his term to run. On the other side of the world, the Chinese Prime Minister might have reflected on the strange ways of Western democracy.

The Socialists had staged a stunning comeback, but the reality behind the voting was somewhat more complex than it appeared—thanks to the genie in the National Front bottle. If the mainstream right had been humiliated, the combined forces of the left still fell short of a majority of votes, with 48.2 per cent in the second round. Once more, the disarray on the right had opened the door to the left. In the past, the division had been in the mainstream; now the wrecker came from the far bank.

Their strong score at the first round of the election had meant that around 130 of the Front's candidates were entitled to stay in the field for the run-offs. As the party celebrated with glasses of sparkling wine at its headquarters in Saint-Cloud on May 25, Bruno Mégret, the unnamed dauphin to Le Pen, preached entryism. He wanted to cut deals with the orthodox right under which each would withdraw some of its candidates to provide a straight run against the left.

Driven by his hatred for Chirac, Le Pen took the opposite tack and insisted on maintaining as many candidates as possible for the second round. His mind was made up. Back in 1986, he had hoped to forge an alliance with the Gaullists during Chirac's second premiership, but had been coldly rebuffed. Now, a decade on, he had a chance to wreak his revenge—a dish, as the French say, best eaten cold, though the red-faced, jubilant Le Pen was hardly the epitome of cool that early summer night. There was no time for the long process of infiltrating the orthodox right as preached by Mégret. The only foe who counted was not Jospin but the man in the Élysée. The greater the chaos the Front could provoke, the greater the chances of the big bang in French politics which might open the gates of power.

In all, the Front put up seventy-six contenders for the second round. Although it won only one seat—in its bastion of Toulon, which it narrowly lost a year later—the party racked up 40 per cent in some straight fights with the left. The former OAS terrorist Jean-Jacques Susini scored 41 per cent in Marseille, and Mégret took 45 per cent in nearby Martigues. (After failing to find a safe constituency, Le Pen himself chose not to stand.) Even in triangular contests where they finished third, Front challengers clocked up 16 or 17 per cent of the vote. The split in the right-wing vote handed around constituencies to the left. If they had gone to the right, Jospin's majority would have been cut from around sixty to around twenty-five. Not surprisingly, some less scrupulous members of the orthodox right began to talk about reaching local agreements with the Front. Le Pen was said to be putting on weight because of all the secret meals right-wing Gaullists were buying him.

By backing Jospin over Juppé, voters had snatched power from the Élysée, a terrible outcome for a Gaullist who stood, above all, for the imperial authority of the presidency, and whose whole career had been dedicated to winning power whatever it took to do so. It was not surprising that reports swiftly spread of Chirac sitting in his palace sunk in the kind of gloom that had enveloped him after his 1988 defeat by Mitterrand. Most important, he no longer had access to the flow of information from government ministries and risked becoming isolated in the Élysée.

The *Canard Enchaîné* quoted a friend of the President as saying, 'He's doing what he always does when things go against him.
He's eating a lot of *charcuterie*, drinking a lot of beer and watching a
lot of television.' Nothing seemed to go right—even the provenance
of an African statue presented to him by his staff for his sixty-fifth
birthday turned out to be of doubtful legality and had to be handed
to a museum for safe keeping. Sympathizing with a defeated Gaullist,
Chirac remarked, 'You have had a slap in the face. I know something
about that: it's often happened to me.' When he asked his former
Finance Minister what his followers were saying about him, Alain
Madelin was reported to have replied, 'They say that you always lead
us to failure, Jacques. They believe you bring bad luck.'

France's third period of 'cohabitation' between a president of one
political party and a government headed by a prime minister from the
opposite camp opened with a Cabinet meeting at the Élysée Palace
on June 6, 1997. The head of state wore what was described by
one reporter as 'a fixed smile of resignation' as he listened to Lionel
Jospin outline his plans to stimulate growth, create jobs and prepare
the country for the European common currency. 'The atmosphere
was both serious and relaxed, no excesses,' said the Prime Minister.
For his part, Chirac told journalists that the constitution assured the
President of 'pre-eminence' and 'something of the last word.'

The two men who vowed to make the cohabitation constructive were very different in character and approach. Chirac confided
to a friend that he did not 'get' the head of government. In his
memoirs, he recalled Jospin was relaxed, seemingly regarding Chirac
as easy game for the presidential battle that they would fight five
years later, a leader past his prime who would not recover from his
recent reverse. François Hollande, who became First Secretary of the
Socialist Party, said later that he thought the Prime Minister underestimated the President's spite and ability to deceive. Jospin told
Socialists not to attack the President, even adding a little joke—'I
forbid you to speak ill of our benefactor.' He was also conscious of
Chirac's age, speaking on one occasion to journalists off the record
on a flight back from French possessions in the Caribbean of the
head of state as being 'old, tired and spent,' a phrase that inevitably

became public knowledge, provoking criticism of the Prime Minister for lacking respect.

Jospin named a twenty-six-strong government; nearly a third of the ministers were women. It was only four years since the last Socialist Cabinet and the ministerial line-up contained some heavy hitters such as Finance Minister Dominique Strauss-Kahn, who enjoyed reasonable relations with business, Foreign Minister Hubert Védrine, who had been Mitterrand's foreign affairs adviser and coined the description of the United States as a 'hyper power' of which France should be wary, and Martine Aubry, second-ranking member of the government and the champion of introducing a thirty-five-hour working week.

There were passages of arms between the Élysée and the new government over foreign affairs, jobs policy and the role of government. Jospin took the President to task in the Cabinet over the interpretation of the constitution, and Chirac used the traditional presidential television interview on Bastille Day to tick off the government on subjects ranging from immigration to the need not to tie down industry with 'obsolete and absurd regulations.' As if the rigours of the Juppé years had never existed, the head of state insisted that the way to fight unemployment was to encourage small- and medium-size firms rather than to create artificial jobs. But when he called the passage to a thirty-five-hour week 'a hazardous experiment,' Chirac opened the door for the obvious response: with a nod at the legislative election, Jospin observed that hazardous undertakings were not unknown in politics.

But, for all that, France's third experiment in having a president of one party and a prime minister of another got off to an unexpectedly easy start. Whatever he had hinted at during the election campaign, Jospin did not renege on the commitment to the Maastricht budgetary requirements, which removed one potential threat to his dual cohabitation, with a Gaullist in Paris and a Christian Democrat in Bonn. Legislation on the sensitive subject of immigration struck a compromise between the demands of the left and the fears of the right. Seven months after his great victory, the Prime Minister even found himself confronted with militant demonstrations of the unemployed across the country, backed by the Communists and Greens who both had ministers in his government. He set up a billion-franc emergency fund to try to soothe the protests, but also declared that he wanted France to be a society of work, not charity. Dealing with the civil servants who loom large in the Socialist electorate, the government managed to get union backing for wage increases limited to 1.3 per cent in each of the two years before the thirty-five-hour week came into effect.

The presidential term was reduced from seven to five years. In a decidedly non-ideological manner, taxes were cut and, despite campaign cries of 'no to privatization,' the sale of state assets was stepped up. There were balancing measures for the left, notably the thirty-fuve-hour working week and increased social security coverage, including more health insurance for low earners and the declaration that health care was a universal right. The system known as PACS legalized civil partnerships, including those between people of the same sex. Women's rights were promoted.

Regional elections confirmed the disfavour that had fallen on the right, though they were not a complete disaster for it. With 35.6 per cent of the vote to the mainstream left's 39.6 per cent, the Gaullists and their centre-right allies were not humiliated, even if they lost control of most regional councils. While the low turnout of 60 per cent indicated continuing disillusion with politics, the right could draw some comfort from the way in which voters had not stampeded to back the Socialists.

Still, Jospin had much to his credit; the favourable economic situation brought down unemployment by almost one million. But Chirac's popularity did not sink. He rode a tide of scandal about his private life, including trips to exotic holiday locations with a woman journalist and tales of visits to the barber's shop in the National Assembly where he supposedly locked himself away with a female assistant. His chauffeur wrote about a safe in his bathroom at the Paris City Hall in which he had kept banknotes from state secret funds.

The old bulldozer was not going to be deterred. A new contest was in prospect: the presidential election of 2002, on which he had been fixed on ever since winning the office in 1995. That was enough to enliven him. Chirac had always been a political killer, and he had a new target in his sights, the Prime Minister who had been forced on him and with whom he felt none of the political vibrations that animated him through his long career.

So the President left Paris to do what he did best—meeting the crowds and drawing strength from his contact with them; on a trip to the city of Troyes, he slept in a bed specially elongated to accommodate de Gaulle. He said he did not read books, but, for the first time in two years, he went to the theatre. His standing in the opinion polls rose when he asserted France's traditional independence from Washington by leading allied opposition to the bombing of Iraq at the beginning of 1998. At presidential elections, he had observed 'the French don't vote for a government record, but for the dream they keep in themselves.' The Socialists could deal with everyday domestic business while the President occupied the high ground of statesmanship, representing France in global affairs, asserting the country's international role and taking the resulting glory for himself. It was a convenient recipe for obscuring past failures and playing the French dream, given an edge by the electoral timetable. Always ready to go into battle if power was to be won, Jacques Chirac, at sixty-nine, still believed he could incarnate that dream, whatever it might turn out to be next time round.

Chirac showed his political touch at home by making efforts to forge links with leading Socialist ministers, to the point that Jospin felt he had to warn them not to get to close to the charm offensive in the Élysée. He also made sure that he blocked anybody in his own camp who might provide a challenge. Foremost among these was Philippe Séguin, a heavyset figure with pouched eyes and the general air of a mournful bloodhound. His fine sense of strategy was accompanied by a quick temper—he refused to take Chirac's telephone calls when he was in one of his periodic fits of anger. Both attributes had long marked him out from the polished ranks of the French political establishment. He had shown his rebellious streak by allying with the rumbustious Gaullist Charles Pasqua in internal Gaullist party revolts, including a campaign against the EU Maastricht Treaty.

Now, Séguin pressed a more populist course, which he called 'social Gaullism,' inveighing against globalization and declaring that the legislative election had been lost because 'Chirac didn't trust' his suggestions that the Gaullists should show greater social concern. He became head of the RPR, but went too far in challenging the President—his first speech to a Party Congress was interrupted by a thirteen-minute ovation from the floor for the head of state, who was not even present. Unsuccessful efforts to become Mayor of Paris, in which Chirac played a sinuous game, further undermined him, and he was forced to relinquish the party post.

As for the centre-right Union de la Démocratie Française (UDF) set up in 1978 to back Giscard d'Estaing, it splintered under the strain of operating in a political context dominated by the Social-ists and Chirac. Some of its provincial barons sought a haven in alliances with the National Front after it scored well in regional elections. The former Education Minister François Bayrou set up a new movement which he hoped would occupy the central ground of politics. The free market champion Alain Madelin and the former Defence Minister Charles Millon went their own ways. The nominal UDF leader François Léotard, who was under investigation in yet another party funding affair, resigned as party leader, while Hervé de Charette, another centre-right dignitary and former Foreign Minister, spoke simply of the 'ruin of the right.'

That left Le Pen. He and Chirac cordially detested one another. The Front leader regarded the triangular constituency battles of 1997, which his party fought against both the RPR-UDF and the Socialists, as a signal of his growing influence. He saw his electorate as the means of bringing down Chirac even if this meant electing Jospin. Nobody envisaged that the old tribune of the far right might, himself, squeeze through into the second round run-off.

For Chirac and his aides, the only battle was against Jospin. As the election approached he hardened his tone, attacking the govern-ment for inaction on reforms and on law and order. Opinion polls showed him marooned at his usual first round score of around 20 per cent but Jospin did no better, with between 17 and 19 per cent, while Le Pen was credited with 12–14 per cent. What was plain was that voters were growing increasingly disenchanted with those who ruled them. The choice was hardly stimulating. On the one side was the old warrior who had failed to deliver on his promises over the long years but who was asking for another chance to glad-hand his way to power. On the other, an earnest but unexciting figure at the head of a party split between its old ideology and the realities of the modern economy, a Socialist who had become suspect to many to his left because of his accommodation with the market. In the cir-cumstances, a limited but decisive slice of the electorate was tempted to cast their ballots for a man who did not even see himself as a potential president, taking France to a political brink whose effects resonate to this day.

The 2002 presidential election was a watershed that showed up many of the strands laid out in this book. The electoral cycle and the broadly unimpressive record of the Chirac presidency during the previous seven years pointed to a turn in favour of the Socialists. At sixty-nine, and after three decades at the top of French politics, Chirac risked being a spent force, as the Prime Minister had incautiously remarked. Jospin was no spring chicken. He was only four years younger than the incumbent. He had been First Secretary of the Socialist Party in 1981 and his first ministerial post dated back to 1988. His government was certainly not without blemishes, some of its measures having lasting negative effects, such as the introduction of the thirty-five-hour working week. But, despite that ideologically driven measure, it had showed a considerable ability to forge a stable and reasonably well-managed economy under Dominique Strauss-Kahn at the Finance Ministry, while the Socialist leader and those around him seemed to offer something a bit fresher than the recipe laid out by the man who had been dubbed 'the resident of the Republic.' Some of the party's managers and much of the rank-and-file still spoke an archaic political language and were intent on preserving the benefits that accrued to them from the state. Yet, a good case could be made that the Socialists had shown themselves to be competent managers of the country whose chief deserved the top job.

So, though lacking charisma or a popular touch, Jospin had seemed well placed to move up to the Élysée in his second presidential joust with Chirac. He rose early on election day, cast his ballot, had an afternoon nap to prepare for the long night ahead and sat down to write a statement he would make about fighting the runoff against Chirac. He told aides he did not want to be informed of early estimations of the vote but preferred to wait until reliable figures arrived in the evening when he drove to his campaign headquarters, held up by heavy traffic. He was greeted by an enthusiastic crowd shouting, 'Lionel, President!' Inside, however, the atmosphere was heavy. An election strategist, bent over the numbers on sheets of paper in front of him, told Jospin that he was running behind Le Pen. Then the gap between the two men narrowed and the Socialists hoped that voting in overseas territories might give their candidate the lead. But at 8 p.m., the television news gave the official outcome. The Prime Minister said nothing, sitting at his desk to write a statement in which he announced that he was quitting politics. Around him, some people wept; others cried out, 'No!'

In 1995, Jospin had been handicapped by the Mitterrand legacy. Now he had been defeated by the divisive nature of French politics. Other countries have evolved broad coalitions that surmount internal differences—the Democrats and, until recently, the Republicans in the United States, the Conservative and Labour Parties in Britain, the German Christian Democrats. But in France, infighting and personal ambition, combined with a particular myopia among the ruling class, came to the fore in 2002 to produce the cataclysm for the left that few anticipated despite the evident danger.

Jospin compounded his woes with a flat campaign which seemed to take victory for granted and took no account of the groundswell of populist rancour that coalesced behind Jean-Marie Le Pen to produce the political earthquake of the first round of the presidential election. The abstention rate was unusually high at 28 per cent; it had been 21 per cent seven years earlier. But the prime reason for Jospin's failure to reach the run-off lay in the irresponsible divisions on the left.

Ten other candidates stood against Jospin for the centre-left-ecologist vote; between them, they took 37 per cent of the first round vote. These politicians, from the serious centrist François Bayrou to the perennial Trotsykite fundamentalists (two of them who totalled 10 per cent of the vote), thought it inevitable that Jospin would get to the run-off. So they could cater to their own ambitions and ideology in the first round, shedding any responsibility to block Le Pen. Most egregious was the former Socialist minister Jean-Pierre Chevènement, who presented himself as a true 'republican and defender of French sovereignty against "the Chirac-Jospin pair."' By taking 5 per cent of the vote he doomed the Prime Minister (and got his come-uppance when the Socialists put up a candidate against him in a subsequent legislative election in his long-time fief of Belfort of eastern France, splitting the left-wing vote and causing his defeat). All in all, it was a formidable illustration of selfishness and divisiveness regardless of the outcome. Serious politics this was not, and the 200,000 vote margin was enough to propel Le Pen into the second round, as the left which had caused such an outcome wailed and sought to avoid acknowledging its own responsibility for what had happened.

Chirac and his close advisers were, as we have seen, astounded and shocked. Jospin's elimination by the old warhorse of the far right attracted all the attention. But there was another message from the numbers. Chirac took just 19.9 per cent of the vote against Le Pen's 16.9 per cent and Jospin's 16.2 per cent. After seven years in office with a major political party behind him and a governmental career stretching back to the 1970s, the incumbent had failed to build a constituency of more than one-fifth of the electorate. He was bound to sweep to an enormous victory in the run-off given the shock at the first round outcome and the lack of fresh votes for Le Pen to attract. So he duly racked up a record 82 per cent on the second round in May. But the victory was hollow. Those most fervent in wanting to block any advance by the National Front leader were on the other side of the political spectrum from the re-elected President. Few of the million people who demonstrated against the Front between the two rounds were his supporters. The abstention rate was the same as in 1995, but many of those who cast their second-round ballots for him held their noses as they did so. 'Vote for the crook, not the Fascist,' went the cry to voters from the left.

That launched Chirac's second term on a shaky note, even though the President's supporters won a majority in parliamentary elections a month later under the banner of the Union de la Majorité Présidentielle (UMP), with Alain Juppé in charge. The adroit and affable provincial politician Jean-Pierre Raffarin, a man with whom the President felt at ease, addressing him as '*tu*,' took the premiership. National Assembly elections in June brought a crushing victory for his supporters. The UMP won 399 seats with 33 per cent of the vote in the first round and 47.3 per cent in the second. The Socialists lost 115 seats to end up with only 140 and 35 per cent in the run-off ballots. The centrist UDF, under François Bayrou, did even worse, with only 29 seats after losing 83 and scoring just 3.9 per cent of the second round votes.

The President felt in optimistic mood; the left was in disarray, he found the new Prime Minister much to his liking. His close lieutenant de Villepin became Foreign Minister, Raffarin embarked on a programme of decentralization in keeping with his provincial roots in the Poitou-Charente region of western France and began a careful attempt to reduce public sector pension entitlements. The re-elected head of state was even told that Giscard had acknowledged that he was 'basically good.' But, below the celebrations of the two victories, many themes which would bedevil the country for the years ahead were becoming all too evident as Chirac launched into his second term.

In May, the national anthem was met with derogatory whistling at the French soccer cup final. EU talks on immigration and border controls broke down. An audit showed the budget deficit rising to 2.6 per cent of GDP from the planned 1.8 per cent; by the following March the forecast was increased again, to 3 per cent. A right-wing extremist suffering from depression fired two shots at the President during the Bastille Day parade in Paris; they went well wide. The government responded to concerns about security by creating 13,500 new police posts and promising tougher legal enforcement, especially against young offenders. Legislation was introduced to modify the thirty-five-hour working week. The retirement age for civil servants was raised, bringing strikes and demonstrations. The government stood firm. Its step in the right direction did not earn popularity.

As the economy worsened, so the President's standing inevitable declined. This was, after all, a politician whose natural constituency amounted to only one-fifth of the electorate. Without the galvanizing effect of a Le Pen as his opponent for the highest office in the country, support for Chirac deflated steadily. France's opposition to the invasion of Iraq earned the administration credit at home and made de Villepin into an international figure. American attacks on the policy laid out by the charismatic Foreign Minister—from the re-naming of French fries as 'Freedom fries' to Vice President Dick Cheney's statement to the French ambassador that his country had committed an 'unpardonable crime in putting US security at risk'—only made the French more sure that they were in the right. Still, the national major concerns were closer to home. A high global profile was welcome, especially when it was executed with de Villepin's panache and meant standing up to the United States at the head of the 'coalition of the unwilling,' but domestic pocketbook issues mattered more.

Regional elections in March 2004 were a disaster for the President's party. The Left took 24 of the country's 26 regions—only Alsace and Corsica resisted the flood wave. Under the management of François Hollande, the Socialists won 49.9 per cent of the second round vote, compared with 36.8 for the UMP and 12.4 per cent for the National Front. The President thought of changing his Prime Minister, but all the candidates suffered from disadvantages that led him to stick with Raffarin. There was a government reshuffle in which Sarkozy became Finance Minister and de Villepin took on the Interior Ministry.

Things got no better for Chirac, whose approval rating plunged to 32 per cent, with 63 per cent judging him negatively. (This would look quite good compared with his successors but, at the time, it was the worst rating of any Fifth Republic head of state.) Alain Juppé resigned as head of the UMP following his conviction for misuse of funds at the Paris Mayor's Office and was succeeded by Sarkozy; the President insisted that the post was incompatible with membership of the government. Sarkozy went for the party post, seeing it as an opportunity to build up a machine for the presidential election three years later. He had not endeared himself to his one-time patron when, on a visit to Hong Kong, he criticized Japan, for which Chirac had a passion, and made fun of fans of sumo wrestling, among whom the President counted himself.

There was a major embarrassment in May 2005 when French voters rejected the new constitution for the EU negotiated in a referendum. The negative vote was 55 per cent on a turnout of only 66 per cent. That made a change at the Hôtel Matignon inevitable, and Chirac plumped for de Villepin after considering his one-time protégé Sarkozy and the Defence Minister, Michèlle Alliott-Marie, who had established herself as a tough operator and a Chirac loyalist. He turned down MAM, as she was known, because of her relatively limited political reach. In his memoirs, Chirac says he rejected Sarkozy on the grounds that there were too many policy differences between them on economic and social policies—though the way the younger man would have used the job to further his own ambitions outside the President's control must have been a major factor. So, he returned to his power base of the Interior Ministry, insisting on retaining the presidency of the UMP against Chirac's wishes, a combination which the head of state was unable to prevent.

With his own approval rating down further to 22 per cent, Chirac hoped that the dashing new Premier would inject new life into the failing government, and there was the usual flurry of plans. But there were urban riots on an unprecedented scale in the summer of 2005 as we saw in an earlier chapter, and de Villepin ran into growing street protests against attempts to reform the labour laws, notably over a proposal to introduce greater flexibility into youth employment. The Prime Minister refused to withdraw the measure but, after a general strike and demonstrations involving more than a million people across the country, Chirac did it for him. That blow to the Premier's credibility was accompanied by the inexorable rise of Sarkozy as the likely standard-bearer in the coming presidential battle.

A murky affair surfaced involving accusations that a French espionage agent had been instructed to conduct investigations into the alleged involvement of de Villepin's main rival for the succession, Sarkozy, in a corruption affair stemming from the sale of French frigates to Taiwan. The President went on television to defend his Premier and to insist that 'the Republic is not a dictatorship of rumors, a dictatorship of lies.' But the rumours continued to fly and de Villepin's status was hit when big demonstrations forced him to water down proposals to reduce job protection for younger workers in the name of greater labour flexibility.

Chirac, who had suffered a minor stroke in 2005, looked increasingly like a monarch who had outlived his time and who surprised nobody when he appeared on television in March 2007 to announce that he would not run for a third term. While including a call for voters to reject extremism at the forthcoming presidential poll, the broadcast did not endorse any mainstream candidate from the centre-right. Chirac may have hoped that de Villepin would somehow manage to get the better of Sarkozy. In his memoirs, he was unsparing about Sarkozy, whose career he had once fostered as the embodiment of the 'bulldozer' attributes which Georges Pompidou had lauded in the young Chirac. On mature reflection, he painted his former follower as 'irritable, rash, impetuous, disloyal, ungrateful, and un-French.'

Though the economic situation was showing improvement, with unemployment down to 8 per cent and the state debt reduced to 2.5 per cent of GDP. But voters wanted change. Despite enjoying Chirac's implicit support, de Villepin was never going to make it to the Élysée. He was doomed to become yet another of the high-grade presidential wannabes who populate French politics. The aristocratic, poetry-writing Prime Minister might play to French nationalistic pride, with his denunciations of the George W. Bush administration over Iraq, and enjoy the sympathy of the head of state, but he could not appeal to the everyday concerns of the French.

The right needed sterner stuff since the electoral cycle meant that, after a dozen years of Chirac, it was time for a Socialist to get into the Élysée—and nobody offered a sterner recipe than Nicolas Sarkozy, a man who made up for his abrasive reputation with his promise of a national revival after years of drift.

14

FROM BLING TO NORMAL

Asked by a television interviewer in 2003 if he thought about becoming President as he shaved in the morning, Nicolas Sarkozy replied with a smile, 'Not only when I shave.' When he put himself forward in early 2007 to a UMP Congress as the party's candidate for the presidency, there was no rival, and he got 98 per cent backing. Chirac gave him the less than ringing endorsement that, since he had been chosen by the UMP, 'it is totally natural that I give him my vote and my support.'

Stepping down from the government in March, the candidate pledged to boost economic growth and employment by reducing taxes and deficits, ignoring his own record; during his time as Budget Minister, public debt had risen by a record amount. He said he would cut the size of government while relaxing labour legislation. There would be tough law-and-order measures and tighter immigration controls. He would rebuild links with the United States while maintaining France's individuality in global affairs—friendship, he remarked, 'means accepting that your friends don't necessarily see eye to eye with you.'

All this went down well with the right but naturally aroused the antagonism of the left and concern in the centre. There was a strong personal element in the campaign—Sarkozyites saw him as a man with the personality and determination to get things done, while many others feared that he would prove an uncontrolled leader, at best pugnacious and at worst a bully, a man in such a hurry that he would trample over others and impose his will regardless.

As it turned out, his campaign style was unexpectedly muted. He sometimes seemed morose and drawn. Instead of mingling with the crowd after finishing a speech, he would lock himself away in a room and start talking on his cell phone. He moved from the family home in the smart Paris suburb of Neuilly to a house owned by a close friend, Dominique Desseigne, head of the Barrière hotel and casino group. His wife, Cécilia, explained that she had arranged this so that he could concentrate on the campaign and get some peace and quiet. She hung photographs of herself and Nicolas on the walls of his room and advised Desseigne on her husband's diet. At breakfast he talked to his host about the role he would like his wife to play when he was elected.

If the centre-right was united this time behind a candidate who had served as Budget Minister, Interior Minister and Finance Minister in a career stretching back a dozen years, the left came up with a much less expected candidate as the result of a decision in 2005 to hold a party primary to pick the presidential nominee. Initially, the front-runners appeared to be the urbane, social democratic former Finance and Economics Minister Dominique Strauss-Kahn, Martine Aubry, the Party Secretary who had overseen the introduction of the thirty-five-hour working week in the Jospin government, and Laurent Fabius, Prime Minister under Mitterrand and leader of the successful 'no' campaign at the European referendum of 2005. Then a new serious contender entered the race: Ségolène Royal, President of the Regional Council of Poitou-Charentes in Western France who had spent a year as Environment Minister in the early 1990s and had been the partner of the Socialist First Secretary, Hollande. (They met at a social occasion when they were both at ENA and had four children together, though, by 2007, they were living separate lives.) The party's top bureaucrat had toyed with the idea of running himself but, after she insisted that she would be the better candidate, he stepped aside and sought to remain neutral between the contenders for the nomination.

Royal called for an expansion of the state sector and public spending. Despite invoking these old themes, she stressed the need for fresh ideas, including reform of her own party. Jospin, who had emerged from his supposed retirement from politics to let his name be put forward, denounced her for 'pure demagoguery'; but he was forced out of contention by his own lack of support, a development greeted by Royal's supporters as a sign of her growing strength. Stylish and eminently self-assured, she proved to be a tireless and charismatic campaigner, building up an intensely loyal following and vaulting into the lead in the opinion polls. The first woman to put herself forward for the presidency as a major party candidate, she was an assiduous user of social media and the Internet with a site called *Désirs d'Avenir* (Desires for the Future). She held on to her lead through a series of internal debates, some televised. When party members voted in November 2006, Royal took 60 per cent of the vote with backing from 101 of the 104 local federations.

Despite this resounding success, and her personal partnership with Hollande, there were reservations about her personality among the Socialist leadership. Some of this was put down to sexism or to her innovative style. What her supporters saw as determination was viewed as authoritarianism by others. Her insistence on running things her way grated with more experienced party politicians, whom her advisers dismissed as 'elephants.' The primary system came in for criticism since it reflected only the views of paid-up Socialist members and ignored the wider non-right national electorate whose support was needed to win the Élysée. One of Royal's leading advisers, Éric Besson, resigned after falling out with her over the cost of her economic programme. Despite having condemned Sarkozy as a 'neo-conservative American who carries a French passport,' Besson joined his campaign and wrote a book accusing Royal of demagogy and of pursuing purely personal aims.

In the first round of the presidential election on April 22, 2007, Sarkozy headed the poll with 31 per cent of the vote to Royal's 26 per cent. The centrist François Bayrou did well among voters who wanted neither of the main party candidates, taking 19 per cent. At 10 per cent, Le Pen failed to come anywhere near his 2002 score; some of those who had been fed up with Chirac in 2002 and wanted tougher policies saw Sarkozy as a man who would deliver on parts of the far right's programme. There were six candidates from the non-Socialist left, including a young Trotskyite postman who did best with 4 per cent; but they mustered only 10 per cent of the vote between them, compared with 37 per cent five years earlier. The once pow-erful Communist Party hit its nadir with 1.9 per cent, and the

Greens did even worse with 1.5 per cent, while the anti-McDonald's maverick José Bové limped in with 1.3 per cent. Royal's tally was 40 per cent more than what her dismissive critic Jospin had recorded in 2002. Even more striking, Sarkozy's first round score was 50 per cent up on Chirac's base support. Turnout was high at 84 per cent, with an unusually intense degree of commitment as the right sought a new start and the left proclaimed 'anyone but Sarkozy.'

The Socialist establishment, including Hollande, ruled out the obvious tactical move, an alliance with Bayrou, who had trebled his 2002 result. The party wanted a clean win on its own. However, despite her advocacy of a new brand of politics, Royal showed herself ready to cut an old-fashioned deal. She telephoned the centrist's home to propose that, in return for his backing, she would make him Prime Minister if she won. Bayrou was not in at the time, and did not reply to the message she left on his answering machine, probably calculating that she would lose and perhaps not savouring the idea of serving under her in any case.

The high point of the run-up to the second round was a televised debate on May 2, when Sarkozy held a 55 per cent lead in the polls. The worry on the right was that its notoriously short-fuse contender would explode and alienate voters. In the event, he kept his cool and used his skills gained from his early career as a court lawyer to make his points; he also had more private reasons for his subdued performance.

It was Royal who went on the offensive, enabling the former minister to lean back and smile reassuringly while she failed to land a body blow. 'I was sometimes a bit surprised by a certain aggression on the part of Madame Royal,' Sarkozy remarked in a radio interview the following day, while his ally François Fillon accused her of being somebody who 'lies shamelessly.' After that, the outcome of the second round on May 6 was in no doubt. Sarkozy did not quite live up to the polls but took 53 per cent of the vote. His victory set off riots in Paris and other cities, with more than a thousand cars torched and government buildings attacked. Five hundred people were arrested.

At fifty-two, the son of an aristocratic Hungarian émigré had won France's supreme political prize at his first attempt and with a clear margin of victory. Mitterrand and Chirac had got to the Élysée only on their third attempt. Giscard had done it at his initial bid but had won by 420,000 votes, whereas Sarkozy led Royal by more than two million. With the right on a roll, the left depressed at having failed to bring about a logical turn in the electoral cycle after twelve years of centre-right rule, and the National Front marginalized, Sarkozy appeared well placed to push through the sweeping reforms that had formed the centrepiece of his presidential campaign. But, four months later, he would tell a friend that May 6, 2007, 'was the saddest day of my life,' not from the anti-climactic sentiment that sometimes follows victory but for a much more private and personal reason.

Self-belief and pride verging on arrogance, a taste for secrecy and drama, a forceful speaking style and a need to show that he was best in class had been the hallmarks of the new President's political career for the past three decades. His father had founded an advertising agency which did well, and the family grew up in a mansion in the elegant 17th arrondissement of Paris owned by his maternal grandfather, a Greek Jew who had converted to Catholicism and who was a staunch Gaullist.

The boy saw little of his father, an absence which he said later helped to shape his character. He also suffered at school for being short of stature. 'What made me who I am now is the sum of all the humiliations I suffered in childhood,' biographer Catherine Nay quoted him as saying. 'Truthfully, I am not more ambitious than the others . . . Only I have chosen not to negate this part of myself that has always driven me to move forward, to try to achieve for myself, to exist.' When he visited the United States as Interior Minister in 2004, he noted to French journalists that he was sometimes called 'Sarkozy the American,' and added: 'I am proud of it, I am a man of action, I do as I say and I try to be pragmatic. I share a lot of American values. You have to love success. Those who succeed must be examples, but sometimes, in our countries, people are suspicious of them.'

Self-assured, impatient and never satisfied, he was unable to stick to an agenda and appeared to believe that, if he ordered something to be done, it would be implemented. He made hasty judgments and did not follow through. He would be the hardest-working president of the Fifth Republic, obsessed by the need to do as much as possible. But he dissipated his energies to a destructive degree, embracing the idea of risk but too often unable to see the task through, pulling back when he should have advanced—in Nay's words, 'a fearful daredevil,' a would-be autocrat in the mode of de Gaulle, but a micro-manager at the same time.

Having been less well off than his classmates at the smart schools he attended after the family moved to Neuilly, he seemed obsessed with money, an unfortunate trait as head of a country which was not at ease with it. 'I will do only one five-year term,' he told early visitors to the Élysée. 'I want to reform France; then I will earn a lot of money.' On winning the presidency, he doubled the annual salary he received as head of state. A friend told Nay that he was always afraid of going short—hence his occasional bouts of compulsive purchasing, for example, buying ten Lacoste sports shirts at a time.

Yet the pursuit of power was his primary motivation; he would have been much richer if he had remained a lawyer but, from his twenties, he was set on rising as far and as fast as he could on the political ladder. Having got to the top, he found it less pleasant than he might have expected. 'I do not like this life,' he told trusted journalists two months after being elected. 'I have few friends. I get too many compliments and too many insults. Now that I have been elected, it is true that I have been freed from a burden, that I no longer have the longing in my stomach. I will do the job, commit myself completely, but I tell you this; I will not end my life in politics.'

Unlike his Socialist opponent, he did not go to ENA and failed to graduate from his college, the Institut d'Études Politiques de Paris (Sciences Po). Instead he studied law and specialized in business and family cases—among his clients was Silvio Berlusconi. He began his political ascension by attracting Chirac's attention as a young councillor in the right-wing fiefdom of Neuilly run by the Gaullist warhorse Charles Pasqua. His mother had been Pasqua's secretary and the young man was taken on to work on his mayoral re-election campaign. But, when Pasqua fell ill, Sarkozy moved in to claim the post for himself in 1983, becoming the youngest mayor of a town with a population of more than fifty thousand.

In the tradition of national politicians who keep a local base, albeit in a chic Parisian suburb rather than in the usual provincial bastion, he

held on to the job until 2002. In 1988, he was elected to the National
Assembly for the area and rose to be appointed Budget Minister in
the Balladur government. In the 1995 election, he backed the Prime
Minister, earning him a period in the wilderness when Chirac won
the Élysée and consigning him to Madame Chirac's blacklist. He was
also said to have dated Chirac's daughter and further antagonized the
First Lady when that broke up. But he was not the kind of politician
who can be kept down and, apart from a brief passage as Finance
Minister, he made the Interior Ministry his own with his forceful
law-and-order message and strident support for the police. He revelled
in headlines and television coverage, starting with the 'Human Bomb'
episode in 1993, when a man took children hostage in a kindergarten
in Neuilly and threatened to blow them up; the Minister hurried to
the scene and supervised operations, which ended after two days with
police stealing into the premises and killing the attacker.

His career went through ups and downs. He became boss of the
RPR in succession to Philippe Séguin in 1999, but the party slumped
to only 13 per cent of the vote in the European Parliament election
that year and Sarkozy had to step down. He bided his time for
three years, content with a new marriage, and returned to the fore
when Chirac pardoned his support for Balladur and appointed him
as Interior Minister in 2002. Two years later, as Finance Minister, he
pushed through the reduction of the government ownership stake in
France Télécom from 50.4 per cent to 41 per cent and the partial
nationalization of the Alstom engineering group, as well as reaching
an agreement with retail chains to lower prices.

Still, despite the earlier patronage of the older man, he and
Chirac did not get on. 'Sarko' wanted to chart his own path to
the top, and the head of state found it hard to control a politician
who, as the President wrote, always moved ahead without hiding his
intentions. When Sarkozy became leader of the ruling UMP party
with 85 per cent of the vote at a convention, Chirac forced his resignation as Finance Minister, but the younger man showed his resolve
and forcefulness by coming back to government as Interior Minister
under his main presidential rival, Dominique de Villepin—without
resigning from the UMP leadership.

Polls showed him as the most divisive conservative politician
in France, a reputation he enhanced with his up-front reaction to

the urban riots of 2005. He sought a wider audience with calls for changes in economic policies, castigating past governments of right and left. In an interview with *Le Monde*, he said the French people had been misled for thirty years by false promises. To correct the situation, he called for a simpler and fairer tax system with a maximum total payment of 50 per cent of revenue, reduction of welfare payments to the unemployed who did not take up offers of work, and a reduction in the state deficit. He celebrated the way in which France was finally getting over the student upheaval of May–June 1968 'and all its slogans' about excessive freedom. He advocated immigration quotas to admit only skilled workers and tighter selection of students from abroad. His language was direct—'Nobody has to live in France,' he said in early 2007. 'But when you live in France, you respect its rules.'

His first marriage in 1982 to the daughter of a Corsican political dynasty ended in divorce in 1996, and later that year Sarkozy married Cécilia Ciganer-Albéniz, a former fashion model working in public relations. He had first caught sight of her when he officiated at her wedding to television star Jacques Martin at the Neuilly town hall in 1983. He said he had been 'struck by lightning.' When they married after her divorce from Martin, the witnesses at their marriage were two of France's richest men, Bernard Arnault, head of the LMV luxury goods empire, and Martin Bouygues, who had expanded the family construction group into television as boss of the main national station, TF1. The couple had a son as well as four children from previous marriages.

In a country where political wives usually keep in the background or pursue separate careers, the striking Madame Sarkozy was unusually prominent. She acted as her husband's personal aide, taking an office alongside his at the Interior Ministry and appeared with him at public occasions. But she said she did not see herself playing the role of a First Lady—'It would bore me. I'm not politically correct.' In 2005, she began an affair with Richard Attias, the French-Moroccan head of an events management and marketing company based in New York.

The story was broken in August by the magazine *Paris Match*, which ran a cover photograph of Cécilia with Attias on the balcony of his

New York apartment and reported that she had spent the summer with him. The magazine's owner, Arnaud Lagardère, a friend of Sarkozy, sacked the editor. But the story was out, and Dominique de Villepin, Sarkozy's principal rival on the centre-right, seized on it to intone that 'a man who cannot keep his wife cannot look after his country.' Sarkozy, meanwhile, was said to be in a relationship with a journalist from *Le Figaro* with whom he spent a break in Corsica. Another story told of an affair with a prominent actress. The politician's private life was becoming an integral element in his public persona.

Cécilia returned to Paris and to her husband as he geared up for his presidential bid. Writing about his private life in a fashion that was highly unusual for a French politician, he confided in a volume of personal observations, 'Cecilia and I have gotten back together for real, and surely forever. I'm talking about it because Cécilia asked me to speak for both of us . . . by asking me to do so, she showed her modesty, her fragility, and maybe also her confidence in her husband.' He did all he could to win back her favour, including a shopping trip to luxury stores at the rue du Faubourg Saint-Honoré. However, she told him she wanted to divorce, arranging for him to move out of the conjugal home in Neuilly to stay with their friend during the presidential campaign and resisting all his telephone calls, including those made behind closed doors after political meetings to try to get her to change her mind.

To go together to vote at the first round of the election, Sarkozy had to sneak into a parking lot under their Neuilly residence in order to be able to emerge with his wife to head for the polling station. A report spread that she abstained at the second round. Most significantly, on the victory night of May 6, she organized a celebration at Fouquet's, the plush restaurant on the Champs-Élysées which belonged to the group run by her husband's erstwhile host, Dominique Desseigne.

The guest list was her doing, and it became notorious. Though the former Prime Minister Jean-Pierre Raffarin and the future occupant of the Hôtel Matignon François Fillon were invited, most of top campaign staff was excluded; she felt they had abandoned her when she went to New York. Instead, there was an array of rich business people, including the wedding witnesses Arnault and Bouygues, plus show business personalities, among them the singer Johnny Hallyday and the actor Jean Reno. It was the beginning of the image of the new President as a man who courted the company of billionaires and stars at a time when the French were experiencing economic woes. But, despite having arranged the evening, Cécilia nearly did not attend, claiming that she had nothing to do with the occasion. Her husband pleaded with her, and she eventually relented, but arrived after he had left to address supporters in a hall and then attend a celebratory rally on the Place de la Concorde.

Addressing the jubilant crowd, he presented his election as a radical new departure. 'The French have chosen to break with the ideas, habits and behaviour of the past,' he declared. 'I will restore the value of work, authority, merit and respect for the nation. . . . I want to give French people back the pride of being French—to finish with repentance, which is a form of self-hate.' Watching on television in the nearby Élysée Palace with his family, Chirac waited for a mention of himself. None came. 'I held back from showing the slightest reaction,' the outgoing President recalled. 'But deep inside I was affected, and I knew what to expect.'

As the victor spoke, his wife sidled on to the platform. Wearing trousers and a pull-over, she looked bored, pale and drawn. The Gaullist minister Michelle Alliott-Marie had to take the couple's hands in hers and raise them in a shared gesture of triumph. When she returned to Fouquet's, Cécilia was in tears.

The following morning, after a night in a Parisian hotel, the Sarkozys flew off together for a Mediterranean vacation on a luxury yacht owned by another of their very rich friends, the industrialist and corporate raider Vincent Bolloré. The image spread of the new head of state as an enthusiast for conspicuous consumption of the most expensive kind and a crony of the wealthy, summed up in the 'bling bling' soubriquet attached to him. On their return, he allowed Cécilia to give her advice on Cabinet appointments, opposing those who she thought were not sufficiently supportive of her in her personal troubles and pressing the case for her friend, lawyer Rachida Dati.

On May 15, the new President was inaugurated at the Élysée, pledging, 'I will defend the independence of France; I will defend the identity of France. I will ensure respect for state authority, and above all its impartiality. There is a demand for change. Never have the risks of inertia been so great for France as they are now in this world in flux, where everyone across the world is trying to change quicker than the others, where any delay can be fatal.' He spoke of his desire to foster a 'Mediterranean Union,' which France would lead as a new regional grouping to balance the power of Germany and the north European states. He promised to make 'the defence of human rights and the struggle against global warming priorities of France's diplomatic action in the world,' concluding: 'The task will be difficult and it will take time.'

His wife vetted the guest list, excluding those she regarded as less than friends. She got the band of the Republican Guards to play an air written by her great grandfather, Isaac Albéniz. Wearing an ivory satin Prada gown, she was at the centre of attention, holding Louis, her ten-year-old son by Nicolas by the hand, surrounded by the children from their other marriages. It looked like a family occasion with the couple reunited, but observers noted that the table plan which Cécilia drew up for the small lunch party which followed placed a woman friend of Robert Attias next to the new President.

The next day, Sarkozy named François Fillon, a former Labour and Education Minister who had been a campaign adviser, as Prime Minister. The two men were photographed jogging together in the Bois de Boulogne, not so much as a symbol of their moving ahead in step as a sign that this was to be a younger, more active administration than the one which had preceded it, their vim putting Chirac into the shade and presaging the 'rupture' with past habits promised by the President.

The fifteen-strong Cabinet contained seven women. Only two of its members were Enarques. There was continuity in the person of Alain Juppé who, despite his conviction three years earlier for mishandling public funds, was named the second-ranking member of the government as Minister of State and Minister of Ecology and Sustainable Development and Planning. The centrist Jean-Louis Borloo, who had first made his name as the socially aware Mayor of the depressed northern town of Valenciennes, became Minister of the Economy, Finance and Employment, and announced his target of reducing unemployment to 5 per cent by the end of Sarkozy's mandate in 2012. Alliot-Marie was appointed as the first woman

Interior Minister in charge of implementing the President's pet theme of law and order. A pro-Sarkozy centrist, Hervé Morin, succeeded her as Defence Minister.

Another of the President's preoccupations lay behind the creation of a Ministry of Immigration, Integration, National Identity and Co-Development, headed by his close associate Brice Hortefeux. A dedicated Sarkozyite, Éric Wœrth, was put at the head of the ministry for the Budget, Public Accounts and Civil Administration, with the task of replacing only a third of retiring civil servants—the President said he wanted fewer public officials but wished them to be better paid.

Sarkozy set out to enlarge his administration by bringing some Royal supporters into the government. In an echo of de Gaulle's aspiration to rule above party lines, he said he wanted those who had followed him faithfully to leave him 'free to reach out to others, towards those who have never been my friend, who have never belonged to our camp, to our political family, who have sometimes fought against us. Because when it is a matter of France, there are no longer any sides.' That might be seen as a cynical attempt to undercut the opposition and cause dissention on the left; but the idea of launching a personal initiative to reach over the left-right divide that had characterized French politics for so long was a natural step for a self-made leader who had known how to use the party institutions to his benefit but had never allowed himself to become their prisoner, and who fancied himself as a mould breaker. He reasoned that, if he was to introduce fundamental reforms and radically shake up the way France was run, he would need backing from beyond the ranks of the UMP.

The most unexpected appointment was that of Bernard Kouchner, the Socialist founder of the Médecins Sans Frontières organization, as Foreign Minister. He had been Health Minister under both Jospin and Mitterrand and had backed Royal. He was promptly expelled from the Socialist Party.

Another Socialist, Jean-Pierre Jouyet, godfather to one of the Hollande-Royal children, was given responsibility for European Affairs; the new President called him 'my favourite Socialist.' Éric Besson, the former member of the Socialist Party's political bureau who had changed camp, was rewarded with a junior ministerial post. Sarkozy approached other Socialists; most turned him down. Two women from immigrant families joined the administration. Cécilia's good friend Rachida Dati became Justice Minister, the youngest person to hold that post at the age of forty-one and the first politician of African immigrant origin in a full government post. Senegalese-born Rama Yade, from a small moderate party, was the new Junior Minister for Human Rights.

Though the flamboyant Kouchner made headlines with controversial statements, Sarkozy fully intended to perpetuate the Fifth Republic tradition of the President dominating foreign policy. On his first trip abroad as head of state in early June to attend a G8 summit in Germany, he asserted his presence with a strong ecological note, setting a target of a 50 per cent cut in France's CO_2 emissions by 2050. His wife accompanied him; observers noted that at the summit dinner she wore jewellery with intertwined hearts which Attias had given to her. He had told journalists that his relationship with her was a thing of the past, but she clearly intended to send him a message that this was not the case as far as she was concerned.

Back in France, the President told a meeting of UMP deputies at the Élysée that he would 'get France going again' through a coordinated set of reforms as he urged them on for legislative elections in which he sought a parliamentary majority that was personally loyal to him, further breaking down the curtain between the presidency and the legislature contained in the original structure of the Fifth Republic. He stayed above the campaign, making only one address in which he recalled de Gaulle's insistence that 'France is not the right; France is not the left; France is all the French people.' But, like the General, he had every interest in a loyal majority emerging to provide a solid foundation for his individualistic approach to the presidency.

With the left demoralized and subject to backbiting about Royal's defeat, the UMP went into the campaign with the winds in its sails. Polls forecast that it would win well over four hundred seats to fewer than a hundred for the Socialists. The first round seemed to bear that out as Sarkozy's supporters captured 45.6 per cent of the vote to the left's 35.6 per cent. But then, in a television programme as the results came in, Laurent Fabius asked Jean-Louis Borloo how the government was going to finance its plans and reduce the state debt. In his reply, the Finance Minister mentioned a possible increase in the 19 per cent VAT sales tax. Quizzed about the size of the rise in another television interview two days later, Fillon did not disagree when a 5 per cent augmentation was put to him as a possible figure.

Talking of a tax increase between the two rounds of voting was terrible political tactics. The Socialists went to town to denounce the 'anti-social tax' as opinion surveys showed that 60 per cent of people opposed such an increase. The UMP campaign was thrown off balance. A significant number of its first round voters boycotted the run-off, producing a 40 per cent abstention rate. In all, 5.5 million people who had cast ballots the first time round stayed away from the polling stations.

François Bayrou's centrist Mouvement démocrate (Democrat Movement, or MoDEM), which had taken 7.6 per cent of the first round vote, rallied to the opposition. The left ended up with 227 seats, 184 of them for the Socialists. Sarkozy's followers still scored a big victory with 346 places in the National Assembly, but it was not the expected triumph. In terms of the second round popular vote, the left finished just 0.55 percentage points behind the majority. Sarkozy was furious as the results came in on June 17. 'If I don't do things myself, it doesn't work,' he exclaimed as he watched the Prime Minister and his colleagues on television that night.

Still, Fillon kept his job in a new ministerial line-up. Juppé had lost his parliamentary seat in Bordeaux and so had to step down. Despite his tax gaffe, and to the surprise of many deputies, the mop-haired Borloo was promoted to second place in the government as Minister of State responsible for ecology, sustainable development and planning. The lawyer Christine Lagarde, who had been successively in charge of foreign trade and agriculture, stepped up as Minister of the Economy, Industry and Employment. The President was said to be impressed both by the quality of her interventions at Cabinet meetings and by her command of English, perfected during a dozen years with the US law firm, Baker & McKenzie. Alliot-Marie, Kouchner, Hortefeux, Woerth and Dati all kept their jobs. It was a team that combined expertise with the taste for change the President wanted to incarnate, with the apparently unflappable Fillon at the Matignon enjoying the support of the UMP deputies.

The head of government was a very different character from his boss. He was a private man who moved in a deliberate manner, an inheritor of the socially conscious stream of Catholicism and Gaullism. He was never seen to lose his temper, a cold fish for some, a reassuringly thoughtful leader for others. He had been the youngest deputy in the National Assembly when first elected in 1981 at the age of twenty-seven and became a minister at thirty-nine. But, unlike his new President, he had never appeared to be a careerist in a hurry. Despite a taste for mountain climbing and motor racing, he cast a reassuring aura around him, drawing on his roots in the deeply rural province of the Sarthe and keeping to himself his private life with his Welsh wife and their five children. He was said to have remarked of himself and the new President, 'He will be the legs and I will be the head.'

To add to the image he wished to propagate as an inclusive leader, Sarkozy set up a committee to draw up proposals to 'modernize the Fifth Republic,' chaired by Edouard Balladur but also including the Socialist former Culture Minister Jack Lang. He commissioned reports from the Socialists Michel Rocard, Jacques Attali and Hubert Védrine who warned against 'the Atlanticist temptation.' He proposed Dominique Strauss-Kahn as the European nominee to head the IMF, a choice that got broad backing and saw his election in September. It was a deft domestic move in sending a potential challenger abroad and weakening the Socialist ranks.

Living up to his image as somebody in a hurry who revelled in upsetting conventions, Sarkozy was seen in shorts and trainers running up the stairs at the Élysée with his cell phone glued to his ear. He gave his first big television interview not from behind the usual desk but sitting at a low table with his legs crossed.

So he had every political reason for satisfaction as he took the salute at the great ceremonial occasion of the Bastille Day parade in Paris. His poll ratings showed a positive 60 per cent, with 56 per cent of respondents backing his ideas of reform. 'I have a plan,' he told associates. 'I want to fill all the space.' On another occasion he remarked, 'There is nobody above me. I have never felt so free.' But personally, he was caught up in a nightmare.

Cécilia was with him on the reviewing stand, wearing a sleeveless grey Dior dress, but she spent much of the time staring at her Blackberry as if awaiting a message. At the Élysée reception that followed she appeared distant, and, when her husband paid tribute to her beauty, replied, 'It's not worth the trouble.' That night she refused to accompany the President to a concert, going instead on her own with one of the daughters from her marriage with Jacques Martin. 'At the end of the day, my only real worry is Cécilia,' the President told journalists.

Ten days later, she took on an unexpected role in going to Libya to help bring back five Bulgarian nurses who had been sentenced to death there, accused of injecting more than four hundred children with the AIDS virus. France had taken up their cause and got an agreement to free the Bulgarians after tortuous negotiations which led to agreements on security, health care and immigration, plus the sale of Milan anti-tank missiles to the tune of $230 million, the first arms Libya had obtained since 2004. Sarkozy arranged for his wife to fly to Tripoli where she met the Libyan leader, Muammar Gadaffi, and then flew out with the nurses. The affair led to criticism that France should not have made a weapons deal with a rogue state and that the freeing of the nurses was a job for diplomats not for the President's wife.

In August, the Sarkozys travelled to New Hampshire for a summer vacation with friends living there. George W. Bush invited them for a burger and hot dog lunch at his family compound in Maine. The Frenchman who had pledged to improve relations with the United States after the chill of the Chirac years arrived forty-five minutes late. Still, the two Presidents got on well. 'Do we agree on everything?' Sarkozy told reporters afterwards, reprising a line he had taken during the election campaign. 'No, but even within families there are disagreements, but we are still the same family.'

The reason for Sarkozy's late arrival was that, before leaving their friends' house for the Bush compound, he had spent time trying to persuade Cécilia to accompany him. She refused, pleading a sore throat. The next day, she was photographed in good health shopping in a nearby town. 'Cécilia has set a new record for making a swift recovery,' a news reader commented dryly on French radio. The business newspaper Les Echos said the incident heightened her reputation as 'secretive, unpredictable, even disconcerting.' Attias must have taken note.

Back in France, the President plunged into a round of engagements remarkable even for somebody who declared, 'I want to be minister of everything.' He unfurled reform plans for agriculture, social policy and the working of the state. Receiving ambassadors at a ceremony at the Élysée, he criticized Russia and China (which had cancelled a Sino-EU summit after he met the Dalai Lama), spoke of a possible bombing of Iran if it continued its nuclear programme and said he would never equivocate on the security of Israel. He flew to New York to address the United Nations General Assembly, calling for an 'ecological New Deal for the Planet.' He then went to Bulgaria, where he was greeted as a national hero for having obtained the liberation of the nurses from Libya. To general surprise, his wife did not accompany him to Sofia despite her role in bringing the nurses out—though his party included the Bulgarian-born evergreen pop singer Sylvie Vartan. The official explanation was that Cécilia had been hurt by the controversy stirred up by her role. Nobody was fooled. As soon as he had finished the official ceremonies, Sarkozy flew home, looking far from happy.

The state of his marriage put the President on edge; he arrived for meetings with telltale red blotches on his face and exploded in anger at small failings of those around him. But there were other fundamental problems. His management style pushed presidential involvement to the extreme. He became, in effect, his own Prime Minister. The Élysée sought to control everything. Ministers found themselves subject to the powerful staff around the President at the Élysée headed by the omnipresent Secretary General, Claude Guéant, who put in sixteen-hour days and seemed to know every dossier, setting a barrier even between the President and Prime Minister.

The attempt to construct a large-circle administration ran counter to tradition and did not go down well with many UMP members of parliament who felt that the President had a weakness for political gimmicks instead of rewarding his supporters. Right-wing voters were at a loss, particularly since the government lacked coherence in bringing together individuals from different political families—a few long-time Sarkozy supporters to be sure, but also remnant Chiracians, Balladurians, centrists and those with no clear allegiance, not to mention Socialists renegades. The President did not wish to be accused of creating a 'UMP state' as Chirac had been attacked for heading a 'RPR state,' but this was just what a lot of his followers desired in the old tradition of monopoly politics. For them, his insistence that he wanted to embody the country's diversity at the summit of government was not what they had fought elections for. Most of them regarded power sharing as an aberration to be avoided. The traditional demarcations and divisions had to be maintained.

Not that the President's action lived up to his rhetoric. He proved anxious to avoid clashes with the unions and vested interests, often adopting a softer line than that advocated by Fillon. He acted like the lawyer he had been trained to be, seeking compromise solutions and maintaining private lines of communications with apparent opponents such as Bernard Thibaud, chief of the Communist-led CGT federation. He achieved some real successes, notably in raising the retirement age in the state sector, but the public was not greatly impressed. The fuss over the sales tax had reinforced the charge from the left that the President was ready to make the population at large pay for his plans while partially ending the inheritance tax and introducing top-end income tax reductions that favoured the wealthy, personified by the tycoons he and his wife frequented.

The lowering of the total rate for the biggest taxpayers from 60 to 50 per cent resulted in the reimbursement of 458 million euros for the year and contrasted embarrassingly with the much smaller amount allocated to a programme to encourage employment and boost growth. The left could only rejoice when it became known that the Treasury had reimbursed thirty million euros from her tax payments to Lilliane Bettencourt, the L'Oréal beauty products heiress who was ranked as the third-richest woman in the world, because the total amount she had paid was above the threshold.

Coming at a time when the minimum wage rose by only 2.01 per cent a year, the President's decision to double his own salary created another fuss, even if the increase took him only to parity with the Prime Minister, whose long career in the legislature, ministries and provincial politics meant that he benefited from advantages that did not accrue to his boss. Promises to slim down the state were not reflected in a meaningful reduction in spending, opening the way for an increased deficit, which earned the disapproval of the Commission in Brussels. The administration annoyed motorists convicted of parking fines by abandoning the tradition of amnestying their tickets on Bastille Day. Shopkeepers were concerned by proposals to liberalize retail price controls. Unions were up in arms over changes in labour regulations to encourage overtime through tax breaks that weakened the thirty-five-hour working week. Compulsory biometric profiling in airports aroused criticism from civil rights bodies. Constitutional reforms seemed to go in opposite directions, both increasing presidential authority and giving the legislature a veto over some presidential appointments.

It was all quite disorganized and out of kilter with the determined programme of change laid out during the election campaign. Rather than following his intentions to their logical conclusion, the President sought alternatives that resulted in confusion. The row over the tax threshold for the rich could have been avoided by abolishing the wealth levy introduced under Mitterrand, but Sarkozy believed it had become part of the fiscal landscape which could not be tampered with. Equally, rather than having a straightforward debate about dismantling the thirty-five-hour working week, the preference was to introduce tax breaks for those who did overtime; the result was a double cost to the economy calculated at twenty-five billion euros a year.

Progress included a reduction of privileges enjoyed by public sector workers in the railway system, where some train drivers had been entitled to stop work at the age of fifty under rules dating back to 1909. But significant wage increases were granted in return and fresh retirement grades were introduced; the administration's success came only after the Communist leadership of the CGT union federation took fright that militants were outflanking it and brought a series of major strikes to a close. Another of Sarkozy's electoral pledges—to introduce a law providing for basic public services, especially transport, to be maintained during a strike—was watered down to a set of requirements for forty-eight-hour notice of stoppages and a ballot of workers eight days after the start of any action. It did have an effect but aroused union accusations that it was an unconstitutional assault on workers' rights, while transport operators were saddled with paying compensation to passengers if they did not provide minimum service levels.

Alain Juppé's fate when he tried to force the pace after 1995 was not forgotten. Reform was pushed when the President judged that a majority of people were ready to accept it, but he held back or modified those likely to arouse widespread opposition. For Sarkozy, reform seemed to consist primarily in announcing new measures.

Movement for its own sake was all—led by political tactics rather than long-term strategy.

Playing on Mitterrand's description of de Gaulle as carrying out 'a permanent coup d'état,' Hollande branded the President's style of governing as 'a permanent coup d'éclat.' The familiar charge that Sarkozy was too much short-term action and not enough longer-term thinking seemed to be playing out. His friendships with media proprietors who could ensure he got favourable coverage were badly viewed by the public. By September 2007, a 54–37 per cent majority of respondents in a poll for the newspaper *Libération* said they were dissatisfied by policies to promote economic growth, while the margin was even larger, 65–31, when it came to unhappiness with the standard of living.

As the global economic crisis which broke in 2007 deepened in 2008, the President declared that 'laissez-faire capitalism is over,' and denounced the 'dictatorship of the market.' There would be no austerity programme, he told UMP deputies, 'because that would be a renunciation and I was not elected for that.' Had he become a Socialist, he asked himself in an interview. 'Perhaps,' he answered. The politician who had come to high office promising to slim down the public sector now promised to create 100,000 state-subsidized jobs. Despite this, the unions took to the streets to demonstrate in mid-October against the proposed changes in the pension retirement age.

The day before the march, Sarkozy attended a ministerial meeting to decide how to respond. He left the room three times, returning with blotches on his face. The next day, at lunchtime, the French news agency *AFP* ran a statement: 'Cécilia and Nicolas Sarkozy have decided to separate by mutual consent.' Cécilia telephoned the Élysée to insist that the word 'divorce' should be used. A second despatch two hours later specified this.

Even those close to the President expressed surprise. They had known of the tension in the marriage but had thought that, like the wives of Mitterrand and Chirac, Cécilia would keep up appearances. Some on the left saw a political manoeuvre, alleging that the statement had been issued in a cynical attempt to distract attention from the next day's demonstration. That was nonsense, but showed what his opponents thought of the head of state.

Sarkozy went off to Lisbon for an important EU summit, which he used to reassert his country's position in Europe after two years of policy inaction following the referendum rejection of the Constitutional Treaty in 2005. To get through the resulting roadblock, he proposed a new agreement between the members to facilitate more decisive joint action, especially on economic, social and climate change matters, as well as strengthening the Community's foreign policy. Television cameras caught Angela Merkel taking him aside to express her sympathy at the news from Paris. Asked about the divorce by journalists, the President replied angrily, 'I was elected to bring solutions to the problems of the French people, not to comment on my private life.' In a newspaper interview, his about-to-be-ex-wife explained that, 'what happened to me happens to millions of people. One day, you no longer fit in the couple.' The weekly magazines, *Paris-Match* and *Elle*, ran cover stories on her—the latter recorded its biggest street sales for three decades.

The President, a man who was normally never ill, had to go for medical treatment of throat trouble on his return from Portugal. He left a UMP meeting to celebrate the Lisbon summit as soon as he could and was distant from ministers accompanying him on a visit to Morocco the following week; in his wife's absence, her friend Rachida Dati played the role of First Lady at the royal banquet. At the next Cabinet session, Sarkozy assured ministers that his personal frame of mind was of no importance—'Life goes on. I am head of state. I owe myself to the French.'

However, the downward path of Sarkozy's popularity became a feature of the political landscape as 2007 drew to a close. Strikes against government policy persisted, especially by railway workers. Legal personnel marched against changes put forward by Dati. Students stayed away from classes and professors protested against reform of the higher education system to give universities financial autonomy to make them more competitive internationally and to increase their links with the labour market; critics said the changes would lead to inequality between colleges, introduce unfair selectivity and lead to decline of disciplines that were not in demand by employers. A big march in Paris criticized the introduction of DNA tests for immigrant families. *Tabac* operators protested at legislations to stop smoking in public places.

There was a recurrence of urban disorder in the Val d'Oise outside Paris after two teenagers died when their motorcycle hit a police car. Rioters used firearms in the fighting; sixty-nine police were injured. There was also a storm when Colonel Gaddafi made a visit to Paris and was allowed to set up his heated tents in the grounds of a former Rothschild mansion. Contracts, including one for the purchase of twenty-one Airbus aircraft and another for nuclear power co-operation, were signed to the value of ten billion euros. Among the critics was the Junior Minister for Human Rights, who told a Paris newspaper that '[o]ur country is not a doormat on which a leader, terrorist or not, can come and clean the blood of his misdeeds off his feet. France should not accept this kiss of death.'

The government was not without substantial support. Polls showed that most people disapproved of the rail stoppages. A majority of those questioned backed the administration on law and order. Defeat had not brought unity to the Socialist Party. Royal published a book attacking the 'elephants' of the Party who had not given her sufficient support; Hollande accused her of 'incoherence.' But growth fell to 2.3 per cent for the year and unemployment increased to 8 per cent. Despite the President's undertakings to cut spending, the social security deficit rose from 8.7 billion euros in 2006 to 9.5 billion the following year.

However, the President's spirits revived. He had fallen in love.

The occasion was a dinner in mid-November 2007 at the home outside Paris of Jacques Séguéla, an advertising guru who had dreamed up slogans for Mitterrand in his 1981 and 1988 presidential campaigns, though he never joined the Socialist party. Among the others present was the Italian supermodel turned singer Carla Bruni.

Just after the President arrived, his cell phone rang.

'Love?' Bruni asked him, according to the account written by the host.

'No, work,' he replied, leaving the room.

It was Bernard Thibault of the CGT labour federation calling about the railway strikes.

Returning to the dining room, Sarkozy, who was still wearing his wedding ring a month after his divorce, pivoted his chair toward

Bruni and spent the rest of the meal talking to her. As he left, he said he would be in the front row when she opened her show at the Casino de Paris the following year 'and we will announce our engagement.'

'Engagement? Never,' Bruni replied. 'I will only live with a man if he has a child with me.'

In the ensuing weeks, senior staff at the Élysée found their boss far easier to work with, jocular and with a shine in his eyes. He sometimes skipped the daily 8:30 a.m. conferences at the palace and no longer summoned them for weekend working sessions at his presidential residence at Versailles. 'I felt straight away that I shouldn't let that man go,' Bruni told Catherine Nay later. 'It was the first time that I gave and received so much.' For his part, Sarkozy called Carla 'a miracle.'

But there were echoes of problems of the recent past. When Sarkozy flew to Egypt on an official visit followed by a holiday with Bruni and her six-year-old son from an affair with a philosophy professor, they travelled in the private Falcon jet of the business magnate Vincent Bolloré, on whose yacht he had spent his post-election break with Cécilia. Magazines ran page after page of the vacation and went on to rake over her past affairs. A nude photograph of her surfaced, her hands crossed over her crotch. Sarkozy's personal life was back at the front of the stage. He was questioned on the subject at his first full Élysée press conference in January 2008. He contrasted the media attention paid to him and Bruni on their journey to Egypt with the lack of coverage of separate trips Mitterrand had made there with his two families. 'Being President of the republic does not bring with it a greater right to happiness than enjoyed by others,' he went on, 'but not to less than theirs.' Then he added, 'With Carla, it's serious.'

On February 2, the couple took the wedding vows at the presidential palace. Under the marriage settlement, they shared their assets. 'Do you realise, she has given me half her fortune,' Sarkozy remarked to a friend. (Cécilia and Attias were married the following month at a ceremony at the top of the Rockefeller Center in New York.)

The President might have found new contentment in his private life, but his approval rating was going downhill at an accelerating pace, falling in one survey from half in late 2007 to one-third in the month of his marriage. The sharp decline was attributable at least in part to his personal life, which simply did not fit the image the French wanted to have of the man who was meant to represent the nation. A poll reported that 63 per cent of those questioned thought he showed too much of his private affairs in public. Nearly as many said he should adopt a style more fitting for a head of state. The importance of the personal factor was shown by the way Fillon, who was pushing the same policies, saw his approval rating rise to 60 per cent.

The UMP majority became even less inclined to follow the Élysée—this at a time when the President had been in office for less than a year, with four more years to go until the next election. The majority party's discontent increased when Sarkozy said he accepted 'the essential elements' of a lengthy report he had commissioned from Jacques Attali, Mitterrand's one-time adviser. It proposed to liberalize commerce and alienated professions ranging from pharmacists to taxi drivers who feared for their monopolies—just the kind of voters he needed.

That helped the left to stage a strong revival at municipal elections in March 2008, gaining control of such big cities as Amiens, Rheims, Saint-Étienne and Strasbourg, as well as holding on to Lyons and Paris, where Bertrand Delanoë's Socialists took 99 of the 163 council seats. In a rare success for the right, Alain Juppé was re-elected Mayor of Bordeaux with 56 per cent of the first round vote. Jean-Claude Gaudin won a narrow victory in Marseilles.

Though local factors played their part, and the left was due a rebound from its previous poor score, much of the blame was put on the President. He reacted badly, forming a small inner group of ministers with whom he conferred regularly, without the Premier. At a dinner for George W. Bush, the Prime Minister was not given a seat at the top table and had to be persuaded by his wife not to walk out. Rebelling against such treatment, Fillon finally insisted on more direct contact with the President, without the presence of Claude Guéant or the inner circle.

In a ninety-minute televised conversation with a small group of journalists, the President acknowledged that he had made mistakes. But he said he had been dealing with a country which had gone to sleep under his predecessor and which did not realize the changes brought by globalization. He had introduced reforms to bring France into the modern world, and that had inevitably led to problems. But he would not give up, and asked to be judged at the end of his five-year term. As for his private life, he said that was now in order, but objected that no president had ever been treated by the media as he had, which was perfectly true. However, politically, his barbs directed at Chirac alienated Gaullist deputies, while left-wing sympathizers were not going to be impressed by anything he said.

The domestic decline contrasted with an upbeat performance abroad. Visiting Washington, he received eight standing ovations during a speech to Congress. He and his wife made a successful trip to Britain, where they slept at Windsor Castle and she dazzled the press. His plan for a union of Mediterranean states which would be led by France was watered down; it faced the opposition of Turkey, was viewed with a cool eye in Berlin and Brussels as a fragmentation of the EU and was subject to Middle East tensions. But the French six-month presidency of the European Union that began on July 1, 2008, was a success.

It started under a cloud with Ireland's rejection of the modified Lisbon Treaty—the new version had been designed so that it could be approved by parliaments without going to the electorate as a whole (which got it adopted in France). The Irish decided to hold a referendum all the same and the vote was negative. Sarkozy insisted on staying the course with a second vote held the following year, which was positive.

He played a central role in getting joint action from the major European players to deal with the financial crisis that escalated rapidly after the collapse of Lehman Brothers in September 2008, even if he sometimes had to cajole a cautious Merkel. He called for the end of self-regulation and laissez-faire to achieve 'the moralization of capitalism' in terms that Royal might have adopted in their electoral battle the previous year.

With his EU hat on, Sarkozy acted as peacemaker in the war between Russia and Georgia. He pushed a pact to toughen immigration rules, and successfully encouraged action on climate change to cut greenhouse gas emissions by 20 per cent, boost renewable energy by the same proportion and increase energy efficiency, all by 2020. He pressed for a stronger European security and defence policy and took France back into the integrated military structure of the NATO alliance which it had quit under de Gaulle. He talked of reform of the common agricultural policy, but was careful not to put his country's farming interests at risk.

This certainly put France back in the European game, but, as at home, Sarkozy sometimes seemed to be doing too much without a clear focus and to accord himself sometimes premature praise, an approach that irritated others, especially the Germans. He infringed on the preserves of the European Central Bank and the EU Trade Commission. His insistence on rejecting Turkey's adhesion to the EU annoyed those who want to work with a moderate Islamic nation. His stress on enabling Europe to protect itself economically was in keeping with his rediscovery of the big state at home but ran counter to the more market-minded EU members from the north of the continent.

Underlying the specific issue was a return to a Gaullist conception of Europe, in which member states would hold the whip hand and take authority back from the Commission in Brussels, with France playing a leading political role. The President showed impatience with the endless EU procedures and a variable degree of respect for its institutions. On one occasion, he insisted that Jean-Louis Borloo take part in a meeting of state leaders and pulled up a chair himself for his minister. On another, he remarked of a proposed all-night bargaining session, 'I don't see the interest in negotiating until 4 a.m. for a few peanuts.'

His target of restoring France's status through his personal efforts was bound to be compromised as Angela Merkel had no intention of returning to the relationship between de Gaulle and Konrad Adenauer at the time of the signing of the France-West German friendship treaty in 1963. The careful, calculating temperament of the pastor's daughter brought up in Communist East Germany and the mercurial French politician denoted different mindsets. Germany and France did not see eye-to-eye on Sarkozy's pet projects, including dealing with climate change, the Mediterranean Union and limiting the independence of the European Central Bank. As the crisis spread to the euro currency zone through Greece and other Mediterranean members, they favoured contrasting responses. Berlin put a premium on reduction of budget deficits and state debts, even if that meant nasty medicine for member states, while Paris stressed the need for growth, even if it risked spurring inflation.

Sarkozy had a long and arduous job persuading the Chancellor to unbend, given the hostility of German opinion to bailing out spendthrift southern Europeans. His desire to maintain a common front in public meant that he was all too easily depicted as Berlin's poodle, especially by the left where anti-German sentiment was not hard to detect. The phrase 'Merkozy,' coined to describe the two leaders, might have depicted an enviable state of trans-Rhine unity, but for many in France it stood for a subordinate role not in keeping with the nation's image of itself. Still, for the six months that France held the EU presidency, Sarkozy walked tall. Foreign affairs once again proved a welcome diversion for a leader under attack at home. But he could not escape from the reality in the Hexagon.

His response to that confirmed the remarkable transformation in his thinking. For the first time, he used the word 'fraternity' in his speeches while words such as 'rigour' were dropped from the administration's vocabulary. He opted for stimulus measures regardless of their impact on the state deficit, which was forecast at 8.5 per cent for 2010. In his 2007 campaign he had said that France's system of social protection was 'running out of breath'; two years later, he claimed that the country had come through the storm in better shape than other countries precisely because of the generosity of its welfare provisions. Rather than a politician pledged to break with the past, he sounded very like the voice of the status quo insisting on the central role of the state. Or like somebody who would grasp at any available branch as the re-election battle loomed.

State payments to the unemployed and poorer families were raised, as were tax breaks for six million households. An unpopular levy on companies was abolished. The sales tax paid by restaurants and bars was sharply reduced. No matter that the Commission said it would start proceedings against France for the size of its deficit and that restaurants kept the benefit of the reduction for themselves rather than lowering prices and taking on more staff as the government had hoped. The President was on a new course and pursued it with his usual energy.

A government reshuffle at the end of 2010 saw the appointment of the long-time Sarkozyist Brice Hortefeux to the Interior Ministry and the departure of Cécilia's good friend Rachida Dati from the Justice Ministry. The ever-dependable Alliott-Marie replaced Bernard Kouchner at the Foreign Ministry, but international affairs remained very much the President's own domain. The UMP troops were reassured with this closing of ranks so long as Fillon stayed at Matignon. The President sought to reach out to the hard right with a toughening of policy on immigration and attacks on the 'Rom' travellers from East Europe, who had become a subject of popular concern. But family matters kept popping up. The latest was when his twenty-three-year-old son, Jean, who led the UMP group on the Neuilly local council, went for the chairmanship of an urban development authority and allegations of nepotism flared—the young man gave up the attempt, but his father was hit, too. His approval ratings fell to 21 per cent.

Another poll placed him thirty-second among the most admired political figure in the country; at the top of the list was Chirac, whose reputation was, however, soon tarnished when he became the first former head of state since Pétain to be put on trial—for misuse of public money while Mayor of Paris by authorizing the payment of cash from municipal funds to associates, nominally for twenty-eight non-existent jobs, but actually to be used for party political purposes. Found guilty, he was given a two-year suspended jail sentence; he did not attend the trial because of neurological problems. Sarkozy also faced a problem of persistent allegations, pursued by a dogged investigating magistrate, that he had taken illicit funds for his presidential campaign from his Neuilly neighbour, Liliane Bettencourt, taking advantage of her poor mental health. The accusations were not finally put to rest legally till 2013.

The causes of discontent continued with rolling demonstrations against pension reform and university unrest about changes that made life more testing for students. The pension issue was always going to be a touchstone for the Sarkozy presidency in putting the administration at loggerheads with the unions and the conservatism of the public sector. The final formula put forward in 2010 by Éric Woerth, the Labour Minister, was relatively mild, raising the retirement age from sixty to sixty-two and the age for a full state pension from sixty-five to sixty-seven, but it unleashed mass demonstrations and strikes, especially by militants in the oil industry, who closed down refineries and cut off supplies to petrol stations. Nor was Woerth's position facilitated by media allegations that, as UMP Treasurer, it was he who had received illegal cash for Sarkozy's 2007 campaign from Liliane Bettencourt and that, as the Mayor of a town outside Paris, he had authorized the sale of a racetrack to a group with close connections to the party for a suspiciously low price. The pension reform was passed by parliament, but the Minister stepped down in a government reshuffle.

With growth remaining low and unemployment hitting a ten-year record of 9.6 per cent, cantonal elections in 2011 gave the left 49 per cent of the vote and 1,212 seats to the right's 32 per cent with 753 seats. The very high abstention rate of 56 per cent showed the disaffection felt by voters on the right for the President and his style and policies. The same trend was evident in a revival of support for the National Front, which took 15 per cent of the first round vote.

Four years after winning his ultimate goal, Sarkozy was caught in the worst of all worlds. The centre-left was lost to him from before the start, but the centre-right also now had deep reservations. Elected as a leader who would bring strong new policies, he had failed to deliver. The parliamentary majority owed its loyalty to Fillon rather than to him. The way in which the financial crisis had led him to abandon his initial market-friendly approach and to embrace the big state that he had formerly rejected raised the question of what the point of Nicolas Sarkozy was. The outlook for the economy offered no relief, with polls showing a 60 per cent disapproval rating even after the switch towards state protection. The crisis had reinforced the pre-eminence of Germany and its Chancellor. His very public private life diminished the status of the presidency in a way many people found either a matter for ridicule or a tarnishing of the nation the head of state was meant to represent. The more active he was, the more provincial trips he made, the more speeches he delivered, the more hands he shook, the less impact he had. He was simply doing too much and all too often looked like a man running scared of his next big electoral test.

'Malediction,' declared the cover of the news magazine *Le Point* after the cantonal results came in. 'Has he already lost?' asked another weekly, *Le Nouvel Observateur*. Pollsters in Paris said the rating to watch was not Sarkozy's popularity but his unpopularity. They reckoned that he was so unloved that he could not claw his way back. One survey found that 63 per cent of respondents did not want him even to stand for re-election. With such a wind in their sails, the Socialists had only to wait, their prospects burnished as it became evident that, far from staying at the IMF in Washington, Dominique Strauss-Kahn intended to return to France to lead the Socialist Party in the presidential election due in 2012 to seek to end seventeen years of centre-right presidencies.

Born into a comfortably off Jewish family, DSK, as he was known, had failed to get into ENA, but pursued an academic career while starting the political ascension that took him to the Finance and Economics Ministry in 1997. Married to Anne Sinclair, the very rich heiress to an art fortune who had been one of France's best-known television journalists and who had been described as a 'Kosher butcher' by Jean-Marie Le Pen, he was far from the left-wing archetype. The former minister was urbane, high-living, a 'champagne Socialist' with a taste for expensive cigars; he and Sinclair had luxurious homes in Paris, the Riviera and Marrakesh. He worked for a time with a group of high-powered business associates in Paris who loaned him a 100,000-euro Porsche. He was known as a skirt chaser and was dubbed by a Sunday newspaper as *'le grand séducteur'* (the Great Seducer). Before he went to take up the IMF job, Sarkozy had warned him to be careful about his sexual activities, adding, '[T]he Americans, you know, are not like the French.' 'If he runs,' Sarkozy remarked on another occasion, 'you will see that Carla and I will seem quite austere beside him.'

Still, DSK had built up a political base in the poor Paris suburb of Sarcelles and had a serious international reputation that few of his compatriots could rival, with expertise in the subject that most preoccupied the electorate: the economy. He might not be the most natural candidate for a political party militants often saw the rich as enemies of the Republic, but, with polls reporting support of around 60 per cent from voters, he looked like the winner the left needed after ten years out of power since the end of the Jospin government.

Then in May 2011, sensational news came from across the Atlantic. A maid in the Sofitel Hotel in Manhattan alleged that the IMF chief had sexually assaulted her as she went to clean up his suite. After being subjected to a 'perp-walk,' he was indicted and put on $1 million bail, plus a $5 million bond. He was held under armed guard in his New York apartment. A semen sample was found on the maid's clothing, and DNA tests matched it to a sample submitted by the Frenchman. After doubts had been raised about the woman's testimony, the charges were abandoned. In a television interview, the former Minister admitted 'inappropriate' behaviour, but said he had 'not used violence'; he later reached a settlement with the maid.

Other allegations emerged, including one by a woman journalist and writer who accused him of attempted rape five years earlier—he said he had only tried to kiss her and the case was abandoned. An allegation of gang rape in Washington collapsed, but Strauss-Kahn was caught up in 2012 in an investigation into a prostitution ring in Lille, which led prosecutors to announce that he would be tried for 'aggravated pimping.' Sinclair divorced him. Undaunted, he re-emerged with plans for a $2 billion hedge fund.

With their favoured candidate destroyed by his own behaviour, the Socialists faced a choice that narrowed down to François Hollande and Martine Aubry, who had succeeded him as Socialist First Secretary. Four other candidates entered the lists, including Royal. The voting qualifications had been widened from 2002, and 2.7 million people cast their ballots after three televised debates between the contenders. Hollande took 39 per cent of the vote, Aubry 30 per cent and the fiery Arnaud Montebourg, who called for 'a new democracy' and was critical of the EU and globalization, 17 per cent. Royal finished fourth, with 7 per cent. She and two other first-round laggards, Manuel Valls and Jean-Michel Baylet, called on their supporters to rally to the Party Secretary in the second round. Montebourg gave no advice but said he would vote for Hollande, who got the nomination with 57 per cent of the vote in a run-off with Aubry.

Born into a middle-class family with an extreme right-wing doctor father in the Norman city of Rouen, François Hollande moved with his parents when he was thirteen to Neuilly, the smart Paris suburb which would be Sarkozy's electoral fief. He worked for Mitterrand's losing presidential campaign in 1974, and joined the Socialist Party while at ENA, where he met Royal. He undertook the sacrificial role of standing for the National Assembly in Chirac's fiefdom of the Corrèze in 1981. After working as a government adviser and Socialist operative during the Mitterrand presidency, he won a parliamentary seat in Corrèze in 1988. At the party headquarters in an elegant mansion on the Left Bank rue Solférino in Paris, he preached unity as Socialist barons went to war for the Mitterrand heritage, such as it was. He was already the man who preached sweet reason amid the endemic civil wars of French politics.

When Lionel Jospin became Prime Minister in 1997, Hollande was elected First Secretary of the Socialist Party, a post he held for eleven years before stepping down after the loss of the presidential poll of 2007. Though he lacked any experience in national government, his time as the party's top manager from 1997 to 2008 meant that he knew how the Socialist machine worked. He had avoided making enemies—his low-key style led to the nickname of 'Flanby,' after a brand of custard pudding. He had performed well in the debates—and showed a sense of humour. He had the necessary provincial bastion in the Corrèze. All in all, he was the backroom operator ready to emerge into the limelight.

The national tide was clearly moving leftwards; Senate elections produced a left-wing majority in the upper house for the first time during the Fifth Republic. By early 2012, surveys credited Hollande with a second round margin of anywhere from six to ten points. Sarkozy denounced the polls as 'lies'; but he faced the perennial desire of the electorate to try somebody new as the economic growth forecast was cut to 1.75 per cent for the year and the ratings agency Standard & Poor's downgraded France, something which the President had vowed to prevent happening.

As it turned out, the presidential battle was closer than many had expected, with Sarkozy once again showing his mettle as a political infighter. His long government record contrasted with the lack of experience of his Socialist challenger. In a television interview, he said Hollande was an intelligent man, and 'I do not have a problem with him.' But he then added, 'The only thing is, he has never held office at the state level. Honestly, can you imagine Francois Hollande as President of France? Imagine it!'

Whatever his hesitations domestically, it was quite true that the incumbent could display a considerable international record, an important consideration for a country as jealous of its global status as France. After initially failing to react to the Arab Spring of 2011, he had championed the NATO intervention in Libya that led to the fall of his one-time guest Gaddafi and had not yet had its sour consequences. Involving himself personally in the planning of the air action, he put himself and France forward as 'on the side of the oppressed.' He had worked feverishly and to good effect to stave off the collapse of the eurozone, weaning Merkel away from her initial absolutist stance of refusing help for Greece and other debt-laden nations. He had been a major engineer of EU coordination, working effectively with Prime Minister Gordon Brown although Britain was outside the common currency region. An important G20 summit which he chaired in Cannes pointed the way to a stabilization of the global financial situation and earned him a fulsome prize from Barack Obama at its conclusion. But while a strong foreign policy is a source of national satisfaction, it does not win elections.

Ten candidates ran in the first round. Apart from the President and Hollande, the principal contenders were Marine Le Pen from the hard right and Jean-Luc Mélenchon from the hard left, while François Bayrou made yet another run from the centre.

Sarkozy argued that, poor though the economic situation was, it would have been worse without the changes he had introduced, and that the cause of France's problems lay abroad—at one point he said he would push the EU to adopt more protectionist policies. He homed in once more on immigration, saying that he would cut it in half. This son of immigrants called for tougher frontier controls, threatening to pull the country out of the Schengen Area, whose citizens can move freely across internal borders. He proposed tougher measures to force the unemployed to find work, opposed legalizing homosexual marriage and said he would not grant voting rights for foreigners living in France.

In a programme designed to appeal to voters of the right who might be tempted to flirt with Le Pen, Sarkozy pledged that he would ensure a presumption of self-defense when police were involved in the killing of suspects. He criticized the EU's lack of mention of Europe's Christian roots in its constitution. 'Without borders there is no nation, there is no Republic, there is no civilization,' he told a rally in Toulouse. 'We are not superior to others, but we are different.' Homing in on his principal opponent, he issued a message to those who did not vote for him: 'Don't complain when Francois Hollande is elected and regularizes all illegal immigrants and lets foreigners vote.' His problem was that voters tempted by hard-line policies on law and order and immigration had the real thing in Marine Le Pen; as her father used to say, 'why vote for Le Pen light when I am the genuine article?' That, plus the disaffection of mainstream right-wing voters meant that, however great his election-eering skill, the incumbent was still facing an uphill battle.

The Socialists laid out a manifesto of sixty propositions, includ-ing higher taxes for big companies, banks and the rich. Retail and investment banking were to be split, and a public bank estab-lished to promote industry. There were to be 60,000 more teaching jobs. The retirement age would be brought back to sixty from sixty-two. Same-sex couples were to gain marriage and adoption rights. French troops would leave Afghanistan by the end of the year. The share of electricity generated by nuclear power in France was to be cut from 75 per cent to half by boosting renewable sources. Giving details of his economic plans in a later speech, Hollande said he would bring in a marginal 75 per cent tax on annual incomes above one million euros, reverse tax cuts introduced for the wealthy during the previous five years and wipe out the national debt by 2017. Sarkozy warned that the left-wing programme would bring economic disaster within two days of his contender taking office.

Policies aside, the real fight was over the judgment voters would make of the two men, the mercurial attack dog President and his more reassuring rival with his round face, owlish spectacles and reasonable manner. Hollande played on this, contrasting his person-ality with that of his opponent; he would, he vowed, be a 'normal president,' and would stick to his promises. Whatever that meant, it tapped into the widespread distrust of a hyperventilated leader who revelled in a world of luxury with his glamorous wife and wealthy friends while the mass of the population had growing problems pay-ing the bills—and who had failed to deliver.

Le Pen and Mélenchon provided the grit in the campaign, the latter calling the former 'half-demented.' While softening her father's brutalist style, she hammered away about the need for 'national pref-erence' for access to jobs and social welfare, a 95 per cent cut in immigration and the restoration of the death penalty. The swagger-ing left-winger, backed by what remained of the Communist Party as well as his own Left Party, proposed raising the minimum wage, a 100 per cent income tax for earnings above 360,000 euros, full reimbursement of health costs by the state, easier naturalization rules for immigrants, a reduction of presidential powers in favour of the legislature and proportional representational voting with gender parity for candidates. Both favoured protectionism and were hostile to the EU and the common currency.

Le Pen established herself in the campaign, but it was Mélenchon who delivered the main surprise as polls showed his support rising from an initial 5 per cent to 15 per cent and even above. While the threat from the National Front ensured that Sarkozy maintained a tough ideological line, bringing criticism from de Villepin, Raffarin and Juppé for pandering to extremism, the one-time Socialist minister did the same for Hollande, abetted by anti-EU jibes from Montebourg. Bayrou appeared even more of a lonely voice in the middle, calling for a public spending freeze to reduce the state debt, lowering of tax exemptions and a greater focus on teaching reading and writing in schools.

Unlike 2002, the fringe candidates were not going to cause problems for either of the front runners. They consisted of Eva Joly, the formerly prominent examining magistrate and hammer of Elf, and Bernard Tapie, who had trouble getting to 3 per cent in the polls. The four even less well favoured runners consisted of a man standing as an 'anti-euro souverainist' at the head of the Arise the Republic movement, a car plant worker representing the New Anticapitalist Party, a teacher member of the Trotskyite Workers' Struggle and a candidate of the French branch of the movement headed by far-out US activist Lyndon LaRouche, who hovered just above zero support.

In the first round of voting on April 21–22, Hollande took 28.6 per cent and Sarkozy 27.2. Le Pen did better than her father had in 2002 with 17.9, but Mélenchon fell short of his fondest hopes at 11, though this still represented nearly four million voters. After his strong showing in 2007, Bayrou was a poor fourth with 9.1 per cent of the vote. The other candidates attracted 6 per cent between them, Joly scoring 2.3 per cent and the LaRouche adept 0.25.

By finishing ahead of the incumbent, Hollande put himself in a strong position for the run-off, given the additional votes the left could pick up from eliminated candidates, especially from those who had backed Mélenchon—though he refused to issue an explicit endorsement, he told his electorate to vote against Sarkozy. Bayrou said he would vote for the Socialist. There was an unexpected intervention from Berlin when Angela Merkel said she supported Sarkozy and saw nothing 'normal' in Hollande. While she might not always be on the same wavelength as the incumbent, Hollande's proposal to tax and spend out of recession was even further from the policies she favoured. But that, however, was not going to sway many votes in a France which had had quite enough of lectures from across the Rhine.

The two men met in a televised debate on May 2. It was a tense occasion. Hollande accused his opponent of failing to lower unemployment and of dividing the French people while promising to stand for social justice, economic recovery and national unity. Sarkozy, who now tacked away from the hard right which was not going to vote for his opponent in the second round, said the Socialist's lack of government experience on a national level made him unfit for the task of leading France in the midst of a globally ignited crisis. As the second round approached, *Le Monde* noted Hollande's 'consistency,' but pointed to 'the vagueness of some of his proposals' while taking Sarkozy to task for 'his inconsistency, first running after the National Front . . . before moving back towards the centre to avoid a breakdown with his own side.'

In the end, some voters seemed to have heeded Sarkozy's warning, though not in sufficient numbers to bring him victory. Hollande got 51.6 per cent of the vote in an 80 per cent turnout, three points below the total of votes for anti-Sarkozy non-National Front candidates in the first round. The defeated President, on the other hand, had increased his support from 27 per cent to 48.4.

For all the euphoria as the winner celebrated with his partner, the journalist Valérie Trierweiler, in the Corrèze before flying to a rally in Paris, it was a slim victory after a long period out of presidential power in which two successive non-Socialist leaders had made themselves highly unpopular. Once again, the French wanted change but were none too enthusiastic about the politician who would bring it.

The pattern had been set back in the 1960s by de Gaulle, who had won the first election of a Fifth Republic President by universal suffrage in 1965 only to run into the debacle of a general strike and student riots three years later. Mitterrand and Chirac had also found that victories at the presidential ballot box did not ensure smooth rule thereafter. But now the dynamic was speeded up. The electorate was even less forgiving; it seemed to want to put up leaders only to pull them down. They had been disappointed in Sarkozy and needed to be inspired by his successor; but 'Monsieur Normal' was not much into the inspiration game.

Shortly before his election, Hollande told British journalists that he wanted to 'pacify' France. As soon as he took office, he sought to reassure the country that the days of 'bling' were over with the reduction in government salaries and by getting ministers to sign a code of ethics. This was fine as window dressing, but the real issue was how to address the growing economic challenges as the state's debt to GDP ratio rose to 90 per cent and was forecast to top 93 per cent in 2013. The main weapon adopted by the new President of a round of tax increases soon stoked the protests we saw at the start of this book.

The planned doubling of capital gains tax to 60 per cent sparked an online petition signed by 65,000 people dubbing themselves '*les pigeons*' (suckers)—most of them younger businessmen with starts-ups. They explained to the government that entrepreneurs investing in new firms into which they put all their working time were not the same as holders of 'sleeping share capital,' whom the left wanted to penalize. By the President's second year in office, the tax revolt had spread much more widely as increases of 16 per cent over two years hit most households and people saw their purchasing power falling for the first time since 1984.

With four more years in office, the administration steadily lost credibility, creating a serious divide between rulers and ruled. The lack of resolution was surprising since the Socialists not only held the Élysée and had majorities in both houses of the legislature but also dominated regional government. Yet they seemed not to know what to do with such authority. As one Socialist politician put it, Hollande 'wanted to create a kinder, gentler, less frenetic presidency. Instead he is often absent when he should have been active or gets involved too late and makes things worse.' At the end of 2013, the President stood forty-ninth in a survey to name the most esteemed people in France. Jacques Séguela commented that he had 'succeeded in making every category of French voters unhappy.'

Policy retreated in the face of demonstrations earned the administration disrespect both for the initial measures and then for its surrender to protests. On occasion, the volte-faces only added to the unconvincing impression; for instance, having rejected suggestions of a reorganization of the arcane tax system, the government suddenly announced that it would hold discussions on the matter—by no coincidence doing so as protests welled up against increased levies. But what it offered, a 'transparent' overhaul to get rid of the system's complexities, was not what people wanted, which was lower rates. Though Hollande made an attempt in the middle of 2013 to get on better with business and persuade entrepreneurs that he was not hostile to them, many remained unconvinced and the Socialist Party faithful still preferred an unreconstructed view of society and economics rather than embracing the model of Social Democracy which the President said he believed in. Unlike Sarkozy, he was not going to risk alienating his troops.

Ministers fell out over policies in public. Having not held the presidency since 1995, and having been out of government since 2002, the Socialists lacked top-level national experience—the Prime Minister, Jean-Marc Ayrault, had been parliamentary leader for the party in the National Assembly and Mayor of the Breton capital of Rennes, but lacked national clout. The machine of government seized up with breakdowns in coordination and confused messages for the public. Seven separate ministers, four of them with Cabinet ranks, dealt with economic policy. While the Finance Minister, Pierre Moscovici, talked a reassuring language to soothe concern in Brussels and Berlin about the deficit, Arnaud Montebourg mounted his bully pulpit at the Industry Ministry to speak of nationalization and protectionism, attacking European Union rules restricting state aid to industry as obsolete and fundamentalist and, in a reference to seventeenth-century protectionist policies, proclaiming that 'Colbertism is back' as he announced a scheme to pump 400 million euros into a global state-owned mining company. Though in charge of the most important government portfolio, Moscovici ranked only twenty-sixth in a survey of the popularity of French politicians. By far the most popular member of the Cabinet, Interior Minister Manuel Valls came under attack from left-wing colleagues for his tough law and order policies. Ministers from the Green Party showed an independence of spirit that reassured their followers they had not sold out, but disrupted government business. By-election losses meant that the Socialists became more dependent on the tiny coalition party in parliament. From outside, Mélenchon hammered away with accusations that Hollande had betrayed the left and organized demonstrations that showed the perennial potency of the politics of the street.

A highly embarrassing scandal for the moralizing President broke at the end of 2012 when an online news service reported that the Budget Minister, Jérôme Cahuzac, had a secret bank account in Switzerland. He issued denials. The government stood by him. The following March, prosecutors began proceedings against him for fiscal fraud. which it had been one of his responsibilities to fight.

The Minister eventually admitted to the existence of the Swiss account. He resigned and stepped down from the National Assembly. Hollande announced measures to strengthen the fight against corruption and increase transparency. Ministers were required to declare their wealth; there were no big surprises—Fabius came top of the list with more than six million euros—but the declarations were entirely voluntary with no controls on their veracity. For all the President's expressions of shock and his announcements, the damage had been done as the administration lost some more of its credibility. In the subsequent by-election in Cahuzac's constituency, the Socialist candidate was knocked out in the first round and the UMP took the seat in a run-off with the National Front.

The revolt against transport taxation in Brittany in 2013 became symbolic of the national unhappiness. Farmers, fishermen, shopkeepers, industrial workers, owners of small businesses and traders donned red bonnets of the kind worn by protestors against royal taxes in the seventeenth century and set fire to piles of hay by roadsides, brought down bridges and destroyed surveillance sensors used to monitor traffic for the tax. In the city of Quimper, they fought with riot police and used heavy vehicles to break through the fence of a government building—this in a region where the Socialist held twenty-two of the twenty-seven seats in the National Assembly. Hundreds of farmers blocked roads around Paris to protest against the tax and against changes in European subsidies that worked to their disadvantage—a policeman was killed in an accident at one blockade. Owners of equestrian centres disrupted traffic by riding their horses through the capital, calling for the government to renegotiate a tripling of the tax on their businesses mandated by the Commission in Brussels; their leaders said it would result in the loss of 6,000 jobs and lead to 80,000 horses being slaughtered.

Soon afterwards, it was the turn of taxi drivers, who blocked roads in Paris and other major cities by driving at a snail's pace to protest at competition from chauffeur-driven vehicles (VTCs) using the Internet to receive orders from passengers and not subject to the licensing system which applies to taxis for hire in the street. The taxi drivers said their jobs were being destroyed, though they operate 18,000 vehicles compared with only 3,500 VTCs. Appealing to the mantra against globalization and international finance, the taxi drivers attacked the competitors as being 'financed by Google and Goldman Sachs.'

Despite the central and generally cherished role of the state, there was also growing hostility towards its central actors, the 2.2 million civil servants who were seen both as unproductive and as imposing unpopular measures on behalf of authorities seen as being out of touch with ordinary life. Both resentments were evident in a survey carried out for the business newspaper *Les Echos* in November 2013. It asked which measures people supported to reduce state spending. Top of the list was requiring state workers to put in longer hours, followed by a freeze in welfare entitlement payments and a reduction in the number of civil service jobs—all three suggestions got more than 50 per cent backing.

Protests, sometimes turning violent, erupted from workers at plants which were being shut or slimmed down, though these were often more muted than expected, as if those concerned realized the inevitability of what was happening. A big urban riot broke out in the northern city of Amiens that lasted for two days and caused damage put at ten million euros. Surveys reported that a growing number of people felt their standard of living was slipping and that they could no longer count themselves as belonging to the middle class.

There was also the institutional problem which had been apparent under Sarkozy. The bringing together of the five-yearly elections of the president and the National Assembly meant that the head of state was more closely implicated in the legislative battle than before as the distance between him and the prime minister was narrowed. De Gaulle and Mitterrand had been able to sacrifice premiers when they judged this opportune, as with the General's abrupt ditching of Georges Pompidou after he had won the 1968 Assembly election, and Mitterrand's chopping and changing with the occupants of Matignon.

In contrast, despite their differences and his desire to run a one-man band from the Élysée, Sarkozy kept François Fillon at the Hôtel Matignon throughout his presidency. Hollande repeatedly got himself involved in matters that would have been delegated to ministers in the past and seemed to have a symbiotic relationship with Jean-Marc Ayrault, who appeared as his damage-limitation doppelgänger, earnest, well-meaning but short on lustre and unable to anticipate events (when the urban riots broke out at Trappes it took him three days to condemn the violence). The President was in the front line and had no convincing answers to the hostile fire coming in at him except to counsel patience until things improved.

A year after his election, Hollande's popularity rating was down to 25 per cent. It slumped even further to one-fifth of those questioned in late 2013, the lowest level for a head of state of the Fifth Republic. The mainstream right got a boost from good results in the 2014 municipal elections, but Fillon and his more abrasive rival Jean-François Coppé accused one another of fraud in an election for the UMP leadership which had to be annulled. Juppé hovered on the margins. But the only real question was whether Sarkozy would return.

He flirted with the idea of heading an investment fund bankrolled by Qatar to the tune of 250 million euros; that could have achieved his long-term of aim of becoming rich, but would have ruled him out from a political role and he wanted to keep that option open. Polls showed 70 per cent of right-wing voters wanting him to stage a comeback.

There was a blip when a ruling that his presidential re-election campaign had exceeded the spending limits for political parties, meaning the loss of eleven million euros in state funding. An online petition raised the money within weeks of being launched. Though the case against the former President over alleged contributions by Lilliane Bettencourt was abandoned, some of his associates faced allegations of misdemeanours; the most serious appeared to be those against Claude Guéant, who revealed an old habit of Interior

Ministers of dipping into secret ministerial funds and was surrounded by stories of having accepted cash for his leader from Gadaffi, as well as receiving a mysterious payment from Malaysia shortly before buying an apartment in Paris.

Some former members of his administration broke cover to lament Sarkozy's timidity in pursuing reform, in seeking a balance between business and the union and in accepting the thirty-five-hour working as a measure that had to be modified rather than abolished. Fillon sought to put distance between himself and his former boss, declining to applaud Sarkozy's speech to party members about campaign overspending and declaring them to be 'in competition.' But then this essence of the moderate centre-right plunged into hot water by saying UMP voters could back National Front candidates against Socialists if they considered them better.

Successes in the municipal elections of March 2014, where the UMP gained one hundred forty towns and cities, boosted Coppé's status as the party leader, but he, Fillon and Juppé lagged far behind Sarkozy in popularity among the electorate of the right. The ex-president aroused visceral hatred on the left, but he ranked as the country's most popular politician in an annual poll conducted in August 2013. 'He is totally idolised by Right-wing sympathisers,' said the head of the IFOP polling organization. 'Given the state of the UMP, they believe only Sarkozy can save the party from stagnation.'

At the end of the year, the magazine *Le Point* quoted the ex-President as telling visitors, 'The question is not to know if I want to return; it's whether I cannot not return. I don't have a choice. It is inevitable'—a spokeswoman issued a denial, but it seemed very plausible. Chirac's wife, Bernadette, told a radio interviewer in early 2014 that he was, indeed, planning a political comeback, though she added that he would tell her off for saying so. With three-and-a-half years to go to the next election, the question was the timing and how Sarkozy could position himself as a man of experience who would return to guide the nation. He had to undertake a marathon watched every kilometre of the way by the band of enemies from within his own camp.

Through it all, Hollande retained a Zen-like calm. Delivering his New Year wishes for 2014, he was the epitome of Mr. Normal, entirely reasonable and entirely without emotion, like a marionette speaking the right lines. A Socialist deputy, Jean-Marie Le Guen, put his tranquility down to his belief in the cycles of history, saying that 'he believes things will improve, growth will return and problems will be solved.' Presenting his New Year greetings for 2014 on television, he acknowledged that he had underestimated the length and gravity of the economic crisis and repeated that cutting unemployment would be his overriding concern. He stressed the need to increase the country's competitive edge and admitted that the tax burden had grown too heavy. But he had an uphill struggle ahead of him. A poll showed that very few of the French thought the recession was finished.

His New Year broadcast of 2014 signalled an acceptance that a new direction was needed which would be less onerous for companies and reduce spending on the state that France could not afford. Coming after the sorry record of his first eighteen months in office, he could hardly have done otherwise. He finally acknowledged the excessive nature of the financial demands the state made on a weak economy. But, as the head of the Senate Finance Commission, Philippe Marini, observed, spending cuts in France mean moderating spending increases rather than actual reductions, and the state audit commission doubted if the deficit targets set by the administration could be met, pointing to further unpopular cuts in spending.

Valls offered a change of tone when he moved into Matignon on April 1, 2014, promising a 50 billion euro reduction in state expenditure and tax cuts. Polls gave him 58 per cent support, four times that of Hollande. A Catalan immigrant naturalized in 1982, his record as Interior Minister marked him as a politician who got things done. He was not popular on the left—Green Party members of the previous government refused to serve under him. But the bad losses at the municipal elections the previous month and consistently high unemployment made a change inevitable. In the new government, Royal returned as Environment and Energy Minister and Hollande loyalist Michel Sapin was named finance minister. A left-winger, Benoit Hamon took the education portfolio while the proponent of state power and critic of the EU Arnaud Montbourg was handed responsibility for the economy and industry as the President launched another call for growth rather than austerity. He could console himself with the thought that his term still had three years to run, but he faced the prospect that, if Valls restored the administration's popularity, he would be a potential rival for the presidency. Vested interests—from taxi drivers to white collar civil servants who make up the big battalions of Socialist voters—are as strong as ever. Ballpark pledges still have to be translated into practice after a string of policy fudges from a leader who seems to want to avoid the harsh choices needed to get the ship of state sailing on a more even keel.

Employees at some big firms feel under growing stress as work rhythms are stepped up—at the Orange telecom company, thirty-five staff killed themselves in 2008–9—apparently because of pressure to perform on the job. The boss suggested that suicide had become a 'fashion' at the firm; he resigned after an official report spoke of 'brutal management methods.' Then, in the first three months of 2014, ten more employees took their own lives.

Pollsters speak of the exasperation felt by working people at the amount they pay to the state and at their feeling that the cash is being used to subsidize those who cannot make the effort to find employment. The editor of the middle-of-the road news magazine *L'Express* was moved to speculate about the possibility of a broad revolution in which working people would dodge tax, managers would refuse to fill up forms and the unemployed would revolt against a system which did little to help them find jobs.

This is not the threatened civil war of 1958 or the frontal challenge presented by the student riots and general strike of 1968 but something much more insidious. De Gaulle's assumption of power warded off military action from the generals in Algeria, while time exhausted the university rioters and Pompidou's deal making bought off the trade unions. Today, the discontent is much wider and more deeply rooted. The authority of the state is at stake. 'One sees very different social groups mobilising . . . and the traditional remedies have reached their limits,' the head of one leading polling firm noted. 'It is as if grassroots France is in rebellion against the central state.' With that comes the sentiment of morosity and hopelessness. 'A climate of pain and a feeling of despondency reign which block any self-projection into a better future,' was the way a leaked report by the Interior Ministry at the end of 2013 put it.

15

ON THE BRINK

There is, of course, another and much more reassuring way of look-ing at France. The lure of the country remains as strong as ever. Its great regional centres—Toulouse, Nantes, Bordeau—grow faster than Paris and encourage local culture. The British colonize the Dordogne and set up second homes in areas served by low-cost airlines and in the Channel Tunnel hinterland of the Pas de Calais. Chinese invest in Bordeaux vineyards. Rich Russians populate the Riviera. Gulf sheikhs buy top Parisian hotels and make them even more palatial. A village in the Drôme becomes a corner of Belgium, and reports of prehistor-ic beings emerging at the foot of the gorges of the Ardèche turned out to be Dutch nudists cavorting in the river. France is still by far the world's top international holiday destination, attracting eighty-three million visitors each year. Its economy is the world's fifth-largest and, whatever their problems at home, Nicolas Sarkozy and François Hollande showed determination in foreign affairs and a readiness to insist on *l'exception française* in a world which many see as slipping away from the old powers of the West. Bond dealers who have invested in anticipation of a slump in French government securities have lost money on what is known, after an *Economist* cover critical of the Hexagon, as the 'baguette bomb.'

So where's the worry? *Tout va très bien, Madame la Marquise*, or no worse than in other comparable nations. A tribe of official spokes-people will always tell you how the country has pulled itself out of its difficulties and is set to help lead Europe into the next century.

Its leaders insist that the Hexagon has weathered the eurozone crisis better than most other members thanks to its strong state system and republican values.

The rosy side of France, set out at the start of this book, has been clouded by subsequent chapters. But one would be unfair and a fool not to make the most of the riches the Hexagon has to offer, starting with its capital, which may be dismissed by ultramodernists as a museum city, but what a museum it is, even if pollution reached dangerous levels in the spring of 2014, caused mainly by vehicle emissions. Moving away from the famous attractions and looking back on trips to different and lesser-known parts of the countryside in the last two years, I remember with the greatest pleasure strolls at sunset along the boardwalks of the Opal Coast resorts on the northern shores; lying in the grass of bucolic Norman pastures; visiting the castle home of the great Marquis of Turenne and the red-stoned villages nearby; and staying in a perfect gem of a sixteenth-century château outside Tours, as the owner clipped roses from the classical French garden and opened 1982 Lynch-Bages claret from the cellar in the limestone cliffs to go with jellied chicken, roast lamb and goat's cheese.

In a hidden corner of the Limousin, a hotel on a millpond was a perfect hideaway. A hamlet near the village of Calvinet, mentioned in chapter 4, shows the weakening of the rural world. Its two shops have closed down. The café exists only thanks to a subsidy from the commune and is usually deserted. There is a distinct shortage of anybody between school-leaving age and retirement. But there are signs of life all the same; an entrepreneur has set up a biomedical research unit in a château on the other side of the valley. Pigs roam free by the woods, and mushrooms sprout beneath the trees. Then there was the pretty, sun-dappled port of Collioure, with its castle built by Louis XIV's military architect Vauban, which became a haunt of Picasso, Braque and Matisse, and the historic town of Uzès, with its great ramparts, winding streets and great Saturday market. And so on, and so on across the Hexagon, a country that includes more variety and more new discoveries even to the seasoned visitors than anywhere else I know.

Apart from such pleasures, look behind the curtain of gloom and doom as we have done from time to time during this book and one sees a nation that can still play a global role, which has status thanks to its position at the United Nations and in the European Union, which houses world-class companies and is a major agricultural economy and which, for all its relative cultural decline, can win an Oscar for a silent film.

So, is everything really all right, Madame La Marquise? Has France just become a national incarnation of Molière's *Malade Imaginaire*? Have the problems of the last three decades been an illusion, a series of passing phases which the Hexagon and its people have been able to absorb as they retain their special status in the world? Are the negative opinion poll figures a self-fulfilling exercise in depression which exceeds the reality of the difficulties facing the Hexagon? An argument can be made on all fronts, especially if you regard the French as a people given to dramatic exaggeration.

But, if you look at the data and listen to the country's leaders over those past thirty years, the concerns seem very well justified. As he made his third bid for the presidency in 1995, Jacques Chirac warned that France was 'suffering from an illness that goes deeper than the political class, economic leaders, fashionable intellectuals or the media stars realize. The people have lost confidence. Their feeling of helplessness inclines them towards resignation; it also risks arousing their anger.

'Too many of the French feel that they are not understood, and are looked down upon . . . The gap is widening dangerously between the man in the street and a political class which offers the French people the spectacle of an interminable costume ball at which the waltzers parade in front of the cameras before going off to foment their little plots . . . France is being sucked down because it is exploiting its trump cards badly. The French people have a wealth of intelligence, combativity and virtues. What our elites lack is the intellectual courage to call into question outdated beliefs and obsolete practices.'

After twelve years of the Chirac presidency, Nicolas Sarkozy clearly felt that there was a huge job to be done to revive the nation and to 'break with the ideas, habits and behaviour of the past.' They needed to have their national pride restored, which he proposed to do by enhancing 'the value of work, authority, merit and respect for the nation.' Fast-forward five more years and there was François Hollande declaring that the 'republican promise' of a better life for each succeeding generation had been betrayed—a verdict borne out by the Pew poll of 2013 showing the low number of French people who thought their children would live better than they did.

Part of the problem lies in the high expectations the French have of their nation-state. When trouble strikes, they expect the state to bail them out; that is what it is there for. They are educated to have a special reverence for the Republic, founded on all the historical elements laid out in this book and glossing over the darker periods of the past. They do believe in France's exceptionalism and do not regard themselves as inhabiting a medium-sized nation which has to work its way in an increasingly competitive world. 'The French have such a high image of France that it always seems to them to be less than it should be,' the sociologist François Dubet remarks, adding ironically, 'If France does not win all the Olympic medals and all the Nobel prizes, the French think it is no good.'

To that, add the descent from the good living around 2000 and the long postwar period of the *Trente Glorieuses* which was, in fact, marked by high inflation, a wobbly currency, lack of modernization and other problems, but is now looked back on as a golden era in a typical exercise in nostalgic false memory. For all their failure to deliver on their promises, Mitterrand and Chirac were both re-elected, but voters have become more demanding since, rapidly showing their discontent with presidents, most recently and notably in the swift descent in ratings for François Hollande. Still, once those politicians are out of office, they often experience a revival in popularity.

This happened with Chirac and, in the summer of 2013, a little over a year since he was ejected from the Élysée, Sarkozy was ranked in an annual survey by the IFOP polling organization of France's favourite people as the most popular active politician—admittedly only twentieth in a list dominated by show business stars, but still twenty-four places ahead of his successor. (The only political figure to appear in the top ten was the long-retired Simone Veil, the concentration camp survivor who introduced abortion reform in the 1970s and acquired a stature above politics.)

That suggests a certain irrationality or, at least, a lack of coherence. Sarkozy had not changed in the year after his defeat. Chirac did not suddenly become a better leader once he had stepped down. But nostalgia is powerful in a nation that looks to its past through rose-tinted spectacles.

This may be natural given the challenges of the present, but it is dangerous. For all the hardships caused by the process of change launched in comparable European nations, Germany and Britain, the reforms that were introduced have led to a greater adaptation to the twenty-first century world than has been the case in France. Many French people would say that has been to the disadvantage of their neighbour across the Channel—Margaret Thatcher has not had a good press in the Hexagon, and Tony Blair is widely dismissed as George W. Bush's poodle. It is more difficult to gainsay the effect of the reforms introduced by Gerhard Schröder and continued by Angela Merkel, even if Germany now finds itself in the dock for not spending enough and exporting too much.

Still, its economic predominance and the relative recovery of growth in Britain contrast sharply with French insistence that it had a better crisis than its neighbours. How could this be admitted? If bond traders began to price in risk at the start of 2014 and the purchasing managers' index fell to 47.3 (a number below 50 signals contraction), that was simply due to the typical machinations of international finance aimed against France and an unreliable statistical survey. To acknowledge that the French model might have gone wrong, that, for all its benefits, it was proving a handicap, would mean an adjustment of the national mindset that could only be unwelcome to so proud a country. Hollande might admit that he had underestimated the severity of the economic crisis but he pulled a veil over the manner in which he had been forced to abandon his attempt to rally eurozone members behind a non-austerity programme and had been obliged to see Germany rule the roost.

When a London financial newspaper ran an article at the start of 2014 arguing that "France's failed socialist experiment is turning into a tragedy,' the embassy in London shot back a ten-point refutation, branding the piece 'an ideological mix of prejudice and error.' Specifically, the embassy highlighted the European Commission's growth forecast for France of 0.2 per cent for 2013 and 0.9 per cent for 2014 and quoted business surveys pointing to a rebound at the end of 2013 of 0.4–0.5 per cent. 'France's redistributive system is a political and social choice and one for which the French government takes full responsibility,' it added, noting Hollande's pledge to introduce reductions. As for public spending, the embassy declared that 'when you live in France—from health to infrastructure and from energy costs to transport—you get bang for your euro.' It noted investment inflows that made the Hexagon the sixth-biggest recipient of foreign direct investment in 2012.

There was not a word about unemployment, and, even if the growth projections are met, which has not been the case in recent years, they looked anaemic, leaving France significantly behind both Germany and Britain. One sign of the malaise was evident in the city where the embassy is located, as growing numbers of French people moved across the Channel in search of jobs and to pay lower taxes, giving the British capital the sixth-biggest aggregation of French people, ahead of Bordeaux, Nantes and Strasbourg. In all, the number of France's graduates seeking employment abroad doubled to 27 per cent in two years. But the embassy was insistent that 'the French government has opted for serious, sustainable and socially fair policies in a very clear road map.' Though the economy is at the core of the malaise, the problem goes much deeper, as we have seen.

'In order to succeed and flourish, states and nations need an attractive idea of what they are,' as the British historian Linda Colley has observed. For that lover of France and critics of its people, Charles de Gaulle, 'The French need to be proud of France. Otherwise, they fall into mediocrity.' But, today, in the words of a leading historian and commentator, Michel Winock, 'The French are afraid.' Or as the sociologist François Dubet puts it, 'The French have never reconciled themselves to not being the universal, imperial country; for them, going into a state of normalcy is to go into decline. It is obviously logical for new powers to emerge and for France to be weakened, but, for our national mindset which is built around the idea of grandeur and sovereign power, it is a real fall.' For an increasing number of the French, Europe became the culprit. The editor and author Franz-Olivier Giesbert wrote in early 2014 that the country's belief in its universalist vocation lay at the root of its refusal to face up to reality. This entrenched belief had, he wrote, 'ended by convincing France that it had nothing to learn from others. . . . Consider what more and more of the French think about the big tests facing them. The debt bomb? The fault of the euro. The unemployment rate? Again, the fault of the euro. Deindustrialization? Always the fault of the euro. This in a country which had led the European project for decades and persuaded Germany to agree to its vision of the common currency.'

Similar sentiments of malaise are apparent elsewhere in Europe; political parties similar to the National Front are on the rise in other countries. But the challenge is that much greater in France because of the expectations built up over the decades, and the reluctance of successive administrations to tell citizens the truth; it is no coincidence that

de Gaulle saw himself primarily as a teacher who brought the people of
the Hexagon face-to-face with reality, however unpleasant it might be.

So the French cling to their model of society and their view of their
special nature, but, for all the reasons laid out in this book, they fear for
it and lack faith in those elected to be its guardians, feeding what the
leaked Interior Ministry report at the end of 2013 called 'extremist arguments about the powerlessness of the authorities.' They want to retain
the state which they see as having guaranteed their way of life, but no
longer believe in it. They cling to the past and present but want a
different future. The result is an existential crisis which is apparent
week by week, but which neither the people nor the rulers seem able
to deal with in this nation on the brink of even greater uncertainties.

It is illusory to expect France and the French to change their natures.
Those who ask, on the lines of Professor Higgins, why can't the French
be more like us, are running after moonbeams. The people who live
between Calais and Marseilles, Bordeaux and Grenoble, are not going
to admit that they lulled themselves into complacency, that they lacked
the will to accept necessary if testing reforms, that, for far too long,
they took the attitude that the system was not broken, so why fix it.

While each generation is different from the last, and the immigrant
population brings new elements, the people of the Hexagon will remain
largely as they are as individuals: fundamentally committed to a unitary,
providential republic, but deeply divisive, modern-minded and traditional,
charming and haughty, patriotic and chauvinistic, grandiose and petty;
in other words, deeply human in their own way and specifically French.
They are not an introspective people like the Germans, nor are they
given to Slav melancholia or to the insularity of the British. But, like
their fictional national templates from the Musketeers onwards, they are
self-regarding. How they see themselves is important, and what is currently on view in the national mirror has become less and less to their
taste, even if it is they who create that image and the reality behind it.

The glass is cracked; the basic problem is that the republican
state on which all is based is fractured. The bigger it grows, the
less it seems able to perform its proper function, producing what
the commentator Jean-François Revel once described as 'a country
which is more and more statist, and less and less governed.' Corporatist
resistance to change leads to a climate of civic and moral disintegration,
and produces a readiness to take direct action that splinters the system

into myriad competing interest groups. Too often, high rhetoric about solidarity is a mask for selfishness, which lowers expectations. Pandering to pressure groups undermines the democratic rights of the majority. The privileges of the elite are not limited to the rich whom Hollande set out to bash through tax increases, but includes many more who enjoy perks and privileges handed down from different times.

The political elite has failed to come up with answers, or, if it has them in mind, has failed to sell them to the people. But, despite the arrival of new faces with Hollande, the perennial parade of the same figures continues as Sarkozy is spoken of as a potential winner at the next presidential election. The supposedly clockwork efficiency of the bureaucrats headed by the Énarques has not proved impressive in practice as witnessed by the ballooning of the social security deficit beyond forecasts and the repeated failure to achieve growth targets. Recurrent scandals have shown how corruption and profiteering has been able to take root under administrations of both right and left; it is not often that one head of state chooses a crook as a close friend and another friend is sentenced for embezzlement and misuse of public funds.

This top-down society constructed on rules, hierarchies and power handed between two different entrenched groups finds itself out of touch with itself and with a ruling class that, in the fashionable phrase, has become 'delegitimized.' But the power of the elite remains crushing, an irony more than two centuries after the Revolution, even if the quest for equality is still held up to vindicate the state's authority and reach. As the political journalist Alain Duhamel has put it, France is 'living in a culture of power which distinguishes it from other democracies and handicaps it. The crushing primacy of government on parliament—unique in Europe—the privileged position of Mayors in relation to their municipal councils, of the Presidents of regional councils to their regional assemblies, and also, until recently, of the Chairmen of public and private enterprises to their boards, all that bestows a great advantage on the executives vis-à-vis those who are meant to control them and act as counter-balances.'

Another prominent commentator, Guy Sorman, depicts the French model as 'a society with no money, no risks, no victims and where chance plays no part,' while the economist Pascal Salin has argued that 'The failure of classical liberal ideas in France is not a case of these ideas being abandoned so much as them never having been really understood.' The Holy Grail of equality all too easily fosters a dependency culture under the protection of the Big Brother state. All that has been taken to embody *l'exception française*—but what if, as Duhamel asked, it actually constitutes 'the French handicap'?

The traditional suspicions of the 'forces of money' has been heightened by widespread fear of the free market society and of the outside world, dating back to the end of the twentieth century and epitomized by a fearsome, near-paranoid but bestselling and award-winning book entitled *L'Horreur économique*, which traces France's woes to the way in which 'cosmopolitan foreign thought has taken over our familiar world, and destroyed it.'

'We have our model and we plan to stick to it,' Chirac declared while Jospin drew a fine distinction between 'saying "yes" to the market economy, but "no" to market society.' Nicolas Sarkozy, the one-time enthusiast for breaking the mould and slimming down the state, ended up by claiming that France's welfare system had enabled it to get through the post-2008 crisis in better shape than other nations. In his major campaign speech in 2012, Hollande warned that markets and globalization put the sovereignty of the Republic at stake, and in the ensuing presidential elections Euro-sceptic, anti-globalization candidates got a third of the first round vote.

'When people ask the reason for my journeys, I usually reply that I know what I'm getting away from, but not what I am looking for,' the sixteenth-century sage Michel de Montaigne wrote in words that apply to contemporary France. It knows what it wants to escape from, but not what it seeks—or what it is ready to leave behind on its journey. The last three decades have left it rudderless in this pragmatic new century where the global balance is changing, technology shapes lives more than ever before, rules are going to have to be refashioned and national identity rethought. But, if the old verities on which the Republic was based for so long no longer hold much water, new ideas are often marginalized or not adopted in the first place, and the extremes flourish in the resulting vacuum.

There is no shortage of suggestions for change, but they are not implemented or only partially taken up. Profiting from the wide and deep disillusion with mainstream politicians, the National Front has moved into a political space by stressing the importance of traditional values and patriotism while proffering what it sets out as a defence mechanism against globalism, finance and multinational institutions, and promising to defend wage-earners and public services against international bankers and a rootless international elite. Its success is a measure of the failure of mainstream politics.

But there need be no fatalism about this. The problems of France stem, overwhelmingly, from the lack of self-belief accumulated in the long grind since the Mitterrand era—in 2014, José Manuel Barroso, President of the EU Commission, compared it to Molière's hypochondriac *malade imaginaire*. Above all, its political class has shown a depressing degree of conservative caution, reflecting the remark of the nineteenth-century politician, Alexandre Ledru-Rollin, 'There go the people. I must follow them, for I am their leader.'

Ministers and presidents know what needs to be done, but they shrink from the challenge of convincing an electorate which, as a result, clings more and more to the status quo. The system gives them greater authority than that conferred on their counterparts in other democracies. The President of the Republic has enormous powers at his disposal. The administrative machine is omnipotent. What is needed is for those on whom the Republic has conferred such weight to use it constructively to chart a new course for the country, which retains all that is precious in France but is not confined by outdated elements of the heritage or constrained by fear about taking risks for the future.

They need to take advantage of the long political cycle produced by the coincidence of presidential and legislative elections, and not to be diverted by passing events or by sectoral protests. Presidents and governments need to stand up to protests and reverse the profoundly anti-democratic tradition of street action taking precedence over legislative action, a tradition which far too many French people who should know better see as a source of pride compared to the 'sheep-like' British and Germans who accept the primacy of their parliament and their elected leaders.

That said, ministers and legislators have to acquire a greater degree of respect and a credibility that they are acting in the national interest, even if it is from partisan political positions. Of course, politicians are in the game of fighting one another for office. Of course, politics always involves deals and compromises and activity which those concerned would rather keep from public view. Of course, there will be those who sail too close to the wind and use their positions for profit. The public accepts that. The trouble in France is that it has gone too far, that the whole process has been brought into disrepute leading to an era of cynicism which feeds on itself as trust in leaders melts and a SOFRES poll reported that 72 per cent of the public thought their politicians were corrupt.

This longer-term vision needs to acknowledge the way in which the world has changed even if that has been to the Hexagon's disadvantage. Self-deceptive 'national Bovary's' dreaming is of no use. François Hollande speaks in lofty terms of the 'French dream,' but what is needed is a practical approach to address more down-to-earth realities starting with unemployment and social tensions. While democratic competition should continue, a new approach ought to include a move away from the petty, personalized warfare of the past; France may not do Grand Coalitions on the German model, but the fusing of common purpose between the moderates of left and right in defiance of the traditional divisions would be the best sign of a new and exceptional model to present to the world, and, far more important, to itself.

The role of the state has to be rethought—in the words of the economist Alain Minc, to be 'less of a shield and more of a sword of justice.' Government has to see itself an enabler of the individual genius of its people. The political class has to rediscover its public service role. The elite has to become more open to the world and its ideas.

For, despite the uncertainties crowding in on it, France remains special, and special places need to be able to rise to special heights to retain their exceptional nature. It has been walking on the brink for too long, saved from tipping over by its innate strengths but dissipating them as social cohesion fragments, unhappiness mounts, mainstream politics loses its credibility, international competitiveness declines and the state deficit ratchets up.

It is high time for a fresh, non-violent revolution, a consensual association of the nation to set out a clearly determined path which embraces the modern world while preserving the best of the past. There will be losers along the way, but their loss must be made into the nation's gain under a leadership which does not flinch from the task. Otherwise, the beacon from this lighthouse nation will grow dim as France sinks under the weight of problems it cannot bring itself to face—and Europe and the world will be poorer as a result.

BIBLIOGRAPHY

Agulhon, Maurice. *La République au village*. Paris: Plon, 1970.

Alexandre, Philippe. *L'Elysée en peril*. Paris: Fayard, 1969.

———. *Le Duel De Gaulle-Pompidou*. Paris: Grasset, 1970.

Alexandre, Philippe, and Roger Priouret. *Marianne et le pot au lait*. Paris: Grasset, 1983.

———. *Paysages de campagne*. Paris: Grasset, 1988.

Ardagh, John. *The New France*. London: Penguin, 1977 and later editions.

Attali, Jacques. *Verbatim*, 2 vols. Paris: Fayard, 1993–96.

———. *Urgences françaises*. Paris: Fayard, 2013.

Bacqué, Raphaëlle. *Chirac ou le Démon du pouvoir*. Paris: Albin Michel, 2002.

Bacqué, Raphaëlle, and Denis Saverot. *Seul comme Chirac*. Paris: Grasset, 1997.

Barnett, Correlli. *Bonaparte*. London: Wordsworth, 1997.

Baveretz, Nicolas. *Réveillez-vous!* Paris: Fayard, 2012.

Benamou, Georges. *Le Dernier Mitterrand*. Paris: Plon, 1997.

Booth, Martin. *Opium*. London: Simon & Schuster, 1996.

Bredin, Jean-Denis. *L'Affaire*. Paris: Julliard, 1983.

Boisard, Pierre. *Le Camembert, Mythe national*. Paris: Calmann-Lévy, 1992.

Blom, Philipp. *The Vertigo Years*. London: Weidenfeld & Nicolson, 2008.

Brigouleix, Bernard. *Histoire indiscrète des années Balladur*. Paris: Albin Michel, 1995.

Broers, Michael. *Napoleon,* vol. I. London: Faber & Faber, 2014.

Brogan, Denis. *The Development of Modern France.* London: Hamish Hamilton, 1940.

Caron, François. *Histoire économique de la France XIXe–XXe siècle.* Paris: Armand Colin, 1995.

Charle, Christophe. *Histoire sociale de la France au XIXème siècle.* Paris: Seuil, 1991.

———. *Les hauts fonctionnaires en France au XIXème siècle.* Paris: Gallimard, 1980.

Chirac, Jacques. *La France pour tous.* Paris: Nil, 1994.

———. *Mémoires,* 2 vols. Paris: Nil éditions, 2009, 2011.

Colley, Linda. *Acts of Union and Disunion.* London; Profile, 2013.

Colombani, Jean-Marie. *La France sans Mitterrand.* Paris: Flammarion, 1992.

———. *Le Résident de la République.* Paris: Stock, 1998.

Dallas, Gregor. *At the Heart of a Tiger.* London: Macmillan, 1993.

De Gaulle, Charles. *Le Fil de l'épée.* Paris: Berger-Levrault, 1932.

———. *Mémoires d'espoir,* 2 vols. Paris: Plon, 1970–1.

Deligny, Henri. *Chirac ou la fringale du pouvoir.* Paris: Editions Alain Moreau, 1977.

Domenach, Nicolas, and Maurice Szafran. *Le Roman d'un Président.* Paris: Pion, 1997.

Dubief, Henri. *Le Déclin de la IVème République.* Paris: Seuil, 1976.

Duhamel, Alain. *La République giscardienne.* Paris: Gallimard, 1980.

———. *La République de Monsieur Mitterrand.* Paris: Gallimard, 1982.

———. *Le Complexe d'Astérix.* Paris: Gallimard, 1985.

État de la France. Paris: La Découverte, 1992.

Evans, Martin. *Algeria: France's Undeclared War.* Oxford: Oxford University Press, 2011.

Fenby, Jonathan, *The General.* London: Simon & Schuster, 2007.

Ferniot, Jean. *De Gaulle et le 13 mai.* Paris: Plon, 1965.

Forrester, Viviane. *L'Horreur économique.* Paris: Fayard, 1996.

Giesbert, Franz-Olivier. *François Mitterrand, ou La Tentation de Victoire.* Paris: Seuil, 1987.

———. *Jacques Chirac.* Paris: Seuil, 1987.

———. *Le Président.* Paris: Seuil, 1990.

———. *François Mitterrand: Une Vie.* Paris: Seuil, 1997.

Gildea, Robert. *Children of the Revolution*. London: Allen Lane, 2008.

Giscard d'Estaing, Valéry. *Démocratie française*. Paris: Fayard, 1976.

———. *Deux Français sur trois*. Paris: Flammarion, 1984.

———. *Le Pouvoir et la Vie*. Paris: Interforum, 1988.

Gubler, Claude. *Le Grand Secret*. Paris: Plon, 1996.

Hayward, Susan, and Ginette Vincendeau. *French Film*. London: Routledge Kegan Paul, 1990.

Hobsbawm, E. J. *The Age of Capital*. London: Weidenfeld & Nicolson, 1975.

———. *The Age of Empire*. London: Weidenfeld & Nicolson, 1987.

Horne, Alistair. *To Lose a Battle: France, 1940*. London: Macmillan, 1969.

———. *A Savage War of Peace*. London: Macmillan, 1977.

———. *Seven Ages of Paris*. London: Macmillan, 2002.

Hussey, Andrew. *The French Intifada*. London: Granta, 2014.

Imbert, Claude, and Jacques Julliard. *La Droite et la Gauche*. Paris: Laffont/Grasset, 1995.

James, Colin. *France*. Cambridge: Cambridge UP, 1994.

Jamet, Dominique. *Demain le Front?* Paris: Bartillat, 1995.

Jarreau, Patrick. *La France de Chirac*. Paris: Flammarion, 1995.

———. *Chirac: La malédiction*. Paris: Stock, 1997.

Jarreau, Patrick, and Jacques Kergoat. *François Mitterrand: 14 ans de pouvoir*. Paris: Editions Le Monde, 1995.

Jeanneney, Jean-Noël. *L'Argent caché*. Paris: Fayard, 1981.

Johnson, Michael. *French Resistance*. London: Cassell, 1996.

Julliard, Jacques. *La Cinquième République*. Paris: Seuil, 1976.

Kedward, Rod. *La vie en bleu*. London: Allen Lane, 2005.

Klein, Richard. *Cigarettes are Sublime*. London: Picador, 1995.

Lacouture, Jean. *De Gaulle*, 3 vols. Paris: Seuil, 1984–86.

Larkin, Maurice. *France since the Popular Front*. Oxford: Clarendon Press, 1988.

Lavigne Family. *Cousins d'Auvergne*. Auriliac: Association Cousins d'Auvergne, 1995.

Levy, Claude, and Paul Tillard. *La Grande Rafle du Vél d'Hiv*. Paris: Laffont, 1992.

Magraw, Roger. *France 1815–1914*. London: Fontana Press, 1987.

Maitres Cuisiniers de France. *Les Recettes du terroir*. Paris: Laffont, 1984.

Maspero, Francois. *Les Passagers du Roissy-Express*. Paris: Seuil, 1990.

Mauriac, Francois. *De Gaulle*. Paris: Grasset, 1964.

Maza, Sarah. *The Myth of the French Bourgeoisie*. Harvard University Press, 2003.

McLynn, Frank. *Napoleon*. London: Jonathan Cape, 1998.

Mermet, Gerard. *Francoscopie*. Paris: Larousse, 1994 and later editions.

Mine, Alain. *Le Nouveau moyen âge*. Paris: Gallimard, 1993.

Mine, Alain, and the Commissariat General du Plan. *La France de Van 2000*. Paris: Odile Jacob, 1994.

Mitterrand, Danielle. *En toutes liberies*. Paris: Ramsay, 1996.

Mitterrand, François. *Le Coup d'Etat permanent*. Paris: Plön, 1964.

———. *Ma Part de vérité*. Paris: Fayard, 1969.

———. *La Rose au poing*. Paris: Flammarion, 1973.

———. *La Paille et le Grain*. Paris: Flammarion, 1975.

Moïsi, Dominique. 'The Trouble With France' in *Foreign Affairs*. New York, May/June 1998.

Le Monde. *La Droite sans partage: Elections législatives, 1993*. Paris: Editions Le Monde, 1993.

———. *La Cinquième République*. Paris: Editions Le Monde, 1995.

Monnet, Jean, *Mémoires*. Paris: Fayard, 1976.

Montaldo, Jean. *Mitterrand et les 40 voleurs*. Paris: Albin Michel, 1994.

Morrison, Donald, and Antoine Compagnon. *The Death of French Culture*. Cambridge: Polity Press, 2010.

Nadeau, Jean-Benoît, and Julie Barlow. *Sixty Million Frenchmen Can't Be Wrong*. London: Robson Books, 2004.

Nay, Catherine. *Le Double Mépris*. Paris: Grasset, 1980.

———. *Le Noir et le Rouge*. Paris: Grasset, 1984.

L'Observatoire français des conjonctures économiques. *L'Economie française, 1997*. Paris: La Découverte, 1997.

Paxton, Robert. *Vichy France*. New York: Columbia University Press, 1972.

———. *French Peasant Fascism*. Oxford: Oxford University Press, 1997.

Péan, Pierre. *Une Jeunesse française: François Mitterrand, 1934–47*. Paris: Fayard, 1994.

Peyrefitte, Alain. *Le Mal français*. Paris: Plon, 1977.

———. *Quand la Rose se fanera*. Paris: Plon, 1983.

Pingeot, Mazarine. *Premier Roman*. Paris: Julliard, 1998.

Polèse, Mario, Richard Sheamur, and Laurent Terrail. *La France avantagée*. Paris: Odile Jacob, 2014.

Pompidou, Georges. *Pour Rétablir une vérité*. Paris: Flammarion, 1982.

Robb, Graham. *The Discovery of France*. London: Picador, 2007.

Rol-Tanguy, Henri, and Roger Bourderon. *Libération de Paris*. Paris: Hachette, 1994.

Ross, George, Stanley Hoffmann, and Sylvia Malzacher. *The Mitterrand Experiment*. Oxford: Polity, 1987.

Short, Philip. *Mitterrand*. London: Bodley Head, 2013.

Tournoux, Jean-Raymond. *Pétain et De Gaulle*. Paris: Plon, 1964.

———. *La Tragédie du Général*. Paris: Plon, 1967.

Viansson-Ponté, Pierre. *Histoire de la République gaullienne*, 2 vols. Paris: Fayard, 1970, 1971.

Weber, Eugen. *The Hollow Years*. New York and London: W. W. Norton & Company, 1996.

———. *Peasants into Frenchmen*. Stanford, CA: Stanford University Press, 1976.

Werth, Alexander. *De Gaulle*. London: Penguin, 1965.

Willard, Claude. *La France ouvrière*. Paris: Éditions Ouvrières, 1995.

Williams, Charles. *The Last Great Frenchman*. New York and London: Little, Brown, 1993.

Williams, Philip, and Martin Harrison. *Politics and Society in De Gaulle's Republic*. London: Longman, 1971.

Winock, Michel. *Histoire de l'extrême droite en France*. Paris: Seuil, 1993.

———. *Parlez-moi de la France*. Paris: Plon, 1995.

Zeldin, Theodore. *France, 1848–1914*, 2 vols. Oxford: Clarendon Press, 1973–77.

———. *The French*. London: Collins Harvill, 1983.

I have also drawn extensively on the French press. Apart from the daily recording of events by *Le Monde*, *Libération* and *Le Figaro*, various passages in this book owe a particular debt to the weekly reporting and analysis by *L'Express* and *Le Point* news magazines.

INDEX